WATERMAN

Waterman

*The Life and Times of
Duke Kahanamoku*

DAVID DAVIS

UNIVERSITY OF NEBRASKA PRESS
Lincoln

Library of Congress Cataloging-in-Publication
Data
Davis, David.
Waterman: the life and times of Duke
Kahanamoku / David Davis.
pages cm
Includes bibliographical references and index.
ISBN 978-0-8032-5477-0 (cloth: alk. paper)
ISBN 978-1-4962-0600-8 (paper: alk. paper)
ISBN 978-0-8032-8512-5 (epub)
ISBN 978-0-8032-8513-2 (mobi)
ISBN 978-0-8032-8514-9 (pdf)
1. Kahanamoku, Duke, 1890–1968.
2. Swimmers—Hawaii—Biography.
3. Surfers—Hawaii—Biography.   I. Title.
GV838.K35D38 2015
797.2'1092—dc23
[B]
2015006562

Set in Minion by Westchester Publishing Services.

To my parents. Thank you.

Ua lehulehu a manomano ka ʻikena a ka Hawaiʻi.
Great and numerous is the knowledge of the Hawaiians.
—Hawaiian Proverb

Water is a kind of destiny.
—Gaston Bachelard

Swimming cultivates imagination; the man with the most is he who can swim his solitary course night or day and forget a black earth full of people that push.
—Annette Kellerman

To describe a wave analytically, to translate its every movement into words, one would have to invent a new vocabulary and perhaps also a new grammar and a new syntax, or else employ a system of notation like a musical score or algebraic formulas with derivatives and integers.
—Italo Calvino

To write properly about the Olympic Games of the twentieth century is to write about almost everything in the twentieth century. About plastics and politics and racism and the demise of the rigid Bible morality and the rise of situation ethics. About avarice and airplanes and vitamin pills and chauvinism and free love and selling refrigerators on television and urban renewal and electricity.
—William Oscar Johnson

"The history of Hawaii is the history of loss."
"Paradise lost?"
"Paradise stolen. Paradise raped. Paradise infected. Paradise owned, developed, packaged. Paradise sold."
—David Lodge

I really don't know why it is that all of us are so committed to the sea, except I think it is because in addition to the fact that the sea changes and the light changes, and ships change, it is because we all came from the sea. And it is an interesting biological fact that all of us have, in our veins, the exact same percentage of salt in our blood that exists in the ocean, and, therefore, we have salt in our blood, in our sweat, in our tears. We are tied to the ocean. And when we go back to the sea, whether it is to sail or to watch it we are going back from whence we came.
—John F. Kennedy

WATERMAN

Prologue

If you spend any amount of time on Oahu, the third largest of the Hawaiian Islands, you cannot help but notice the name Duke Kahanamoku everywhere. There's Duke Kahanamoku Lagoon, Duke Kahanamoku Beach, and the Duke Kahanamoku Aquatic Complex. There's the annual Duke Kahanamoku long-distance canoe race and the annual OceanFest carnival, which raises money for scholarships for the Duke Kahanamoku Foundation and is held near Duke's, the popular tiki-themed restaurant and bar with a superb view of the ocean.

Not far from the restaurant, on the beach at Waikiki, stands an oversized statue of Duke Kahanamoku. He is depicted wearing swimming trunks, with a surfboard behind him. His arms are extended as if to welcome the many visitors—tourists in T-shirts and sunglasses, surfers with dreadlocks, military personnel in uniform—who have stopped to take photos and read the accompanying plaque.

As statues are wont to do, the bronze figure casts an enormous shadow over its surroundings, sort of like the man himself. While he was alive, Duke Kahanamoku was Hawaii's favorite son. Until Barack Obama came along, no one born in Hawaii was more famous or revered than Duke Kahanamoku.

Legend is a tricky thing. Director John Ford, a friend of Duke's from his stint in Hollywood in the 1920s, addressed this conundrum in one of the last (and best) Westerns that he directed. The plot of *The Man Who Shot Liberty Valance* revolves around an extended flashback concerning the fates of the two main characters in the movie (played by Jimmy Stewart and John Wayne).

A journalist asks Stewart, a successful elder statesman in the film, to discuss the long-ago incident during which he allegedly killed a scurrilous outlaw named Liberty Valance (Lee Marvin). Stewart proceeds to give the truthful account of what happened and, in so doing, corrects the inaccurate version. After listening to the story, the reporter destroys his notes. "When the legend becomes fact," he relates, "print the legend."[1]

Soon after his death in 1968 (or, perhaps, even before he passed away), the legend of Duke Kahanamoku supplanted the flesh-and-blood version. He officially competed in three Olympics, but reporters routinely stretched that number to four or five without supplying any concrete evidence. His famous "Long Ride" on a surfboard went from approximately one mile to one mile-and-a-half. He is said to have introduced surfing to Australia and the East Coast of the United States, even though others surfed there before him. Relatives of the world's richest heiress, Doris Duke, claimed that Kahanamoku impregnated her, although that seems unlikely. Others have argued that he fulfilled a prophecy spoken by King Kamehameha, the unifier of the Hawaiian Islands, but it is doubtful that this prophecy was ever uttered.

As one of Kahanamoku's relatives told me, with only some exaggeration, "All that you now read 'bout the Duke is false, and for me to divulge the facts would place him in a shallow of the family worth. Let beliefs be if they help the progress of the entities of surfing and aloha, as they need a historical hero for commercialization. . . . Best to leave them to their wallows for it brings no harm and he is left the image of a hero."[2]

It's easy to understand why Duke Kahanamoku continues to inspire such talk. His life was one epic ride. In 1890, when Kahanamoku was born, Hawaii was an independent nation. He was just a youngster when Hawaii's queen was overthrown in a hostile takeover that remains controversial to this day. He first gained fame while swimming for the United States at the 1912 Stockholm Olympics, at a time when nonwhite athletes were barred from competing at the elite professional and amateur levels (with the exception of a few boxers, jockeys, and collegiate stars).

A dark-skinned man who represented the hopes and dreams of a predominantly white nation, Kahanamoku encountered and traversed racism and ignorance well before the likes of other pioneers (including Joe Louis, Jesse Owens, and Jackie Robinson). As his swimming success continued into the 1920s, he integrated private and public pools as well as surfing spots at exclusively white beaches. Photographs of Duke holding white women in his arms while they swam, or bearing them aloft on his powerful shoulders while they surfed tandem, appeared in newspapers around the country. He became the living embodiment of Hawaii and its "exotic" culture—and what a symbol! He was seen as the distillation of everything that was believed to be good about the Hawaiian people: humble yet powerful, sensual and healthy, gracious and noble.

Most athletes excel in only one sport. Kahanamoku was also the best surfer of his era. He used his fame as a swimmer to promote surfing, the indigenous pastime of Hawaii and one that few people outside of Waikiki had ever witnessed, much less experienced, before Duke helped to export it. He became the Johnny Appleseed of the waves, collecting acolytes around the globe—from Atlantic City in New Jersey to Corona del Mar in Southern California to Freshwater Beach in Australia. He formed the earliest surfing club in existence and helped formulate the "rules" that govern surfing etiquette even today. He practically invented the "Hey, Brah" lifestyle and, despite his lack of business acumen, was among the first sports stars to open an eponymous restaurant-nightclub, to market his own fashion and sneaker lines, and to "brand" himself.

Consider the multiple sports that Kahanamoku directly pioneered: surfing and competitive swimming, most prominently, but also beach volleyball, waterskiing, rowing, sailing, paddling, and stand-up paddling (SUP). Consider, too, the myriad activities that surfing has spawned in its wake: skateboarding, snowboarding, and their offshoots. When one adds to that mix his contributions to race relations and to the development of modern tourism in Hawaii, as well as his career in Hollywood, it is clear that few athletes, alive or dead, can claim a broader legacy.

"Duke is Babe Ruth and Jack Dempsey combined down here,"[3] syndicated columnist Bob Considine once wrote. That was not much of an exaggeration.

Duke Kahanamoku's uniquely American journey rivals any tale that Horatio Alger concocted—and it resonates more than any lifeless statue. The story begins, as it often does in Hawaii, with its most enduring and beguiling feature: water.

1

The precise moment when Duke Paoa Kahanamoku slipped into the shimmering blue waters of the Pacific Ocean is lost to history. Duke himself recalled only that he was around four years old when his father, so proud of his namesake, the first of the Kahanamoku children to survive infancy, tossed him over the side of a canoe somewhere off Waikiki Beach.

"It was save yourself or drown," he said, "so I saved myself."[1]

This was no mere introduction. This was a baptism. Water binds the Hawaiian Islands. It is no exaggeration to say that, in Duke's era, water was the lifeblood of Hawaii and its people. It cleansed their bodies after work and was a transportation source. It was their playground, for surfing, swimming, and canoe races, and it was a hallowed sanctuary. Fishing brought them sustenance, from the *hee* (octopus) and *papio* (trevally) and *oio* (bonefish) to the *akule* (scad) and *amaama* (mullet) that they caught, ate, and traded with neighbors for vegetables and meat.

On that momentous but unrecorded day, young Duke splashed, flailed, and swallowed water until he discovered his buoyancy and equilibrium, caught his breath, and trusted in the ageless sea that engulfed his body, like his father and uncles and grandfathers before him. Until he felt comfortable enough to stretch his arms beyond his head and pull his hands through the water, his sticklike legs kicking and churning. Until he was moving, self-propelled, his black hair glistening in the sunlight, a little black shadow shimmering in blue liquid. A water bug, soon to be a water boy, soon to be a waterman.

Duke Paoa Kahinu Mokoe Hulikohola Kahanamoku was born on August 24, 1890, in downtown Honolulu, near the corner of King and Bishop Streets. He referred to his birthplace in different ways, depending on his audience.

To younger folks, he might say, "I was born where the Bank of Hawaii is now," or to a contemporary, he might say, "I was born where the Arlington Hotel was." If he was talking to an old-timer, he'd say that he was born at Haleakala ("House of the Sun"), which they knew to be the homestead of Princess Bernice Pauahi Paki Bishop, the last of the Kamehameha royal line and the largest landowner in the kingdom.

The two-story structure, fashioned from pink coral by Princess Bernice's father, was all of those incarnations. Duke's father, it is said, was born on the site, in July of 1869, to parents identified as Kapiolani Kaoeha and Kahanamoku. As *kahu* (retainers) of Princess Bernice, the proud parents sought her advice about naming their baby.

The story goes that the Duke of Edinburgh, Alfred Ernest Albert, the second son of Queen Victoria of England, was making a stopover in Hawaii on a voyage to the British colonies in the Pacific. Princess Bernice, who had traveled to Europe and considered herself an Anglophile, suggested that the newborn be named to commemorate the royal visit. Thus, Halapu Kahanamoku became Duke Halapu Kahanamoku.

"Mrs. Bishop took hold of me and at the same time a salute to the Hawaiian flag from the British battleship in which the (Prince Albert) Duke of Edinburgh arrived," the elder Duke put it. "And after I was washed by Mrs. Bishop she gave me the name 'The Duke of Edinburgh.' The Duke heard and was glad and came to house and I was presented to him and tooke [sic] me in his arms. And that is how I got this name."[2]

Years later, he and his wife, Julia Paakonia Lonokahikini Paoa, gave the same first name to their son. Strictly speaking, Duke was only a name. The family was not related by blood to Kamehameha the Great, the monarch who conquered the islands and established the Kingdom of Hawaii in 1810. But genealogy in Hawaii is as tangled as the gnarled roots of a banyan tree because it involves other factors besides direct bloodline. Duke's paternal grandparents, through their domestic relationship with Princess Bernice, who was the great granddaughter of King Kamehameha, were considered adjunct members of the royal family and thus had valid claims to nobility. Further, the name "Kahanamoku" reputedly "had been given to [Duke's grandfather] by Kamehameha or a powerful *alii* [nobleman] to commemorate the 'putting together of the Islands of Hawaii to form the Kingdom,'" according to one source.[3]

The ancestry of Duke's mother, Julia Paakonia Paoa, also involved nobility. The Paoa family had a reputation for being storied watermen. Through the Paoa side of the family, originally from the Big Island of Hawaii, "Duke is a descendant of Kinau [a regent] of the Kamehameha line," according to one cousin. "Also [Duke's grandmother] was the granddaughter of Makue and Halapu . . . who are descended from the ancient Alapai family. . . . The ancestors of Duke—through both his father and mother—were warriors of Kamehameha the Great and no doubt fought to bring Oahu into the Kingdom."[4]

All of this would lead to confusion after Duke Kahanamoku achieved Olympic fame, as many journalists and fans assumed that he had blood-ties to Hawaiian monarchy. When asked if he was related to Hawaiian royalty, Duke was wont to reply, "My understanding [is] that we are in a line of the royal family."[5]

Conflicting evidence exists about his parents' birthdates. One census states that Duke's father was born in July of 1870—a full year after the visit by the Duke of Edinburgh. Information from the same census states that Duke's mother was born in May of 1873 (making her seventeen years old when her son was born). Other reports give her birth year as 1870. It is also unclear exactly when Duke Halapu and Julia were married. According to official reports, they wed in Honolulu in April of 1907.

What is clear is that Duke was his parents' oldest surviving child. One infant, a girl, died before him. In handwritten notes, Duke called her variously "Miss Lea" and "Miss Kala." In total, Duke's mother lost three infants to stillbirth.[6]

In 1890, when his eldest son was born, Duke Senior was a hack driver and clerk for the United Carriage Company. He had a stand on King Street just across from the Arlington Hotel. He then found work as a deliveryman for the W. W. Dimond Company in Honolulu.

In 1893 Duke Senior was hired by one of the most powerful men in Hawaii, Lorrin A. Thurston, to perform at the world's fair in Chicago. World's fairs were perhaps the most popular form of mass entertainment during the latter half of the nineteenth century. They were rollicking extravaganzas that combined elements of today's technology conventions, Middle Eastern bazaars, art walks, amusement parks, and county fairs. Some twenty-seven million visitors attended the "White City" edition in Chicago, where Thurston and his troupe extolled the splendors of Hawaii and showed off an enormous cyclorama of the Kilauea volcano. Duke Senior later traveled with the group to New York.

While her husband was away on an extended trip to the mainland, Julia and young Duke, then three years old, moved from Honolulu to Waikiki. Her side of the family, the Paoas, had title to 3.22 acres of land, formally awarded them after the Great Māhele (land division) of 1848. The Māhele introduced private ownership of land in Hawaii, a radical notion in a kingdom where, by tradition, the lands were controlled by the chiefs but were also considered communal property for use by the commoners. The premise behind this reform was to give Hawaiians possession of the kingdom's lands, but instead foreigners took advantage of the opportunity and purchased vast tracts of invaluable property.

The distance from downtown Honolulu to Waikiki is but a few miles, but it might as well have been one thousand miles. Honolulu was devoted to commerce, shipping, and politics—"a humming city with shops and palaces and busy wharfs, plying cabs and tramcars, telephones in operation and a railway in building," according to Robert Louis Stevenson, a visitor to Oahu in 1893.[7] And, ever since the days of the whaling ships, Honolulu was known as a den of easy pleasures. The Chinatown area was considered to be the center of gambling and opium use; the local police force was widely reputed to be "on the take."

Waikiki means "spouting waters." The area was formed from the natural convergence of inland waters flowing from the Palolo, Manoa, and Makiki valleys, which then fed into the Pacific Ocean via three freshwater streams: the Kuekaunahi, the Apuakehau, and the Piinaio. This confluence created an aquatic never-neverland of rice fields and banana plantations, coconut trees and hau groves, duck ponds, lily ponds, and fish ponds stocked with mullet and milkfish, limu (seaweed) that attracted crabs and shrimp, and patches of taro root that, when mashed, produced Duke's favorite food: poi.

In this bountiful idyll, young Duke was soon joined in 1895 by his brother, David Piikoi, followed by his oldest sister, Bernice, in 1897, William in 1900, and Samuel Alapai in 1902. Then came three siblings in quick succession: sisters Kapiolani (1905) and Maria (pronounced "Ma-RYE-a," 1907) and Louis

(1908). Duke went by "Paoa" among family and friends, to distinguish him from his father.

Their mother spoke little English, but Julia was active in the community, joining the Daughters of Hawaii and the Kaahumanu Society (the latter was named for the favorite wife of King Kamehameha). Slender and devout, Julia ran the day-to-day household with quiet love, and Duke credited her with the luscious hair of the Kahanamoku clan. "Mother used to get herbs and put them in a cloth and squeeze them on our hair," he remembered.[8]

Tall and handsome, Duke Halapu "laid the law down," according to one of his sons. He had joined the Honolulu Police Department, first with the special bicycle force before being assigned to the patrol wagon and then appointed as receiving clerk. He was promoted to sergeant on March 7, 1910, a happy day that coincided with the birth of the last "bruthah," Sargent. With the arrival of Sargent, Duke now had eight younger brothers and sisters.

The Paoa and Kahanamoku families lived in simple wooden cottages in the neighborhood of Kalia, on the western edge of Waikiki, extending from the intersection of Kalia Road and Ala Moana Boulevard to the beach. They were surrounded by aunts and uncles, dozens of cousins, in-laws, and extended family: the Sterlings, the Piikois, and the Harbottles. Young Duke always had companions to play with, to explore the marshes and coconut groves with, and to fish with. If someone picked up a guitar or a ukulele, the others joined in. "[Kalia] was a beautiful place to live," said Mary Paoa Clarke, one of Duke's cousins. "We were just like one big family there."[9]

Like many people in polyglot Hawaii, they learned to straddle different worlds. They spoke Hawaiian, English, and Pidgin. They joined the Reorganized Church of Jesus Christ of Latter Day Saints, which had made inroads in the community, but Duke and the other children were also infused with Hawaiian traditions and values. *Aloha*, meaning love and welcome, was central to their lives. Worldly possessions and wealth were deemed not as significant as *mana*, a form of spiritual power. The togetherness of *ohana*, or family, bound them in unity.

The natural world loomed significant. Not only was taro a plant used to produce poi, a staple in the diet of both chiefs and commoners, but in Hawaiian lore taro was a brother to the people. Each family had its *aumakua*, or animal guiding spirit; the *mano* (shark) was the *aumakua* of the Kahanamokus. Duke was taught to respect sharks but never to fear them because they provided protection. His father later told one reporter that he was given "a direct promise" from the chief shark of Honolulu harbor and Puuloa (near Pearl Harbor) that "in Duke's favorite distances he would never be defeated."[10]

Their backyard was water: the wide expanse of the Pacific Ocean, a seemingly infinite horizon, along with the streams that fed into it. Waikiki's largest fishpond, Kaihikapu, was nearby. The omnipresent sunshine and the balmy temperatures, interrupted only by cleansing rain showers, encouraged the water-focused lifestyle. When the trade winds blew, and the aroma of papaya mixed with scents from coco palms, mangoes, luxurious ferns, and the jasmine-like perfume of the *pikake* flower, Kalia felt like heaven.

One of Duke's uncles owned fishing canoes that helped in supplying the family with food. Another uncle helped lay the submarine cable that, in 1902, linked Hawaii with the mainland by telegraph. All of the children learned how to catch dinner. "We had a lot of crabs down there, too, that we caught," Duke's brother Louis Kahanamoku said. "Then we used to use a little cord with a good hook on the end. And we get the [coconut leaf], we tie the hook on like that and we stick 'em in the eel hole. Eel take a bite at 'em. That's how we caught our eel. You really got to know how. Never miss."[11]

Being in the water was as central and basic to their lives as eating and sleeping. Duke's father and uncles taught their progeny to swim, but his mother, too, encouraged her children. "Mother said, 'My boys and girls, go out as far as you want. Never be afraid in the water,'" Sargent Kahanamoku said. "All we did was water, water, water. My family believes we came from the ocean. And that's where we're going back."[12]

There was never much money, not with so many mouths to feed, but the family never went hungry. And, as they grew older and bigger, the kids found ways to bring in extra cash. When ships ferrying tourists, sailors, and merchants arrived in Honolulu, Kahanamoku and his cousins hustled down to the harbor. From the decks high above the water rained money that was thrown overboard by the visitors—nickels, pennies, dimes, and even foreign coins. The kids gulped mouthfuls of air and then dove into the water, plunging deep as they learned to control their breath, the reward commensurate with their efforts. The best divers, according to lore, could tell in a flash which coins were pennies and thus to be ignored, and which shined with precious silver.

The aquatic lifestyle that Duke Kahanamoku and so many Hawaiians enjoyed derives from Hawaii's unique origin. Indeed, one cannot understand Kahanamoku and his times without knowing about Hawaii's history. Hawaii has had, in essence, three distinct births. The first was geological. The islands were formed millions of years ago from eruptions of deep, underwater volcanoes. The lava eventually hardened upon contact with water. Over time, these masses grew large enough to break through the surface, producing a chain of eight major islands (Niihau, Kauai, Oahu, Molokai, Lanai, Maui, Kahoolawe, and the Big Island of Hawaii) as well as numerous atolls, reefs, and shoals that stretch over 1,500 miles.

Then came man. Seafaring Polynesians in double-hulled canoes were the first to arrive, perhaps from Tahiti or the Marquesas, perhaps as early as 400 A D. They discovered an Edenic paradise: glorious weather, a bountiful sea, and no predators. They worshipped their own gods and developed their own rituals and laws—known as the *kapu* system—that regulated every aspect of daily life, from religious rites to marriage, from preparing meals to land ownership, from sex to surfing.

As the most isolated archipelago in the world—separated by water some 2,500 miles from the West Coast of the United States and about 3,800 miles from Japan—Hawaii existed without outside contact after the Polynesian expeditions ceased around 1200 A D. Scholars believe that Spanish explorers in the sixteenth century were the first to reach Hawaii, but truly significant interaction with foreigners began in January of 1778 with the arrival of Captain James Cook, a British explorer seeking the Northwest Passage. Cook dubbed them "the Sandwich Islands" after his patron, the fourth Earl of Sandwich.

Hawaii's third and most dramatic transformation had begun. Cook's accidental discovery coincided with the rise of Kamehameha, a chief from the island of Hawaii whose relentless military campaign conquered and ultimately united the islands under his rule. King Kamehameha retained many of Hawaii's ancient traditions even as he relied on an influx of foreign advisers to open Hawaii to the outside world. (Cook was not one of those; he was murdered when he returned to Hawaii in 1779.)

Successive waves of visitors brought radical changes to the freedoms embedded within Polynesian culture. Bible-toting missionaries came from America to convert the natives to Christianity. They helped translate the local dialect into written form (in no small part so as to create a Bible in Hawaiian) and boosted literacy to rates higher than that enjoyed on the mainland. The missionaries maintained a healthy disdain for what they considered to be the hedonistic lifestyle enjoyed by Hawaiians, but that didn't stop their sons and daughters from marrying into *alii* (or, royal) families, thus giving this generation control over vast tracts of once-communal land.

Whaling ships and merchant vessels plying the Pacific Ocean, primarily from the United States and Europe, used Hawaii as a convenient port for refueling and trading (not to mention partying and drinking). Later, from different countries throughout Asia, came shiploads of laborers to work the sugar plantations that were becoming such a lucrative industry for Hawaii. "The white man's ships have arrived with clever men from big countries," Hawaiian historian David Malo wrote around 1837. "They know our people are few in number and our country is small, they will devour us."[13]

Malo's comment proved prescient. The centuries-long period of seclusion left the Hawaiian people defenseless to the deadly contagions carried by sailors, traders, and visitors. Smallpox, measles, venereal disease, and Hansen's disease, among others, ravaged the native population, estimated to be around 300,000 (or more) on Cook's arrival. That number fell to approximately 30,000 by 1900, with an additional 10,000 part-Hawaiians.

As late as 1876, Hawaiians and part-Hawaiians made up nearly 90 percent of the population. By 1900 they comprised only one-quarter of the population, with Asians registering nearly 57 percent (thanks to the vast numbers of laborers imported for the sugar plantations) and Caucasians registering nearly 18 percent. Hawaiians were now forced to adjust to being a minority within their homeland.[14]

The layer cake of ethnicities created a cultural mishmash unlike any other, forging inimitable couplings of people, cuisine, music, religion, and more. (The hybrid slang of Pidgin, otherwise known as "Hawaiian Creole," became the unofficial language of the Islands.) Close quarters brought grudging acceptance: when you live together on an island, you cannot afford to make many enemies.

But while Hawaii's cultural diversity encouraged a level of tolerance not found in much of the world, it did not eliminate racism or prejudice. The Hawaiian word for "person," *kanaka*, was often used by the *haole* (white) community as a derogatory slur that was roughly the equivalent of "nigger" on the mainland.

Hawaii might have been able to retain its independence into the twentieth century but for the fact that the world powers, notably Great Britain, France, Germany, and Japan, were jockeying for control of the Pacific Rim. The strategic worth of Hawaii, and its geographic position, now assumed enormous importance.

Hawaii's closest neighbor, the United States, was perhaps the most interested party. The country was in the process of shedding its long-standing isolationist stance. The 1890 publication of Alfred Mahan's treatise, *The Influence of Sea Power upon History*, deeply swayed many politicians, including a youthful Theodore Roosevelt. Mahan's disciples believed in extending American influence beyond the continental United States, with the buildup of a powerful navy to accomplish this goal.

President William McKinley, no doubt influenced by Roosevelt, his assistant secretary of the navy, noted that "we need Hawaii as much and a good deal more than we did California. It is manifest destiny."[15]

In Honolulu, McKinley's thoughts were echoed by proannexation supporters from the *haole* community. One prominent supporter was lawyer-businessman Lorrin A. Thurston. A descendant of missionaries, Thurston pronounced in 1884 that "when these Islands cease to be self-governing, the United States government will take possession."[16] He and other like-minded citizens lobbied hard for passage of the Reciprocity Treaty in 1887. This gave the United States exclusive concession rights to the port of Pearl Harbor and thus provided American ships with a tactical advantage. They also won approval for a new constitution for Hawaii, dubbed the "Bayonet Constitution" for how it was achieved, which placed the monarch under their control and reduced the voting power of the native people.

It was Thurston who hired Duke's father to perform at the Chicago world's fair of 1893. The Columbian Exposition, named in honor of Christopher Columbus, was an extravaganza of red-white-and-blue pride, beginning with the unveiling of the Ferris wheel. The lectures of historian Frederick Jackson

Turner regarding the closing of the frontier underlined a growing notion that the country was exceptional, a time when, as historian Evan Thomas writes, "Americans extolled, sang about and versified national pride. The 'Pledge of Allegiance' was written in 1892, 'America the Beautiful' in 1895, and Memorial Day celebrations were becoming increasingly popular. The bitterness of the Civil War [was] a fading memory."[17]

Amid the flag-waving came the final, inevitable collapse of the Kingdom of Hawaii. After Queen Liliuokalani attempted to quell the incipient power grab by Thurston and his allies, proannexation forces stripped the queen of her authority. The monarchy was replaced, first by a provisional government and then by the newly formed Republic of Hawaii, headed by Sanford Dole, another *haole* business leader. Hawaiians were defenseless against what the *New York Times* described as "a shameful conspiracy."[18]

Hawaii's fate was sealed with the onset of the Spanish-American War, which Secretary of State John Hay called the "splendid little war." The United States gobbled up Cuba, Guam, Puerto Rico, and the Philippines; in the climax to this imperialist jag, President McKinley signed the resolution to annex Hawaii on July 7, 1898. Two years later, the Organic Act established the Territory of Hawaii under the sovereignty of the United States, the culmination of what one historian called "one of the most audacious land grabs of the Gilded Age, in which 1.8 million acres of land now worth billions of dollars was seized from native Hawaiians and claimed by American businessmen."[19]

Commented former president Grover Cleveland, who had opposed annexation: "Hawaii is ours. As I look back upon the first step in this miserable business and as I contemplate the means used to complete this outrage, I am ashamed of the whole affair."[20]

The status of Duke Kahanamoku, and of all native Hawaiians, had changed three times in the span of one decade. In 1890, the year he was born, Queen Liliuokalani reigned over the Kingdom of Hawaii. In 1893, when he and his mother fled the turbulence of Honolulu for tranquil Waikiki (in what was surely no coincidence), Queen Liliuokalani was forcibly removed from power. In 1900, as Duke was learning to balance on a surfboard, he became an American.

At age ten Kahanamoku was too young to understand all of the implications of what had transpired. He had no comprehension of how Hawaii was being transformed into a uniquely American outpost: a multiethnic, multicultural, multilinguistic territory with competing business, religious, and political interests. But the quietude that he and his family found on the Paoa estate in Kalia was about to change—and fast—leaving Duke and others to navigate the chasm between the vestiges of traditional Hawaiian culture and the coming American century.

2

Duke Kahanamoku's life was completely centered in Waikiki. He walked from home to the heart of town, near the old Ainahau estate, to start his formal education at Waikiki School. After the lessons ended, he only had to walk across the street to be at one of the most pristine beaches in the world. After third grade, he attended Queen Kaahumanu Elementary School, walking from Ala Moana Boulevard to Piikoi Street and then to school.

He was shy and reticent, noticeably so at an early age. "He was not what you'd call a scholar," his cousin, Irmgard Harbottle Perkins, said. "He never gave the teachers a hard time, but his mind seemed to be far away; he would rather have been outdoors. . . . He was happiest with the family but even then he was quiet, to himself."[1]

In 1904, when he was fourteen years old, Duke was sent to Kamehameha School for Boys for training in the industrial arts. His admittance was an honor for the family, as the funds used to establish the school came from the estate of Princess Bernice Pauahi Bishop, the woman who gave Duke's father his name and thus gave Duke his name as well.

Princess Bernice had passed away in 1884. Three years after her death, the first of the Kamehameha schools opened in the Kalihi neighborhood, west of downtown Honolulu. There would eventually be three schools: one for boys, one for girls, and one for youth.

The Kamehameha Schools were modeled after institutions on the mainland that educated Native American Indians. The most prominent of these was the Carlisle Indian Industrial School, founded in 1879 in Pennsylvania. Its superintendent, Captain Richard Henry Pratt, believed that an immersive experience was the best way to assimilate the "savage" Indian into mainstream American culture. His philosophy is best summarized by his chilling words: "Kill the Indian and save the man."

Likewise, the Kamehameha Schools were designed to inculcate religion, discipline, and education in native Hawaiians. According to Charles Bishop, the late Princess Bernice's husband, the schools would help "her own people [so that they] might have the opportunity for fitting themselves for such competition, and be able to hold their own in a manly and friendly way, without asking any favors which they were not likely to receive."[2]

Speaking Hawaiian was banned in the Kamehameha Schools, with English deemed the only acceptable language spoken in the classroom. Religious faith and loyalty to the United States were emphasized. Students dressed in military-style uniforms and boarded on campus. Discipline was strictly enforced. One president noted that, since Hawaiians are "conceded to be fonder of ease than of toil," then "Christian industrial training is the key."[3] A 1910 report concluded: "To prepare boys and girls for life, in the largest sense, is our problem."[4]

Students took English and math classes, but the Kamehameha Schools emphasized the manual trades. Duke was taught hand- and machine-sewing skills to become a tailor. He learned how to make buttonholes, jackets, and trousers. He also received training in blacksmithing and carpentry. His handwriting improved to such a degree that he became a voluminous letter writer throughout his life.

Like Carlisle Indian Industrial School, which was gaining a national reputation for its football teams, starring Jim Thorpe, Duke's future Olympic teammate, Kamehameha Schools leaders held that sports should be a vital part of the students' lives. Duke tried them all: football, track, baseball, basketball, soccer, and softball.

He earned his first public plaudits for playing halfback on the soccer team (referred to as "socker" in the local papers). Duke helped the Kamehameha squad compile a 4-1 record as they whipped the "Buff & Blue" private-school boys from Oahu College (later known as Punahou School) in the 1908 interscholastic championship. His future would not be found on the soccer pitch, however, but in the water.

Kahanamoku liked to say that surfing is "as old as the hills." The first lucky person to grab a board and get stoked has never been identified. Surf historians believe that the Polynesians and Pacific Islanders who settled Hawaii brought the tradition with them, but that it was the Hawaiians who took it to the next level and who recognized surfing as exhilarating, primal, addictive fun, tasting the salty spray while moving through coils of liquid, feeling the wind and the sun and being at one with the mysterious universe. Like the notes coming from a musical instrument, that moment disappears without a trace—and all you want to do is catch another wave and then another.

There was no "surfing god," but "wave-riding" (as it was originally called) was entrenched within Hawaiian culture. It became the favorite recreational pastime of kings (including Kamehameha the Great) and chiefs, but commoners, including women, also took part. Surfing contests were held during the Makahiki festivities, an annual affair that lasted several months and honored Lono, the god of agriculture and fertility.

Long before Kahanamoku was born, Waikiki Beach earned a reputation as the sweetest spot for surfing off the south shore of Oahu. Waikiki enjoyed every natural advantage for surfing, beginning with the prevailing northeast trade winds. The long sliver of beach formed a cozy amphitheater, sheltered by the promontory of Diamond Head at one end and stretching west toward the harbor. The ocean floor sloped gradually out to sea, where a large coral reef about a half-mile from shore protected the cove. Summertime was especially magical, when swells generated by storms from the Southern Hemisphere created sets of long breakers that rolled in and broke as steadily and rhythmically as a heartbeat—a cradle for surfers, with waves that were good for novices and experts alike.

As a boy, Kahanamoku learned to recite the original names of the surf breaks off Waikiki like his counterparts on the mainland memorized the batting order of baseball lineups: "Ai-wohi, Ka-lehua-wehe, Ka-pua, Ka-puni, and Mai-hiwa." Each of these, he said, "seems to have a ring of excitement to it."[5] Every type of wave, or *nalu*, was given its own description: *nalu halehale* was a "large, towering wave," while *nalu haki poko* was a "quick-breaking wave." If the desired waves were nowhere to be found, surfers gathered strands of vines, swung them around their heads, and lashed the water with them while reciting a *mele* (chant):

Arise! Arise, ye great surfs from Kahiki [Tahiti],
The powerful curling waves.

Arise with *pohuehue* [a coastal vine].

Well up, long raging surf.[6]

Hawaiians surfed wearing only a *malo* (loincloth) or sarong, or "clad simply in Nature's robes." Different styles of boards—or *papa*—were employed, with the thick *papa olo* extending sixteen feet long and weighing as much as one hundred and fifty pounds. These boards were handcrafted from local woods, most often koa, wili wili, or ulu. The scarcity of wili wili wood meant that these boards were generally reserved for the chiefs.

The assembly of each board followed ritual. After a tree was cut down, a prayer was said and a fish was left as an offering. An adze made from stone was used to roughly shaped the board, and then, as Duke recalled, "coral of the corrugated variety, termed *pohaku puna*, which could be gathered in abundance along the sea beach, and a rough kind of stone (called *oahi*) were the commonly used articles for reducing and smoothing the rough surfaces of the board until all marks of the stone adze were obliterated."[7] A natural stain, often made from the root of the *ti* plant, gave it a polished finish and some protection against the corrosive effects of salt water.

Surfing was uniquely Hawaiian. So, when the first outsiders arrived in Hawaii, they couldn't help but comment on this seemingly bizarre activity. After Captain Cook met his death, his successor, James King, wrote about his encounter with "twenty or thirty of the natives, taking each a long narrow board, rounded at the ends, set out together from the shore. . . . The boldness and address, with which we saw them perform these difficult and dangerous maneuvers, was altogether astonishing, and is scarcely to be credited."[8]

In *Mardi and a Voyage Thither*, Herman Meville's novel about traveling in the South Seas, the author observed natives gamboling in the waves. "For this sport a surf-board is indispensable; some five feet in length; the width of a man's body; convex on both sides; highly polished; and rounded at the ends. . . . An expert swimmer shifts his position on his plank; now half striding it; and anon, like a rider in the ring, poising himself upright in the scud, coming on like a man in the air."[9]

Mark Twain journeyed to Hawaii as a correspondent for the *Sacramento Union* newspaper in 1866. Not far from where Cook was murdered, Twain came upon "a large company of naked natives, of both sexes and all ages."

Related Twain: "Each heathen would paddle three or four hundred yards out to sea (taking a short board with him), then face the shore and wait for a particularly prodigious billow to come along; at the right moment he would fling his board upon its foamy crest and himself upon the board, and here he would come whizzing by like a bomb-shell! It did not seem that a lightning express train could shoot along at a more hair-lifting speed.

Twain, then in his early thirties, decided to try surfing. "I got the board placed right, and at the right moment, too, but missed the connection myself," he wrote. "The board struck the shore in three quarters of a second without any cargo, and I struck the bottom about the same time, with a couple of barrels of water in me."

Concluded Twain: "None but the natives ever master the art"[10] of surfing.

The Reverend Henry Cheever described surfing in 1851 as "so attractive and full of wild excitement to Hawaiians, and withal so healthful, that I cannot but hope it will be many years before civilization shall look it out of countenance, or make it disreputable to indulge in this manly though dangerous exercise."[11]

This literary exposure notwithstanding, by all accounts surfing suffered a steep decline during the second half of the nineteenth century. This was primarily attributable to the precipitous death rate suffered by Hawaiians. The missionaries, too, quelled enthusiasm for surfing. They chopped up surfboards to use as desks and seats in school and discouraged displays of naked and near-naked flesh in the water.[12] They convinced Hawaiians to wear clothing at all times, which "greatly diminishes their practice of swimming and sporting in the surf, for it is less convenient to wear it in the water than the native girdle," missionary Hiram Bingham wrote, "and less decorous and safe to lay it entirely off on every occasion they find for a plunge or swim or surf-boat ride."[13]

Surfing also languished because outsiders did not "get" it. Surfing was unstructured, ephemeral, and without written rules. There were no goals to score or points to make; there were no innings or strikeouts; no quarters, halves, or game clocks. Like the original game of lacrosse, its Native American cousin on land, there were no boundaries in surfing. Further, it was so connected to Hawaii that it did not seem exportable. There was only one documented occurrence of surfing on the mainland before 1900. Three Hawaiian princes attending school in California were spotted surfing near Santa Cruz in 1885.

Other newly minted sports, like basketball (created in 1891) and volleyball (invented in 1895), were gaining disciples because of their ties to the popular Young Men's Christian Association (YMCA) movement. The mainland's most popular sport, baseball, was spreading faster than a surfboard could be carved, its popularity in Hawaii hastened after the man who helped formulate the rules of the game, Alexander Joy Cartwright, moved there in 1849 and became the head of Honolulu's fire department. Cartwright introduced the sport throughout the Hawaiian Islands and built Oahu's first diamond, in the neighborhood of Makiki.

Mark Twain himself was a hardball proselytizer. In a speech delivered to the Chicago White Stockings team upon their return from a worldwide tour in 1888–89 (which included a stop in Honolulu), Twain remarked that baseball was "the very symbol, the outward and visible expression, of the drive and push and rush and struggle of the living, tearing, booming nineteenth century!"[14]

By 1892, amid the political and societal crises facing the Hawaiian people, surfing was declared an endangered species. "There are those living, perhaps some present, who remember the time when almost the entire population of a village would at certain hours resort to the seaside to indulge in, or to witness, this magnificent accomplishment," wrote Nathaniel Emerson in an essay titled "Causes of the Decline of Ancient Hawaiian Sports." "We cannot but mourn its decline. But this too has felt the touch of civilization, and today it is hard to find a surfboard outside of our museums and private collections."[15]

Duke Kahanamoku did not graduate from the Kamehameha Schools. He left not long after helping the soccer team win the title. One biographer has related that Duke quit over a dispute with the principal concerning an absence. This account cannot be confirmed because the official registers from his five-year tenure at the school cannot be located. What remains from that time are black-and-white photos: Duke in his formal uniform, Duke and his soccer teammates in street clothes, Duke growing from young boy to young man.[16]

His connection with the school's namesake, on the other hand, would endure. After he achieved athletic success, Kahanamoku was occasionally "cast" as King Kamehameha and made to don a warrior costume during celebrations that honored the king's legacy. He also reportedly signed to play King Kamehameha in Hollywood, but the movie was never produced.

Later, others linked Kahanamoku to the deathbed "prediction" purportedly made by King Kamehameha: "Someday my people will lose their freedom and their nationality. Some day they will be supplanted in their own islands and sickness will spread among them and their strength will pass away. But before they are entirely gone there will come one in my image who shall have within himself all the glorious strength of a dying race, and he shall be honored throughout the world, and he shall bring fame to my people."[17]

Whether King Kamehameha uttered this prophecy is unknown. But it's instructive that, with his otherworldly achievements, many saw Duke Kahanamoku as the embodiment of the modern hero in the Hawaiian Islands.

What is known is that, in the fall of 1909, Duke left Kamehameha School for Boys behind and enrolled at Oahu's oldest public high school. Honolulu High School had recently changed its name to William McKinley High School to honor the late president. If Kahanamoku ever commented on the irony of transferring from a school named for the Hawaiian king who unified the Hawaiian Islands to one named for the American president responsible for signing the decree that annexed them, he did not do so publicly.

Now nineteen years old, Kahanamoku's athletic reputation preceded him. The school's student publication, *Black and Gold*, noted: "Three Kam boys have joined the McKinley ranks and are out for football practice . . . [including] Kahanamoku, with soccer, swimming, and rowing fame."[18]

But Kahanamoku did not stay long enough to impact the teams' fortunes. The campus of McKinley High School, located east of downtown Honolulu at the corner of Beretania and Victoria streets, was much closer to the temptations of Waikiki than Kamehameha. Because he was no longer a boarding student, Duke spent every afternoon and all weekend at the beach.

Soon, Kahanamoku dropped out of McKinley High altogether. He never finished high school; nor did he contemplate going to college. He would fathom his future in the watery depths of Waikiki.

3

Duke Kahanamoku left high school without any employment prospects but not without work. He sold newspapers on trolleys and street corners, shined shoes, carried ice, and did "just about anything that would bring in some pocket money"[1] for the family. If he needed to get somewhere quickly, he borrowed his grandfather's horse.

He ventured from Kalia, where the U.S. Army was filling in portions of the wetlands to build a vast military base for Oahu's coastal defense, and headed for the area down the beach near the Moana Hotel. He earned tips as a beachboy, taking tourists out on his surfboard or in canoes, allowing them to experience the frenzied rush of the waves.

Kahanamoku and a group of his pals, mostly Hawaiian lads like himself, gathered daily under the shade of a *hau* tree by the Moana Hotel. They spent countless hours listening to stories from experienced watermen and studying the ways of the water. It was the education of a waterman, with the sort of knowledge that one did not learn in school: wave formation and its tendencies, the effect of the reef on the different breaks, where the best fishing areas were located.

"Their sense of their environment was unusual," said Kenneth Brown, a longtime friend of Duke's. "They didn't differentiate much between what was above and below the sea. They had place names for all the hills and bays like we do, but they also had place names for things *down* in the water. That's the way it was with Duke. The ocean was such a familiar, friendly environment for him. He was no more afraid of what might happen to him at sea than you or I would be of getting hit by a car crossing the street. The ocean was his home."[2]

Like most of his contemporaries, Kahanamoku started off bodysurfing—riding waves without the help of any board. The first "boards" he used were improvised: "kerosene cans that we'd beat flat with stones," he said. He graduated to using the wooden bottoms of Standard Oil containers.

"One of the first things I remember is taking a cracker box board and pushing it ahead of me to swim out into the surf, using it like a surfboard," he later told columnist Robert Edgren. "You can take a small board and go a long way. I used to swim out, turn around, and come back through the surf."[3]

As Kahanamoku grew older and bigger, he switched to using a longboard for surfing. He fashioned this from redwood planks, learning by trial and error what size, shape, and weight worked best for him. The woodworking skills he learned at Kamehameha Schools inadvertently helped him become adept with the tools that were needed for board shaping: saws, planers, and sandpaper.

In 1910 he built himself a new board that measured close to ten feet in length, with a tail that was 19 inches wide. He proudly carved "DUKE" into the wood, outlined in white, near its rounded top edge. "I was fired up with a mania for improving the boards and getting the most out of the surf," he said. "I was constantly redoing my board, giving it a new shape, new contours, new balance. . . . [and] spent uncounted hours working at every phase of controlling my boards in the waves, trying new approaches, developing new tricks."[4]

His style was unadorned compared to today's surfers. He stood proud and erect, his knees slightly bent. The massive board, which was shaped roughly like a coffin lid and did not have a skeg (fin), was not maneuverable enough for modern-day tricks, like hotdogging or riding inside the tube.

Surfer Albert "Rabbit" Kekai, who was much younger than Duke, remembers that Kahanamoku and his peers used to "just stand and do what we call 'pose.' They used to hold their pose for a mile. At times you'd see them bend down to just take a little drop, then pick up speed again. But they never did cutbacks. It was all angle. They'd shout, 'Comin' down!' or 'No drop-in!' if we looked like we were thinking about going in front of them."[5]

For kicks, Duke stood on his head or grabbed a youngster and placed him or her atop his shoulders for a tandem joyride. That's what surfing was about: fun. His philosophy was as plain as his wooden board. "We had a board and there were waves," he said. "So I surfed. When there were no waves, I swam and played baseball."[6]

But surely surfing also provided Kahanamoku with an escape from the chaos and changes engulfing Hawaii. In the water he didn't have to answer to anyone. The waves represented freedom, and he just happened to be the best surfer around. "On a board I felt like the bossman," he said. "I'm in charge when I make the big wave do what I want."[7]

In May of 1907, Jack London and his second wife, Charmian, were sailing the South Seas on their yacht, *The Snark*, when they stopped over in Hawaii. London was at the height of his literary fame, with *Call of the Wild* (1903), *The Sea Wolf* (1904), and *White Fang* (1906) among his recent successes. With *The Snark* safely moored at Pearl Harbor, they decamped to the Seaside Hotel, which was managed by a friend of Jack's from his Yukon days.

A slender, goateed man latched onto the couple and, for the next two hours, bent their ears. Alexander Hume Ford, then thirty-nine years old, was a South Carolinian by birth. Like London, Ford was a relentless traveler and prolific writer, although he admitted to London that his fiction was "rot."

Ford was himself a *malihini* (a newcomer) to Hawaii, but he excitedly related to the Londons the changes coming to the area. An electric tramline running from downtown Honolulu to Waikiki was replacing the horse-drawn streetcars of Kahanamoku's youth and improving accessibility to the surf. On Waikiki itself, wedged between a smattering of private residences and bungalows, were two new beachfront hotels. The Seaside, which opened in 1906, and the deluxe Moana (1901), with a breezy lanai and a 300-foot wooden pier that extended into the ocean, were bringing visitors to within steps of the sparkling white sand.

Businessmen with the Hawaii Promotion Committee were marketing the splendors of the island life, having recognized that vacationers cared only so much about the debate over sugar tariffs. What visitors wanted to do when they stopped over in Hawaii was relax and enjoy its natural rhythm. The Hawaii Promotion Committee began to plaster images of surfing on travel posters and advertisements in order to "sell" this version of Hawaii. They hired cinematographer Robert Bonine, from Thomas Edison's company, to shoot scenes for his "actuality" series. Bonine's black-and-white films, among the first flickering images to capture surfing in motion, were exhibited throughout the mainland.

An inveterate schemer and striver, Alexander Hume Ford formed the Hawaiian Trail and Mountain Club, the Pan-Pacific Union, and the Hands around the Pacific organization with one purpose: to aid the *haole* population in asserting greater control over Hawaii and the region. Curiously, it was Ford's passion to promote Hawaii as the "land of opportunity for the quick, courageous white man"[8] that led him to surfing.

Sport, Ford well knew, was cultural currency. Like many in his social circle, Ford took his cue from Great Britain, then the world's superpower, where the privileged gentlemen who were inventing the structures of modern sport believed that it was the intoxicating glue that marshaled national spirit and bound together the far-flung empire. They had invented cricket and then exported it to India and the Caribbean. They had created rugby and taken it to South Africa, Australia, and New Zealand. They had designed tennis, table tennis, golf, and soccer—and soon these were played everywhere. At the very moment that Alexander Hume Ford met Jack London, the city of London was building the first great modern sports stadium and English athletes were preparing to meet their up-and-coming rival in empire building, the United States, at the 1908 Olympic Games.

Ford himself flopped in his first attempts at surfing. He kept at it until a local expert, George Freeth, taught him. "I learned in a half an hour the secret I had sought for weeks,"[9] Ford proudly related.

Surfing turned Ford into a proselytizer. "As a healthful sport and exercise, surf-riding has no equal in the world,"[10] he exclaimed. With that, he added a new goal to his long to-do list: make surfing, which he contended was "for so long believed to be possible of acquirement only by the native-born, dark-skinned Hawaiian,"[11] palatable to the *haole* population, including youth, adults, and tourists.

In Jack London, Ford saw an opportunity to make a convert—one who just happened to be a best-selling adventure author with a penchant for "manly" challenges. It probably did not take long for Ford to entice London to give surfing a whirl, and he came by several days later with an enormous wooden surfboard.

Ford's plan worked. Jack London's "Riding the South Sea Surf" appeared in *Woman's Home Companion* magazine and, later, was reprinted in *Cruise of the Snark* and other publications. Unlike Herman Melville and Mark Twain, London brought his readers into the surf from the moment he espied "the white-headed combers thrust suddenly skyward out of the placid turquoise blue and come rolling in to shore. One after another they come, a mile long, with smoking crests, the white battalions of the infinite army of the sea. And one sits and listens to the perpetual roar, and watches the unending procession, and feels tiny and fragile before this tremendous force expressing itself in fury and foam and sound."[12]

Suddenly, in the distance, London observed a figure:

> Where but the moment before was only the ocean's wide desolation and invincible roar is now a man, erect, full-statured, not struggling frantically in that wild movement, not buried and crushed and buffeted by those mighty monsters, but standing above them all, calm and superb, poised on the giddy summit, his feet buried in the churning foam, the salt smoke rising to his knees, and all the rest of him in the free air and flashing sunlight, and he is flying through the air, flying forward, flying fast, as the surge on which he stands. He is a Mercury—a black Mercury. His heels are winged, and in them is the swiftness of the sea. In truth, from out of the sea he has leaped upon the back of the sea, and he is riding the sea that roars and bellows and cannot shake him from its back. But no frantic outreaching and balancing is his. He is impassive, motionless, as a statue carved suddenly by some miracle out of the sea's depth from which he rose. . . . He is a Kanaka—and more; he is a man, a natural king, a member of the kingly species that has mastered matter and the brutes and lorded it over creation.[13]

London never identified the surfer by name, although it was likely George Freeth. Later, Freeth personally helped London stand upright on his board. The writer suffered extreme sunburn and a bump on the head, but unlike Melville and Twain, he succeeded in catching his first big wave:

> I saw it coming, turned my back on it and paddled for dear life. Faster and faster my board went, until it seemed my arms would drop off. What was happening behind me I could not tell. One cannot look behind and paddle the windmill stroke. I heard the crest of the wave hissing and churning, and then my board was lifted and flung forward. I scarcely

knew what happened the first half-minute. Though I kept my eyes open, I could not see anything, for I was buried in the rushing white of the crest. But I did not mind. I was chiefly conscious of ecstatic bliss at having caught the wave.[14]

Experience the "ecstatic bliss" of surfing, was London's message, delivered in purple prose that challenged members of the white race to match the Hawaiians. "You are a man, one of the kingly species, and what that Kanaka can do you can do yourself. Go to. Strip off your clothes that are a nuisance in this mellow clime. Get in and wrestle with the sea; wing your heels with the skill and power that reside in you; bite the sea's breakers, master them, and ride upon their backs as a king should."[15]

In the summer of 1907, George Freeth left Hawaii to pioneer surfing on the mainland, taking with him letters of introduction from Jack London and Alexander Hume Ford, support from the Hawaii Promotion Committee, and, presumably, his surfboard. He was soon spotted surfing at Venice Beach in California. Railroad magnate Henry Huntington then hired Freeth to showcase surfing in the nearby town of Redondo Beach, a promotional ploy that was designed to attract customers to Huntington's real estate venture and to generate business for his Pacific Electric Railway line (the ubiquitous "Red Cars").

Billed as "The Hawaiian Wonder," George Freeth was actually *hapa-haole* (of mixed heritage). He performed his "walk on water" act twice a day in front of the Redondo Hotel, wearing a tight green woolen suit and drawing enormous crowds that stayed to indulge in Huntington's beach empire (which included an indoor saltwater pool and an enormous oceanfront ballroom). Freeth concluded his performances by standing on his head while riding the surfboard to shore.

Freeth became the first confirmed surfer off California since the Hawaiian princes had surfed Santa Cruz in 1885. He soon set about exploring the Southern California coast, a large and diverse surf zone that would stretch from Mexico north to San Diego and then to San Onofre and Newport Beach, to Huntington Beach and Long Beach, and then to Manhattan Beach and Malibu and Santa Barbara, eventually becoming the world's most popular and influential surfing region outside of Hawaii.[16]

Alexander Hume Ford, meanwhile, used the momentum from Jack London's propitious visit to start the Outrigger Canoe Club on Waikiki Beach in May of 1908. He leased one-and-a-half acres of land from the Queen Emma Estate, a parcel located between the Moana and the Seaside hotels, agreeing to pay ten dollars a year for a twenty-year lease.

The Outrigger Canoe Club's mission was about "preserving surfing on boards and in Hawaiian outrigger canoes."[17] The club purchased canoes and surfboards, and members dragged two authentic grass houses from an old zoo in Kaimuki to the beach to serve as a bathhouse and a place to store surfboards. Soon, Ford was organizing surfing and rowing contests.

Ford respected surfing's indigenous roots, but he barred Duke Kahanamoku and other native Hawaiians from joining his whites-only domain. The Outrigger Canoe Club was "practically an organization for the *haole*,"[18] conceded Ford, who did little to hide his glee. "The white man and boy are doing much in Hawaii to develop the art of surf-riding," he wrote. "Games and feats never dreamed of by the native are being tried."[19]

Kahanamoku described it another way. "The Caucasians began to take to surfing—and that was a real switch," he dryly noted.[20]

The Outrigger Canoe Club's snub was not the first time that Duke had encountered prejudice in Hawaii; nor would it be the last. But it stung, not only because he was one of the best surfers at Waikiki (and thus the world), but also because he and the other regulars considered surfing to be the ultimate pleasure, without distinction of race, gender, religion, nationality, or class. "The best surfer out there is the one having the most fun," he said.[21]

4

The Outrigger Canoe Club was not the only local sports organization to exclude Duke Kahanamoku from membership. In 1910 Bill King of the Healani Boat Club in Honolulu encouraged him to come to Honolulu harbor and practice with the swimming team. Duke anchored the Healani's six-man relay team during a race against their rivals, the Myrtle Boat Club.

George "Dad" Center of the Myrtle Boat Club had about a 20-yard edge when Duke dove into the water for the last lap. "I caught up to [Center] and just beat him by a touch," Kahanamoku recounted. "That's when they noticed there was something in me to become a great swimmer."[1]

But neither the Healani Boat Club nor the Myrtle Boat Club invited Duke to join. Instead, he played on a pickup water polo team captained by his surfing pal, George Freeth, who had returned to Hawaii a hero for his rescue work in California. Kahanamoku was high scorer in a match against soldiers stationed at Fort Shafter; their triumph was so one-sided that it was the only match they were able to schedule.

In the summer of 1908, when Duke turned eighteen, he and two pals, Kenneth Winter and William "Knute" Cottrell, who hung out by the Moana Hotel, decided to form their own club. The "Very Lazy Surfers" was one name that they initially came up with. The trio eventually settled on a name that stuck, "Hui Nalu"—one they discovered while they were in the water.

Kahanamoku and Cottrell were sitting on their surfboards, by the reef, watching the waves come in sets. Duke got to thinking: "Well, gee, if we only can form a club and this would be the word—'Hui Nalu'—because 'hui' is 'to get together' or 'organization'—and 'nalu' is 'surf.'"[2]

Hui Nalu—"the club of the waves" or "surf club"—was organized in response to the exclusionary policy practiced at the Outrigger Canoe Club, according to Cottrell. "I had heard something said by one of the fellows at the Outrigger Canoe Club at that time which disgusted us quite a bit," he said, "so Duke, myself and Kenneth Winter . . . started the Hui Nalu."[3]

They had no clubhouse, but they met daily beneath the hau tree on the beach. They were the original "Bathhouse Gang," with space in a locker room of the nearby Moana Hotel. Dues were one dollar a year. "It was a poor man's club, but it was made up of dedicated surfers," Kahanamoku said. "Suddenly we seemed to belong to something important. At least it was to us."[4]

What set the club apart was its diversity: members were Hawaiians, *hapa-haole*, and *haole*, with a sprinkling of *wahine* (girls). They included Jonah Kuhio Kalanianaole, one of the three princes who surfed Santa Cruz in 1885; prominent businessman Harold Castle, whose family headed Castle & Cooke (one of the "Big Five" companies that dominated Hawaiian commerce); Harry Steiner, later a district court magistrate; the Hustace brothers, Curtis and Harold, whose family lived on the beach; George "Tough Bill" Keaweamahi and his brother "Steamboat Bill"; and Duke's cousins and younger brothers.

First and foremost they were watermen and waterwomen. The ocean and the beach were at the center of their existence. To them, learning to read currents, tides, and wave patterns were more important skills than deciphering a novel. "A waterman is a fisherman, to start off," surfer Richard "Buffalo" Keaulana said. "You have to know the grounds—the bottom, not just the top. You know where's the flat area, where there's coral, where the channels are, where the sand is."[5]

Hui Nalu members swam together, surfed together, paddled together, talked story together, plied the tourist trade together, rescued the lives of flailing swimmers together, and fished together. At night, they gathered with their guitars and ukuleles for *kanikapila* (loosely translated as "playing music together on the beach"), sitting on the end of the Moana Hotel's landmark pier.

There was a decided hierarchy, with Duke and the older, more experienced watermen creating the unwritten rules that have come to constitute surfing etiquette: paddle around the wave going out, so you don't get hit by another board; the surfer who's on the wave first has the right of way; don't pick a wave in front of someone who is already on the wave; aid any surfer in distress; help retrieve a fellow surfer's lost board (in the days before ankle leashes were invented); and, finally, perhaps most important of all, never turn your back to the water.

"We'd know [which youngsters] can't handle the big waves and we'd send them back to shore," Kahanamoku said. "And we'd say, 'You stay there until you're big enough and then you come out.' . . . And every time we see them getting into difficulty in handling the board or getting into the wrong spot, we used to tell them, 'You go over there or you go over there, which is easier for you.'"[6]

Kahanamoku's exclusion from the Outrigger Canoe Club did not stop Alexander Hume Ford from publishing a photograph of Duke on the cover of the inaugural issue of *Mid-Pacific Magazine*, a glossy mouthpiece that Ford used to promote the natural wonders and business potential of the region. Local photographer A. R. Gurrey Jr. took the black-and-white photo of Kahanamoku surfing without a shirt, his stomach muscles flexed. Other photos accompanied the long article, titled "Riding the Surfboard" and published in January of 1911.

The byline was simply "Duke Paoa." Duke's last name was also not used on the second part of the story (published in the following issue). It is obvious from the stilted and hyperbolic language that Ford himself served as the ghostwriter. "I have never seen snow and do not know what winter means," the article begins. "I have never coasted down a hill of frozen rain, but every day of the year, where the water is 76, day and night, and the waves roll high, I take my sled, without runners, and coast down the face of the big waves that roll in at Waikiki."[7]

Then, echoing Jack London's prose, the article builds:

How would you like to stand like a god before the crest of a monster billow, always rushing to the bottom of a hill and never reaching its base, and to come rushing in for half a mile at express speed, in graceful attitude, of course, until you reach the beach and step easily from the wave to the strand? . . . I mastered the art of riding the surf-board in the warm Hawaiian waters when I was a very small child, and I never gaze out upon the ocean in any part of the island that I do not figure out how far each wave, as it comes rolling in, would carry me standing on its crest.[8]

Before 1911 Duke Kahanamoku's name was mentioned several times in the local newspapers, but only in passing. The published thoughts of one "Duke Paoa" were different. "Riding the Surfboard" introduced Kahanamoku and surfing to an audience beyond Hawaiian shores. It also marked the first time that Kahanamoku and his athletic skills and physique were used to promote Hawaii.

That point is worth noting in the ongoing debate about Alexander Hume Ford's role in the renaissance of surfing around 1908. Many believe that, if not for Ford's tireless promotion, surfing in Hawaii would have continued its slow march into obscurity. Ford was able to staunch surfing's demise, his advocates say, with proactive machinations: seizing the opportunity to put Jack London on a surfboard, founding the Outrigger Canoe Club and placing surfing at the center of its mission, legitimizing surfing among *haole* citizens, writing numerous articles that touted surfing's benefits, and publishing a photo of Duke on the cover of *Mid-Pacific Magazine*.

Others feel that Ford as marketer exaggerated surfing's decline to cement his own reputation. They note that surfing was enjoying a grassroots resurgence on Waikiki Beach—led by Freeth, Kahanamoku, and Hui Nalu members—and that Ford usurped surfing to further his goal of promoting American interests in the region.

Savior? Revivalist? Usurper? Somewhere between these viewpoints is where Ford and his reputation deserve to rest. Perhaps the most salient point is that, unlike many of the rituals practiced in ancient Hawaii and then abandoned after contact with outsiders, surfing survived into the twentieth century.

Up until about 1910, Kahanamoku focused primarily on surfing and rowing. Surfing was fun; it was social, but it was also deeply personal. Rowing was about competition. The local clubs involved in "barge racing" in Honolulu harbor and throughout Hawaii competed for bragging rights and gleaming trophies, with Regatta Day, held every September, celebrated as a public holiday.

Swimming, on the other hand, was something Kahanamoku did every day at Waikiki, sort of like breathing. He told one interviewer that his goal was "to become the world's champion single sculler. I did not think much about becoming a swimming champion back in 1908 and 1909, although I knew I was pretty fast then. However, I could not afford a scull."[9]

Unlike running, competitive swimming was slow to catch on. The sport began in the early nineteenth century with, almost exclusively, the breaststroke. John Trudgen, an Englishman who spent his youth in South America and learned to swim by watching native Indians there, made the next leap. His stroke combined the overarm movement associated with the freestyle and the sidestroke (or scissors) kick. The "trudgen" was a hybrid that was anything but smooth, but it was considered the best option for distance events.

Still, competitive swimming remained an afterthought. The world's most famous swimmer was a former British naval officer named Matthew Webb. But Webb wasn't renowned for his speed or for racing; in 1875 he was the first person to swim the English Channel.

At around the turn of the twentieth century, Alick Wickham, a Solomon Islands native, was credited with using a "crawl" motion and a straight-legged kick. Members of the Cavill family in Australia put these components together, adopting Wickham's kick in a two-beat rhythm with the overhead arm motion; hence the "Australian crawl"—and, hence, speed in the water.

By 1904 Charles Daniels was employing a more continuous, six-beat kick en route to becoming America's first swimming star. A member of the New York Athletic Club, Daniels won the 200- and 400-meter events at the 1904 St. Louis Olympics, as well as the 100-meter event at the London Olympics in 1908.

The Cavill family and other Australians (including Annette Kellerman, swimming's first female superstar) deserve much credit for their pioneering contributions toward popularizing swimming. Several Australians toured Hawaii in 1910; many experts maintain that Duke Kahanamoku developed his stroke after he observed these swimmers in Honolulu.

Kahanamoku claimed that he never "learned" to swim—that is, he did not receive formal training beyond the encouragement of his father and uncles. He said that he used established practices of Pacific Islanders. "A funny thing about my swimming," he said, "is that from the time I was a kid I used a modern crawl kick. That's supposed to be a modern invention, but I used it naturally—always used it. Nobody ever showed it to me. I swam that way the first time I pushed a cracker-board ahead of me and swam out into the surf."[10]

His arm movement was not radically different from others', except that he swung them overhead at a slower, more deliberate pace. What was original was his flutter kick. He moved his limbs up and down in short, powerful bursts, six times for every stroke that he took with his arms. He kept his legs underwater, while his enormous feet acted like "propeller blades,"[11] according to one account.

The "Kahanamoku kick" came about, Duke said, because he swam outside and in open water. He had to adjust to the natural elements and navigate wind, waves, reefs, and tides. With his head held high out of the water and his powerful chest acting like a prow, he moved like a sleek, graceful projectile.

Being a consummate waterman benefited his swimming. Rowing built up strength in his arms, chest, legs, and lungs. Surfing offered a full-body workout: muscling his one-hundred-plus-pound board in and out of the water, paddling out in different conditions, and balancing on a board in the ocean. Even retrieving wayward surfboards improved his swimming. "It was in steering these boards to shore that [we] discovered the tremendous drive that we might get from our legs by thrashing them up and down, stiff-kneed, with a short, vigorous kick," he said. "This is the origin of the Hawaiian kick."[12]

About the only thing that slowed him down was the two-piece bathing suits that the conservative (some would say prudish) mores dictated swimmers should wear. These "costumes" exposed as little bare skin as possible. A tank top virtually encased their bodies, from shoulder to midthigh. Underneath that, they had to wear the equivalent of boxer shorts. The material used was either woven cotton or wool. When soaked through and waterlogged, the suits weighed down the swimmers and markedly slowed their times. "One reason that swimming had failed to develop as a sport was simply that no one could move in the damn things," journalist Paul Gallico recalled. Women swimmers, whose costumes were even more restrictive, dressed "more for going down into a mine than entering the sea."[13]

Alexander Hume Ford was the first to publicize Duke's prowess on a surfboard, but it was another *haole*, William Rawlins, who pushed Kahanamoku into the national spotlight via swimming. The Yale Law School-educated assistant U.S. district attorney for Hawaii espied Kahanamoku and a couple of friends during their daily swims off Sans Souci Beach at Waikiki. Rawlins introduced himself and had the boys swim a 100-yard course while timing them with a stopwatch.

Rawlins was intrigued by Duke's raw speed and potential. Kahanamoku was quiet and had no vices: he didn't smoke cigarettes or drink alcohol. His boyish frame was developing into the physique of a mature muscleman, with broad shoulders and a burly chest that tapered to thick thighs. His gigantic hands and size 13 feet—"the paddle-like appendages wished on him by nature"[14]—pulled him through the water like a motorboat.

"He had the biggest hands, the biggest feet," his brother Sargent said. "I'll never forget when I was a young boy and he slapped me—that was enough to know not to do something anymore. When his hand came out—whoosh. . . . No foolin' around."[15]

Well connected and with political aspirations of his own, William Rawlins was a leader within the newly formed Hawaiian chapter of the Amateur Athletic Union (AAU). The men who were taking control of the apparatus of modern sports—and they were all men—believed that it was necessary to regulate the increasingly complex and unwieldy nature of organized competition. They formed the AAU and its brethren, including the International Olympic Committee (IOC), the American and National leagues in baseball, and the Fédération Internationale de Football Association (FIFA) in soccer, to codify sports. They drew up rules, created game schedules, oversaw officiating, provided for accurate measuring and timing devices, maintained records and statistics, built stadiums and pools and other facilities, and governed the behavior of the athletes.

Under the leadership of James E. Sullivan, the tsar of amateur sports in America, the AAU required that athletes join sanctioned clubs to enter its meets, including the all-important national championships. These events were regarded as the fundamental stepping-stone for the Olympics. Sullivan himself had coordinated the 1904 Olympic Games in St. Louis, the first held on American soil, and had selected and managed the U.S. team for the 1908 Olympics in London.

Rawlins and bandleader-lifeguard-beachboy Edward "Dude" (pronounced "Doo-die") Miller pushed Kahanamoku and other Hui Nalu members to think beyond mere recreation. Soon, Hui Nalu was registered with the AAU, and thus its members were eligible to compete in the upcoming AAU swim meet in Honolulu harbor. They duly elected their first set of officers—with Rawlins as president and Miller as captain—and adopted a distinctive uniform of "black shorts and black tank tops with a gold or yellow stripe around the waistline, like a wide belt."[16]

Of course, they couldn't enter the competition without a rousing fight song:

We love you, Hui Nalu
Our club of the ocean wave
And we shall never cease to love you
Or our colors so brave.
Firm friendship will entwine you
From our hearts where e're you go
We shan't forget our fellows
Who adore and love you so.

Chorus: Where the wild ocean waves are foaming
Our fellows are sure to be
Where the big rollers burst
And the surf is the worst
We'll be there and yell with glee!

With our surfboards we always are ready
To leap in the deep blue sea
Our royal black and gold
In victory will unfold
Always on top!
Hui Nalu![17]

5

Duke Kahanamoku and Hui Nalu made their first official appearance as a swim team on August 12, 1911. Their opponents were rival clubs from Honolulu, the Healanis and the Myrtles. The Outrigger Canoe Club reportedly had cold feet and decided not to enter the competition once they scanned the entry list.

Curious spectators flocked to Honolulu harbor at the foot of Alakea Street, the men dressed in white shirts, ties, and straw hats, and the women dressed in white linen dresses holding umbrellas to shield themselves from the sun. The excitement was palpable as the crowd lined the walkways between piers 6 and 7, where the interisland coal slip was located.

For this, the first AAU-sanctioned sporting event held in Hawaii, the conditions were perfect. The "murky, flotsam-filled" water was calm, with little current, accompanied by a slight cooling breeze. The straightaway course "stretched from a barnacled old barge into what was called the Alakea Slip,"[1] with a thick rope stretched taut over the water to mark the finish line.

Standing six feet one inch tall and weighing a muscular one hundred and seventy-five pounds, Duke Kahanamoku was in top shape. He climbed down to the wooden starting plank and calmly awaited the starter's pistol. Twelve days shy of his twenty-first birthday, his life was about to change forever.

The tone was set during the opening race, when Kahanamoku took the 220-yard event by thirty yards in 2:42.4, whipping "Dad" Center of the Myrtles. Later, he was part of the victorious 300-yard, six-man relay squad that cemented the points competition for Hui Nalu.

In between those races, in two sprints, Kahanamoku swam to history. The 100-yarder was his best event, and he did not give his main opponent,

Larry Cunha of the Healanis, a chance. Duke was so far ahead by the half-way mark that it was just a matter of how fast he could go. And he was fast! He drove to the finish, toppling the hapless Cunha by ten yards. His time of 55.4 seconds was 4.6 seconds faster than Charles Daniels's American record of 1 minute flat.

The 100-yard event was mere warm-up for the 50. Kahanamoku was the third man to hit the water, but he overtook Cunha and forged ahead to win by five yards. His time of 24.2 seconds was faster than the American mark, held by Daniels, by 1.6 seconds.

In less than ninety seconds of action, Duke had turned an improbable trifecta. He trounced one of the local clubs that had snubbed him for membership; shattered two records set by the premiere swimmer on the mainland; and announced his arrival to the far-flung swimming fraternity, from San Francisco to New York City to London to Sydney.

Bill Rawlins and Dude Miller rushed to congratulate him. As he would for the rest of his career, Kahanamoku treated the occasion with understated modesty, preferring to celebrate the overall triumph of Hui Nalu above his personal victories. He later gave credit to the *water* in Honolulu for his success. "Our water is so full of life, it's the fastest water in the world," he said. "That's all there is to it."[2]

In the days that followed, local reporters and photographers scurried in search of the mysterious and modest beachboy, who was "not well known among the people of Honolulu, but is remembered by many tourists who have visited Hawaii and taken a dip in the surf of Waikiki."[3]

One newspaper sent a correspondent to interview Kahanamoku on the beach. At the appointed hour, Duke was found asleep under a palm tree wearing nothing but bathing trunks. Awakened, Duke was asked to stand his giant surfboard erect and, directed by the photographer, dutifully pose in front of it against the backdrop of Diamond Head. The tableau indelibly linked him with Waikiki and Hawaii—and would become almost a trademark: surfing's primal image.

Kahanamoku pledged "body and soul" to Hui Nalu and then suffered a battery of questions with charm. "How does it feel to be able to swim faster than any other man on earth?" he was asked.

"I don't notice anything different," was his deadpan reply.

When Duke took his surfboard into the water for action photographs, the reporter noticed a distinct change. "On land he is like a fish out of its element. In the water he is a seal, or a whale, or a shark, or anything else that is popularly supposed to be born in the briny deep."[4]

The first article to identify Kahanamoku as a swimming phenomenon set the tone for the media coverage that he received throughout much of his life. Reporters then (and later) commented on Duke's reticence and mocked his terse, stilted answers. They did not understand that he was a private person who was wary about revealing personal information. "We used to say, '*Mahape a ale wala'au*,' and that means 'Don't talk—keep it in your heart,'" his brother Sargent said. "And that's what [Duke] did."[5]

Duke's friend Kenneth Brown put it another way. "People could say to you that Duke was simple—'the bugga must be dumb!'" he said. "No way. That's an easy way of explaining that. Duke was totally without guile. He knew a lot of things. He just knew 'em."[6]

Those in Hawaii who followed the results of the Honolulu meet were proud of Duke and his accomplishments. But when Bill Rawlins sent the times to AAU officials on the mainland, Kahanamoku's performance registered a very different (and probably apocryphal) reaction: "What are you using for stopwatches? Alarm clocks?"

Rawlins forwarded supporting documents from the timekeepers and course measurers to AAU headquarters in New York City. Two months later, a lengthy response arrived in the form of a letter from Otto Wahle, James Sullivan's chief adviser and official record keeper for swimming.

Wahle was an Austrian-Jewish swimmer who had taken second place in the 200-meter obstacle course at the 1900 Olympics in Paris and third place in the 400-meter breaststroke at the 1904 St. Louis Olympics. He emigrated to the United States and was hired by the prestigious New York Athletic Club (NYAC). Together with Italian-born Louis de Breda Handley, Wahle guided the NYAC to national championships in swimming and water polo, helped develop the "American crawl" stroke, and coached superstar Charles Daniels, who, coincidentally, held the very records that Duke had purportedly smashed.

Wahle was bluntly suspicious about Duke's times. He couldn't fathom Kahanamoku breaking Daniels's 50-yard record by nearly two seconds or his busting the 100-yard mark by almost five seconds. Wahle chastised Hawaiian officials about every aspect of the process, beginning with the timekeeping. "The fact that four watches, two of which are handled by the same person, should on two occasions agree absolutely is a very rare, almost unusual occurrence," he wrote before adding, "Some information regarding the anchoring of the floats should have been given. If they were not well secured they may have floated nearer to each other with the tide and a course which measured 100 yards may have been considerably shorter an hour or two later."[7]

From his mid-Manhattan aerie, Wahle presumed to lecture Hawaiians about the effects of the tide in Honolulu. "The information that the swimmers had the tide against them is based on the reasoning that the tide was coming in whereas the swimmers swam from shore towards the open," he asserted. "No greater mistake could be made than to accept this supposition as a general rule. In a bay with inlets and channels the current runs in irregular directions."[8]

The most incriminating evidence, according to Wahle, was Duke's anonymity. "The fact that an absolutely unknown swimmer should swim 100 yards considerably faster than the world's champion is still more rare or to be correct it is unheard of," he noted. "If his 55 2/5 sec. were accepted and he should afterwards compete in the United States or Europe and be beaten by swimmers whose best times are considerably slower, the correctness of his 55 2/5 sec. would be strongly questioned as well as the good faith of the AAU."[9]

Wahle declined to accept Kahanamoku's times. But he also dangled hope, intimating that the AAU would validate the records if Kahanamoku were to travel to the mainland and race against the nation's best swimmers. Wahle stated another motivation to see Duke in person: the upcoming Stockholm Olympics. "If Kahanamoku really can do 100 yards straightaway or even in a bath [indoor pool] in 55 2/5 sec. he is a man whom the AAU needs to replace Daniels in the Olympic games, 1912," he noted.[10]

The outrage in Hawaii over the AAU's haughty attitude was palpable. Many wondered whether Duke's skin color was the reason for the denial. Others pointed to Hawaii's territorial, outlier status.

"We are some sporting nation," one journalist fumed, "but it must be admitted that that part of 'we' which hangs around the corner of Tecumseh,

Maine, and Forty-fifth street, New York, are sometimes inclined to turn a collection of supercilious noses skyward over any American or world's amateur record of any sort being held by a 'South Sea Islander,' whom they might actually think at this moment is blowing the ashes under a pot destined for the par-boiling of a missionary."[11]

Perversely, the snub awakened Hawaiians to Duke's plight. In Kahanamoku, they had a bona fide phenomenon whose family could not afford to send him to the mainland, much less to Europe, should he qualify for the Olympic team. Local boosters and sportsmen rallied around their Hawaiian hope and decided to raise the necessary money, estimated to be about $1,000, for his travel expenses to the national swimming championships, scheduled for February. Rawlins, Miller, and Hui Nalu members organized a benefit dance that brought in $311. Receipts from a two-day athletic carnival raised another $277.60. Individual donations starting at $1 poured in from rich and poor: from Hawaiians, Asians, and *haole* (including Alexander Hume Ford); from Maui to Molokai.

The Hawaii Promotion Committee, spearheaded by none other than Lorrin A. Thurston, embraced the cause. The publisher of the *Pacific Commercial Advertiser* newspaper and president of the local branch of the AAU, Thurston likened Kahanamoku to an export product that was as alluring as a crate of pineapples—and potentially as lucrative. Sponsoring Duke's efforts was "an advertising scheme" that would bring "the most valuable sort of publicity for the Islands," according to the *Advertiser*.[12]

Beginning with the Kahanamoku Fund, the relationship that developed between Duke and an ever-changing cast of patrons, including the *haole* powerbrokers who controlled Hawaii's economy, was unique in modern sports. No individual athlete was so closely identified with his homeland as Kahanamoku—and no community ever championed one athlete as assiduously as Hawaii championed Kahanamoku. The bond was mutually beneficial, but Duke always felt pressure to perform well and represent his homeland with dignity. The nature of this arrangement would occasionally fray, leaving both parties vexed and disillusioned.

For now, Kahanamoku appreciated the backing, financial and otherwise, that he received. All he wanted, he maintained, was an opportunity to compete at the highest level. "Give me a chance and I'll do my best to make good," he said. "I think I can do it."[13]

It was determined that Kahanamoku needed an escort to handle the travel chores and the demands of competition. Surfer George Freeth volunteered his services, but officials nixed that idea over worries that Freeth's connections to professional athletes might taint Kahanamoku's amateur status and harm his chances to qualify for the Olympics. Duke recommended that Hui Nalu distance swimmer Vincent "Zen" Genoves accompany him because "he would be able to hold his own in endurance races and add to Hawaii's credit."[14]

Money was quickly raised for "Zen" to make the trip. Rawlins himself had personal business concerns in Hawaii, so Lew Henderson, a draughtsman at the Pearl Harbor naval station, was chosen to be the tour manager. "Dude" Miller was added as trainer–companion because the commodore of Hui Nalu had previously traveled to the mainland as a bandleader.

To stay in shape Kahanamoku swam and surfed daily, and also helped Hui Nalu win the four- and six-man canoe events on Regatta Day. He and Genoves gave a free swimming exhibition at the Bishop slip to thank the public for their support. Duke also aided Alexander Hume Ford in the rescue of a drowning woman at the beach. "I saw her struggle in the water and at once rushed in and put my tights on, got my surfboard and started out after her," he said. "I got the woman's arms around my neck and was helped in with her by the others. . . . Then I went out again as I heard there was a man missing. I and other Hui Nalu boys saw two sailors on surfboards a long way out and drifting out to sea. They were unable to get back and so I and the others went out and brought them back."[15]

Finally, on February 8, 1912, Duke, Genoves, Henderson, and Miller boarded the ss *Honolulan* for California. The Matson wharf was crowded with friends and family, and the four were decorated in pungent, colorful lei. Duke's mother cried quietly as Hui Nalu's quintet sang their version of "Aloha Oe" ("Farewell to Thee"), written by Queen Liliuokalani.

And then, with the foghorn whistle blowing, they were off. Kahanamoku had packed little more than his bathing costume, an ill-fitting summer suit, and a hat. It was his first trip away from Hawaii. He had no way of knowing it, but he would not see his family again for eight months.

6

Duke Kahanamoku's first impression of the United States was one of cease-less bustle. Duke and his three companions' immediate destination, San Francisco, was rebuilding itself after the devastating earthquake and fire that occurred nearly six years previously. The entire country was gearing up for the 1912 presidential race, a three-way affair involving President William Taft, former president Teddy Roosevelt, and Democratic chal-lenger Woodrow Wilson. The newly formed National Collegiate Athletic Association was tinkering with the rules of football, reducing the length of the field to one hundred yards (from one hundred and ten yards) and increasing the number of downs to four (from three). Media attention was focused on the upcoming maiden voyage of the RMS *Titanic*, the world's largest ocean-liner.

"Everything seemed very strange to me," was Duke's initial reaction to the mainland. "I thought if I ever got as far as San Francisco I would have seen the world."[1]

Almost immediately, Kahanamoku, "Zen" Genoves, Lew Henderson, and "Dude" Miller left California and boarded the Overland Limited train to Chicago. Looking out the window as they passed through the Rocky Mountains, Kahanamoku saw snow for the first time. The scene recalled the opening line from the essay that Alexander Hume Ford ghostwrote for Duke in 1911: "I have never seen snow and do not know what winter means."

He soon learned that winter and snow meant cold. The clothes he brought from Honolulu were no match for the Windy City in February. He stuffed cardboard to line the inside of his coat until some Chicago clubmen took him to Marshall Field's department store and purchased more appropriate outerwear. He stayed busy writing letters to his family.

Kahanamoku and his companions left Chicago for Pittsburgh, where Kahanamoku was scheduled to make his mainland debut in the 220-yard national championship race on February 22. American swimming officials were anxious to see how the heralded Hawaiian handled the rigors of top competition. There was one catch, however: he would have to prove himself indoors.

Duke had only swum outdoors—either on the straightaway courses in Honolulu harbor or in the Pacific Ocean. Indoor pools were a relatively new phenomenon in America. With the exception of public baths, they were almost exclusively built and reserved for members of private clubs. The dimensions of these "tanks," as they were called, were not uniform, with the pool length measuring anywhere from twenty-five feet to fifty yards. Getting a good start was important, but so was navigating the turns, especially in the sprint races. If a swimmer incorrectly timed his approach, that could prove to be the difference between winning and losing.

There were other challenges. Pools from that era were not divided into lanes; nor were there markings on the pool's floor to guide the swimmers. Races often devolved into jostling collisions between competitors who drifted from their designated lanes.

The ventilation at these facilities was downright ruinous. "The place was filled with smoke right down to the water," Duke recalled about one of his first indoor races. "They had to stop everyone from smoking, they had to open all the windows up and use the fan to push all the smoke out of the pool. Then we went on. . . . It [was] terrible. You [could] smell that smoke right down on the surface of the water."[2]

The cigar smokers packed into Pittsburgh's indoor swimming pool as Duke and Genoves readied for their first test. They had no opportunity to swim during the voyage from Hawaii to San Francisco—and scant hours to get accustomed to swimming indoors. Kahanamoku was entered in the 220-yard race—a distance somewhat outside his comfort range—in front of a crowd that likely had never previously encountered a Hawaiian.

Duke's start was good, and he was in the lead for several laps. Then, suddenly, for perhaps the first time in his life, the water no longer was his best friend. Everything caught up with him at once: the rigors of travel and the long layoff, his first time being away from home and on the mainland, the indoor conditions, the cold weather, and the pressure of carrying Hawaii's hopes for winning in the Olympic Games. His legs tightened. He gasped in pain and swallowed water. He floundered as if a powerful tide were surging toward him. He had to be pulled from the pool, nearly unconscious.

Cramps had nearly sunk Kahanamoku, likely caused by dehydration and the lack of an adequate warm-up. Poor Genoves fared little better, finishing fifth in his heat of the 500-yard race and failing to qualify for the finals.

Their showing was an ignominious disaster. "Kahanamoku the Hawaiian has discovered that there's all the difference in the world between surf riding and a 75-foot tank," jeered Pittsburgh reporters.[3]

An impromptu ukulele session with Toots Paka's touring ensemble relaxed Duke and eased his mind about the dispiriting performances. He returned to the pool to practice and, later that week, raced two exhibitions against Kenneth Huszagh of Chicago, one of the nation's premiere swimmers. These were 50- and 100-yard sprints—distances that better suited him—and Kahanamoku won both races with a forceful verve. Impressed by his physique and his friendly demeanor, event organizers embraced him. They wrapped his body in an American flag and introduced him to an appreciative crowd that roared its approval. He was given two gold medals designed by Victor David Brenner, the artist who designed the Lincoln penny, and when the ukuleles were brought out that night, this time they were tuned to the key of victory.

Lew Henderson escorted the crew to Philadelphia. His family lived in the area, and the home cooking helped the Hawaiians get comfortably situated. Henderson then made an invaluable contribution, introducing Duke to George Kistler, the swim coach at the University of Pennsylvania.

Born on the west coast of England, Kistler was an open-water champion distance swimmer who had come to the United States in the late nineteenth century. Penn was upgrading the quality of its athletics program—Michael Murphy, the flinty track coach, being the most prominent hire—and employed Kistler to develop aquatics training. Kistler's swim and water polo teams were among the first collegiate squads to be established in the country, and Penn soon became a regional power.

The portly, mustachioed Kistler agreed to coach Kahanamoku gratis. He tutored him in three areas. His starts were poor, so Kistler had Duke dive into the water over and again, teaching him to harness his forward momentum during the crucial opening stanza. Duke also received lessons in negotiating the turns, including the all-important approach and follow-through. Finally, Kistler helped Kahanamoku coordinate his stroke with his oxygen intake. "I didn't know how to breathe, and I didn't know how to turn," Duke admitted.[4]

Every other day, under Kistler's direction, Kahanamoku swam a half-mile at Penn's new indoor pool at Weightman Hall, with its cramped dimensions of 30 x 100 feet. "I'm getting familiar with fresh water," Duke wrote to his father, "but I had an awful time with it at first. The turns, of course, bothered me, but I'm getting accustomed to them. Kistler says I have them down pretty well."[5]

Between workouts he competed in seven races in a span of twenty-three days, in various cities on the East Coast. He defeated R. E. Frizell in a 100-yard invitational at the City Athletic Club pool in New York and whipped two of Kistler's own stars, John Shryock and F. H. Sanville, at Weightman Hall. Kistler crowed that Kahanamoku was capable of becoming the first swimmer to bust the seemingly impregnable one-minute barrier for 100 meters.

In mid-March, in a pool that measured sixty feet, Chicago hosted the second stage of the AAU indoor championships. Kahanamoku took second place in the 50-yard event after he blew the lead by accelerating too fast approaching the final turn. For the 100, he held back and finished second in his heat. The final was close, coming down to the last length, but Duke held on to win his first national title.

His string of strong performances and Kistler's glowing praise impressed James E. Sullivan, Otto Wahle, and the U.S. Olympic brass. In a meeting held at his New York City offices, Sullivan assured Kahanamoku that he would represent the United States in the 100 meters at Stockholm. The only question left to consider was, would Duke have enough stamina to make the 4x200-meter relay team?

Their duties complete, Dude Miller, Zen Genoves, and Lew Henderson left for Hawaii. Kahanamoku stayed on with the Henderson family to prepare under Kistler. He had time to travel to the Hygeia Pool in Atlantic City for more indoor practice and was credited with saving the life of a man who fell unconscious and sank to the bottom of the pool, reportedly under the influence of alcohol.

Atlantic City, the prime resort along the Jersey Shore, made a powerful impression on Duke. He was itching to get into the water with a surfboard, but the chilly temperature of the Atlantic Ocean in April, in the decades before the invention of the wet suit, was far too daunting. Kahanamoku vowed to surf there in the summertime, when he returned from the Olympic Games in Europe. He wrote to Lew Henderson, who was now back in Hawaii, and arranged to have two surfboards sent to the mainland.

Kahanamoku promised one board to members of the Philadelphia Canoe Club, who had befriended him and allowed him the use of their facilities. Their headquarters along the Schuylkill River proved to be a fine place for him to swim once the weather turned warmer. He played rescuer again when two sailors upset their racing canoe on the Schuylkill River and flailed in its currents. Duke jumped in and fished them out.

When he was not saving lives in the water, Kahanamoku was discovering that his features, in and out of the water, fascinated and confounded opponents and newspaper reporters. "It was startling, the reaction when he swam," said Mike McDermott, the Chicago-based breaststroker. "Nobody had ever seen a Hawaiian before. And he swam differently. He lifted his head higher than we were taught and his arm curved as it went into the water. It wasn't that he was unorthodox. His stroke was symmetrical and easy. And he had plenty of rhythm. Besides he was strong, had a good heart, and he had big feet. I think that's where they got the idea to manufacture those swim fins to make you go faster."[6]

"His form has been a revelation to experts," the *Boston Globe* raved. "A noticeable feature of Kahanamoku's work is the manner in which he takes swells. Our own men swim low and go through them, experiencing a sudden and unmistakable check. He instead—due unquestionably to the marked slant of his body—sweeps gracefully over them, without apparent loss of momentum. Breasting the rollers and breaking surf of his native land has probably taught him to hold the position he does and it is bound to give him a great advantage in rough water, such as he is likely to find in Sweden."[7]

Even his prerace routine was deemed unconventional. Kahanamoku originated the practice of jumping into the water before the start of a race. "I would stop and go, 'Starter, could I go in for a swim?'" he said. "All those swimmers would sit on the edge of the deck . . . biting their nails and getting nervous [while] I'm in the water relaxing. . . . I know the temperature of the water. I know how cold and how hot [it is] when I jump in. I never get shocked, see? The starter would say, 'Are you ready?' I'm all ready."[8]

McDermott recalled that Duke brought his ukulele to the pool. "It was really a sight to see him before a race, plunking on the uke while the other swimmers were biting their fingernails," he said. "He was the first great bombshell to hit swimming."[9]

Many cited his heritage as an explanation for his success. Kahanamoku, as "a native Hawaiian, with a natural inclination toward the water, and a boyhood passed largely in that manner, has a marked advantage,"[10] one journalist wrote. "Nature has endowed him with such tremendous natural strength and surrounded him with so many encouragements to swim that he simply can't help himself,"[11] another later opined, as if Duke did not need to train.

Newspapers repeated a tall tale that "proved" he had an unfair edge. When Duke was a youngster, the story went, he and some other children and their parents embarked on a Sunday School picnic party aboard an old schooner. A squall arose unexpectedly, and the ship was tossed on its side. Duke and the occupants were thrown into the water, but "there was not one drowned for men, women, boys, girls, and babies paddled two miles back to shore and safety. The distance was nothing to the Hawaiians, who swim as easily as they walk."[12]

The incident did not actually happen to Duke, but Kahanamoku's "otherness" encouraged such exaggeration. "Foreign Swimmer Competes at Penn," one headline read, implying that Hawaii was not part of the United States.[13] Another paper reported that "there has been some criticism as to whether the Hawaiian should compete as an American [during the Olympics], but it is pointed out that he is in exactly the same position as the Indian Ranji, who for years represented England in cricket."[14]

Kahanamoku's name, too, perplexed reporters. With monarchical rule being the norm outside of the United States, they debated whether Duke was royalty. They routinely referred to him as "The Duke," while the *Chicago Almanac* dubbed him "Count Kahanamoku."[15] In "The Sporting Oracle" column of the *Chicago Examiner,* a reader asked: "Please give me the correct pronunciation of the name of Kahanamoku." The snarky answer: "The 'b' is silent, as in "geranium."[16]

This type of reaction was not surprising. The number of nonwhite athletes competing at the elite level was extremely limited due to the ingrained racism of the times. Perhaps the most prominent African American athlete of the era was boxer Jack Johnson. White promoters across America shunned the mercurial Johnson, the son of slaves, whose iconoclastic ways often upstaged his brilliance in the ring. Reporters who covered boxing (including Jack London) vilified him; footage of his triumphs was banned in certain sections of the country for fear of inciting riots. Johnson was forced to travel to Australia in 1908 to challenge (successfully) for the heavyweight championship, sport's most prestigious individual crown.

Kahanamoku was no firebrand like Johnson. But his presence at private, all-white athletic clubs was groundbreaking, all the more so because he was outfitted in bathing suits that, despite being dowdy by today's standards, were quite revealing when wet. He was accepted at these clubs because of his stature and gracious nature, but that did not shield him from hurtful and unseemly comments. Kahanamoku was repeatedly mistaken for an American Indian or an African American. He was refused service at one restaurant in Pittsburgh because of his skin color and reportedly also on other occasions.[17] He was publicly derided as "Kanaka," a term that was used pejoratively by non-Hawaiians.

Those who admired him often saw only the exotic. R. Tait McKenzie was a childhood friend of James Naismith, the inventor of basketball. An amateur sculptor who worked alongside George Kistler as the head of the Physical Education Department at Penn, McKenzie was awed by Kahanamoku's muscular body. He brought Duke into his studio on Pine Street, photographed his body, and completed a small sketch model. Kahanamoku was, McKenzie exclaimed, "the finest human specimen" he had ever seen.[18]

Kahanamoku never publicly complained about the demeaning treatment he encountered. He realized early on that the best possible retort was to win in the pool—something Jack Johnson had learned in the ring. But instead of taunting his detractors and flaunting his prowess, as Johnson did, Kahanamoku sloughed off insults like a wave. In his regal acquiescence, he wielded a different sort of power.

In Hawaii, interest in Kahanamoku was soaring as high as the Stangenwald, the six-story building on Merchant Street that was Honolulu's first high-rise. Letters that Duke sent to his father and Lew Henderson were published verbatim in the local papers. His value as "Hawaii's greatest publicity agent" and "the best advertisement Hawaii has ever had"[19] was confirmed with every newspaper clipping.

"The sending of Kahanamoku to the mainland to take part in the tryouts will turn out to be one of the most important advertising features that these Islands have ever had," one newspaper noted.[20]

June 11 is an annual holiday in Hawaii: Kamehameha Day honors the ruler who was responsible for conquering and unifying the islands. On Kamehameha Day in 1912, all of Hawaii awaited word from New Jersey as Kahanamoku and eleven other American swimmers gathered for one final test before the Stockholm Olympics.

With the retirement of Charles Daniels in April, Otto Wahle was seeking a fresh quartet for the only relay race on the Olympic swimming program. On a course that was surrounded by Lake Verona's weeping willow trees, Kahanamoku covered 220 yards in 2:40. His time broke Daniels's record for open-water swimming, even though he stood frozen for seconds after the pistol was fired for fear of making a second false start, and reversed his poor initial showing at the same distance in Pittsburgh.

That night, Kahanamoku was officially named a member of the U.S. Olympic team in the 100 meters and the 4x200-meter relay. His achievement was historic. He had overcome poverty and prejudice to become the first Hawaiian athlete to qualify for the U.S. Olympic team. He was going to Sweden to represent not only all of America (most of whom could not pinpoint Honolulu on a map) but also the Hawaiian Islands.

On the eve of his departure to Europe, Kahanamoku wrote an open letter to his backers, sending his "sincerest and grateful thanks for their splendid financial assistance and encouragement, by which I am enabled to take part in the great Olympic Games. I am very mindful of this splendid opportunity offered me, and in the contests for which I am entered, will put forth my best efforts to win, and add to the athletic glory of the United States and Hawaii."[21]

7

On the night before they sailed to Stockholm, members of the U.S. Olympic team assembled at the New York Athletic Club to receive their dress uniforms and listen to a pep talk from Colonel Robert Thompson, the president of the American Olympic Committee. On the following morning, June 14, they met at 23rd Street and Sixth Avenue and then marched west toward the Hudson River, where Duke Kahanamoku and some 160 athletes boarded the SS *Finland* of the Red Star line.

The ship was awash in flowers and red-white-and-blue bunting, from masthead to deck, as approximately 5,000 well-wishers converged on the Hudson River pier at 21st Street to wave American flags and ribbons reading "Bring Home the Bacon." As the *Finland* pushed off, every ship, ferry, and tugboat in the vicinity sounded its foghorn at full blast.

James E. Sullivan of the AAU, the leader of the Olympic team, was bullish about his chances. "I look for an American triumph which will overshadow the achievements of any band of athletes which has ever left the States," he declared. "I fancy that our men will score more points than the combined nations of the world."[1]

For much of the next two weeks, the sweat of Sullivan's men mixed with the brine of the Atlantic Ocean. The *Finland* had been converted into a floating gymnasium. The upper deck was covered with a cork track for the runners, while the cyclists rode stationary bikes. Workouts for the "mer-men," as newspapers commonly called swimmers in those days, were relegated to the forward deck, where two makeshift tanks made from sail-cloth, about fifteen feet in length and five feet in width, were filled with cool water replenished daily from the ocean. Their care was left to Otto Wahle, the same AAU official who had advised Sullivan to deny Duke's records from the races in Honolulu harbor.

Tethered in place by a harness that fit snugly around his waist, Duke Kahanamoku sloshed about uncomfortably in what was a glorified bathtub. He practiced with swimmers he'd met and raced against in Pittsburgh, Chicago, and elsewhere: Harry Hebner, Kenneth Huszagh, Perry McGillivray, and Mike McDermott, representing the powerhouse clubs from the Midwest.

They were occasionally joined by a young lieutenant in the U.S. Army who was competing in the modern pentathlon, a new event for military officers that included a swimming test of 300 meters. Practicing onboard the *Finland*, George S. Patton Jr. later wrote, was "much more distressing than ordinary swimming, and we had to cut down the length of time we worked."[2]

"Some traveling, Daddy," Duke wrote in a letter home, mentioning that his teammates were a "fine bunch of athletes."[3] In turn, they marveled at Kahanamoku's demeanor. "We were most impressed by his graciousness," breaststroker Mike McDermott said. "He was a clean competitor and always a gentleman."[4]

Miler Abel Kiviat remembered that Duke "was a strange person to us. None of us ever saw a Hawaiian or Philipino [*sic*]. You know, what they look [like] except in pictures in the paper. So we were very respectful of him and he proved him [*sic*] to be a wonderful, a real chap. As good as any of us."[5]

When Ralph Rose, the giant shot-putter from San Francisco, was asked how he'd practice his throws on deck, he replied that he was going to hurl the shot as far as possible into the ocean. "The Duke's going to swim out and catch it," he joked.[6]

In the athletes-only dining cabin, Kahanamoku watched in awe as Rose, Matt McGrath, and Pat "Babe" McDonald, the behemoth weight men known as the "Irish Whales," devoured enormous portions of food. Boredom was relieved by the discovery of a stowaway (who became the team mascot) and endless games of shuffleboard and quoits. Duke took photographs with a small camera that he had bought in New York.

As part of the nighttime entertainment program supplied by the passengers, Kahanamoku broke out his ukulele and sang Hawaiian tunes. Colonel Thompson shook his hand and congratulated him for his moving version of "Aloha Oe." He then witnessed a commonplace occurrence: several of the white athletes blackened their faces with shoe polish and performed a minstrel show that was met with laughter and applause.

Kahanamoku bonded with another outlier on the team, Jim Thorpe, who was born in a cabin in the Oklahoma Territory three years before Duke. He was of mixed heritage: part Irish, part Sac and Fox, and part Potawatomi. Like Kahanamoku, Thorpe attended schools that were designed to "civilize" Native American Indians by teaching them a trade and helping them assimilate into mainstream America. His athletic career blossomed on the gridiron at one of those institutions, the Carlisle Indian Industrial School in Pennsylvania, where he first demonstrated his slashing backfield moves under coach Glenn "Pop" Warner, leading them to an 11-1 season in 1911.

Thorpe was preparing to compete in the ten-event decathlon and the five-event pentathlon. Contrary to popular myth, he did not train for the two grueling events by lounging in a hammock during the overseas trip. Rather, with direction from "Silent" Mike Murphy, the bowler-wearing coach from the University of Pennsylvania, Thorpe exerted himself in readying for competition.

Thorpe's wondrous athleticism was obvious to everyone. Kahanamoku asked him: "Jimmy, I've seen you run, jump, throw things and carry the ball. You do everything, so why don't you swim, too?"

Thorpe grinned. "Duke, I saved that for you to take care of. I saved that for you," he said.[7]

The modern Olympic Games were the brainchild of Pierre de Coubertin, a diminutive French baron who believed in the power of sport and competition to reinvigorate a world that was becoming increasingly mechanized and urbanized. In this he was part of a global social movement of "athletic missionaries" who advocated for a more vital physical culture, a viewpoint echoed by such figures as George Williams and Robert Baden-Powell, the originators of the YMCA and the Boy Scouts, respectively, as well as Teddy Roosevelt, a pen pal of Coubertin's.

Coubertin took this passion a step further. He single-mindedly orchestrated the events that led to the revival of the Olympic Games in 1896, based on the precepts and traditions of the quadrennial competitions held at Olympia, in ancient Greece, from 776 BC to 346 AD. His vision was singularly novel: large-scale and international sporting events did not exist before

1896. The inaugural editions of the Davis Cup tennis competition (1900), the Tour de France (1903), and the World Cup (1930) were in the future, as were the first Rose Bowl game (1902) and the first World Series (1903). So, too, Coubertin's International Olympic Committee (IOC) was a precursor to the many governing bodies that were formed to organize and regulate sport, including the Fédération Internationale de Football Association (FIFA, 1904) and the National Collegiate Athletic Association (its predecessor, the Intercollegiate Athletic Association of the United States, formed in 1906).

The 1896 Olympics took place in Athens, selected so as to burnish an indelible connection to their roots. These Olympic Games were a modest undertaking, with 245 men from fourteen nations gathering in Greece, including all of fourteen athletes from the United States. Its primary achievement was one of conception, not the uneven competition, although these Olympics did see the invention of the long-distance race that became known as the marathon.

Coubertin had succeeded in replanting the Olympic seed, but the next two iterations, Paris in 1900 and St. Louis in 1904, were fiascos. Both were so subsumed by concomitant world's fairs that many athletes did not realize that they had participated in the Olympics. In 1904, when James E. Sullivan himself organized the sports program at the St. Louis Olympics, he devised a "Special Olympics" competition among the native peoples working at the fairgrounds, including Filipinos, Sioux Indians, African Pygmies and Zulus, and Patagonian Tehuelches. They were not trained athletes and, not surprisingly, performed poorly on "Savages' Day."

The scheme was an ignominious folly, but Sullivan trumpeted the results as evidence of the white race's supremacy. "The whole meeting proves conclusively that the savage has been a very much overrated man from an athletic point of view," he noted. "Lecturers and authors will in the future please omit all reference to the natural athletic ability of the savage, unless they can substantiate their alleged feats."[8]

Coubertin, ever the aristocratic and cosmopolitan idealist, shunned Sullivan and took solace in the selection of Rome as the prospective host for the 1908 Olympic Games. But then came another near death knell: the eruption of Mount Vesuvius, causing the Italian government to hastily withdraw its support and funding. As Coubertin retreated to his home in the summer of 1906, his nascent Olympic Movement was in danger of collapsing.

To the rescue came the city of London. British Olympic organizers, led by another sporting aristocrat, Lord Desborough, were determined to show off their athletic muscle to the world. Despite being the last-minute replacement, the 1908 London Olympics offered up a template for how the Olympic Games would be staged in the twentieth century, starting with the construction of the first Olympic stadium. The concrete-and-steel marvel at Shepherd's Bush featured a 586-yard running track encircled by a banked cycling track of 660 yards; capacity for as many as 80,000 spectators; and private areas for the royal family and the press corps. The oval was so vast that there was room enough to sink a 100-meter pool in the infield, complete with a retractable diving tower.

The 1908 London Olympics also broke ground as the first in which nations selected their own squads (as opposed to collections of individual athletes), the first to begin with a formal opening ceremony, the first to be extensively photographed and filmed, the first to be widely written about in newspapers and magazines, and the first to showcase the best amateur athletes from Europe and North America.

One other factor ensured their success: rivalry. James E. Sullivan brought over a scrappy team comprised largely of working-class, Irish American athletes. These upstarts locked horns with the world's reigning superempire in everything from the tug-of-war to the marathon. The so-called Battle of Shepherd's Bush turned the Olympics into an event worth caring and arguing about, from Nenagh in County Tipperary to Hoboken in New Jersey to Sydney in Australia.

The dramatics in London saved the flailing Olympic Movement and transformed Coubertin's Olympic Games into a high-stakes athletic contest suffused with national pride. The triumphant return of Sullivan's boys from England was cause for celebration. The athletes were feted with a ticker tape parade in New York City and greeted personally by then-President Teddy Roosevelt, himself an outspoken advocate of "manly" physical culture, at his summer home on Long Island.

Swimming events were not contested during the ancient games at Olympia, and aquatic activity was an afterthought at the first two modern Olympic Games. Four swimming events were held in the Aegean Sea in 1896, all on the same day, including one held solely for Greek sailors. No water polo or diving events were held. There were seven swimming events, held in the River Seine, in 1900. These included such one-offs as the 200-meter obstacle course and underwater swimming.

The 1904 Olympics in St. Louis attracted considerable international participation in the pool—actually, a man-made lake—and introduced diving and breaststroke events. When Charles Daniels, representing the New York Athletic Club, emerged with five medals, the United States had its first "mer-man" star.

The 1908 London Olympics set a new standard. With the pool centrally placed within the Olympic Stadium, just opposite the royal box, it was "likely the best international swimming meet to this date,"[9] according to one expert, drawing top swimmers from Britain, Australia, Sweden, Hungary, and the United States. World records were established in all six events, with Daniels and British distance man Henry Taylor crowned as major stars. Swimming's growing popularity was such that the sport's leaders met during the London Olympics to establish their own international governing body (Fédération Internationale de Natation, or FINA) and to formulate common rules.

In 1909 Coubertin and the International Olympic Committee awarded the 1912 Olympic Games to the city of Stockholm. The selection gave aquatics yet another boost, given Sweden's deep connection to water. Stockholm itself is part of an island chain, located on the eastern shore of the country, where Lake Malaren meets the Baltic Sea. Swedish organizers built their own concrete-and-steel stadium for track and field, gymnastics, and the Opening and Closing ceremonies. They deviated from London's blueprint by erecting the first stand-alone venue for swimming, diving, and water polo, albeit a temporary one. Two new events, the 400-meter breaststroke and plain high diving, were added.[10]

The most radical change from past Olympic Games was the debut of women swimmers and divers. Female athletes had been largely excluded from Olympic competition during the first four Games (with the exception of tennis players, golfers, gymnasts, and archers). Stockholm organizers and FINA welcomed the women over the protestations of Pierre de Coubertin, whose preference was to emulate the ancient Greeks and bar women from the Olympics except as spectators.

Sullivan sided with Coubertin on this. He declined to send American women swimmers to Stockholm, although eight other countries did so, because he considered elite competitive sports to be a male enclave. The stout son of immigrants from County Kerry, Sullivan was a self-made man of his time, which is to say, his stance was not exceptional even though it would be considered sexist today.

"It is now an established fact that girls' athletics, when conducted along safe and sane lines, is a real benefit to the health of the girls," he wrote. "They must not be exploited, however, as female [Mel] Sheppards, [Martin] Sheridans, or [Eugen] Sandows, or as show girls. A girls' team must not be trained in the tricks and methods of a man's champion team or play under men's rules; nor should they be sent around the country to exhibit themselves as experts or compete in open competition where gate money is charged. . . . Girls should be kept in their own group and not be permitted to take part in public sports."[11]

Sullivan was also a track-and-field devotee who left swimming matters to Wahle. Over one hundred American runners, throwers, and jumpers traveled to Stockholm, accompanied by just seven swimmers (including Kahanamoku). That was far fewer than the eighteen swimmers representing Great Britain (who had a much shorter trip to make) and fewer than Australia's nine swimmers. (The United States also did not field a water polo team.)

That said, Sullivan was a pragmatist. He so badly wanted to defeat the British, and every other country, that he was willing to ignore race when selecting athletes to represent the stars and stripes. His Olympic team of 1908 featured one African American sprinter (John Baxter Taylor), one Hopi Indian marathoner (Louis Tewanima), and one Tuscarora Indian long jumper (Frank Mount Pleasant).

Sullivan cast a slightly wider net for the 1912 Stockholm Olympics. He selected a Hawaiian in Kahanamoku, a black sprinter in Howard Drew, several Jewish athletes (including standout miler Abel Kiviat), and three Native Americans in Jim Thorpe and distance runners Tewanima (also a Carlisle student) and Andrew Sockalexis, from the Penobscot tribe.

In 1912, when African American athletes were barred from playing Major League Baseball, joining private athletic clubs, or enrolling in most elite colleges, this was progress, if not progressive. *Harper's Weekly*, the self-professed "journal of civilization," delighted in this athletic melting pot that was en route to Sweden. "In the heterogeneous gathering were lawyers, physicians, policemen, Indians, negroes, Hawaiians, college men, school boys, clerks, mechanics, and, in fact, entrants from every walk of life," wrote Edward Bayard Moss. "Sons of wealthy men fraternized with youths of their own age so poor that public subscriptions by citizens of their home towns were necessary in order that they might make the trip to Stockholm."[12]

Other commentators were not as sanguine. "Two Dark-Skinned Athletes with American Team," was the headline in the *Detroit Free Press*, accompanied by photographs of Kahanamoku and Howard Drew. The caption underneath read: "The fellow with the funny name is a Kanaka."[13]

The U.S. team's voyage to Europe took longer than usual. The unsinkable *Titanic* had sunk in April after hitting an iceberg, and so the *Finland* took the southern track to avoid the iceberg zone. Then, they stopped in Antwerp for three days to refill their coal supply. Kahanamoku walked around the Belgian port city to shake off his sea legs. In lieu of another workout in the cramped tank, he dove off the ship's railing into the harbor and swam in the open water.

The *Finland* headed up the North Sea before turning east and entering the Baltic Sea. The team arrived in Stockholm on June 30 to a loud welcome. "We were met early in the morning by a lady reporter of one of the morning papers who climbed up the side of the boat," wrestler George Retzer remembered. "She took quite a fancy to Duke Kahanamoku of the Hawaiian Islands, much to his embarrassment. It was the first Hawaiian she had ever seen. The next morning the paper was full of the 'Duke.'"[14]

The *Finland* was moored in the harbor near the royal palace. Two decades before the first athletes' village was built for Olympic competitors, Kahanamoku and his teammates bunked aboard the ship during the entirety of the Olympic Games. One exception was George Patton Jr. and his wealthy family, who could afford to stay at a nearby hotel.

8

One week after their arrival in Sweden, Duke Kahanamoku and his U.S. teammates converged inside Stockholm's Olympic Stadium. They stood in the infield beneath the midday sun as Pierre de Coubertin presided over the opening ceremony. Prayers were offered and hymns were sung before King Gustaf V, an avid tennis player who fooled nobody when he entered tourneys under the pseudonym "Mr. G," officially welcomed the athletes to Stockholm.

The spectators at the 22,000-capacity stadium applauded as each of the twenty-seven national delegations paraded past the royal box, the U.S. team in step behind flag bearer George Bonhag, a distance runner. The contingent of American fans in Section P yelped a patriotic chant to support them:

Rah! Rah! Ray!
U.S.A.!
A-M-E-R-I-C-A!
U.S.A.

Kahanamoku marched proudly in his snappy uniform—blue blazer with brass buttons, white shirt and dark tie, white flannel trousers, and white shoes—and brought his straw bowler to his chest when he passed King Gustaf. Having sailed across a vast segment of the Pacific Ocean from Honolulu to California, crossed the continent by train, and then voyaged across the Atlantic Ocean and up the North Sea to arrive in Sweden, Duke reckoned that he had traveled farther than any of the nearly 2,400 athletes and the tens of thousands of spectators surrounding him. He was doubly pleased to be representing Hawaii as well as the United States.

Local organizers scouted several bodies of water for the swimming events before deciding on a bay in central Stockholm called Djurgårdsbrunnsviken, at the foot of the hill called Laboratoriebacken. They built a temporary facility, framed by pontoon bridges some twenty meters apart, that offered decent protection against the currents from Nybroviken bay.

So much for all the hand-wringing over Kahanamoku's lack of expertise with indoor swimming. This was an outdoor course that featured a 100-meter straightaway; no turns were involved in races under 100 meters. There were also no starting blocks for the swimmers. The starting place and the opposite turning point consisted of wooden planks driven into the bottom. No ropes divided the water into separate lanes—it was one large, rectangular course—so competitors had to be wary of careening into their opponents.

Officials dredged four hundred cubic meters of clay from the western part of the basin to insure that the depth of the water "was everywhere greater than would cover a man." The water was not particularly clear, and several competitors developed ear infections. Its temperature was chilly, much colder than the water at Waikiki Beach.[1]

The spectator area had room enough for 2,700 people and the royal box in the lower part, with additional room for 1,000 fans in the upper section. Underneath were twenty dressing rooms, two furnished clubrooms (one for ladies and the other for gentlemen), and a press area. The construction cost was just under $11,000.

Kahanamoku had little time to get acclimated to the course because the preliminary heats for his first event, the 100-meter freestyle, were held shortly after the opening ceremony. Besides the swimmers from the Midwest, his main competition was expected to come from Australians Cecil Healy and Bill Longworth and Germany's Kurt Bretting. The latter had recently set a new world record of 1:02.4.

The first round involved eight heats. In the fourth round, Chicago's Perry McGillivray established a new Olympic record of 1:04.8. Kahanamoku swam in the next heat and immediately asserted himself. His time of 1:02.6 bettered the opposition by more than two seconds and shattered McGillivray's mark.

The next afternoon, in the quarterfinals, Duke won his heat in a restrained time of 1:03.8. Two Americans, McGillivray and Ken Huszagh, another Midwesterner, also qualified for the semifinals.

"The phenomenal Kanaka . . . employs a special kind of crawl, with the motor-power derived from the ankles alone, and not from the hip or knee joints," raved the *Official Report*.[2]

Kahanamoku was "the talk of the town," according to the *New York Times* "not only for what he does but for the easy way in which he does it. He has caught the popular fancy."[3] The president of the British Life-Saving organization promised Duke a splendid gold cup if he were to break the sixty-second barrier for the 100-meter freestyle.

Suddenly, however, disaster befell Kahanamoku, McGillivray, and Huszagh. The three had gone back to the *Finland* after the quarterfinals, having been told that the semifinals were scheduled for the next day. They were misinformed. The actual schedule, printed on both a preliminary version given to the U.S. team on the ship as well as the daily program from the venue in Stockholm, stated that the semifinals were to be held on the same day as the quarterfinals—Sunday, July 7—at 8 p.m.

The trio should have been alerted to return to the stadium, but they were not. In their absence, Cecil Healy, Germany's Walter Ramme, and Bill Longworth finished first, second, and third in the first semifinal heat, while Kurt Bretting paced himself to victory in the second semifinal heat.

Kahanamoku, McGillivray, and Huszagh faced immediate disqualification for their nonappearance. Coach Wahle protested that the mishap was due to a "misunderstanding" over the program times. Sullivan stated the problem was due to "ignorance of the Swedish language."[4] These excuses were lame, Olympic and FINA officials pointed out, and as they deliberated the Americans' fates, it appeared that their chance for the gold medal had vanished—that is, until the Olympic spirit prevailed. None other than Cecil Healy of Australia, himself a gold-medal contender, argued that disqualifying the Americans for a scheduling snafu did not constitute good sportsmanship. He gallantly insisted that the victims of the "Asleep on the Deep" incident be given another chance.

The trio waited in limbo as the swim jury, along with Australian and German representatives, debated the situation. Finally, a compromise was reached. An extra heat was scheduled for the three Americans, as well as Italy's Mario Massa (who had also missed his heat). To qualify for the finals, they would have to better the time of the third-place finisher from the first semifinal heat (Longworth in 1:06.2). If all four managed to better that time, only the fastest two swimmers would advance.

On July 9 they all returned to the water. Kahanamoku swam as if he did not want to waste this second chance. He clocked a personal best of 1:02.4 to tie the world's mark set by Bretting. Huszagh nipped McGillivray to qualify for the finals.

The field for the finals of the 100 meters was now set: Kahanamoku, Huszagh, Bretting, Healy, and Ramme. (An ear infection forced Longworth to the sidelines.) Duke returned to the *Finland* and breathed a huge sigh of relief.

Kahanamoku knew that, when he was at his best, he was superior to anyone in the water. But he admitted to feeling added pressure. He wasn't just competing for the United States; he was also swimming to bring honor to Hawaii. "The only thing I was thinking about is, 'I gotta make good,'" he said. "I was thinking of everybody back home, see. The only thing for me to do is to go out and win."[5]

The following evening the finals were held. By 8 p.m., under a northern summer sky that still was bright, the stands along the 100-meter straightaway were packed, with King Gustaf and his wife, Queen Victoria, and the Crown Prince and the Crown Princess seated in the royal box, joined by Lord Desborough, the mastermind behind the successful 1908 London Olympics.

Only . . . Duke Kahanamoku was missing—again. The swimmers were told to get ready for the race, but Kahanamoku was nowhere to be found. They called his name; there was no response.

Desperate teammates scrambled to search for Kahanamoku. Finally, breaststroker "Turk" McDermott found Kahanamoku "stretched out under the bleachers sound asleep. We hustled him to the starting line just in time for the race."[6] Duke stripped off his white bathrobe and hurried to the platform. He stood at the center of the pool, flanked by Huszagh, Bretting, Healy, and Ramme. This was no time to strum the ukulele.

A nervous Bretting caused a false start. Kahanamoku stood motionless, gathering himself. At the pistol's retort, the swimmers set off cleanly. Duke dove deep and surfaced cleanly, grabbing the early lead over Huszagh and the two Germans, with Healy trailing the pack. He surged ahead at the halfway mark, his closest rival ten feet behind him. He seemed to let up after that and cleaved leisurely through the water in complete control. He won by two meters in 1:03.4. A late rally brought Healy to second place, with Huszagh in third.

Healy and Kahanamoku, dripping wet, shook hands. The Australian congratulated the Hawaiian on his victory, and the Hawaiian thanked the Australian for his gentlemanly conduct. Officials and teammates grabbed Kahanamoku, wrapped a blanket around him, and then, with the crowd applauding, used the blanket to toss him in the air three times.

King Gustaf indicated that he wanted to meet the victor. Kahanamoku was escorted to the royal box. The monarch congratulated "Duke de Crawl-stroke," and the two men shook hands. He received yet another ovation as he exited to the dressing room, with the other competitors patting him on the back.

Kahanamoku celebrated quietly. He had survived the start-time controversy and, in maintaining his equilibrium, delivered on his quest to bring glory to Hawaii. But he wasn't done. Two days later he returned to the pool for the first heat of the 4x200-meter relay.

Great Britain held the world's record, but the foursome of Kahanamoku, Huszagh, McGillivray, and Harry Hebner shattered that time by almost 30 seconds in winning their preliminary heat, with Duke smoothly handling the turn at the 100-meter mark. Then they watched as Healy and his mates (with New Zealander Malcolm Champion replacing the ailing Longworth) lowered that time by another twelve seconds in the next heat.

The finals were not much of a contest. Healy and Huszagh went neck and neck in the first leg, but then the Australians took over and built a substantial lead. By the time Kahanamoku dove in as the anchor, he trailed Harold Hardwick by several lengths. The American quartet settled for second place and silver, finishing nearly nine seconds behind Australia.

Kahanamoku and his teammates congratulated Healy and his squad before returning to the *Finland*. Duke changed into his dress uniform and, late in the afternoon, reported to the Olympic Stadium for the closing ceremony. He and the other athletes marched into the arena, with those receiving gold medals gathered in the middle of the infield.

A herald called out the names of the victors. Triple gold medalist Hannes Kolehmainen, the remarkable distance runner from Finland, was rewarded with the loudest ovation from the crowd. Louis Tewanima was awarded the silver medal in the 10,000 meters behind Kolehmainen, but it was his Carlisle teammate, Jim Thorpe, with twin gold medals in the decathlon and pentathlon, who received the second-loudest ovation after Kolehmainen. (Thorpe also finished fourth in the high jump and seventh in the long jump.)

The volume of applause greeting Kahanamoku ranked a not-too-distant third. He approached the raised platform where King Gustaf stood, removed his straw bowler, and bowed. Sweden's monarch was dressed in a grey morning coat and black top hat, a thin cane balanced on his left arm. He placed an oak wreath on Kahanamoku's head and awarded him the gold medal. They shook hands for the second time, and then Kahanamoku retreated to the company of athletes, holding tight to his medal and hat, the wreath balanced atop his head.

Kahanamoku watched as King Gustaf uttered the most memorable quote from the 1912 Olympics. When Thorpe approached the podium to receive his medals, King Gustaf leaned down and told him, without understatement, "You, sir, are the most wonderful athlete in the world." To this Thorpe replied: "Thank you."[7]

Thorpe was so weighed down by medals and trophies that Kahanamoku had to help him haul the hardware back to the *Finland*. Thorpe got roaring drunk that night and, the next day, nursing a hangover, managed to play in an exhibition baseball game. He was indeed the world's greatest athlete—on land.

As James Sullivan had promised, his men had outclassed the opposition and had taken home the most gold medals (twenty-five). Sweden edged the United States, 64–63, in the overall medal count, but the host country enjoyed a significant numerical advantage—446 competitors compared to 174 from the United States—and competed in many more events than did the Americans.

In the aftermath, Coach Wahle attempted to take credit for Duke's success. "When Duke Kahanamoku came on board the *Finland* he was a green and inexperienced swimmer, but the improvement he made in practicing in our small tank was nothing short of wonderful," he said. "The coaching he received in the small rubber cloth tank on the *Finland* was of greater benefit to him than any coaching received before or since."[8]

That statement not only ignores Kahanamoku's record-breaking times from Honolulu, which Wahle had sought to discredit, but also the coaching contributions of Duke's father and uncles, Bill Rawlins, and George Kistler at Penn. Nor did Wahle explain how swimming inside the cramped tank on the *Finland* improved Duke's start; nor did he accept responsibility for the scheduling snafu that jeopardized the Americans' chances in the 100-meter freestyle. Kahanamoku later complained that Wahle had underutilized him by not allowing him to enter additional events in Stockholm (presumably, the 400-meter freestyle).

Still, all agreed that the 1912 Stockholm Olympics had been a smashing success. The weather was glorious, with ever-present sunshine and long, radiant nights, and the organizational duties were skillfully accomplished. The Pacific Rim was represented not only by Kahanamoku, from Hawaii, but also by two athletes from Japan, which became the first Asian country to compete at the Olympics. The bitter acrimony that had disrupted the 1908 London Olympics never surfaced, and only the death of Portuguese marathoner Francisco Lazaro, due to heat exhaustion, marred the proceedings.

What lingered in memory were Thorpe's never-before-seen combination of athleticism and strength; the endurance of "Hannes the Mighty" in the 5,000, the 10,000, and the cross-country races; and Duke Kahanamoku, his taut bathing costume soaked through, water pouring from his jet-black hair as he emerged from the pool, smiling with gracious appreciation as applause rained from the stands, a Hawaiian champion for all the world to admire.

On the eve of the conflagration that would soon engulf all of Europe, any talk that Pierre de Coubertin's Olympic Movement was flailing was summarily dismissed.

9

Duke Kahanamoku's services were in high demand immediately after the 1912 Stockholm Olympics. He was invited to swim in Moscow and Algiers. Australian official William Hill pressed Duke to come to Sydney over Christmas. Germany's swim association wanted revenge after the 100-meter finals, so Kahanamoku journeyed to Hamburg and, over a straightaway course, outdueled Kurt Bretting again. In the process he lowered the world's record to 1:01.6.

Kahanamoku extended his stay in Europe and swam in exhibitions in Paris and London. Then he sailed from Southampton on the SS *New York*. When the ship broke down midway across the Atlantic Ocean, Kahanamoku, Mike McDermott, and a few swimmers decided to go for a dip. They dove into the ocean and splashed around, until they noticed that the current was causing the ship to drift away. They had to holler for help. "The captain had to send out a lifeboat to get us," McDermott laughed. "Was he mad!"[1]

Duke went to Philadelphia and reunited with the Henderson family and with Coach Kistler. He thanked them for their support and showed them his medals. He was tickled to find that two surfboards, shaped from California redwood, had arrived while he was in Europe, sent from Honolulu by his brother David. His favorite of the two measured two-and-a-half feet wide, nine feet long, and weighed seventy-five pounds.[2]

Eager to test them out, he decamped to nearby Atlantic City, the millionaires' summer playground on the New Jersey shore. There, at the intersection of the famous wooden boardwalk and Arkansas Avenue, Captain John Young had built a vast entertainment and amusement arcade that stretched into the Atlantic Ocean. Young's "Million Dollar Pier" was its own attraction, with theaters, dance halls, a poultry show, an aquarium, and Young's own home. Now, Young added America's newest swimming star to his stable.

Kahanamoku's first order of business was to apply for a permit from Commissioner William Bartlett, with the local Public Safety office, because the city apparently had banned the use of surfboards. Duly licensed, he was given permission to surf for two hours a day.

On a sunny August day, Duke carried his surfboard onto Atlantic City's Steel Pier. Throngs of tourists, who paid a single-admission fee to gain entrance to the pier, watched and waited. Most, if not all of them, had never seen a surfboard before, much less witnessed someone surfing.

Kahanamoku stood high above the water and studied the surf below. The Atlantic Ocean's rollers broke a quarter of a mile away, and the sets didn't roll in like he was used to at Waikiki. But waves are waves. He flung his board into the ocean and dove in after it. He recaptured his board by the pier and then straddled it.

During his first time surfing on the East Coast, during his first time surfing outside of Hawaii, and during his first time surfing since leaving Honolulu in February, Duke took his time in order to get accustomed to the conditions. He turned his board to paddle out, all the while eyeing the waves. Then, he was ready. He paddled, leapt to his feet, balanced himself on the board, and rode it toward shore.

The crowd, at first stunned, applauded loudly as Duke skimmed across the water like a dancer. He smiled—it felt great to be surfing again—and when the wave died, he lowered himself into the water, turned, and paddled out again. As he became more comfortable, he performed a repertoire of tricks: standing on his head, riding backward, roaring in with a youngster balanced on his shoulders. The crowd lapped up his showmanship.

Kahanamoku augmented his surfing exhibitions with a swimming show at Atlantic City's indoor Hygeia Pool.[3] He also explored other surfing spots in the area while staying with Joe Ruddy, a swimmer and water polo player who coached with Otto Wahle at the New York Athletic Club. Ruddy lived in Far Rockaway, in Queens, and he and Kahanamoku ventured into the water there for what one newspaper described as an "an interesting swimming exhibition"[4] at Rockaway Beach. It is unclear whether Duke used his surfboard in the Rockaways, or just swam and bodysurfed. No photographs of him in action in the Rockaways have surfaced.

Still, many surfing historians contend that Kahanamoku's appearances in Atlantic City (and perhaps in the Rockaways) were the first episodes of surfing on the East Coast. They note that his exhibitions helped introduce surfing to an audience beyond Hawaii and California. Dissenters include Duke's friend George Freeth, who claimed that he surfed in Atlantic City as early as 1903—and was arrested for doing so.[5] That account has not been verified.

Two years before Kahanamoku came to the East Coast, however, an article published in the *New York Times* cited evidence of surfing in Asbury Park, New Jersey, located some sixty-five miles north of Atlantic City. "There is a new fad that is being taken up with decided interest by the summer people," the writer proclaimed in 1910. "It is coasting in on long rolling swells on boards or skidders. The sport was introduced here a week ago by a number of Hawaiians, and every bathing party now has one or more skidders."[6] (The "Hawaiians" were apparently a group of touring musicians.)

Ultimately, whether Kahanamoku was the first surfer on the East Coast, or the third or the tenth, matters little. His multiple-day stint in Atlantic City was noteworthy because, as a newly crowned Olympic swimming hero, he attracted huge publicity. People who had never witnessed surfing before, people who had never dreamed of traveling to Hawaii, now knew about surfing.

And, as would be the case with many of Kahanamoku's earliest surfing exhibitions, he directly influenced the life of at least one individual. Sam Reid, seven years old, happened to be in Atlantic City with his parents when he witnessed Duke take off in the ocean on a long piece of wood. "The wave towered over him, but perfectly balanced, like a statue of Poseidon, bronze god of the sea, he was challenging the power of the wave, daring it, taunting it," Reid remembered. "At the end, he won; and when he stepped off smiling from his board to the sandy beach, the once overpowering wave was now a harmless ripple, conquered and tamed by this brown man from the sea."[7]

Awed by the "poetic beauty and suspense of man winning out against the sea," Reid swiped his mother's ironing board to catch waves the next day and then used that makeshift surfboard for the next four years. A hard-core surfer was born, and a love affair sparked. Reid reconnected with Kahanamoku in Southern California in the early 1920s, eventually moved to Hawaii to surf there, and became a lifelong friend of Duke and the Kahanamoku family.

Duke celebrated his twenty-second birthday in style. He woke early on the morning of August 24, 1912, in New York City, for a "monster parade" organized by James E. Sullivan for the American Olympic team. A fleet of thirty open touring cars awaited the athletes at 41st Street and Fifth Avenue, in front of the newly opened New York Public Library. Kahanamoku shared the backseat of the fourteenth car with Penn distance runner Wallace McCurdy.[8]

Some 20,000 or more people marched or rode along with them as they proceeded downtown to Waverly Place, crossed to Broadway, and then went down Broadway to City Hall. The sidewalks were lined with well-wishers and fans, perhaps as many as one million of them, cheering and waving American flags. Workers threw confetti and ticker tape from the windows of office buildings, while groups of schoolchildren vied to produce the loudest version of the ubiquitous chant:

Rah! Rah! Ray!
U.S.A.!
A-M-E-R-I-C-A!
Olympic, Olympic, Olympic!

They yelled loudest and longest for Jim Thorpe, who received the singular honor of being placed solo in an automobile, the accumulated trophies piled around him. "Oh, you Jim!" they howled. Thorpe nodded solemnly beneath a snappy white fedora.

Sullivan, New York City mayor William Gaynor, and a slew of dignitaries that included the Swedish consul, Magnus Clarkson, met the athletes at City Hall. About the only politicians who were absent from the podium were the three men running for president: incumbent William Taft, challenger Woodrow Wilson, and former president Teddy Roosevelt. Each sent polite regrets and exuberant congratulations to Sullivan and the Olympians.

That night, the team dined at a banquet at the Terrace Garden restaurant on East 58th Street. It was a fitting climax to a memorable birthday for Kahanamoku. He enjoyed the company of his teammates, and he enjoyed holding his two Olympic medals that were so tiny and shiny. He carefully preserved the oak wreath given to him by King Gustaf.

He was also broke. Hawaii's promotional committee forwarded him money, as did Hui Nalu members, so that he could find his way back home. He made a final stopover in San Francisco in late September, his arrival greeted by the headline: "World's Greatest Swimmer Is Here."[9]

Kahanamoku visited the swank Olympic Club in San Francisco and admired the one-hundred-foot indoor pool, with its elegant fittings and decoration. "Gee, but this is some tank!" he exclaimed, and then proceeded to sprint 100 yards in 59 seconds, the fastest time ever recorded on the West Coast. He was almost home.

Separated from Stockholm by two oceans, one continent, various landmasses, and thousands of miles of telegraph cable, Hawaii's newspaper editors had published confused and inaccurate accounts about Kahanamoku and the controversial semifinal heat of the 100-meter race.

After reports finally confirmed that Kahanamoku had been reinstated and won the gold medal, all of Hawaii exulted that the high-school dropout from Waikiki had succeeded on sports' highest international stage. Then, all of Hawaii rushed to claim credit for "Our Duke." McKinley High School's student newspaper boasted, "It is interesting to note that Duke Kahanamoku, the world's champion swimmer . . . is an old High School boy," conveniently omitting that Duke's stay at the school was brief and that he did not graduate.[10]

"DUKE wore tights from our stock when he made his Honolulu record," McInerny department store boasted in an advertisement. "He is probably wearing them while getting international fame. What suits DUKE will suit anyone."[11]

Publisher Lorrin A. Thurston's newspaper, the *Pacific Commercial Advertiser*, editorialized that Kahanamoku was "a credit to his race, to his native islands and to those who started him upon the road of sobriety, without which his name would not today be blazoned upon the athletic honor roll."[12]

Enterprising reporters interviewed Duke's father, now Captain Kahanamoku of the Third Watch. "He's the same *keiki kane* (young boy) today that he was last week," the elder Duke allowed. "He's still our young Paoa. . . . He's a pretty good boy."[13]

The Outrigger Canoe Club was criticized for not inviting Kahanamoku to join. "The reason for his absence from membership to the Outrigger Club has never been made public and will not be on this occasion," the *Honolulu Star-Bulletin* sniffed. "It would seem to most Honolulu residents that to have had him a member of the canoe club would have been a good thing from the point of view of the promoter of tourist travel to the islands. The Outrigger Club now has a wide reputation. It may be presumed that it is international and to have it known that this young son of Hawaii, and best of all a pure Hawaiian type, is a member of the club, would be good advertising for Outrigger without in any way detracting from the boy himself."[14]

Having raised money to send Kahanamoku to compete, Hawaii's Territory leaders hastened to set up a fund to reward him, urging Hawaiians to donate money for the cause. Hand-painted postcards of Kahanamoku were printed and sold for ten cents apiece, with the proceeds added to the collection. The total soon topped $2,500. Hui Nalu's Bill Rawlins vowed to use the money to purchase a home for Kahanamoku. Others suggested that the sum pay for Duke's college education so that he could retain his amateur status and compete at the 1916 Olympics.

Finally, after his return was postponed by parades, banquets, exhibitions, and appearances on the mainland, Kahanamoku arrived home on October 1, 1912. The pride of the Matson shipping line, the *Wilhelmina*, chugged slowly toward her berth at Honolulu harbor as whistles from boats, trains, and bands sounded all over town.

Kahanamoku, from the upper deck, waved his hat to the gang below. "Luau tonight, Duke!" one friend cried out. He responded by dipping two fingers and raising them to his mouth, pantomiming the scooping motion for eating his beloved poi.

The welcome that greeted him when he stepped ashore was much different than the patriotic exuberance he experienced in New York City. This was an outpouring of pure *aloha*. His mother, sobbing with joy, clung to him. His father hugged them both and wiped away tears. His brothers and sisters wrapped numerous lei around him—so many that he could scarcely turn his neck—before the members of Hui Nalu hoisted him on their shoulders, carried him down the pier at a run, placed him in a waiting automobile, and drove him to Waikiki.

First things first: Kahanamoku went for a homecoming swim in the ocean. "Gee, but this feels good," he said. "Tank swimming is all right in its way, and I had some good plunges in the surf at Atlantic City, but there's nothing like Waikiki in the whole world. I've been thinking of this for months and months. Ever since I went away, I guess."[15]

That night, his family and Hui Nalu threw a toothsome luau, with loads of roast pig, pots of poi, and plenty of seared fish. Ukuleles and guitars were brought out, and everyone joined in singing and dancing hula. Duke's mother could not stop beaming or fussing over her son. The party lasted one week.

Most amateur athletes in the early part of the twentieth century quietly resumed their lives after the Olympics. They had to: they had to earn a living. Kahanamoku's situation, however, was different. He was not just a sports champion; he represented all of Hawaii.

Gurrey's photo studio in downtown Honolulu displayed his medals and trophies for the public to admire. When Kahanamoku toured the islands of Maui and Hawaii to thank residents for their support, he was embraced as the mightiest hero since King Kamehameha. "He seems as modest as a child and greets everyone pleasantly," the *Maui News* reported. "Social affairs are given in his honor and he seems to know how to act. He even eats peas with his fork."[16]

The exhaustive, often patronizing coverage underlined how Kahanamoku's status had changed. He was now "Our Champion," universally admired and loved. But because every segment of Hawaiian society had invested money and faith in him, he was accountable to these same people. Each held a definite opinion about, and a vested interest in, his future.

Haole businessmen hoped to expand Hawaii's nascent tourism industry by capitalizing on Duke's fame. Politicians eager for statehood wanted to use his renown to press their case. Sports officials yearned to make Hawaii the aquatics center of the Pacific Rim by leveraging Duke's name and organizing an Olympic-style swim meet in Honolulu. Promoters looking to make a splash for their products saw dollar signs in his handsome visage.

The individuals would change over time, but Kahanamoku would be enmeshed in this tug-of-war for the rest of his life. At the crux of the debate was this question: how does a waterman without job prospects or a high-school diploma find his way outside the water?

10

In January of 1913, as Duke Kahanamoku was basking in the afterglow of the 1912 Stockholm Olympics, disturbing news percolated from the mainland. The *Worcester (MA) Telegram* newspaper reported that Jim Thorpe had played semiprofessional baseball in North Carolina during the summers of 1909 and 1910. He made little more than pocket change, but with restrictions in place that prohibited amateur athletes from competing against professionals and earning a salary, the ramifications were clear-cut.

"If Thorpe is found guilty the trophies will have to be returned and his records erased from the books," thundered AAU chieftain James E. Sullivan. "For the greatest athlete of them all to be dragged down in the mire of professionalism would cast a gloom over the American competitors in future Olympic meets."[1]

An investigation followed, but the facts were not difficult to uncover. During an interlude when Thorpe was not enrolled at the Carlisle Indian Industrial School he played baseball for the Rocky Mount Railroaders (1909–10) and the Fayetteville Highlanders (1910) in the Eastern Carolina League (Class D). That Thorpe won his Olympic medals in track and field and not in baseball (which was not an Olympic sport) mattered little.

Thorpe never tried to hide his identity or use a pseudonym. As he put it, "I liked to play ball. I was not wise to the ways of the world and did not realize this was wrong, and that it would make me a professional in track sports."[2]

Prompted by Glenn "Pop" Warner, his coach at Carlisle, Thorpe apologized to Sullivan in a letter that read in part: "I hope I will be partly excused by the fact that I was simply an Indian schoolboy and I did not know all about such things."[3]

Sullivan and Warner met to discuss the situation without Thorpe being present. They dispatched their version of justice by distancing themselves from the "mire of professionalism." Sullivan ordered Thorpe's trophies and medals to be surrendered, sent them to Sweden, and voided the athlete's records.

Thorpe was at the height of his fame. Only a handful of athletes—baseball stars Ty Cobb and Honus Wagner, boxer Jack Johnson, marathoner Dorando Pietri—carried such name recognition outside the stadium. But in about the time it took Thorpe to compete in a decathlon, his reputation was sullied. The stripping of his medals and records was harsh punishment for a minor-league transgression that harmed no one except the athlete himself.

"I went to play baseball in North Carolina for a couple of summers and paid for it for the rest of my life," Thorpe later said.[4]

Fellow athletes rushed to express their sympathy for Thorpe. When Martin Sheridan of the Irish American Athletic Club was informed that Thorpe's admission meant that the all-around points record reverted to him, he replied, "I don't want that record back and I would give most anything to see Jim cleared."[5]

Duke Kahanamoku was so bitter over his friend's downfall that he could barely bring himself to speak about the incident. "Jimmy Thorpe was the greatest athlete there ever was," he later said. "He could do everything. And what happened to him was a bad break for sports and for everyone."[6]

As Kahanamoku was discovering, amateurism was the hot-button issue in sports in 1912, akin to the controversy over gambling by athletes in the latter part of the decade and the stormy debate over performance-enhancing drugs today. The ideal of amateurism had emerged from Great Britain, the birthplace of modern sport, and, in particular, Great Britain of the Victorian era. The public school-educated leaders of this movement wished to exclude the lower classes from mixing with the moneyed and titled on the pitch. They devised strict rules that divided athletes into two categories: amateurs, who could afford to play for the love of the game and were expected to comport themselves as gentlemen, and professionals, who were generally working-class joes who accepted money and were likened to mercenary strivers.

Amateurism in Great Britain replicated the country's class system. In the United States, amateurism took hold as a puritanical morality play. Amateurs were considered pure, and professionals were perceived as tarnished. Athletes in sports that allowed for monetary compensation, including boxers and jockeys, were looked down on. Even those involved in the national pastime, baseball, endured this sort of snobbery. Major League Baseball players were seen as coarsened immigrants or country bumpkins with little social standing.

"The evils of professionalism, so called, are not merely the taking of money," moralized one advocate in the *New York Times* in 1907; "it is the spirit which this contending for money produces, the taking advantage of every subterfuge, of every device, honest or dishonest, in order to win. To straighten out the difficulties in their way the [athletic] clubs and the men are willing to misconstrue facts and misrepresent! This is the evil, dishonesty."[7]

The rules that amateur athletes like Thorpe and Kahanamoku encountered were prohibitive. They were barred from earning money doing what they did best—running and swimming—either in competition or in exhibitions. They were allowed to receive travel expenses for meets and events, but only a minimal amount, and they could not profit from their fame via endorsements. They were even prevented from coaching the very sport they had mastered. How elite, working-class athletes like Thorpe and Kahanamoku were supposed to train while simultaneously holding down a full-time job was never addressed.

"Peerless Mel" Sheppard, the top-notch middle-distance runner, wrote that banning athletes from coaching defeated "the very basic principals [*sic*] of amateur athletics, which, as I understand it, should be considered strictly from the standpoint of providing recreation and athletics for everybody. And how can an aim of this sort be better accomplished than by starting at the very beginning—with the youngsters of the country? And who is more qualified to instruct these youngsters of the art and science of playing than those who are actively engaged in that very pastime themselves?"[8]

And, if these athletes veered from the straight and narrow, James Sullivan was there to regulate the amateur beat like a baton-twirling policeman; in one year he suspended 288 athletes for various offenses. Long before elite athletes could be represented by agents, they had little recourse for appealing the punishment.

What made the system all the more perplexing was that it was replete with loopholes. Athletes who received watches or silver cups knew exactly which merchants would quietly buy these shiny baubles. Well-heeled supporters (who may well have profited from their wagers) often slipped them money under the table or gave them no-show jobs.

Swimmer Johnny Weissmuller, who emerged as Kahanamoku's greatest rival in the pool in the 1920s, described how his coach, Bill Bachrach of the Illinois Athletic Club, bent the regulations. "When Bachrach and I would go to meets, we were supposed to get eight dollars, nine dollars a day from the AAU," he said. "Bachrach got around that. He'd tell a meet promoter, 'Listen, I'll get Johnny to break a record for you. It'll get lotsa publicity for your pool. Then you give me a hundred dollars.' They'd wonder if that wouldn't make me a pro, but Bachrach'd say, 'No, you're giving the one hundred dollars to me. I'm the pro, not Johnny.' With the one hundred dollars, we'd eat steaks instead of mush and sleep in hotel suites instead of cots in a dormitory."[9]

Duke Kahanamoku did not have Bill Bachrach in his corner; in 1913 he had all of Hawaii. That spring, immediately after the news broke about Jim Thorpe, Hawaiian citizens were debating what to do with the money that they had raised to reward Duke for his successes at the 1912 Olympics. Some supporters wanted to use the money to pay for his college education. But the talk in Honolulu was that Kahanamoku had been promised a house and property in Waikiki. If that promise was kept, Duke presumably would be declared a professional and forced to leave the amateur ranks.

Hawaii's sport officials and tourism boosters wanted him to remain an amateur, for reasons both selfish and altruistic. Kahanamoku was valuable to them "as a promotion asset"[10] because his prowess in the pool and his endearing personality helped to publicize the Islands at swim meets and appearances around the world. They also reasoned that, with Duke's inexperience in business matters, turning pro might not yield the lasting fortune that fast-talking promoters were whispering about in his ear.

The delay made Kahanamoku "peeved" and "good and mad," according to published reports, as he was getting "nothing but the small bits doled out by tourists for his service as a steersman in the canoes on the beach." A plaintive Duke asked one reporter, "Is it best to be an amateur without a house or would it be better to turn professional and have at least a house of my own?"[11]

On March 14, 1913 a group of prominent civic leaders that included Honolulu mayor Joseph J. Fern and U.S. District Attorney of Hawaii A. L. C. Atkinson convened at the office of attorney Bill Rawlins, Duke's chief adviser and the president of Hui Nalu. The purpose of the meeting of the Duke Kahanamoku Fund Committee was to make arrangements "for the purchase of a suitable home at Waikiki [for Duke] and to see that the property was put in proper shape."[12]

The proposed house belonged to attorney William R. Castle, a *kamaaina* (longtime resident) whose family had amassed considerable wealth and power in the Hawaii Territory. (His son, Alfred, was a member of the committee.) The location was near where Kahanamoku grew up, on the southeasterly side of Ala Moana Street, near the corner of Kalia Road, next to land owned by the Paoa family. Castle fixed the price at $1,800.

In May, Castle granted the 6,500-square-foot property not to Kahanamoku himself, but to the Henry Waterhouse Trust Company. The purpose for setting up the trust arrangement was twofold. The committee wanted to make it impossible for Kahanamoku to sell the property for a quick buck. The primary factor, it was later revealed, was to preserve his "status as an amateur athlete to the end that he would not, by reason of acceptance of the gift, be deemed a professional athlete for purposes of national and international athletic competition."[13]

This contrivance was openly discussed. The money raised by the contributions, the *Honolulu Star-Bulletin* noted, was "a suitable reward for Kahanamoku in representing Hawaii at the Olympic Games last year and his work in winning the world's championship." The newspaper reported that the committee had "finally gained the consent of the champion and his father to accept the house which has been chosen."[14]

"The people of the islands have been very generous to me," Kahanamoku himself told the *Los Angeles Times* in 1913. "They gave me a handsome house when I got back from Stockholm."[15]

Even though Hawaii Territory's top amateur sports officials negotiated the transaction, they apparently did not report the deal to the national authorities. Or, if they did, the AAU declined to investigate the matter. Kahanamoku was able to keep his Olympic eligibility and the property even as he flouted the strict rules about amateurism. Thanks to his savvy benefactors, he was able to avoid the same fall from grace that beset Jim Thorpe.

It is impossible to criticize Duke over this deal; he was simply looking after himself and his family's needs as best he could. But the arrangement also left him beholden to the desires of Hawaiian sports officials, which was something they never let him forget.

The specter of professionalism would linger for the remainder of Kahanamoku's competitive swimming career, a span of nearly twenty years. Knowingly or not, he broke the sacred rules on numerous occasions. It is likely that he profited from his surfing appearances in Atlantic City in 1912, with payments either from agents connected with the Million Dollar Pier or from the Hawaii Promotion Committee. In addition, in the same year that he was deeded the property in Waikiki, Duke endorsed a brand of chewing tobacco (even though he neither smoked nor chewed the stuff).

American and British tobacco companies had long printed illustrated cards of athletes (and entertainers) and inserted them within the packaging. These cards, which became popular collectibles, were one of the earliest examples of sports marketing. A trading card featuring Kahanamoku was found in packages of Pan Handle Scrap tobacco—"The Finest Chew That Has Ever Been Offered"—in a fifty-card series titled "World's Champion Athletes" and featuring such Olympians as Mel Sheppard, Louis Tewanima, Abel Kiviat, and Avery Brundage (Jim Thorpe's erstwhile rival in the decathlon and, later, the head of the International Olympic Committee).[16]

Kahanamoku was one of two swimmers pictured in the series. He was photographed in a white bathing suit, his arms clasped behind him. The text on the back read in part: "Duke Kahanamoku ... is a Hawaiian, and, like all his countrymen, has been used to the water almost from his very birth. Caucasians have little chance against the Hawaiians." It is not known how much money, if any, Duke received for this advertising plug.

Pan Handle Scrap was part of the American Tobacco Company, controlled by magnate James B. Duke, whose family established Duke University in North Carolina. This was Kahanamoku's first known connection to the "other" Duke family. It would not be his last.

Kahanamoku's travels to the United States in 1912 primarily took place on the East Coast: swimming in that disastrous race at Pittsburgh, training in Pennsylvania before the Olympics, marching in the victory parade in New York City, and surfing at Atlantic City.

Now, as the public's demand for him to perform increased after the 1912 Olympics, he gravitated to the West Coast. California was a better fit for him, given its temperate climate and relative proximity to Hawaii. An added bonus was the excellent waves that George Freeth had discovered along the coast. Kahanamoku made extended forays in Northern and Southern California in 1913, accompanied by Hui Nalu teammates and escorted by William Rawlins. Over the July 4th weekend, he won five swimming events at the Pacific Coast championships, held at San Francisco's Sutro Baths, and then broke records at the city's Olympic Club pool in August. He returned in the fall for the Portolá Festival, which commemorated the "discovery" of the city by the Spanish explorer, Don Gaspar de Portolá, and again Duke excelled in the Sutro tank.

"There's the greatest swimmer the world has ever known or ever will know," said Sid Cavill of the Olympic Club, watching Duke win the 440, his fourth straight win in the Portolá meet. "All distances seem alike to him and he is surely possessed of wonderful endurance. I have seen all the best of them. But I have never seen anyone who even compares with him."[17]

Kahanamoku journeyed down to Santa Cruz for another swim meet, but the people who flocked to see him were more excited about the exhibitions of surfing that were advertised in area newspapers. This was Duke's first visit to the birthplace of surfing on the mainland—where, in 1885, three Hawaiian princes rode surfboards—and likely his first surfing excursion on the West Coast. He and his large wooden board were the center of attention as he surfed "in the famous style of [his] native land." He sang at the evening banquet after the swim meet, filling the big trophy cup he won "with a delightful beverage and all drank heartily."[18]

Venturing south, he was introduced to Les Henry, an influential figure in amateur swimming in Southern California. Kahanamoku defeated members of Henry's club, the Los Angeles Athletic Club (LAAC), at their sparkling new downtown facility, with an indoor plunge on the sixth floor that measured thirty-two by one hundred feet. Afterward, he and his teammates went looking for George Freeth, their surfing pal from Hawaii who had moved back to California.

Freeth had been denied a spot on the 1912 Olympic team because, with his job as a lifeguard and swimming instructor at the Redondo Plunge, an oceanfront palace billed as the world's largest saltwater tank, he was deemed to have violated the amateur rules. Duke told reporters that Freeth surely would have won an Olympic medal in diving if he had been allowed to compete in Stockholm.

They met in the South Bay, where Freeth was shooting a scene for a short movie, titled *The Latest in Life Saving*, for producer Mack Sennett. The waves weren't great that day, so Kahanamoku used the opportunity to explain to reporters that the phrase "Hui Nalu Club" was redundant because *hui* itself means "club." He later nipped up-and-coming prospect Ludy Langer, of the LAAC, in a rough-water race of three-quarters of a mile.

Freeth told Kahanamoku about the best surfing spots along the coast, from Venice Beach to Redondo Beach and down to Huntington Beach, and he checked out as many of them as possible. At Long Beach, Duke "gave a thrilling exhibition of swimming and surf-board riding, standing erect on a large surf-board. Thousands of people enjoyed the exhibition and cheered his work."[19]

Kahanamoku has given surfing "a great stimulus" in California, raved one newspaper. "Whenever Duke appeared with [his board] a great crowd gathered on the beaches to marvel at the ease with which he stood upright and rode the bucking waves as skillfully as a cowboy rides a bronco. Everywhere he was besieged with pupils anxious to learn his methods and his skill with the board is already a popular legend in a dozen great resorts."[20]

Reporters extensively covered Duke's trip in 1913 as he surfed at Santa Cruz, Long Beach, and other places. Late in his life, Kahanamoku indicated that he first surfed the Southland in 1913, when "there was nothing there but oil wells."[21]

And yet, reliable sources have since claimed that Kahanamoku first surfed California the year before, in 1912, although exactly when and where varies according to the source. Duke's friend Charley Paddock, the track star, wrote, "As a youngster of twelve I rode on his surfboard with him when he made an exhibition tour of the California beaches after the Olympic Games of 1912."[22] Art Vultee, a member of the Los Angeles Athletic Club, wrote that Kahanamoku became the first person to surf in Newport Beach—"en route to Olympic Games" of 1912.[23] Surfing historians Tom Blake and Ben Finney offer similar, if also disparate, stories.

These accounts notwithstanding, there are no published reports in local newspapers like the *Los Angeles Times* and the *Redondo Reflux*, or in the *Mercury*, the weekly newsletter of the Los Angeles Athletic Club, indicating that Kahanamoku surfed in Southern California in 1912. Newspaper articles from that year reported that, on his way to Stockholm, Kahanamoku traveled from Honolulu to San Francisco and then directly to Chicago for swim meets on the East Coast, without detouring to Southern California. It is doubtful that he would have interrupted his pre-Olympic training in Philadelphia under coach Kistler to make a cross-country trip to Los Angeles on the eve of the Olympic Games. Kahanamoku reportedly retraced the same route when he returned to Hawaii after stops in New York City and Atlantic City.

It seems likely that Duke first surfed California in 1913, as he himself noted. But unless other, more definitive evidence is uncovered, the exact date and place of Kahanamoku's surfing debut in California will remain a mystery. Still, the relationship between the Golden State and the "Bronze Duke" proved to be genuine, deep, and long-lasting. He journeyed there often to compete in swimming, to surf, and to renew friendships—and later established Los Angeles as his home away from home in the 1920s.

11

Duke Kahanamoku's new home in Waikiki, while small, helped accommodate the large Kahanamoku family. He took a job as a draftsman in the Public Works department, where his excellent penmanship came in handy. The position was practically a sinecure, allowing him ample time to train.

He came to the beach every afternoon at about 4 o'clock, diving into the water off the Moana Hotel pier or working on his surfboard. Duke's pal, Dude Miller, ran the beachboy concession at Waikiki, and many Hui Nalu members supported themselves this way, giving surfing and swimming lessons to tourists and taking them for rides in the outrigger canoes for a dollar a person.

Their duties extended beyond mere instruction. The beachboys made sure visitors didn't get too sunburned and were there to aid inexperienced swimmers. They taught tourists how to eat poi and cooked them crab and squid over open fires. They put pungent *lei* around their necks, rubbed oil on their backs, weaved hats for them, and soothed their aching limbs with the vigorous and sensual massage known as *lomi-lomi*. Then, as the sun disappeared over the horizon, they took out their ukuleles and crooned soothing melodies on the pier.

They were jesters and musicians, philosophers and tour guides, with nicknames like "Steamboat," "Splash," "Panama," "Turkey," "Chick," and "Mystery." They worked for tips and meals and more, symbols of the casual hedonism of sunshine, swimming, and surfing found only in Hawaii. "Without these remarkable people the island would be nothing," the novelist James Michener once observed. "With them it is a carnival. . . . They are perpetual adolescents of the ocean, the playboys of the Pacific."[1]

An attitude of "what happens in Waikiki, stays in Waikiki" became part of beachboy lore. Louis Kahanamoku, one of Duke's younger brothers and a beachboy himself, remembers going to Honolulu harbor to welcome the new arrivals. "We size up the girls that come in," he said. "You look, 'Ey, that one up there, the one with the blue dress, that's mine, okay?' That's it. No fight, no nothing. And we know they going to be on the beach, we know they going stay in the hotel. We meet 'em, that's ours. That's mine, you know."[2]

After Duke's death, Sargent Kahanamoku related that his brother preferred one particular surfboard "because it floated better and he take out many *haole* girls surfing. But he no surf. He keep on paddling way outside and 'ges' dem one good Hawaiian fucking."[3]

A snapshot of Kahanamoku's life at this time came from Minnie Leola Crawford, a young tourist from the state of Washington. Crawford penned a series of letters to her mother that, in 1913, publisher Howard D. Berrett compiled into a book titled *Seven Weeks in Hawaii*. Crawford related that she had engaged "the services of the champion swimmer of the world" to go riding on an outrigger canoe:

> [Duke] is a grand fellow, only twenty-one years old, about six feet tall and as dark as an Indian. He told me many interesting things about the fishes and the coral and offered to teach me to ride on the surf-boards. I told him I would love to learn if I could keep from getting wet. He thought this a great joke, and when we finally returned, before I knew it, the Duke was carrying me to shore to "keep the lady from getting wet," as he said, and how he laughed and showed his pretty white teeth. I am quite fond of the Duke![4]

Kahanamoku eventually persuaded Minnie to take a surfing lesson. She collided with a canoe and was thrown into the water, only to be rescued from the coral below by Duke. "He clutched me by the back and spreading me out upon a surfboard gave me the famous Hawaiian *lomi-lomi*,"[5] she wrote. Restored, she limped back to her hotel and, in her next letter, enclosed photographs of Duke.

The erotic, hands-on approach was sometimes misinterpreted. In the fall of 1913, Kahanamoku was cited as a corespondent in a divorce case filed by Noel Deerr, a technologist with the Hawaiian Sugar Planters' Association.

Deerr was married to a young British woman named Rhoda Wilson. He alleged that his wife had committed adultery with Kahanamoku and denied the paternity of their as-yet-unborn child.

A scandal erupted, and Rhoda Deerr publicly denied the charges. "You and only you are the father of the child that is coming," she told her husband. "I can only hope and pray that before the poor little mite is born its father will repent of his evil actions and will manfully and honorably own and support his own child and also his faithful wife."[6]

Kahanamoku shrugged off the accusation, saying that his relationship with Mrs. Deerr "was that of a swimming instructor."[7] But dealing with the legal fallout was one reason why he canceled a trip to Australia for swimming exhibitions.

His newfound prominence attracted other rumors. When San Francisco beauty queen Mae Josephine Bennett traveled to Hawaii, Kahanamoku was identified as a suitor who "paid not a little attention to Miss Bennett." After he showed dancer-entertainer Verna Mersereau "a very fine time" in Hawaii, she felt compelled to write a letter to the society columnist at the *Hawaiian Gazette* newspaper denying that Duke had made a proposal to her.[8]

The stories sometimes went beyond the fantastic. While swimming at Waikiki, Kahanamoku supposedly engaged in a "battle to the death" with a four-foot, man-eating eel. The monster clamped its fangs on his hand and wrapped its body around his waist in a boa constrictor-like embrace. Ten feet beneath the surface of the water, Duke had to strangle the beast in order to escape its death grip.

"I guess it will be some time before I can use my finger," he was quoted as saying, "but I do not think it is serious. The eel got a big piece of flesh out of one joint, though, and I feel thankful that it did not get the entire finger."[9]

The incident turned out to be a yarn—Kahanamoku was cut slightly by the rocks—but the "silly fake" was reprinted in newspapers around the nation.

One writer managed to incorporate romance, rescue, sharks, and surfing all in one story. Under the headline, "Matrimony and Man-Eater Both Dodged by Duke," the *Honolulu Star-Bulletin* related that Addie Dunbar, a singer-dancer from the mainland, was swimming in the waters at Waikiki Beach when "a huge man-eating shark" attacked her.

"A dark flash in the water, a scream and then her rescuer appeared in Duke Kahanamoku, the famous swimmer," the newspaper related. "A short tussle and the shark was put to flight."[10]

Later, the canoe carrying Miss Dunbar capsized. She struck her head on the gunwale of the boat and was rendered unconscious. "But the Duke was at hand," the paper reported, "and she was again safely landed on the beach."

"Of course there was no proposal," she said. "The Duke is awfully nice, and I think it was lovely of him to help me."

While Kahanamoku was fending off imaginary marriage proposals and shark attacks, preparations for the next Olympic Games, scheduled to be held in Berlin in 1916, were proceeding. German organizers constructed multipurpose Grunewald Stadium, in a forest about a half-hour west of Berlin, which was dedicated by Kaiser Wilhelm II himself in June of 1913.

"That the Olympic Games at Berlin will surpass all previous events of the kind goes without saying," James E. Sullivan noted that year. "With the patronage of Emperor William, whose enthusiasm for everything that tends to the betterment of the German race is well known, no effort will be spared to show the world the superiority of the German athletes. . . . May we all be there to again cheer when 'Old Glory' is hoisted to denote an American victory."[11]

The following year, Baron Pierre de Coubertin marked the twentieth anniversary of the founding of the International Olympic Committee with a celebratory meeting in Paris. With the Berlin stadium complete and with the 1912 Stockholm Games considered to be the most successful of the Olympics to date, the baron was in an exceedingly optimistic mood. He used the occasion to unveil a flag of his own design, showing five interlaced rings of different colors against a white background. The symbolism was readily apparent: the continents of the world, united in harmony by the Olympic spirit.

The conference was winding down when news reached Paris that Serbian nationalist Gavrilo Princip had assassinated Archduke Franz Ferdinand, the heir to the Austro-Hungarian throne, in Sarajevo. The serene mood inside the Palais de la Sorbonne vanished, and the cataclysm of war suddenly loomed over Europe.

Germany refused to relinquish control as host of the 1916 Olympics, in the apparent belief that the war would be concluded swiftly. Coubertin, so proud of his creation, stubbornly did not countenance canceling the Olympics. His main action was to move IOC headquarters from Paris to Lausanne, Switzerland, which became its permanent home after the war.

A stalemate developed. "No decision has yet been reached regarding the holding of the Olympic games in 1916," the *New York Times* reported in early 1915. "The matter has been left in status quo pending the termination of the war. . . . So many conflicting reports have been received here regarding the disposal of the 1916 Olympic Games that reliance can be placed on none of them."[12]

Neither the IOC nor Germany officially announced the cancellation of the sixth Olympic Games. They simply did not happen.

Duke Kahanamoku resumed competition at the Mid-Pacific Carnival in Honolulu in 1914. Hawaii's promotional agency used the annual event to publicize the Islands' charms, complete with a floral parade, circus acts, and sports contests. And who better to represent Hawaii than Duke? The colorful carnival poster featured him surfing without his shirt, his fists and chest muscles clenched in a powerful pose offset by a welcoming grin.[13]

Before 6,000 people at Honolulu harbor, Kahanamoku set a world's record in the 100-yard straightaway, with a time of 54.8, and won the 220 and 440 events. The real news, however, was his upset loss to Robert "Bud" Small in the 50-yard event. "Someone had to win," he said graciously as he congratulated Small, "and I don't feel a bit bad about being beaten in world's record time."[14]

Duke's defeat to the unheralded Small was a blip, but it instantly brought out the critics. "There must either be something the matter with Kahanamoku or he is already deteriorating," wrote William Unmack of the *San Francisco Call.* "It is as plain as the nose on one's face that Duke got all the competition he wanted last Saturday, and it is just as plain that he was found wanting in his speed. He was not equal to the occasion."[15]

Arthur Cavill, of the famous Australian swimming family, echoed those sentiments. "Kahanamoku is certainly a great boy and still has some good swims in his system," he said, "but I would be willing to wager that within a year the Hawaiian will have passed out of the limelight."[16]

A slipup during the Honolulu meet in June did not improve matters. Kahanamoku apparently misjudged the finish line for the 50-yard event and stopped swimming at forty yards. Three others passed him by.

Kahanamoku recuperated by spending much of the latter half of 1914 in California. He flirted with the idea of staying on the mainland as his friends in Southern California, including Les Henry, tried to convince him to join the Los Angeles Athletic Club. George Freeth, now ensconced as the club's swim instructor, tutored Kahanamoku on his start and turns, the two weakest parts of his indoor regimen. Duke had developed a bad habit of diving into the water too close to the starting platform. Freeth encouraged him to utilize the power of his legs and, at the gun, leap as far as possible while extending his body. On the turns, Duke tended to resurface too quickly afterwards. Freeth worked with him to stay underwater as long as possible in order to take maximum advantage of the shove off from the wall.

The advice paid off at the swimming championships in San Francisco in July, when Kahanamoku and Hui Nalu members faced off against the team representing the Illinois Athletic Club. The Midwest ranked as one of the nation's most formidable aquatic regions, with the Illinois Athletic Club (IAC) leading the way, thanks to a Jewish maestro with thinning red hair. At 340 pounds, William "Big Bill" Bachrach resembled former president William Howard Taft in girth. His habit of watching his swimmers train while chewing on a cigar and pacing alongside the deck of the pool in leather dress shoes and a threadbare bathrobe that barely covered his immense chest belied one of the world's keenest coaching minds.

After a stint at the Chicago YMCA, Bachrach had replaced Frank Sullivan at the IAC. He piloted the club's water polo team to four consecutive national titles. One of his training precepts was that competition brought out the best in elite athletes. He liked to take his "finny marvels" on the road to challenge the nation's top amateur swim teams: the Olympic Club in San Francisco, the Los Angeles Athletic Club, and the New York Athletic Club.

Harry Hebner, the IAC captain and backstroke gold medalist, described Bachrach as the "Miracle Man" of swimming. He molded championship teams "as no other man could do, settled all differences, fixed difficulties, fathering the boys until [Olympic swimmer] Jamison Handy has named him 'Padrone.'"[17]

Local newspapers breathlessly covered every angle of the IAC-Hui Nalu matchup. A *San Francisco Examiner* reporter was amazed at the amount of sun-dried octopus being consumed by the Hawaiian swimmers, noting that Kahanamoku "smiles like a schoolboy when he munches devilfish."[18]

"Can Duke Hold His Title Against Yankee Marvels?" was the question posed by the *Oakland Tribune*.[19] He soon supplied the answers at the Sutro Baths. Despite losing to Ludy Langer in the half-mile, Duke nipped Arthur Raithel in the 100 and defeated McGillivray in the 220. Duke's "remarkable, fish-like turn on the laps gave him both races," according to the *Los Angeles Times*.[20] Kahanamoku took revenge on Bud Small in the 50, but he lost the finals to Raithel.

Kahanamoku had prevailed as America's top individual swimmer, but the IAC prevailed over Hui Nalu in the points competition. The burgeoning rivalry would consume both parties. Bachrach and his talented IAC teams—featuring, soon enough, Johnny Weissmuller—would constitute Duke's main competition, both at national meets and at the Olympics, for the remainder of his competitive career.

Before returning to Hawaii, Kahanamoku made his motion picture debut in *The Beachcomber*, shot on an unidentified beach in Southern California. The one-reel silent film was directed by its star, Hobart Bosworth, a pioneer in Hollywood's nascent movie industry. (Bosworth also was a friend and business associate of the author Jack London.) Duke did not have to stretch much to play a native islander who swims out to rescue Bosworth's character from drowning. Publicity photos showed him wearing nothing more than a sarong. Bosworth had to delay releasing the film, however, after it was discovered that "the champion might lose his right as an amateur if swimming for money," according to *Motion Picture News*.[21] It is unclear whether *The Beachcomber* was ever shown or distributed in the United States, although foreign audiences reportedly were able to view the stirring flick.

Between the excellent surfing conditions and his many new acquaintances, Kahanamoku felt increasingly comfortable in Southern California. But in 1915, with the war continuing in Europe, he was not yet ready to leave his family, or Hawaii, behind. He sailed home that fall on the *Matsonia*. The steamer slowed to a halt midocean after a stowaway was discovered. The captain arranged to meet a sister ship sailing east so that they could transfer the stowaway and exchange mail. Duke was writing letters below, but the ocean looked so inviting that he thought it would be "a nice thing" to take a swim.[22]

Kahanamoku and Bill Inman, a baseball player from Hawaii who briefly pitched for the San Francisco Seals in the Minor Leagues, decided to go in together. Duke changed into his one-piece suit and came topside. No Inman. Finally, Inman showed up, but without a bathing suit. Duke shrugged. He slipped off his robe and stood for a moment on the railing. Then he took the plunge. "When I got into the water," he said, "gee, oh boy, it was wonderful. And more buoyancy, too, out there in deep water. I was swimming around there, this way, that way. . . . No sharks. Just good, nice Pacific Ocean for a swim."[23]

Kahanamoku cavorted in the depths, measuring the distance between the two ships. To his surprise, the *Matsonia* powered up and drifted away. He found himself dangerously far astern, bobbing in rough seas and, despite his training, tiring. Thankfully, passengers were able to get the crew's attention. Captain Charles Peterson lowered a lifeboat for Duke, who helped the sailors row the rescue vessel back to the ship before the *Matsonia* resumed its journey to Hawaii.

"Kahanamoku Was Almost Marooned," related the *Los Angeles Times*. Duke was able to laugh about the incident, especially when Captain Peterson told him that it provided "good publicity" for the Matson Navigation Company.[24]

12

The war in Europe had displaced the quadrennial timetable of the Olympic Games. In the prime of his career, Kahanamoku missed out on defending his Olympic crown. He searched for other outlets to hone his talents. Swimming-mad Australia beckoned next. William Hill, the secretary of the Australia Swimming Union, had worked to arrange a visit ever since he watched Duke perform at the 1912 Stockholm Olympics, even stopping over at Honolulu to meet with him.

After several aborted attempts, plans were finalized for Kahanamoku to go to Australia in the winter of 1914, when it would be summer in the Southern Hemisphere. He departed aboard the SS *Ventura* on November 30. "Duke Kahanamoku, the famous Hawaiian swimmer, has left for Australia. He went by boat,"[1] deadpanned the *Los Angeles Times*.

Australians were shedding their old fears of the ocean—for years, beach swimming was banned during daytime hours—and the newly established commonwealth was churning out elite swimmers at a disproportionate rate to its small population, including Cecil Healy and William Longworth, Duke's rivals in Stockholm; Fred Lane, the first man to break the 60-second barrier for 100 yards; and the Cavill family of swimming gurus. Annette Kellerman, the first woman to attempt to swim the English Channel, had parlayed her glamorous image—she wore a black one-piece bathing suit that revealed every curve of her voluptuous body—into a film career. Fanny Durack and Mina Wylie paid their own way to Stockholm, finished first and second, respectively, in the 100 meters, and instantly became national heroes.

As the first foreign Olympic gold medalist to visit Australia, Kahanamoku was an object of fascination from the moment he arrived in Sydney on

December 14, accompanied by George Cunha, a top swimmer from Hawaii, and Francis Evans, who replaced William Rawlins as tour manager.

There to greet them was Cecil Healy, serving as the reporter for a sporting newspaper. "You're getting fat!" Duke joked to Healy. "We're all getting fat."

After discovering that Cunha was "not an Hawaiian native as was thought, but a white man," Healy turned to Duke and asked, "Oh! Did you bring your surfboard with you?"

"Why, no, we were told the use of boards was not permitted in Australia," he replied. Seeing Healy's disappointment, Duke quickly added, "But I can easily make one here."[2]

The party was whisked off to a reception at the Hotel Australia in Sydney. Kahanamoku's formal statement was brief: "I'm not as good a speaker as the rest of the bunch here," he said, "but, in the water, I'll do my best to please everybody."

His trip occurred at a time when the Australian government was forcibly removing aboriginal children from their families so as to "recivilize" them. In this era of "stolen children," local reporters seemed required to comment upon Duke's skin color. He was described, variously, as the "brown marvel," the "dusky champion," the "bronzed islander," and the "dark-skinned Hawaiian." When he surfed, he stood "like an ebony statue."[3] One wag called him "Kokobanana."

Australia, it should be noted, was not insensitive concerning race and sports. Promoters in Sydney gave boxer Jack Johnson the opportunity to challenge Tommy Burns, the white champion, for the heavyweight crown in 1908, when no opponent or city in the United States allowed him that chance. Johnson defeated Burns on, appropriately enough, Boxing Day.

Kahanamoku himself was treated courteously in Australia. He avoided any hint of controversy or conflict—even on those occasions when he encountered racist jibes and snubs—an attitude that the press corps applauded. "All my glowing impressions of the Duke (as a man) were reestablished," Healy reported. "I had managed to get a chance to shake hands and have a chat with him. He is a splendid dispositioned fellow, and I cannot conceive the thought of anyone taking other than an instant liking for him. I make bold to predict that he will have ingratiated himself into the affections of a large number of Australians before departing on his homeward voyage."[4]

Healy's prediction proved to be correct, and crowds clamored to see Kahanamoku in action. Francis Evans juggled the swimmers' schedule as the tour expanded to include the cities of Melbourne, Newcastle, and Brisbane, the northern beach towns of Queensland, and then on to New Zealand. Posters promoting "The Human Fish" were plastered everywhere: "Is Duke the Best? Book your seats!"

Once Kahanamoku confirmed that surfing was legal at Australia's beaches, he was directed to a local lumberyard owned by timber merchant George Hudson. Duke penciled out a rough template design for a board. There was no available redwood of that size, but Hudson was able to supply him with an elongated piece of one-hundred-year-old sugar pine.

Kahanamoku finished the shaping by hand, likely with an adze, a knife, and sandpaper. He then coated the board with varnish so that the surface was "as slick as a dancing board." The result was a solid plank that weighed roughly eighty pounds: a rough-hewn, round-nosed, square-tailed board that was about eight-and-a-half feet long, nearly two feet wide, and almost three inches thick.[5]

Australians were eager to watch him surf. When one newspaper published a brief note that Duke was to give a surfing exhibition at a local beach, about 3,000 people showed up, only to be left extremely disappointed when he did not appear.

Over Christmas Kahanamoku, Cunha, and Evans were guests of the New South Wales Amateur Swimming Association at the Boomerang Camp at Freshwater Beach, outside of Sydney. On December 24 Duke gave an unannounced surfing exhibition, viewed by reporters and members of the local club. In waves that weren't all that special, he paddled out into the breakers about a quarter of a mile and then rode them back to shore, arms crossed against his chest as he moved across the water at top speed.

He surfed backwards at one point, causing the board "to describe a half circle or turn completely round without spoiling the shoot," and then startled onlookers by standing on his head.[6] Disbelief turned to jaw-dropping amazement. Kahanamoku was the "human motor boat," wrote one observer. "So lightning like was the movement that all one could see was a dark figure—it might have been a post for all that the spectators knew—flying through space. We had known him only by repute; we had seen him in pictures in one of his famous attitudes—standing on his surf board, being borne shorewards on the crest of a wave, a smile on his dusky countenance, and there were a lot of us who imagined the poster to be grossly exaggerated; too theatrical, in fact. But we are wrong. The man on the poster is the Duke all right, but the picture errs on the side of modesty."[7]

Kahanamoku surprised his hosts by ignoring the threat of sharks that inhabited the waters. "The lifeguards asked him, 'Did you see any sharks?'" his brother Bill recalled Duke telling him later. "Duke said, 'Yeah, I saw plenty.' 'And they didn't bother you?' the lifeguards asked. 'No,' Duke replied, 'and I didn't bother them.'"[8]

A horse-and-buggy carriage was employed to ferry Duke's board to other surfing excursions. At a session at Dee Why Beach, north of Freshwater, Kahanamoku motioned for Isabel Letham, a fifteen-year-old schoolgirl, to join him. "To say I was dumbfounded was putting it mildly," Letham later recounted. "[I had] never seen a surfboard before in my life—[and now] to go out with a raging sea with the world's greatest surfboard rider, and ride tandem with him on this great big killer wave."

Duke paddled out with Isabel and picked out a wave. "I said, 'OH NO! NO! NO!'" Letham remembered. "He said, 'OH YES! YES! YES!' and he got me by the scruff of the neck and yanked me up in front and of course I got this wave."

When she reached shore, all she wanted to do was do it again. "I was sold on surfboard riding then," Letham said.[9]

Whenever Kahanamoku heard about excellent waves—at Dee Why, at Cronulla, or at Manly—he detoured to catch them. "I was staggered," said Charles "Snow" McAlister, then 11, after watching Duke's surf-riding exhibition. "Everyone just clapped and clapped."[10] The son of a mailman, McAlister was so excited that he immediately procured the necessary wood to shape his own surfboard.

Journalist W. F. Corbett sought out Kahanamoku to talk about his "surf shooting" experiences. "You have hundreds more surf shooters at work in one day around Sydney than we see in a week, or perhaps a much longer stretch of time, at Honolulu," Duke told him, "but I think the old island has the pastime at greater perfection, which is only to be expected considering its antiquity with us.

"You ask me if I held the championship as a surf shooter," he continued. "I did not, because we had no competitions, but I do not mind telling you that there were none around Honolulu whom I knew anything about able to shape [surfboards] better than me."[11]

Kahanamoku interrupted his surfing escapades in early January for the first swim meet on the Australian tour. Upwards of 8,000 people packed the extensive grandstands at the Domain Baths in Woolloomooloo Bay, outside of Sydney, to watch Duke take first place in the 220-yard event, beating Longworth and Cunha, and second place in the 440, behind only Tommy Adrian of Manly.

In his specialty, the 100 yards, Kahanamoku started slowly on the straight-away course. Then he accelerated, leaving Longworth, Cunha, and Albert Barry behind. His clocking of 53.8 seconds broke his world record by nearly one second. He seemed so relaxed in the water, according to one eyewitness, that the time "seemed preposterous, so easily had been the accomplishment of it. One could not help but wondering how few seconds Kahanamoku could swim 100 yards in if he swam 'all out' all the way."[12]

It was not the first or the last time that reporters commented on Kahanamoku's habit of easing up during races. Some believed that Duke's stroke was so smooth that he looked like he wasn't trying. Others whispered that he slowed down so as not to humiliate his opponents. Kahanamoku shrugged and kept winning.

Kahanamoku, Cunha, and Evans traversed thousands of miles along the east coast of Australia, drawing massive crowds and filling the coffers of local clubs. Duke did not win every race on the tour due to arcane "handicap" rules that gave opponents a considerable advantage from the start, but his form dazzled. "The feet revolve like the blades of a steamer's propeller," according to one newspaper.[13]

At banquets, he preferred to "manipulate" the ukulele than speak. "The swimming giant burst into song to the accompaniment of the weirdest strains one ever listened to," the *Sunday Times* reported. "It was something between the high-pitched notes of a mosquito and the angry hum of a swarm of bees on its wing, but it earned a wonderful reception. 'Give us more!' yelled the gathering. This time the Duke came down to civilization and sang 'By the Sea.'"[14]

The trio journeyed to New Zealand in mid-February, making stops in Auckland, Christchurch, Wellington, Dunedin, Timaru, and Rotorua.

Kahanamoku surfed the chilly waters of New Brighton Beach, outside of Christchurch, and at Lyall Bay, near Wellington. At Muriwai Beach, on the west coast of Auckland, Duke only had access to a "flimsy pineboard," but he still wowed the locals. "It was a magnificent sight to see him cleaving his path upwards over a big blue sea, the sunlight flashing on his brown arms and shoulders as he alternately lifted them clear of the water."[15]

When Duke came to surf at Lyall Bay, Chief Tureiti Te Heuheu Tukino V welcomed them to Aotearoa (the Maori name for New Zealand) with *hongi* (the traditional greeting of nose and forehead pressing). A feast followed, and then came a display of the Maori ancestral war dance.

Later, Chief Tukino signed Kahanamoku's autograph book with a message that connected two Polynesian cultures separated by thousands of miles of water. "We are very glad in our hearts to see you and to meet you at our house," he wrote. "Your people have never moved from the old country called 'Hawaiki,'" referring to the traditional place of origin for the Maori, "and your *mana* [spiritual energy] like the *rangatira* [chieftain wisdom] has never changed from the olden days to the present time."[16]

Kahanamoku delighted in connecting with his Polynesian roots. But even in Australia there was no escape from suspicions about professionalism. One anonymous critic questioned the nature of Duke's expenses on the months-long journey, writing that he "did not believe a man like Kahanamoku would come so far away from his home unless he was liberally remunerated."[17]

Journalist Corbett made inquiries and reported that the AAU had "vouched" for Duke. "Neither Kahanamoku nor any one of the two visitors accompanying him received a penny," he answered. "They were guaranteed first-class traveling to and hotel expenses from Honolulu to Honolulu, and promised a tour through Australia in so far as it could be arranged."

At the end of March, when Kahanamoku left Australia for Hawaii, he had been away for nearly four months. He swam in sixty events and surfed at numerous beaches, providing a bright note at a time when scores of men—including Cecil Healy, as it turned out—were leaving home to fight in Europe. When he bequeathed the surfboard that he had made to a teenager named Claude West, the design became the default model for a generation of shapers down under—its Rosetta stone, as it were.

The trip also initiated Kahanamoku's deep connection with athletes from Australia and New Zealand, which he repaid with *aloha* whenever their surfers and swimmers came through Hawaii. Duke himself returned to Australia several times, most notably in 1956, as a revered guest at the Melbourne Olympics.

His surfing excursions in 1914–15 were later mischaracterized or, at the least, enshrouded in legend. The narrative set forth was that Kahanamoku was the first person to ever surf in Australia and New Zealand. Numerous historians and journalists have repeated this like a mantra, including Duke himself. "My memories of Australia go back to 1915 when I was world freestyle champion and gave the first demonstration of surfboard riding in Australia," he later wrote."[18]

Contemporary scholars, while respectful of his stature, have exposed the Duke-as-originator story to be a myth. They point out that several locals, including William and Tommy Walker (who acquired his surfboard when he visited Hawaii), surfed in and around Sydney before Duke's arrival in 1914 and have displayed photos and newspaper clippings as evidence.

That said, Kahanamoku was the first expert to surf in Australian waters. And, as he had done previously in places like Atlantic City and Southern California, his skill at "walking on water" inspired numerous followers. At least three of the young people whom he directly touched on the 1914–15 trip—Claude West, "Snow" McAlister, and Isabel Letham—grew up to become influential figures in Australian surfing circles. Once again, Duke had played the role of apostle, seeding the ancient pastime of surfing in distant locales and generating positive publicity for Hawaii.

13

Duke Kahanamoku was greeted with unsettling news upon his return to Hawaii. His father had abruptly quit his job with the Honolulu police force. Duke Halapu had been charged with "conduct unbecoming an officer and gentleman," according to one published report. The veteran police captain "volunteered his resignation rather than face a civil service hearing" concerning the series of allegations filed with the sheriff's office.[1]

"Captain Kahanamoku asked to be relieved from further duty," Sheriff Charles Rose said. "About all I have to say is that I have accepted the resignation. As far as I know any charges that may have been filed against the officer in the department have been dropped."

What transpired to cause Duke Halapu's sudden resignation was never revealed; nor did the family address the charges publicly. Duke comforted his father as best he could and then went back to work with the Hawaii Territory's Public Works department. The enormous amount of goodwill that he produced during his tour of Australia, for swimming and surfing and for Hawaii, had done little more than pay his expenses.

Duke plunged back into training for the 1915 national swimming championships, held in conjunction with the Panama-Pacific International Exposition in San Francisco. The world's fair commemorated two events of supreme significance to Hawaii: the "discovery" of the Pacific Ocean by European explorers in the sixteenth century and the completion of the Panama Canal in 1914. The latter eliminated the need for ships to go around Cape Horn in order to reach the Pacific Ocean and thus made the Hawaiian Islands more accessible for commerce and tourism and more strategically important.

The Panama-Pacific International Exposition was also San Francisco's coming-out party after the city was leveled by the earthquake and fire of 1906. The most famous of the nineteen million visitors to the expo was former president Teddy Roosevelt, who had wrested control of the Panama Canal project for the United States and ensured its completion. But its two biggest draws were the Liberty Bell, which arrived from Philadelphia by train, and the fourteen-ton Underwood typewriter that churned out headlines daily at the Palace of Liberal Arts.

Territory boosters from Hawaii used the event to cement ties with the Bay City and to promote the Islands' splendors. They constructed a building on the expo grounds, complete with an "action sculpture" by Gordon Usborne that depicted three surfers from Waikiki, and stocked a massive aquarium with tropical fish. Mornings and afternoons, a native quintet played "weird, unworldly melodies" amid palms and tree ferns from Kilauea.

Picked to head the expo's athletic program was James E. Sullivan. The AAU leader had held a similar role at the world's fair in St. Louis, where the sports competition doubled as the program for the 1904 Olympics. For San Francisco, Sullivan outlined an ambitious carnival that included state, regional, and national championships in swimming, wrestling, rugby, soccer, gymnastics, tennis, and other sports. He made overtures to have supplementary World Series baseball games played in the city, and he traveled to Europe to recruit foreign athletes. He even persuaded Pierre de Coubertin to award an Olympic medal to the winner of the modern pentathlon.

Then, with the onset of war in Europe, Sullivan lobbied to have the 1916 Olympics shifted to American soil. "The United States is the logical country in which to hold the games and the American committee will carry out the schedule as planned by Germany without a hitch of any kind," declared Sullivan in August of 1914. "Should it prove desirable to postpone the Panama-Pacific exposition planned for San Francisco next year until 1916, the Olympic games would undoubtedly be held there in connection with the fair. If the exposition is held according to schedule, Chicago, Pittsburgh, New York and Boston are all available for the following year. New Haven and Syracuse, with their big college stadiums, might also be available."[2]

Sullivan unexpectedly died one month after issuing this statement. His death left amateur sport in America without its most influential leader. The sports menu of the expo—once considered "the grandest ever conceived"—was severely curtailed, and the "heavy handicap" of the war eliminated the participation of international athletes.[3] About the only world-class sports event that remained from Sullivan's original plan was the swim meet, featuring Kahanamoku.

Duke tuned up with a standout showing at the local AAU meet in Hawaii, taking first place in the 50-, 100-, 440-, and 880-yard events, and a tie for first place in the 220. He was almost a no-show for the exposition meet because of a disagreement with organizers over expense money. World's fair officials had agreed to pay for him to come to San Francisco, but they balked at paying for other Hawaiians.

After Duke protested the arrangement, business leaders raised money to send five other swimmers, including George Cunha, Clarence Lane, and Harold "Stubby" Kruger, with Harvey Chilton along as coach and trainer. "Kahanamoku is a champion, a world's champion, and the people of Hawaii should contribute as liberally as possible to see that he is kept before the public," noted the Chamber of Commerce's monthly magazine. "It's Promotion. It's boosting for Hawaii. It's helping to place Hawaii more solidly on the map."[4]

The expo swimming championships were held at the Sutro Baths, a familiar place for Duke from his successes there in 1913 and 1914. Located on the western edge of San Francisco just south of Land's End, the massive public facility was the brainchild of one-time mayor and serial entrepreneur Adolph Sutro. The oceanfront water park featured six pools filled with ocean salt water (heated to varying temperatures) and one freshwater plunge, over 500 private dressing rooms, a gigantic toboggan slide, a waterwheel, tier upon tier of amphitheater seating, and a glazed roof consisting of 100,000 panes of glass.

Kahanamoku's main rivals were also familiar. Coach Bill Bachrach of the Illinois Athletic Club brought a group of swimmers from the Midwest who competed as the Central Association squad. On the first night, Duke took the early lead in the 50-yard event and held on for the victory, with Lane and Cunha completing the 1-2-3 Hawaiian sweep.

In the 220, Kahanamoku struggled stroke for stroke with Chicago's Perry McGillivray before winning by inches in 2:26.4, with Cunha coming in third. Bachrach's team picked up crucial points in the backstroke and breaststroke events, leaving the two teams virtually tied going into the final night.

Kahanamoku and Arthur Raithel squared off in the 100-yard event, and the two finished in a dead heat in 55.4. The Hawaiians were convinced that Duke had prevailed, but "there was nothing to do but swim the race over," he said later.[5] And so they did, after a fifteen-minute rest. Kahanamoku summoned the strength to prevail by a body length in 54.4.

The points contest between Hawaii and the Midwest now came down to one race: the 300-yard relay. Bachrach's squad of William Vosburgh, McGillivray, Raithel, and Harry Hebner lined up against "Stubby" Kruger, Clarence Lane, and George Cunha, with Kahanamoku in the anchor slot.

The Midwest took an early lead and maintained its edge going into the last lap. Duke started well behind at the final exchange, with only seventy-five yards to make up the difference. He chased down McGillivray and, with a desperate surge, appeared to have won the race and given Hawaii the meet.

The happy quartet got dressed and prepared to celebrate when the officials declared the relay a dead heat. They ordered the race to be swum again. Trainer Harvey Chilton protested so vehemently that, in an effort to quiet him, he was pushed into the tank, clothes and all.

After a ten-minute break, the eight swimmers readied themselves again. This time, the Lake States prevailed by three yards in 2:42.6, establishing a new world's record. The final tally: Central 34, Hawaii 28. Kahanamoku was again the individual star, but Bachrach had pulled out another team duel. "We got the worst of it in the relay," Kruger protested. "The Hawaii team won it fair and square the first time, and should have had the meet."[6]

Duke's duties were not limited to the pool. He and the other swimmers joined in the effort to publicize the Territory inside the Hawaiian Building, with Kahanamoku performing hula, playing the ukulele, and posing for photos. He then vacationed at Monte Rio, in the Russian River area, before heading home, his reputation as a "great promotion asset for Hawaii"[7] secured. A poet named R. M. Bartley went further, praising him in verse:

They know him for a good sport
   In spindrift wild or slow
He upholds his championship in Honolulu City,
And in San Francisco and Melbourne
   His records meteor-like grow.

Why? He's the swimmer, the champion swimmer,
   Of the measured waters;
He's the sport whose record ne'er grows dimmer—
Having the qualities of a pugnacious trimmer
   In the treasured waters.[8]

On his return to Hawaii, Kahanamoku stepped away from swimming and picked up the oars again. Sculling was a very different experience than paddling an outrigger canoe, and both the one- and two-oar varieties agreed with him. Duke relished the competition, the speed on the water, and the training involved. He rowed for the Myrtles Boat Club in various configurations: on the six-man barge team as well as in the double scull. Later, at a regatta at Pearl Harbor, Duke won in the single scull along a course that ran from Banning's point to the railroad wharf.

Kahanamoku also took part in the introduction of two new sports. Volleyball was a recent invention, concocted in 1895 by YMCA instructor William Morgan. Like basketball, its recreational cousin, volleyball was designed to be an indoor activity during wintertime.[9] Hawaiians moved volleyball outdoors—onto the sand, under the sun, and next to the ocean—after "Dad" Center strung up a net at the Outrigger Canoe Club, "between the surfboard lockers and the canoe shed parallel to the beach."[10]

Freed from hard gymnasium floors and harsh indoor lighting, beach volleyball added different physical challenges to an already demanding sport. Kahanamoku loved the action: running, pivoting, and leaping in the sand kept his legs in excellent shape. One player, Ronald Quay Smith, remembered competing against the Outrigger Canoe Club boys, "who were the best volleyball players that I knew of at the time and it was something to go up against those fellows," he said. "Tom Singlehurst, Duke and Dave Kahanamoku along with some of the other boys could jump five or six feet, and we respected them very much."[11]

Aquaplaning was another new activity that Duke pursued. For this, Kahanamoku balanced on his wooden surfboard and held onto a rope as a motorboat towed him at top speed. He and his brothers later performed this form of "water-surfing"—the precursor to waterskiing and wakeboarding—while being towed in the water by a low-flying airplane. The experience was an adrenaline rush like no other.

If 1914–15 brought acclaim for Kahanamoku, the events of 1916 showed how abruptly success can be reversed. The keenest athletic disappointment occurred with the annulment of the 1916 Olympics on account of the war. This was not a surprising development, but it meant that Duke was not able to defend his 100-meter title from 1912 or add to his medal haul while he was in his physical prime. The efforts to preserve his amateur status, including the subterfuge regarding his ownership of the home in Waikiki, had left him eligible for a competition that never materialized.

Instead, Bill Rawlins arranged for Kahanamoku to compete at a series of events on the mainland in April. The AAU had scheduled races over several days at different locales: Pittsburgh, New York, St. Louis, and Chicago. On Duke's "rest" days, Rawlins scheduled exhibitions for New Haven, Detroit, and Minneapolis.

The result was an unmitigated disaster. In Pittsburgh, Kahanamoku lost the 100, his best event, to Perry McGillivray of the Illinois Athletic Club. Two days later, in New York, he was defeated in the trial heats for the 220-yard event and did not qualify for the finals. He came in second place in the 500-yard event in St. Louis, before gaining revenge over McGillivray and Coach Bachrach by taking the 50-yard sprint at the IAC's pool in Chicago.

Mainland observers blamed Rawlins for not preparing Kahanamoku for the trip. "Duke should have been here a month ahead of time," said George Kistler, who had coached Kahanamoku before Stockholm. "He was in no condition to swim."[12]

Hawaiian singer Henry Clark lamented that Kahanamoku was over-worked and undertrained. The swimmer was "rushed from train to tank without rest or a rubdown or a chance to practice," Clark wrote from New York, because his manager "turned the tour into a sort of vaudeville circuit." Clark added that he had to send his own assistant to Detroit as Kahanamoku was "without anyone to help him."[13]

Famed swim coach Louis de Breda Handley noted that Duke's showing was a "keen disappointment. His style has changed since last seen here. He appears to have lost much of his buoyancy, swimming a good deal lower in the water, and his stroke—a straight six-beat crawl—is not nearly so clean."[14]

Rawlins tried to defend himself. "There is no reason to criticize anyone because Duke did not win all of the fourteen events he entered and swam in," he said. "Duke cannot win every race and he has been beaten before. As to the slighting charge that I traveled on the trip on anybody else's money but my own, that is entirely false. Likewise false are the stories that Duke had a chance to go into vaudeville for the mere bagatelle of a thousand [dollars] a week. Hot air, that's all."[15]

Kahanamoku's comments about the trip were clipped but showed his obvious disappointment. "Too much train travel," he said. "Entered everything. Trouble was in my legs."[16]

At a swim-fest in Honolulu in September, Kahanamoku lost to Ludy Langer in the 500-yard event and finished third to Ted Cann in the 220. He found redemption with victories in the 50 and the 100. Typically low-key, he punctuated his win in the latter by slamming the float at the finish line with a bang that could be heard on the pier.

The string of subpar performances, his family's precarious financial situation, and his dismay over the cancellation of the 1916 Olympics caused Kahanamoku to reconsider his amateur status. On his return from the mainland, he was seen huddling with professional billiards star Willie Hoppe, who was barnstorming with Japanese ace Koji Yamada. Hoppe introduced Duke to Robert Benjamin, his manager.

Rawlins was right about one thing: Kahanamoku was not offered "the mere bagatelle of a thousand a week." Benjamin offered $250 per week, plus one-half of the booking fees, for Duke to tour the vaudeville circuit, with options for one, two, or three years. With the excellent publicity that Duke generated from swimming and surfing—and with his ability to perform the *hapa-haole* music that was becoming so popular on the mainland—the opportunity seemed too good to pass up.

In May, in the presence of his father, Kahanamoku signed an option agreement with Benjamin on the deck of the *Matsonia* liner. He was ready to become a "pro-fesh fish."

"I have decided to become a professional," he told the *Honolulu Star-Bulletin*, "provided that proper arrangements are made whereby I will be guaranteed a certain sum for my work. I regret that I will be forced to leave the amateur ranks, but feel that in justice to myself I should not refuse the tentative proposition that has been offered."[17]

According to Benjamin, Duke was to travel to the East Coast to give exhibitions of surfboard riding at Atlantic City, New York, and Newport.

When the weather grew cold, he would move indoors and hit the stage to show off his myriad skills, including "the novel and strange trick of biting the heads off live fish."[18]

Rawlins's reaction was one of disbelief and indignation. He had arranged for several mainland swimmers to come to Hawaii in order to challenge Kahanamoku. Those plans were now in jeopardy. "It is all news to me," he said. "I regret that I was not let in on the secret."[19]

In early June Rawlins and other Hawaiian sports officials demanded a meeting with Kahanamoku. They argued that it was not in his best interest to sign a promotional contract with an outsider whom he scarcely knew. They also emphasized that he could better promote Hawaii as an amateur swimmer who was eligible for international competitions.

The coaxing worked. Kahanamoku wired Benjamin and canceled the arrangements, thus preserving his amateur status. For work, he became an inspector with the Public Works department. He donned a regulation rubber diving suit and helmet and descended forty feet to the bottom of the harbor in order to check the cylinders under the piers and other under-water features.

In the depths Kahanamoku found solace. "He was down there waiting [for the next piling], and nothing came," a friend, surfer George Downing, later said. "So he took the line he had to secure the piling, and he secured himself. And he fell asleep, sound asleep under water. So these guys had a message line to his helmet that they could jerk on, and they were jerking away and the line was tied up. So they sent a skindiver down to take a look, and Duke was sound asleep."[20]

Consolation came in the form of Duke's first serious girlfriend. Bernyece Smith lived in a bungalow in Waikiki that she rented from Kahanamoku's cousin, Maria Piikoi. According to writer Joe Brennan, their romance started in the water. "Duke taught me to surf, and what a thrill it was when I was able to stand with him on his huge board when catching a wave," Bernyece told Brennan. "I swam with him every day and he helped me with my stroke, and on moonlight nights he would take all three of us for a surfboat ride, after which we would have a swim and go back to our house for light refreshments."[21]

Kahanamoku showed her the scenic beauty of Oahu: the hidden water-falls of the Manoa Valley, the flowers bursting with fragrance in the garden oasis of Princess Kaiulani's estate, horseback riding on trails that only locals knew about. Bernyece described Duke as "simple and unspoiled in spite of all the fuss made over him." Because he was shy and loathed long conversations, she dubbed him "The Bronze Statue."[22]

Bernyece noticed that, whenever a visiting celebrity came to Hawaii, local officials demanded that Duke drop what he was doing and enter-tain them. Kahanamoku was gracious enough to comply—and he usually ended up becoming lifelong friends with these visitors—but it was another reminder that the business elite who controlled Hawaii also felt that they controlled Duke.

"I well remember when Edsel Ford [Henry Ford's son] and his little bride came on their honeymoon, and I accompanied Duke when he took them to his house," Bernyece said. "They wanted to see his cabinet of trophies . . . and afterwards his little brothers played ukulele, guitar, and sang, while his sister, Bernice, served refreshments."[23]

The romance didn't last, but that didn't prevent local newspapers from prying into the personal life of Hawaii's most eligible bachelor. Swimmer Frances Cowells, who met Duke at the 1915 world's fair competition, was forced to issue a denial that they were engaged. "Duke is a perfect gentle-man," she told a reporter. "Those who are always running him down are jealous of him. But, as for marrying him, why, he hasn't asked me, in the water or any other place, and it wouldn't do him any good if he did. I don't care to marry.

"I am very sorry about this business of Duke and I," Cowells concluded. "It makes it embarrassing for me, and also for him, and he is a perfectly grand fellow—none better."[24]

Published reports linked Kahanamoku with Marion "Babe" Dowsett, a young woman from a well-known family in Hawaii. The Dowsetts were among the first nonmissionary white families to settle in the Islands. They initially made a small fortune from whaling boats. When that industry declined, they branched out and became successful merchants and ranchers.

Slender and vivacious, Babe was much younger than Duke. Like many local teens, she and her sister, Beatrice, loved to hang out at the beach.

Kahanamoku took them out on his surfboard; after they got the hang of it, they began surfing on their own and were among the first expert female surfers in the area. Babe was also an excellent swimmer—the "first feminine star who has been honored by being coached by Duke Kahanamoku," according to the *Honolulu Star-Bulletin*. "If Miss Dowsett will pay careful attention to everything her teacher says in the swimming line she cannot help but have a glorious future. . . . [S]he has the Duke Kahanamoku stroke which ought to be good enough to win from the best in America in a few years."[25]

Babe decided not to pursue a swimming career. She and Duke remained close enough that published reports of their engagement appeared in newspapers on the mainland. After Babe went to California to finish her schooling, the relationship fizzled.

Kahanamoku was considered a serious catch. But he was still consumed by competition and, with his low-paying job, did not have the financial means to support himself and his family, much less a wife and children. And, between the beachboy lifestyle on Waikiki and his extensive traveling, he enjoyed the benefits of being single. "Don't get married too young," he counseled. "A man should have his fun for the first 35 years of his life."[26]

14

In the spring of 1917, as German U-boats stepped up their attacks on American shipping interests, the war that had forced the cancellation of the 1916 Olympics spread across the Atlantic. President Woodrow Wilson had won reelection under the slogan, "He kept us out of war," but on April 2, 1917, he went before Congress to proclaim, "The world must be made safe for democracy." Within a week the United States was mobilizing against Germany and its allies in what H. G. Wells called "the war that will end war."[1]

The attention of the country was focused exclusively on the European theater, on "Over There." A tense pall fell over Hawaii. The military tightened control by establishing curfews and regulating travel and communication. Many locals signed up for service, including Duke's brother David, especially after word reached the Territory that five Hawaiian-born merchant marines had died in a U-boat attack.

With tourism stagnant, visitors no longer mobbed Duke to take his photo on the beach. He was unable to schedule exhibitions, either on the mainland or in Australia. He began to wonder if his swimming career was *pau* (over).

That summer, nearly a decade after Alexander Hume Ford founded the Outrigger Canoe Club to revive traditional Hawaiian sports, the organization that had snubbed Duke Kahanamoku asked him to join. He accepted the invitation in large part because his good friend, "Dad" Center, was now the athletic director at the club. Duke valued Center's sage advice for swimming, surfing, paddling, rowing, and beach volleyball.

Duke's membership represented a milestone of inclusion. But the offer wasn't entirely altruistic. In recruiting Kahanamoku, the Outrigger Canoe Club gained the prestige of having an Olympic gold medalist in its locker room and a surefire winner in competitions against Island teams. The club was also eager to align itself with the purest of the full-blooded Hawaiians, someone who gave their grass shacks and weekend luaus a semblance of authenticity.

Kahanamoku donned the distinctive emblem of the Outrigger club (a big red "O" and a canoe paddle), and the working-class kid without a high school diploma began rubbing shoulders with *haole* graduates of Punahou School and Yale University. The Outrigger Canoe Club became his second home, athletically and socially, until the day he died (and, as it turned out, even beyond).

There was some grumbling around Waikiki that Kahanamoku was receiving special treatment, what with the house, the government sinecure, and the Outrigger Canoe Club membership. Duke maintained amiable ties with Hui Nalu. He and the old crew, including his brothers, hung out together in the water. It was around this time that he performed a feat that surfers still regard with awe today. The "Long Ride" is among the most legendary moments in surfing annals. Duke called it "that once in a lifetime ride" and "the Big One."[2] He ranked it among the highlights of his athletic career, even though he received no official recognition for it at the time.

Hard facts about the "Long Ride" are as elusive as an eel. Kahanamoku himself gave differing accounts. In one version, he surfed alongside "Dad" Center. In others, he surfed solo. His board measured ten feet or sixteen feet. The distance of the ride was one mile, a mile and an eighth, or one and a half miles. No contemporary newspaper or magazine covered it, and there are no known surviving photographs. It is the surfing equivalent of Babe Ruth's "called shot" at the 1932 World Series.

The earliest mention of the "Long Ride" in print came in Robert Ripley's "Believe It or Not" syndicated cartoon. The sketch appeared in 1924, portraying Duke with his arms outstretched while balanced on a surfboard, wearing only a pair of billowing shorts and a grin. The caption reads: "Duke Kahanamoku rode the same wave—on a surf board—from Castle's Point in to Waikiki Beach—a distance of more than a mile. Honolulu—1916."[3]

Ripley was wrong about at least one detail. Tom Blake, a close friend of Duke's and among the most profound and original thinkers in surfing, dates the ride to 1917, linking the incident to the "Japanese earthquake surf" of that year. There is no record of a major earthquake involving Japan in 1917, although an enormous quake did strike Samoa in June.[4]

What is known is that the Long Ride began at a mystical break that Hawaiians call "Kalehuawehe," out by Diamond Head. On most days the surf there is as flat as glass. When massive southern swells roll in, however, normal surfing spots are closed out and Kalehuawehe wakes like a vengeful monster, with waves measuring twenty-five feet or more. Sometimes years, even decades, may pass without these conditions.

Kalehuawehe became known as "Castle's" around the turn of the century. The break was named for James Castle, the brother of the lawyer who helped create the trust giving Duke his home after the 1912 Stockholm Olympics. James Castle had built a yellow, three-story mansion that stood at the eastern end of Waikiki. From the ocean, surfers used the distant estate as their landmark for takeoff, hence the sobriquet "Castle's."[5]

On this particular day, word spread across Oahu via the coconut wireless: surf was definitely up—way up—at Castle's. It was nature at its most fearsome. Sets of "bluebirds" (gigantic waves) were rolling in, stretching across the Bay of Waikiki toward Honolulu harbor, impelled by the stiff trade winds from the Koolau Range.

The waves were "the largest I'd ever seen," Kahanamoku said, "easily thirty-plus waves."[6]

He timed the sets, watching them build and build with amazement. Paddling out in these conditions might not be possible. Riding his gigantic, skegless board meant risking serious injury. If he wiped out, he would be submerged beneath an avalanche of water and tossed like a human cocktail. His sodden board would become a dangerous projectile, capable of knocking him out or worse. The coral reef, hidden beneath the surface, was waiting to shred his body.

Duke took a deep breath. The competitor in him took over. "I had to go," he said.[7]

He plunged in and paddled out into the percolating sea. His board was pummeled, but his muscular arms carried him through. When he encountered a wall of water, he "turned turtle" by rolling underneath the combers while hugging the board and holding his breath.

The power of these waves—their sheer energy—was unlike anything he had experienced. He was drenched and winded by the time he reached the takeoff spot, which was so far out in the ocean, nearly to the shipping lane, that he "recognized the captain on the bridge of a passing steamer."[8]

He straddled the board and tried to regain his breath. Elongated humps of water lifted and dropped him like a yo-yo. He bobbed in the depths and waited, a tiny blotch in the emerald-green-and-white froth.[9]

Then he spied it: "the tallest, bulkiest, fastest wave" of them all, "a very personal and special wave—the kind I had seen in my mind's eye during a night of tangled dreaming."[10]

It was now or never. Kahanamoku pivoted his board around and went for it. Lying prone, he stroked hard in the water with his huge hands. Then, timing himself instinctively, he pounced up and found his balance, his left foot placed forward and solidly planted, knees slightly bent.

The board slapped, shimmied, and rattled as he slid along the face of the wave. A high-pitched crashing sound echoed like a freight train. Duke felt like he was riding a watery roller coaster without brakes. His speed approached thirty miles an hour.

He shifted his weight, directing the board to the left, his only possible route. He railroaded through the surf, connecting to the next break, and kept going, allowing the momentum to carry him. He stood tall, embedded in the moment, alive to its potential, with his feet, legs, torso, shoulders, and the board working as one, streaking across toward the next break, harnessing the awesome energy of the waves. His eyes were tearing up, but his vision was clear. He was at one with the water.

One last forward rush, and he was in the familiar waters of Queen's. The board slowed. The waves became ripples. He got off the board in waist-deep water, by the familiar grounds of the Moana Hotel.

His thighs burned. His calves ached. His breath came in heaves and hiccups. Young boys and experienced surfers, *haole* and Hawaiians, surged forward to pat him on the back as he lugged his board up the beach.

"Hey, Paoa, wotta ride!"

Kahanamoku sat down and stared out at the not-so Pacific, tracing the route he had just taken. He felt a shivering tingle pass through his body, almost as if he was still riding on the board. His heartbeat galloped.

He said nothing, but Waikiki was soon abuzz. People who had not been there wondered how he had managed to stay upright for so long. Estimates of the distance that he had covered grew. First it was a mile, and then it was a mile and a half. Others insinuated that the Long Ride was a tall tale and that, given the limitations of surfboard technology, it was not possible for Kahanamoku to have succeeded.

His defenders included Tom Blake, who later wrote about attempting, and completing, a comparable ride in the 1930s. Duke's younger brother Sam caught a similarly epic wave, but his was written about in the local newspapers.

George Downing, an expert surfer who viewed Kahanamoku as a mentor, remembers hearing chatter about "if [Duke] really did it or not—if anyone could actually make a wave from Castles to Canoes. This bothered me, and I wanted to prove to myself that Duke could have done it."[11]

Downing waited years for a day of huge waves at Castle's. When it came, in the early 1950s, he paddled out on a ten-foot surfboard made of balsa-redwood and with a skeg—a much lighter and more maneuverable board than Duke's solid redwood board. "I made the ride three times from Castles to Canoes," Downing said. "I proved to myself that it could be done, and that if the Duke said he did it, he did it."[12]

Kahanamoku admitted that, at the time, he often surfed to impress beachgoers with his skills. "Pride was in it with me those days, and I was still striving to build bigger and better boards, ride taller, faster waves. . . . [V]anity probably had much to do with my trying to delight the crowds at Waikiki with spectacular rides on the long, glassy, sloping waves."[13]

The "improbable ride," as he called it, was different. It occurred spontaneously, and, like so much of what happens in the water while surfing, it was an ephemeral, intensely personal, and humbling experience. He remained thankful for the rest of his life. "I never caught another wave anything like that one," he said. "It is a golden one that I treasure, and I'm grateful that God gave it to me."[14]

On August 2, 1917, Duke's father went out for an afternoon swim. When he returned home, he complained briefly of dizziness and lay down. Minutes later, he suffered a heart attack that killed him almost instantly. Duke Halapu Kahanamoku was forty-eight years old.

The elder Kahanamoku had become a prison guard after resigning his police captaincy. His death left Julia with the sole care of their nine children. The extended clan, including aunts, uncles, and cousins from the Paoa and

Piikoi sides, gathered together at the family property by Ala Moana Road, stunned with grief.

When his father passed away, Duke was on the island of Hawaii, riding horses and branding cattle on the Dowsett family's ranch. He received the news via wireless, rushed to Kona, and caught the interisland steamer home. The family waited to hold funeral services at Oahu Cemetery until the prodigal son returned.[15]

Duke was crushed. He had lost his father, the stoic man who had taught him to swim by throwing him into the waters of Waikiki, the man who had supported him as he journeyed from Oahu to the mainland to the Olympics and back. Whenever and wherever he traveled, Duke found time to write letters and postcards to his father—to connect, as it were, with his roots. Now it was left to him and the oldest siblings—David, Bernice, and Bill—to support their mother and help raise the other children, the youngest of whom (Louis and Sargent) were nine and seven years old, respectively. Duke moved back into the bungalow at Waikiki.

Not long after the death of Duke Halapu, Queen Liliuokalani died from a stroke. She had spent the years since annexation living "in exile" in Hawaii, never ceasing her campaign for the restoration of the Hawaiian kingdom. When she wrote her memoirs, she pleaded with Americans to emancipate Hawaii—words that went unheeded:

Oh, honest Americans, as Christians hear me for my down-trodden people! Their form of government is as dear to them as yours is precious to you. Quite as warmly as you love your country, so they love theirs. With all your goodly possessions, covering a territory so immense that there yet remain parts unexplored, possessing islands that, although near at hand, had to be neutral ground in time of war, do not covet the little vineyard of Naboth's, so far from your shores, lest the punishment of Ahab fall upon you, if not in your day, in that of your children, for "be not deceived, God is not mocked." The people to whom your fathers told of the living God, and taught to call "Father," and whom the sons now seek to despoil and destroy, are crying aloud to Him in their time of trouble; and He will keep His promise, and will listen to the voices of His Hawaiian children lamenting for their homes. It is for them that I would give the last drop of my blood.[16]

The last of Hawaii's monarchs was seventy-nine years old. Duke Kahanamoku was accorded the ultimate honor when he was asked to act as pallbearer at her funeral.

In September of 1917, Honolulu hosted the AAU national championships in swimming. Despite the onset of war, several swimmers came from the mainland to challenge Kahanamoku and the Hawaiians. Most prominent was Norman Ross, the dominant performer on the Pacific coast in 1916 while Duke was slumping.

Born in Portland, Oregon, Ross was just twenty-two years old. He was a hulking brute at six-feet-two-inches and 210 pounds; newspaper columnists dubbed him "The Big Moose." Many were already calling Ross the best American swimmer of all time. He lacked a sprinter's speed—he was best at middle distances—but he feared no opponent or course, from one hundred yards to fifteen miles.

Once, after Ross moved to Chicago and joined the powerhouse Illinois Athletic Club under coach Bachrach, he was seen chugging past the Oak Street beach while training for William Wrigley's marathon swim race at Lake Ontario. Astonished lifeguards blew their whistles furiously and directed Ross to come ashore. As he waded in shallow waters, he was heard to ask: "What town is this?"

"Chicago," one ventured after a stunned silence.

"Chicago? Hell, I thought it was Milwaukee," and with that Norman Ross headed north in search of Milwaukee.[17]

Against Ross, the local newspapers touted not Duke but three young rising stars: John Kelii, a Native sprinter from the Healani Boat Club; Clarence Lane, a stocky sprinter with the Palama Club; and Harold "Stubby" Kruger, who excelled in the backstroke.

Kahanamoku was considered to be an afterthought. He was still reeling from the death of his father. He had also taken a long layoff from swimming, going so far as to anger Bill Rawlins and other local AAU officials by refusing to compete in a meet in Honolulu earlier in the year. Their bitter row made headlines, and Duke was publicly accused of "sulking" in Waikiki.

Ignored and ill-prepared, he thought about pulling out of the contest until "Dad" Center counseled him to embrace the challenge. Center persuaded

Kahanamoku to enter three events. In the first heat of the 50-yard event, he got off to a great start and swamped Kelii and Lane, equaling his own world record. He came back to take the final over Ross, Kelii, and Lane.

"Duke was right, and all doubts being circulated that Duke has gone back will perhaps be discontinued," the *Honolulu Star-Bulletin* harrumphed.[18]

Then, in the 100-yard open, Kahanamoku downed Lane and Kelii and set a new world record. Two for two, with the 220 left.

Ross was the overwhelming favorite as the racers lined up at the harbor course. He powered to the lead at the 50-yard mark, with Kelii right behind and Kahanamoku trailing in third. Ross's long strokes kept him in front at the 100-yard mark and the 150-yard mark.

Duke shadowed, his stroke a study in relaxed motion, until, suddenly, he surged. The fans rose together, stomping their feet and shaking the harbor to its pylons.

Fifteen yards to go. One thought crossed Duke's mind: "He wins!"[19]

Ten yards remained and then five, and now the final touch! Kahanamoku wiped the water from his eyes and looked at the judges. A moment later came their decision. Duke had pulled off the come-from-behind win, beating Ross by a hairbreadth.

Spectators threw their hats into the harbor, blanketing the water with bowlers. The time of 2:24.4 was a personal best for Kahanamoku. He and Ross embraced in a show of sportsmanship, and then Duke was taken off on the crowd's shoulders.

"They say an athlete can't come back," a gentlemanly Ross offered. "Why, this fellow has never been away. He took a layoff for a while, for certain perfectly good reasons he stayed out of competition for a year, but when he got back in again it was quite noticeable that he was not the same Duke. No indeed, he was a newer and better one."[20]

Was the 220-yard matchup between Kahanamoku and Ross "the greatest swimming race in history," as the *Honolulu Star-Bulletin* described it? That's doubtful. But Kahanamoku counted the victory among his favorite moments because it happened at home, when he was said to be struggling.

"The vast assemblage of friends gave the greatest swimmer of all time an ovation," the newspaper reported. "They were all friends of Duke last night. Even those who had claimed that he had gone back were literally forced to cheer. But it was not the triumphant and exultant sound which was carried away in the night. It was something inside which could not be described, and that something inside remained long after the cries for an idol had lost their force in the evening air."[21]

15

The year 1917 had been like a roller-coaster ride for Duke Kahanamoku. He had been accepted into the Outrigger Canoe Club, made a surfboard ride for the ages, and whipped the latest crew of swimming challengers—Norman Ross, John Kelii, and Clarence Lane—in familiar waters. Intermingled with those triumphs was a feeling of gloom. His father was dead at the age of forty-eight, and Hawaii's last queen, whose regency and empire were unjustly stolen, had passed away. The global powers were engaged in a brutal war that was killing and maiming many of his contemporaries.

The United States was mobilizing for war, too, after Congress passed the Selective Service Act (SSA) in May of 1917 to establish a national draft. The SSA divided men between the ages of twenty-one and thirty into five classifications. As an employee of the Hawaii Territory and as a primary supporter of his mother and his younger siblings following the death of his father, Kahanamoku was rated as Class No. 3.

He was safe, temporarily. He did his small part by joining the Red Cross "Knit Your Bit" effort. He started with knitting a muffler for his friend and rival, Norman Ross, who had enlisted and was stationed in San Diego. Then he knitted sweaters for President Woodrow Wilson and Henry Davison, the head of the American Red Cross.

He served the war effort in a more substantive way the following spring, not long after the Red Cross had established a chapter in Honolulu. Red Cross Commodore Wilbert Longfellow had initiated a drowning prevention campaign that featured the teaching of water safety and lifesaving skills. Kahanamoku, Clarence Lane, and Harold "Stubby" Kruger were signed to tour the mainland (and parts of Canada) and give swimming, diving, and lifesaving exhibitions. All funds raised on the trip were to be donated to the Red Cross.

Tour manager Owen Merrick, the sports editor of the *Honolulu Star-Bulletin*, announced before their departure that Kahanamoku's feet had been insured for $50,000. Accompanied by Clair Tait, a fancy diver stationed with the U.S. Navy at Pearl Harbor, the sixteen-city tour started in San Francisco before turning north, with stops in Portland, Seattle, and Victoria, then on to Winnipeg, Duluth, Milwaukee, Chicago, and Detroit, and finally East to Providence, Boston, New York City, Philadelphia, and Norfolk.

Sometimes they performed lifesaving demonstrations for enlisted men at military bases. Sometimes they goofed around, like when the three of them interlocked their arms and legs and swam together as one "body." Sometimes they raced against local talent. They often closed the proceedings with song, taking out their ukuleles and delighting spectators with Hawaiian tunes.

Part fund-raiser, part entertainment, and part training exercise, the exhibitions were the predecessor to the "aquacade" shows that would grow in popularity during the 1920s. Kahanamoku also sharpened his swimming form on the tour. In August, in an exhibition in New York, he was credited with breaking his own world record in the 100 meters, lowering his time to 1:01.4.

The group encountered a huge storm surge at the Castles by the Sea resort on Long Island, conditions that the Hawaiians recognized as perfect for surfing. "Duke took a surfboard out to the last line of breakers, half a mile out, and rode all the way in at express-train speed," Clair Tait recalled. "The waves were the best ever seen. We gave people something new in the line of body surfing when we rode the crest of the waves for 200 and 300 yards. The shore was lined with enthusiastic people and we were nearly mobbed when we started back for the dressing rooms. There were cameras by the hundreds, and Duke was photographed until he was blue in the face."[1]

If Kahanamoku thought that touring the mainland to raise money for the Red Cross war effort would steer him from controversy, he was mistaken. In July officials in Chicago charged the "trio of amphibians" with padding their expenses—to the tune of $950—on their twelve-day, five-city swing through the Midwest. If the accusations were found to be true, Duke would be banned from AAU competition.

Owen Merrick met with the national registration committee of the AAU to review the itemized expense accounts. The swimmers were promptly cleared of any wrongdoing. Not only had they not violated the rules, chair Fred Rubien noted, but their presence "aided in the big swimming boom that has cropped up throughout this country."[2]

Another columnist complained that Kahanamoku was not fighting for his country overseas. "Duke Kahanamoku, a Hawaiian, recently established a tank record at Chicago. The duke would hold a higher place in our estimation if he had established the tank record on the Marne," fumed the *New York Times*.[3]

Attention shifted to Kahanamoku's draft status. He was moved to Class No. 1. He told reporters that he wanted to join the nascent aviation corps and learn to fly. "This branch of army service I have always been very keen to get into," he said. "I am going to see if there is any possibility of landing in the aero corps there."[4]

Kahanamoku lingered in Washington DC, after the conclusion of the Red Cross tour. He had made a personal connection with Lieutenant Colonel Millard Harmon, and he was considering enlisting in the naval aviation service (the precursor to the Air Corps). It seemed just a matter of time until he would be told to report for ground school training, either in Texas or California.

While in Washington DC, he checked into the local YMCA to await word of his induction. Two days before he was to hear the news, he took ill. He couldn't stay warm, even under woolen blankets, and drifted in and out of sleep. His muscles were sore. His head throbbed.

Kahanamoku had apparently contracted a highly contagious form of the influenza virus. Biologists and medical experts have since adjudged the 1918–19 pandemic to be the most fatal infectious event in modern times. Tens of millions of people died worldwide—many more people than were killed during World War I. Curiously, healthy adults like Duke were more likely to succumb than the elderly and the young.[5]

For forty-eight hours, Kahanamoku suffered alone. His condition worsened. His fever climbed, and he developed double pneumonia. He lay on a cot, shivering and unable to keep food down. Merrick was nowhere to be found.

According to author-journalist Joe Brennan, Duke's life was saved by the fortuitous intervention of Bernyece Smith, his former girlfriend, who was said to be working on Territorial matters in the nation's capital. It is unclear how Bernyece discovered that Kahanamoku was ill or how she was able to find him at the YMCA, but when she did, he was unshaven, feverish, and hemorrhaging from the mouth.

Brennan wrote that Bernyece took charge and had Duke moved to a private rooming home. She brought in a doctor to see him daily—and paid Duke's medical bills—and nursed him to something resembling health. Finally, she managed to put him on a train to California.[6]

Kahanamoku was wan and weak, and lucky to be alive. He gave one interview while he was in San Francisco in which he downplayed the severity of his illness. "I had a slight touch of Spanish influenza but am all right again," he said. "It had me scared for a while, but the doctors just laughed at me and said that I would be okay in a couple of days. They were right for I never felt better in my life than I do right now."

He also talked about his plans to enlist. "I want to be a flyer like Norman Ross and have filed my application," he said. "First, I will have to return to Honolulu and report to my draft board and then expect to be transferred to the aviation branch of the service. Believe me, I envy Ross, who is now a Lieutenant, and would like to meet him in the air some time."

Kahanamoku revealed that he was not planning to swim competitively again until after the war. "But don't let anyone tell you I am through," he warned. "I am not trying to make time in the distances any more, but I guess I will be able to hold my own in the sprints for a long time to come. Some of the Eastern critics thought I would have a hard time holding my own against the new crop of swimmers that have developed, but after I lowered a few records they were all willing to admit that I could still go some."[7]

Only later did reports emerge that manager Owen Merrick had deserted Duke and the others. "This tour proved exceedingly disastrous to the swimmers, as all three champions were left stranded in the East [by Merrick]," one columnist commented. "Several good Samaritans came to the aid of the Duke."[8]

The unfortunate ending obscured the merits of the Red Cross tour. Kahanamoku and his mates raised money for a patriotic cause and promoted swimming and water safety across North America. This was especially important after the cancellation of the 1916 Olympics, which had created a temporary vacuum in aquatics and other sports.

"The public was attracted and took more interest than ever before in water sports," the *New York Tribune* noted, "while contestants . . . profited materially by seeing the South Sea Islanders in action and studying their methods. Duke and his fellow stars now have imitators a-plenty wherever they appeared, and the practical demonstrations received by the latter are bound to bear fruit. In every way the sport has benefited through the coming of the Hawaiian stars."[9]

On November 11, 1918, peace came to an exhausted Europe. The news reached Duke as he sailed home to Hawaii aboard the *Shinyo Maru*. He celebrated the armistice with fellow passengers, but was deeply regretful that the ending of the war closed a chapter in his life. "There goes my flying career," he said. "But I'm glad all the killing and dying is over."[10]

There was no midocean swim on this journey. To his mother's horror, he arrived in Hawaii looking like a stick figure, weighing twenty pounds less than his usual weight. "I was a ghost," he said. "Friends hardly recognized me. But I was home—and I knew I would get well. I needed the sun. I needed the surf."[11]

He was reminded of how fortunate he was when local newspapers reported that George Freeth, the Hawaiian waterman who had introduced surfing to California, had succumbed to influenza on April 7, 1919, in San Diego. Duke's longtime friend was just thirty-five years old.

Kahanamoku's recovery from the flu came slowly. He ate plenty of poi, fish, and fruit, and gorged on home-cooked meals prepared by his fretful mother. He returned to his job in the Public Works department and ventured outdoors again, lolling on the beach with his brothers and soaking in the healing waters of the Pacific.

As he regained his strength, his trusted adviser, "Dad" Center with the Outrigger Canoe Club, encouraged him to start training again. Center dangled an intriguing and challenging goal for Duke: defend his crown as the world's top swimmer at the 1920 Olympics, which Pierre de Coubertin had hastily awarded to Antwerp after the armistice.

1. Duke (*in plaid shirt*) with his soccer teammates at the Kamehameha Schools, 1908. Used with permission from Kamehameha Schools.

2. (*above*) The day that Duke's life changed forever: Duke extends his lead in Honolulu harbor, 1911. Courtesy James W. Gaddis.

3. (*opposite top*) The 1912 U.S. Olympic swimming team en route to Stockholm. International Swimming Hall of Fame.

4. (*opposite bottom*) Duke receiving the gold medal from King Gustaf V at the 1912 Stockholm Olympics. Courtesy James W. Gaddis.

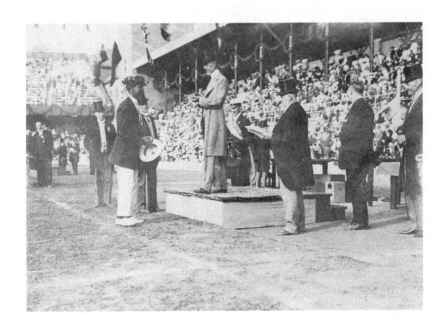

5. (*above*) In *The Beachcomber*, Duke's first film role, with Hobart Bosworth, 1915. Hobart Bosworth Collection, Margaret Herrick Library, Academy of Motion Picture Arts and Sciences.

6. (*opposite*) Duke poses with his wooden surfboard on the beach at Waikiki, circa 1915. Unidentified Artist, gelatin silver print, National Portrait Gallery, Smithsonian Institution.

Duke Kahanamoku

at Freshwater. Jany 1915

7. (*opposite top*) A dark speck in the distance, Duke surfs solo at Freshwater, Australia, in January of 1915. Warringah Library Local Studies.

8. (*opposite bottom*) Duke relaxes with his guitar at the Illinois Athletic Club pool in Chicago, 1918. Chicago History Museum.

9. (*above*) The gold-medal-winning 4x200-meter relay team at the 1920 Antwerp Olympics: (*from left*) Norman Ross, Pua Kealoha, Perry McGillivray, Duke Kahanamoku. International Swimming Hall of Fame.

10. Duke Kahanamoku and Viola Cady surf tandem at Laguna Beach, circa 1925. From *Viola—Diving Wonder*, courtesy the Paragon Agency.

11. Two-sport star: Duke hones his golf game while surfing in Southern California, circa 1925. Security Pacific National Bank Collection, Los Angeles Public Library.

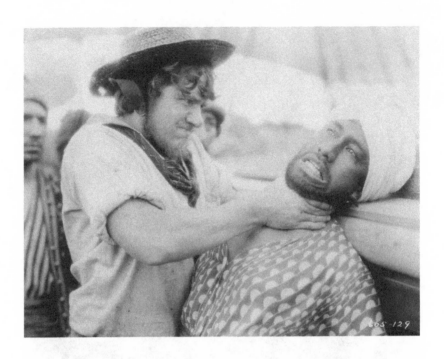

12. (*opposite top*) George Bancroft throttles Pirate Duke in *Old Ironsides*. Paramount Collection, Margaret Herrick Library, Academy of Motion Picture Arts and Sciences.

13. (*opposite bottom*) Ranch-hand Duke and Clara Bow in *Hula*. Paramount Collection, Margaret Herrick Library, Academy of Motion Picture Arts and Sciences.

14. (*above*) Duke and actor Tom Moore in *Adventure*. Paramount Collection, Margaret Herrick Library, Academy of Motion Picture Arts and Sciences.

Duke Kahanamoku
and
Shirley Mason
in
Paramount's "Lord Jim."
Victor Fleming Pic.

15. (*opposite top*) Duke playing an American Indian in *The Pony Express*. Paramount Collection, Margaret Herrick Library, Academy of Motion Picture Arts and Sciences.

16. (*opposite bottom*) Duke teaches actress Shirley Mason how to swim on the set of *Lord Jim*. Hollywood Museum Collection, Margaret Herrick Library, Academy of Motion Picture Arts and Sciences.

17. (*above*) Studio portrait of Duke, circa 1925. The Paragon Agency.

18. The last hurrah: Duke (*left*) with (*from left*) Clarence "Buster" Crabbe, Harold "Stubby" Kruger, Johnny Weissmuller, race officials, Red Cross nurses, and Boy Scouts at the 1932 U.S. Olympic tryouts. Library of Congress, Prints and Photographs Division.

19. Bodysurfing at Waikiki. Courtesy James W. Gaddis.

20. (*above*) Duke and Babe Ruth at Waikiki Beach. Courtesy Linda Ruth Tosetti, Babe Ruth's granddaughter, archives.

21. (*below*) Performing hula with Aggie Auld, circa 1936. Library of Congress, Prints and Photographs Division.

22. (*above*) Doris Duke Cromwell flanked by the Kahanamoku brothers: (*from left*) Sargent, Louis, Sam, Bill (*seated*), David, and Duke, on the grounds of Shangri La. Doris Duke Charitable Foundation Historical Archives, Doris Duke Photograph Collection, David M. Rubenstein Rare Book & Manuscript Library, Duke University, Durham, North Carolina.

23. (*below*) Doris Duke Cromwell and Sam Kahanamoku in front of the Playhouse at Shangri La. Doris Duke Charitable Foundation Historical Archives, Doris Duke Photograph Collection, David M. Rubenstein Rare Book & Manuscript Library, Duke University, Durham, North Carolina.

24. Hawaii's most eligible bachelor and his bride, Nadine Alexander, on their wedding day, 1940. Courtesy James W. Gaddis.

25. With Diamond Head in the background, Duke dunks a youngster as two tourists beam from an outrigger canoe. International Swimming Hall of Fame.

26. (*above*) Duke, brother Sam (*far left*), and friends return from a successful fishing excursion. International Swimming Hall of Fame.

27. (*opposite top*) President John F. Kennedy greets Duke in Honolulu, 1963. Courtesy James W. Gaddis.

28. (*opposite bottom*) Johnny Weissmuller and Clarence "Buster" Crabbe flank Duke at their induction into the International Swimming Hall of Fame in 1965. International Swimming Hall of Fame.

29. Duke and his surfing team in 1965: (*from left*) Paul Strauch Jr., Joey Cabell, Fred Hemmings, and Butch Van Artsdalen. Bob Johnson, *Herald-Examiner* Collection, Los Angeles Public Library.

30. Duke outside his restaurant-nightclub at the International Market Place, circa 1965. Courtesy Joseph L. Brennan and James W. Gaddis.

31. (*above*) Duke with entertainer Don Ho, the top act at his nightclub. *Honolulu Star-Advertiser.*

32. (*opposite top*) Duke breaks down during a press conference with manager Kimo McVay (*left*) and Mrs. Kinau Wilder, 1966. *Honolulu Star-Advertiser.*

33. (*opposite bottom*) Nadine Kahanamoku and Arthur Godfrey (*seated in sunglasses*) at the "beachboy" funeral services, 1968. *Honolulu Star-Advertiser.*

34. Courtesy James W. Gaddis.

16

Duke Kahanamoku's workout regimen in preparation for the 1920 Olympics in Antwerp would be considered cross-training today. It consisted of rowing, paddling, surfing, and swimming, sprinkled with beach volleyball and water polo. Surfing was especially useful in building his stamina and strength, considering that he had to heft his 115-pound board and carry it through the sand, use his arms to paddle out into the ocean, and call upon his legs and core to balance himself and steer the board. Not to mention the time spent sitting on the board between waves, when his mind was free to meditate on the upcoming competition.

Kahanamoku faced a chorus of naysayers who claimed he was past his prime. Many championed Norman Ross, especially after he won five events in distances from 100 meters to 1,500 meters at the Inter-Allied Games, an Olympic-styled sports competition held in Paris soon after the war. Others backed an array of fresh-faced contenders from Hawaii, including Pua Kealoha, Clarence Lane, John Kelii, and Bill Harris.

That summer, after Duke and Kelii raced to a dead heat in the 100 in Honolulu, the *New York Times* reported: "As [Kelii] is Kahanamoku's junior by several years, there seems good reason to believe he may outdo the latter's greatest feats before he attains the limit of his speed. Hawaiians already are predicting that he will be the next international sprint champion."[1]

This sort of speculation was to be expected. After all, Kahanamoku would be nearly thirty years old at the start of the 1920 Antwerp Olympics. What stunned him and his family was an ad hominem attack published in the *Pacific Commercial Advertiser* on October 29, 1919, under the headline: "Duke P. Kahanamoku Quits Cold."

The incident that provoked the article involved a scheduled swim meet in Honolulu. Athletes from the mainland were making plans to go to Hawaii, when Kahanamoku informed event organizers that he was not prepared to compete. This was not the first time that he had refused to participate in an important meet in Hawaii. He had "savagely and emphatically" bowed out of the AAU Championships in 1917 amid reports of a "bitter row" with Bill Rawlins. He was "disgruntled" that Rawlins "prevented him from making what to Duke, who is virtually penniless, would have been a small fortune.... He has no trade, very little education, and his only means of livelihood lies in taking tourists out in a surfboat at Waikiki Beach."[2] Duke eventually separated from Rawlins (who also lost his position as head of the Hawaiian branch of the AAU).

This time, Kahanamoku said, his workouts with the Outrigger Canoe Club's rowing team left him in subpar shape for swimming. His explanation did not please *Pacific Commercial Advertiser* sportswriter Leonard Withington. His withering column charged that the swimmer had offered up "a silly excuse" to the public. "Duke sulks in his tent and talks about muscles. What he needs is backbone," he commented. "The quitting of Duke will be heralded far and wide in the press."

Withington was just getting started:

Some of the committee say that Hawaii has done very little for the Duke. Since when has it become the thing that the world owes an amateur athlete a living for his sport? If it does, the structure of amateur sport falls in ruin. After the present denouement who will have the hardihood to say that Hawaii owes the Duke anything?

Others of the committee excuse the Duke's failure to come across with a clean cut action, and his lack of a sufficient job by saying that he "is a Hawaiian."

The *Advertiser* protests in the name of the Hawaiian people, whose members are self-supporting and many of whom are well-to-do. The race has too much self-respect to let a slur like that go unchallenged. The Hawaiian people will be among the last to back up a slacker or a loafer, whoever he may be.

The Duke has had his chance and he has passed it up. The chance of his being sent to the Olympics in 1920 is gone and Hawaii will be ready to welcome some new swimming idol who is worthy to represent her in the water.[3]

Observers of the labyrinthine customs in Hawaii sensed the influence of Lorrin A. Thurston behind the attack. The powerful publisher of the *Advertiser* had defended William Rawlins in his dispute with Kahanamoku two years previously. Thurston was also hoping to launch a Pacific Olympiad, with Hawaii as the centerpiece, an idea that Alexander Hume Ford had floated years ago. He and other Territorial schemers were counting on Kahanamoku's name and support to drive this proposal to fruition.

Thurston often used the platform of his newspaper to campaign for pet causes. In this case, Kahanamoku was being denounced for not kowtowing to Thurston and for putting his own health and welfare before the cause of Thurston's vision for Hawaii. "Our whole program, intended to make the Crossroads of the Pacific the swimming capital of the world, will fall like a pack of cards when it is known that our swimming idol has feet of clay, and that we are too blind to see it," the article concluded.[4]

Kahanamoku usually shrugged off criticism. If he believed that he had been wronged or insulted, he shunned the person and did not mention his name again. It was how he and his brothers were raised: if you can't find anything good to say about someone, say nothing.

The disparagement within the newspaper article called for a more forceful response, however, especially after the *Advertiser* tried to plead its case with protestations "in the name of the Hawaiian people." Kahanamoku filed a libel suit, asking $50,000 in damages. He charged that the *Advertiser* brought him "into disgrace, abhorrence, odium, hatred, contempt and/or ridicule, among the people of the Territory of Hawaii, the United States of America, and the people elsewhere, and for the purpose of causing him to be excluded from the society of said peoples, and with the intent wickedly, viciously and maliciously to injure him personally in his good name, fame, reputation and character, as a swimmer, amateur athlete and otherwise."[5]

Challenging one of the most powerful personages in Hawaii took considerable courage. But Kahanamoku felt that he had to stand up for himself and his family's name, even at a high personal cost.

If Lorrin A. Thurston wanted to see Duke Kahanamoku in action promoting Hawaii, he need only have gone to the beach on April 13, 1920. That day, the Prince of Wales stopped in Honolulu en route to Australia, anchoring the HMS *Renown* in view of the Outrigger Canoe Club at Waikiki. When word circulated that the heir to the British throne wanted to try surfing, there was only one candidate to help him.

A large crowd gathered on the beach as Prince Edward and his cousin, Louis Mountbatten, changed into swimsuits embossed with the Moana Hotel's logo. Kahanamoku met them at the water's edge with canoes from the Outrigger club. He greeted the pair, steadied the canoe, and allowed Prince Edward to jump in and take his seat. Duke took the steering position at the stern.

They paddled out a mile into the ocean, turned to face the beach, and then barreled toward shore. They repeated this "toboggan ride" several times, to the delight of the prince.

The prince told Duke that he wanted to try surfing next, so Kahanamoku gave him a lesson. They climbed onto a long wooden board together. The prince perched in front, in a prone position, as Duke waited for the right wave. When it came, he paddled hard, jumped to his feet, and together the prince and Duke rode from where Big Surf begins to the Moana pier.

"After riding his wave, the prince said to me, 'This is jolly fun!'" Kahanamoku recalled. "'Do you know, old man, this is the first time I've ever been able to escape the newsreel cameras and the secret service men? I've never had a moment alone till now.'"

The prince decided he wanted to surf solo. After Kahanamoku helped him paddle out, he manfully struggled to his feet and stood erect for a few seconds before losing his balance. He plunged into the surf and, according to Duke, "was tossed about like a toy doll. He came up sputtering but smiling. 'I say, that was a nasty smack on the head. Maybe you'd better call the secret service men after all!'"[6]

They shook hands and made small talk before parting ways. Later that summer, on the return voyage from Australia, Prince Edward demanded that his party return to Hawaii. This time, Duke's brother David handled the teaching chores and, with practice, the prince learned how to stand up on a surfboard.

Thurston's print competitor, the *Honolulu Star-Bulletin*, published a lavish account of the visit. Photos of Duke and the future King Edward

VIII, smiling together on the beach, were transmitted worldwide, helping to spread Hawaii's "Sport of Kings."[7]

The *Advertiser* article that had lambasted Kahanamoku, as scathing and hurtful as it was, did accomplish something. It lit a fire under Kahanamoku. The competitor in him wanted to prove the newspaper—all of his critics—wrong. He redoubled his efforts under "Dad" Center and, as the 1920 Olympics drew near, began to recapture his old form.

His first major triumph was very unexpected. A sprinter by instinct and training, Kahanamoku entered an open-water endurance race of one-and-a-half miles, the course stretching from Castle's Pier at the foot of Diamond Head to the Outrigger Canoe Club headquarters on Waikiki.

At the sound of the gun, the eleven other entrants made for the finish line by taking a direct path. Kahanamoku veered toward shore and, riding the winds and the currents that he knew so well, opened up a large advantage. He won easily, in a time of 27:52.

In April, at the Hawaiian Centennial meet, he defeated Pua Kealoha and Clarence Lane in the 100-yard event, in a time of 54.6. In June, at the Western tryouts for the Olympics that were held in Alameda, California, he dominated the field in the 100 meters. In July, at the final Olympic trials in Chicago, he bested Pua Kealoha and Norman Ross in the 100.

America's Olympic Committee made it official days later, naming Kahanamoku to the U.S. swim team along with Norman Ross. Six other Hawaiians joined him: Pua Kealoha and Warren Kealoha (who were unrelated), Bill Harris, Ludy Langer, Harold "Stubby" Kruger, and Helen Moses. Another familiar face, "Dad" Center, stepped in for Otto Wahle as the swim coach, assisted by Harry Hebner and Bill Bachrach of the Illinois Athletic Club.

The preponderance of Hawaiian swimmers on the Olympic team was a tribute to Kahanamoku and his magnetic influence (and yet another rebuke to the *Advertiser* article). Starting with his breakthrough in Honolulu harbor in 1911, nearly a decade's worth of appearances, exhibitions, and meets had inspired young talent to follow in Duke's wake and aspire to excellence. The swimming competition at the 1920 Olympics would essentially pit Hawaii versus the rest of the world.

As the United States prepared for another presidential election, with Republican Warren Harding facing Democrat James Cox, American sports was preparing to meet the Roaring Twenties. In 1920, Babe Ruth was tearing up American League pitching for his new club, the New York Yankees, and Man o' War was taking two of the three Triple Crown races. Jack Dempsey reigned as the heavyweight champion, and Bill Tilden was becoming the first American to win the singles crown at Wimbledon.

The Olympic Movement was struggling to regain its momentum after the war, however, both in the United States and abroad. The death of James E. Sullivan in 1914 left American amateur sports without its most vocal cheerleader and tireless fund-raiser. In the aftermath of the Great War, the U.S. Olympic organization's coffers were bare and its leadership was rudderless. The result was chaos.

Many U.S. Olympic team members were scheduled to ship out from New York City on the *Northern Pacific* passenger liner. But when the vessel went into dry dock, the team's departure date had to be pushed back by nearly a week. Finally, after a rousing send-off at the Manhattan Opera House, the athletes were transported to Hoboken, New Jersey, to board the *Princess Matoika*, a former German merchant ship that had been seized during the war in Manila harbor and then had been used to transport troops overseas.

The hastily arranged substitute had just arrived in port to unload the bodies and remains of 1,800 dead soldiers. "When the team filed up the gangplank, the caskets were sitting there on the docks, lines and lines of coffins," Olympic official Daniel Ferris said. "It was a shocking way to start. . . . The smell of formaldehyde was dreadful."[8]

Filthy, old, and creaky, the *Princess Matoika* was barely capable of making the crossing. The captain took the southern route, and so a journey that should have taken about one week ended up taking two weeks. The athletes dubbed their ship "The Princess Slowpolka."

Conditions were so unbearable that Duke joined with his teammates in signing a petition of protest addressed to the American Olympic Committee. The "mutiny of the *Matoika*" decried the ship as "entirely unfit for housing the country's best athletes: sleeping either in an ill-smelling hold, overrun with rats, and without sufficient ventilation, or on hard decks in rain; eating food originally good but served improperly due to overcrowded condition of the galley; poor sanitary conditions for the majority of the men; loss of many articles which under the circumstances could not be properly guarded."[9]

The grumbling lasted the entire voyage, but there were signs of progress. With the death of Sullivan, the most vociferous opponent to the participation of women athletes in the Olympics, female swimmers and divers were selected to join the U.S. effort in 1920. They shared the onboard training tank with Kahanamoku and the other men. (Women won another victory while the team was in Antwerp: gaining the legal right to vote.)

The apparatus was similar to the one Duke used in 1912. Diver Aileen Riggin described it as "a square wooden box in which a canvas tank was suspended and filled with sea water."[10] A hose ran from the ocean to the tank, and the athletes swam in place in the shallow water while strapped to two belts. It was just long enough for Duke to stretch out his arms—that is, when it was operable. At one point, the canvas split and had to be dismantled and repaired. Always a gentleman, Kahanamoku made sure the women got their turn in the tank. "Duke was like a father to us," swimmer Ethelda Bleibtrey recalled.[11]

Robert Ripley, of "Believe It or Not!" fame, was on board as a correspondent for the Boston Globe. He spent the trip observing Kahanamoku and the other athletes—including sculler Jack Kelly, the future father of actress Grace Kelly—and sketching his trademark cartoons as they "pray[ed] for land and complain[ed] that the ship was 'just a cattle boat.'"[12]

Ripley thought that "Duke and his yuke" did their most inspirational work in the evenings, when Kahanamoku and the other Hawaiians strummed melodies as the ship slowly plied across the Atlantic. The music helped "free our minds from the strain of the approaching Olympic championships," said sprinter Charley Paddock, who triumphed in the 100 meters in Antwerp.[13]

"They were very accomplished musicians, and everyone seemed to have a beautiful, sweet voice," recalled Riggin, then fourteen years old, the youngest member of the team. "We were entranced listening to them and sitting under the full moon, sailing through the Gulf Stream."[14]

A bedraggled, feisty U.S. team arrived in Antwerp less than a week before the start of the Olympic Games. Their mood did not improve when they had to spend another night on board the ship before they were allowed to go ashore. They soon found that the new accommodations, a schoolhouse filled with rows of cots in classrooms, weren't much of an improvement. When Dan Ahearn snuck off to a hotel so that he could catch up on his sleep, the triple jumper was dismissed from the team. Another row ensued— this one nicknamed "the revolt of Antwerp," with Norman Ross among the ringleaders—until Ahearn was reinstated and a semblance of order was restored.

The "mutiny" and the "revolt" were among the first instances of disgruntled athletes organizing to demand their rights. To those who had endured the hardships of the war—which was all of Europe—the Americans' grousing was undignified and selfish. But to the audience to whom the complaints were directed—namely, the U.S. Olympic officials—the effort was successful, leading to reforms within the organization and improved treatment of the athletes.

17

Duke Kahanamoku and the U.S. team had stopped over in Antwerp en route to the 1912 Stockholm Olympics. Then, it was a bustling port city. Eight years later, after a war in which an estimated 37 million were dead, wounded, or missing, Antwerp was a very different, very damaged place. Olympic diver Aileen Riggin recalled touring the battlefield around Ypres and coming across a German Army boot—only to discover a foot still inside it.[1]

Pierre de Coubertin had persuaded Belgium's leaders to host the 1920 Olympics on short notice after the armistice—a "reward," as it were, for the suffering that the country had endured. With only sixteen months to prepare for the Olympic Games, Antwerp had scant resources to build a grand stadium, much less feed thousands of athletes and entertain tens of thousands of spectators. In fact, the local organizing committee went bankrupt during the Games.[2]

Reminders of the war were everywhere. The entrance to the Olympic Stadium featured a statue of a soldier hurling a grenade, with the date of the armistice inscribed at the foot of the sculpture. Belgium took some revenge by excluding Germany, Austria, Hungary, Bulgaria, Turkey, and Bolshevik Russia from participating in the Games. So much for Coubertin's vision of the Olympics as a beacon of brotherhood.

Bowed but undaunted, Coubertin publicly unveiled the five-ringed Olympic flag that he had introduced in 1914 and released pigeons of peace during the subdued opening ceremony, a gesture that harkened to the ancient Olympic Games. Kahanamoku and his teammates proudly marched behind flag bearer Pat McDonald, the New York City policeman who moonlighted as a medal-winning shot-putter, and then watched as Belgium's King Albert opened the Games.

Organizers hailed the Stade Nautique d'Antwerp, at the end of Van Rijswijck Avenue, as a model of outdoor pool design. The first permanent venue built for Olympic swimming had ample room for spectators and featured a smart-looking, three-story clubhouse. Three parallel pools extended from the building, including a hundred-meter straightaway course for the main events and areas reserved for water polo and diving.

The facilities looked first-rate, but the conditions were a disaster for the swimmers. The water was head-numbingly cold, "considerably below 60 degrees,"[3] according to the American Olympic Committee's official report, and there was "more mud than water." Riggin remembered that the color of the water was "dark, dark black. . . . [T]his had been the city moat. It was a ditch that had been dug with an embankment on one side to be a protection in case of war."[4]

"We had no towels, nothing but cold showers and inadequate dressing rooms," swimmer Eleanor Uhl said. "Some of the girls fainted because of the discomforts, and if it hadn't been for an old German woman who rubbed us with hot olive oil, I believe that more of us would have been seriously ill."[5]

Kahanamoku dreaded going into the frigid water. Training became about survival, followed by brisk massages to keep the blood circulating. As soon as he climbed out from the water, he donned a full-length, checkerboard-patterned bathrobe to warm his body. He was buoyed by "Dad" Center's presence and by the group of Hawaiian swimmers.

The opposition he faced in the pool was underwhelming, primarily because of the effects of the war. A generation of young men had indeed been lost. Germany had won the medal count in swimming in Stockholm, but they were banned from the Games. So, too, the Australians, always a threat in the water, mustered only a small contingent. Cecil Healy, whose chivalry had allowed Kahanamoku to qualify for the 100-meter finals in 1912, was shot to death while crossing the Somme just before the armistice. Albert Barry lost a leg in France. Tommy Adrian, who had defeated Duke at the Domain Baths in Sydney in 1915, was so traumatized by battle that he could no longer compete.

Kahanamoku's main threats in the 100 came from countrymen he knew well: Norman Ross, Pua Kealoha, and Bill Harris. In the preliminary heat, Duke set the pace and recorded the fastest time. He won the first semifinal the next afternoon as Kealoha took second place.

The four Americans faced off against Australia's William Herald for the gold medal on August 24—which just happened to be Duke's thirtieth birthday. He stood at the starting mark, side by side with the other swimmers in front of the clubhouse, awaiting the gun.

Kahanamoku had a clean start and began powering through the water, almost as if he could not wait to leave its chilly depths. He opened up a comfortable lead, but this time he did not tarry, churning to the far end of the pool to win easily. A loud cheer went up at the touch. His time of 1:00.4 broke his own world record by one second—and narrowly missed breaking the one-minute barrier—and led a 1-2-3 Hawaiian, and American, sweep.

Immediately afterward, Herald protested that Ross had interfered with him. The officials concurred and disqualified Ross; then, they ordered the final to be reswum. For the second consecutive Olympic Games, eight years apart, Kahanamoku had to contend with chaos and controversy in the staging of the 100 meters.

Five days later, Kahanamoku coolly prevailed in a time of 1:01.4, with Kealoha coming in second and Harris third. He emerged from the water and joked with the cameraman who was filming the action. He shivered into his bathrobe, accepted the congratulations of his teammates and officials, and went underneath the stands. Then he closed his eyes for a satisfying and celebratory nap.

His snoozing almost caused him to miss the encore. Kahanamoku had to be shaken awake and rushed to the starting line for the finals of the 4x200 meter relay, accompanied by Perry McGillivray, Pua Kealoha, and Norman Ross.

The United States, with Duke, had taken second place in 1912, losing to the Healy-led Australians. The Americans romped this time, with Kahanamoku anchoring the team to a world-record time of 10:04.4, some twenty-one seconds faster than second-place Australia.

His two victories paced America's domination in the pool. The men won five of seven events, with Ross adding wins in the 400 and 1,500 freestyle, and Warren Kealoha capturing the 100-meter backstroke. The American women cleaned up in their first Olympic appearance, led by Ethelda Bleibtrey's three gold medals. Their efforts helped the United States easily win the overall medal count. Somewhere, James. E. Sullivan was smiling.

Unlike in 1908 and 1912, the United States organized a water polo team for the 1920 Olympics. The Americans finished fourth, with Great Britain defeating the hosts in a heated gold-medal match that ended with a crowd of Belgians booing the playing of the British national anthem.

What also remains disputed today is whether Kahanamoku officially competed in water polo for the United States. Several biographers claim that he did. Duke himself indicated that he played briefly in 1920. "It happened that the water was so cold, the day we played," he said years later, "a couple of the boys turned blue . . . [so I] jumped in. Couldn't feel anything was so numb. It's a tough sport. Just got to keep moving all the time."[6]

Diver Helen Meany remembered: "The water was so cold that the American water polo team refused to compete. . . . [W]hen they wouldn't compete, some of the American swimmers—Norman Ross, Duke Kahanamoku, and others—formed a polo team and actually competed against some foreign team. They didn't really know that much about water polo and just kind of clowned their way through the game. . . . The referee, a big, fat man, was laughing so hard he nearly fell off the high chair he was sitting on."[7]

The official records from the 1920 Antwerp Olympic Games are incomplete. An American-published Olympic program from 1920 noted that the polo team consisted primarily of Midwest players coached by Bill Bachrach. This program did not list Duke's name on the team.

"The U.S. rosters are known for all the matches in which the United States competed, except the full roster for the match against Sweden, and Kahanamoku is not listed in any match," historian Bill Mallon concluded in the definitive account of the Antwerp Games.[8]

That leaves open the possibility that Duke played against Sweden (which was the final match for the Americans), perhaps by substituting for a half-frozen teammate, or he may have participated in an exhibition match as part of a makeshift squad. Still, without additional corroborative evidence, it cannot be stated definitively that Kahanamoku played water polo at the 1920 Olympics.

Kahanamoku stayed relaxed in Antwerp thanks to Haig "Hal" Prieste, a stuntman and bit player for Mack Sennett in early Keystone Kops films. Prieste had the entire team laughing on the ship crossing the Atlantic when he performed his "In Hash" routine that he claimed "put Charlie Chaplin out of business."[9]

Prieste and Kahanamoku concocted their own comedic bits during the streetcar ride to the pool in Antwerp. They acted like they were arguing with each other before Kahanamoku, nearly a foot taller than the pint-sized diver, pretended to manhandle Prieste with his huge paws, shaking him to and fro. Prieste would make his escape and chase Duke down the street, to the horror of onlookers and the glee of teammates.

Another routine involved Prieste, who took the bronze medal in platform diving, deliberately mangling Duke's name: "Kakaako," "Kakamaka," "Kama-cola," "Wacky-wacky." Finally, as the Games drew to a close, Kahanamoku dared Prieste to swipe the newly designed Olympic flag that Coubertin had dreamed up and was so proud of. Prieste shimmied up a fifteen-foot pole, secured the Irish linen flag, and slipped the memento into his suitcase.[10]

Afterwards, Kahanamoku and Prieste performed exhibitions in cities throughout Europe. Duke took one of his first airplane rides, flying with Ross and Langer from Paris to Exeter, England, so that they could attempt to break several records. In Paris so many women mobbed Duke that "Dad" Center had to call in the gendarmes. They managed to get in some body-surfing at the beach at Calais.

They sailed home on the *Mobile*, a White Star liner that was a much grander ship than the *Matoika*, and marched in the welcome-home parade in Manhattan. In Detroit, en route to Honolulu, Kahanamoku and other Olympic teammates went to watch newsreel highlights from Antwerp. A young man approached Duke in the theater and asked him probing questions about surfing. Kahanamoku encouraged him to visit Hawaii so that he could experience the sport at its birthplace.

Such was Duke's introduction to Tom Blake. Kahanamoku and Blake would become close friends in the years to come. Blake eventually took Duke's advice and lived in Hawaii for long stretches. After studying the Bishop Museum's collection of historic surfboards in Honolulu, Blake was moved to shape lighter and more maneuverable boards, both for surfing and for paddling, advancing modern board design in ways that anticipated the future of surfing.

Kahanamoku arrived home in November of 1920. The Hawaii Chamber of Commerce lionized Duke, "Dad" Center, and the six other Hawaiian Olympians for so ably promoting the Territory, and then life returned to normal. He moved back into the home he had been given after the 1912

Olympics, at 1847 Ala Moana Road, with his mother and four of his siblings.

At the age of thirty, Kahanamoku had every reason to feel content. The Olympic flame had been reignited. Duke himself had won two more gold medals and personal congratulations from King Albert of Belgium. He had defended his crown after an eight-year hiatus, an eternity in swimming, and proved the naysayers wrong, including one scurrilous newspaper columnist. (His libel suit against the *Pacific Commercial Advertiser* was working its way through the court system.) His comeback—from illness, from obsolescence, from charges of professionalism, and from ridicule— was complete. As peace settled across Europe and the United States swept into the Roaring Twenties, Kahanamoku was again at the top of the sports scene and in pretty good company.

"The winning punch of this country's brightest athletic stars was never more potent than this year," editor Jack Velock wrote. "Take a look at a few of our 1920 heroes. What names to conjure with: Babe Ruth, Jack Dempsey, Man o' War, Stanley Coveskie, William T. Tilden II, Jack Kelly, Chick Evans, Don Lourie, Duke Kahanamoku, Frank Foss, Frank Loomis, Gorge Sisler, Alexa Stirling, Molla Bjurstedt, Charley Paddock, Ethelda Bleibtrey, George Gipp, Rogers Hornsby."[11]

18

Redemption was sweet. But even as Duke Kahanamoku received praise for bringing glory to Hawaii, he realized that he had no long-term career prospects. He took a job as a tracer with the U.S. Army Quartermaster Corps and then worked as a clerk for the governor's office.

He fell back on the old standby of taking tourists and celebrities out into the ocean and showing them the joys of swimming, surfing, and canoeing. It helped that brother Bill was now captain of the Waikiki Beach Patrol, but it was a hand-to-mouth existence for Duke. "I'd like a nickel for every hour of free swimming or surfing instruction I've given to people who didn't stick around long enough to say thanks," he said. "Really trying to make a living out there could be a grubby existence, at least for me."[1]

A bitter thought brewed within him. "Out of the water I am nothing," he would mutter to himself.

He pondered turning pro, which would allow him to make money by endorsing products. Other companies were starting to follow the example of the cigarette manufacturers by signing well-known athletes to promote their wares. Massachusetts-based Converse, for instance, hired basketball player Chuck Taylor to help sell its new "All Star" sneakers.

Duke had been photographed at the 1920 Antwerp Olympics wearing a swimsuit made by Jantzen, a fledgling company based in Portland, Oregon. The following year, Kahanamoku's name (and that of Norman Ross and gold-medal diver Louis "Happy" Kuehn) appeared in advertisements for Jantzen in *Life* and *Vogue* magazines and in newspapers in over twenty cities.

Jantzen's first national marketing campaign, featuring full-page advertisements drawn by noted illustrators Anita Parkhurst, Coles Phillips, and Ruth Eastman, swiftly turned its swimsuits (and its "Red Diving Girl" logo) into an iconic brand. What compensation, if any, Duke received for this work is unknown.

Kahanamoku also endorsed Valspar, a waterproof varnish manufactured by Valentine & Company. This may well have been the first advertisement for a surfing-related product ever published. Kahanamoku's testimonial and photo appeared in magazines like the *Saturday Evening Post*: "Have used Valspar on my surf-boards for several years, and find that it preserves the wood, because it is waterproof and prevents the water from soaking in," the ad copy read above a coupon for the product. "No matter how long the board is used in the water, the Valspar is not affected and does not change color."[2]

One newspaper tried to joke about Valspar's advertising tagline—"The varnish that won't turn white"—at Duke's expense by noting, "It is not the Duke's fault that nature endowed him with a mahogany tint."[3]

This was no joking matter to the Hawaii branch of the AAU. Their officers met to consider whether this endorsement made Kahanamoku a professional. They decided that it did not because they had no jurisdiction over a noncompetitive sport like surfing.[4]

The endorsements signaled that Kahanamoku, with nothing more to prove in the pool, was preparing to exit the amateur ranks. Those rumblings grew louder after several newspapers reported in 1922 that Duke was moving to California.

The decision to leave home was not easy for Kahanamoku. His extended family—mother, brothers, sisters, and cousins, as well as the beachboys and his pals at the Outrigger Canoe Club and with Hui Nalu—gave him unlimited love and support. But the fallout from the *Pacific Commercial Advertiser* lawsuit (in which he prevailed, although the money from damages he received was little) and the lack of decent employment opportunities, despite all he had done for his homeland, left a bitter aftertaste. Hawaii no longer felt like *aloha*.

In May of 1922, on the eve of Kahanamoku's departure for the mainland, Bill Bachrach arrived in Honolulu for the national swimming championships. The rotund coach brought his latest protégé from the Illinois Athletic Club: a gangly teenager whom Bachrach believed just might have the stuff to dethrone "King Duke."

Johann Weissmuller was born on June 2, 1904, in the village of Freidorf, near Transylvania. The region was then part of the Austro-Hungarian Empire. Both of Johann's parents were of German ancestry; Johann grew up speaking German at home, even after the family emigrated to the United States when he was not yet one year old. They settled in Pennsylvania, where Johann (now called John) was joined by younger brother Petrus (Peter), before they moved to the Germantown neighborhood of Chicago.

Like Duke, Johnny was not born in the United States. Like Duke, Johnny came from modest means (his father abandoned the family when Johnny was about twelve years old). Like Duke, Johnny was a high school dropout. Like Duke, Johnny required assistance in navigating the thicket of amateur sport. Fortunately for Johnny, his guide happened to be Bill Bachrach.

The stories of how Weissmuller got started as a swimmer are legion. He contracted polio at the age of nine and took up the sport in order to regain his health. Or, he was competing for a local YMCA club when Bachrach spotted him and enticed him to the Illinois Athletic Club (IAC). Or, he was splashing around in Lake Michigan when Norman Ross discovered him.

However Weissmuller came to Bachrach's attention in the fall of 1920, it didn't take long for Bachrach to realize that he had found an unpolished gem. Johnny stood six feet three inches. He was lanky yet powerfully built, with impossibly wide shoulders. Beneath a mass of gleaming black hair, he sported a cocky, devil-may-care grin that concealed a Teutonic work ethic. Bachrach bemoaned Johnny's horrible thrashing in the water but was impressed enough to present him with a golden ticket: membership to the IAC and access to the indoor pool inside the twelve-story clubhouse on Michigan Avenue.

Then they got to work. Bachrach refused to allow Weissmuller to swim competitively for nearly one year. He broke down Johnny's stroke and rebuilt his mechanics, fixing everything from the angle of his arm's revolution to the rhythm of his kicking. He taught Johnny how to breathe properly in the water and how to use the turns to his advantage.

In the summer of 1921, Bachrach was satisfied enough to unleash his aquatic Frankenstein beyond the confines of the IAC. At an exhibition at Ohio's Buckeye Lake, the seventeen-year-old broke Duke's record in the 100-yard event (open water). In September, at the Brighton Beach pool in

Brooklyn, he shattered Duke's record in the 100-yard event (pool). Other records soon toppled, in distances ranging from fifty to two hundred and twenty yards. Within one year Johnny held dozens of world's records.

Bachrach exulted in his young charge. "Johnny doesn't diet at all," he bragged to reporters. "There's only two things I don't let him eat—chocolates and cucumbers. They're indigestible, especially cucumbers. But he can chew up all the hot dogs and take down all the ice cream he wants. . . . Johnny has never smoked. He doesn't like cigarettes. He has never drunk anything. He has no bad habits to stop. He's clean, through and through."[5]

Others jumped on the Weissmuller bandwagon. "We've had some wonderful Olympic Games material in the past, with champions like Daniels, Spencer, Cann, Hebner and a score more of nearly equal ability, but never an Olympic prospect in the water sports like John Weissmuller of the IAC," wrote influential columnist Robert Edgren of the New York *Evening World*, ignoring the contributions of Duke Kahanamoku and his three Olympic gold medals altogether.[6]

Kahanamoku watched Johnny's progress from afar until May of 1922. A series of swim meets that climaxed with the national championships in Honolulu coincided with a Shriners convention in Hawaii. The Chicago chapter of the Shriners paid for Weissmuller and Bachrach to journey to Oahu, with the intent of challenging Duke head-to-head.

The newspapers played up their differences. Duke was symmetrically muscular with a powerful upper body and thighs that seemed custom-made for sprints. Johnny had "wide shoulders, flat belly, no hips or buttocks, long, slender, smooth-muscled legs and arms,"[7] according to sportswriter Paul Gallico. Duke was a pure sprinter; Johnny was versatile enough to win at distance events up to 500 meters and at other disciplines besides the freestyle.

Duke was old school: reserved and circumspect. Johnny was jazz age: he liked to play the rogue and was an inveterate skirt chaser. "He had this magnificent physique and he was very strong—six feet four inches, with muscles that rippled and flexed as he moved," recalled Esther Williams, who later partnered with Weissmuller in Billy Rose's Aquacade shows. "Heaven knows, he was handsome. He had a classic profile and he loved to pose. He thought he was God's gift to women."[8]

The anticipation that Duke, the human fish, would face off against Johnny, the human hydroplane, was keen. But although the two posed for photographs when Weissmuller arrived in Honolulu, the match never came off. Kahanamoku was leaving for Los Angeles just as Johnny and Bachrach were arriving in Hawaii.

Weissmuller's camp claimed that Kahanamoku was ducking the youngster. Duke was so intimidated after witnessing Johnny practice at the Punahou School pool, they said, that he fled for the mainland on the next boat. One reporter noted that Weissmuller had "driven [Kahanamoku] into retirement."[9]

That was false. Kahanamoku had pulled out of the Hawaii meet, reportedly due to illness, before Bachrach and Weissmuller went to Oahu. "Dad" Center himself announced in May that Duke "had lost 26 pounds . . . and could not get in condition to compete."[10]

More to the point, Kahanamoku was already preparing to move to California. "Duke did not quit the swim game because of Weissmuller," his friend, Charley Paddock, observed. "He quit because of personal reasons, one of them being that it is necessary to work to make a living, and you cannot work while traveling around the country swimming as an amateur."[11]

Kahanamoku took the high road when it came to his young rival. "Weissmuller is the greatest swimmer of all time," he told reporters. "It would be foolish to match him against me. I wouldn't have a chance with him now."[12]

It was left to Duke's precocious brother, Sam, to swim against Weissmuller in Hawaii. Johnny dominated, although Sam finished a close second in several races. Weissmuller did not emerge unscathed, losing to Warren Kealoha in the backstroke. But he was fast rounding into Olympic form. Upon his return to the mainland, Johnny became the first swimmer to shatter the one-minute barrier in the 100 meters, recording a heart-stopping 58.6 in July at Neptune Beach in Alameda, California, and breaking Duke's mark by almost two seconds. Bachrach could almost taste the Olympic gold medal.

For the next two years, Kahanamoku and Weissmuller circled and measured each other. But they would not race until the summer of 1924, with the Olympic gold medal and the title of the world's fastest swimmer at stake.

Kahanamoku's immediate destination was Los Angeles. Like many others before and after him, he hoped to make a splash in the movies, perhaps the only industry that rivaled sports in its star-making ability. Kahanamoku was enticed to Hollywood by a manager-promoter identified as Dr. Oscar Henning. Newspaper accounts emphasized that Duke and Henning met when both competed at the Stockholm Olympics in 1912. However, the breaststroke swimmer who represented Sweden in 1912 is known in the official records as Thor Henning.

Indeed, Henning remains a mysterious figure. He was described as "an explorer and traveler . . . who has encircled the globe five times" and as "one of the richest men in Russia."[13] Whichever Henning this was, his scheme was grandiose. Henning was said to be negotiating for a $10,000 guarantee for Kahanamoku "to introduce the art of surfboard riding at European beaches and possibly have a moving picture produced in England with himself in the central role," he told reporters. "The idea is to stay a month in Denmark, visiting the principal beaches. Then the plan also calls for a tour of Sweden and Norway, and later France and England."[14]

Henning proclaimed that he was going to make Duke "as world famous on the screen as he is a swimmer." A series of movies was going to be shot in Hawaii; the first production was to be an epic bio-pic starring Kahanamoku as King Kamehameha, the conqueror-unifier of the Hawaiian Islands. Henning was said to be raising $750,000 to engage an all-star crew of writers, directors, and cast such that Kahanamoku's pictures "will be as much sought after throughout the world as those of Douglas Fairbanks, Tom Mix or any of the other athletic screen actors who do their 'dare-devil' stunts on land."[15]

Not long after Kahanamoku arrived in Los Angeles, in June of 1922, he visited the set of *The Dangerous Age*, a Louis B. Mayer production. He was photographed with director Sam Wood during the filming of *The Impossible Mrs. Bellew*, starring Gloria Swanson, and helped a bathing beauty with her swimming technique. He told one reporter that he wanted to make "educational films" in which "the teaching of swimming will find a great impetus."[16]

The European surfing tour never happened, however, and the Kamehameha bio-pic was never produced. It is unclear whether financing was the problem or whether Henning could not convince any movie studio to make a big-budget film starring a nonwhite hero.

Perhaps both. The color barrier in film production loomed as large as the newly erected "Hollywoodland" sign in the hills above Los Angeles.

Every movie star in the silent era—male and female—was white, as was every mogul, producer, director, and nearly every extra. Kahanamoku would soon find out that breaking into Hollywood's clubby studio system was as challenging as any race in the water.

For the moment, Kahanamoku shelved his celluloid dreams. He decided to stay on in Southern California—and why not? Los Angeles was booming, fueled by the discovery of vast oil fields, cheap and abundant property, spectacular weather, and the burgeoning motion picture and aviation industries. The semiarid region owed its very existence to the natural resource that Kahanamoku most cherished, water, imported from the northern part of the state via an extensive aqueduct system that opened in 1913.

The far-flung Southland was also becoming a sportsman's paradise. Kahanamoku took up golf and was soon shooting in the low 80s at the many fine courses throughout the area. He fished in mountain streams near Lake Arrowhead and at Yosemite in the Eastern Sierras. He also surfed every chance he could, exploring the top-notch spots that stretched along the coast.

With Henning's plans shelved, Kahanamoku took a job as a lifeguard at the Santa Monica Beach Club. He helped members with their swimming and surfing technique at the posh club. Thanks to his presence, beach volleyball also started to become a popular activity in Southern California. One perk was earning extra money teaching actors how to swim and surf.

Child star Jackie Coogan, all of seven years old, had become so wealthy that he had one of the first private swimming pools installed at his home at the corner of Wilshire Boulevard and Western Avenue. "Being who I was, I had the best swimming instructor—Duke Kahanamoku—the year after he won the Olympics," Coogan boasted. "I surfed from Baja California to San Francisco when there were only 9 or 10 surfers on the entire Pacific Coast."[17]

Kahanamoku was thrilled to discover that Tom Blake, whom he had met in Detroit after the 1920 Antwerp Olympics, was working at the club next door. The pair became close; their conversations and surfing excursions inspired Blake to travel to Hawaii and study the craft of board making. Splitting his time between Hawaii and California, Blake became one of surfing's preeminent historians-ambassadors-innovators.

Duke also renewed his acquaintance with the Henry family. Les Henry, known as "L.A.," was president of the Bank of West Hollywood and vice president with Alvin Frank, an investment securities firm. The two had met back in 1913, during one of Duke's first trips to Southern California, when Duke helped Henry stage an aquatic event.

"[Mr.] Henry was in charge of the bathhouse and in charge of the open swim that day," Duke remembered. "It happened that the whole team was invited and I was the only one who showed up. . . . After I saved Mr. Henry's hide, he thought it was the best thing anyone had done, so the family just took me in as one of them."[18]

Henry's wife, Madge (or, "Ma"), doted on Duke, and he lodged at their home at 824 S. Rimpau Boulevard in the tony neighborhood of Hancock Park. The relationship deepened after Pa and Ma Henry decided to adopt Kahanamoku.

"Yeah, I was legally adopted [by the Henry family] and was baptized there at St. John's Episcopal Church [in Los Angeles]," Duke said. "That was back in '24."[19]

One magazine reported that Pa Henry "was charmed by the simplicity of the Duke and made arrangements to adopt him. When [Bill Henry, their son] was born the two boys were raised as brothers. . . . Bill has made five trips to the Island. His foster-brother has taught him the native language, how to handle a surf-board and an outrigger canoe."[20]

Duke Kahanamoku was baptized on May 4, 1924, according to records at St. John's Cathedral. But no record of an adoption in 1924 involving Duke Kahanamoku or Leslie and Madge Henry was recorded with the Superior Court of the County of Los Angeles. It may well be that Duke considered their relationship to be one of *hanai*—a traditional Hawaiian practice in which a child is "given" to be raised by another family member or close friend.[21]

Pa Henry was a longtime member of the prestigious Los Angeles Athletic Club (LAAC) and ran the club's swim program. The LAAC's top brass, under the leadership of William May Garland, was lobbying Baron Pierre de Coubertin to bring the Olympic Games to Los Angeles, going so far as to start building an immense stadium for that purpose, in nearby Exposition Park, even before the International Olympic Committee (IOC) sanctioned their bid. IOC approval came in 1923, not long after the completion of the Los Angeles Memorial Coliseum, with the Olympic Games scheduled for 1932. The LAAC soon added the Grand Olympic Auditorium for boxing and wrestling matches.

With Pa Henry's guidance, Kahanamoku and Tom Blake joined the LAAC. Duke's athletic and social life soon revolved around the LAAC. He trained in the indoor pool at the club's downtown headquarters and competed for the Mercury at swim meets throughout the region. He donned plus fours and teed off in club golf tournaments—the LAAC was about to build the Riviera Country Club—and played for the top-ranked water polo team. He hobnobbed with the movie stars who worked out or roomed at the club. His fame guaranteed press coverage whenever he represented the LAAC at the opening of new swimming facilities in the region: the Redlands Municipal Pool, the pool at the Encino Country Club, the pool on the campus of UCLA, and the pool and lake at the Norconian Resort Supreme near Corona.

Nearing thirty-three years old, Kahanamoku was still in fantastic shape. There was nobody in the LAAC, or on the West Coast for that matter, who was swimming faster. With the 1924 Paris Olympics fast approaching, the urge to defeat Johnny Weissmuller and his coach, Bill Bachrach, began to grow inside Duke.

He hungered for one last and enormous challenge: to beat the best swimmer that the world had ever seen and to record a "three-peat" in the 100 meters at the Olympics in the process.

19

Duke Kahanamoku plotted to ambush Johnny Weissmuller with help from Fred Cady, a former circus strongman and gymnast with a dapper mustache. Cady had coached women's champ Olga Dorfner, the so-called Philadelphia Mermaid, and had recently arrived in Los Angeles to develop the swimming, diving, and water polo programs at both the Los Angeles Athletic Club and the University of Southern California.

Under Cady, Kahanamoku turned back the clock and posted personal bests at 50 yards (22.6) and 100 yards (52.6). His 50 was even faster than Johnny's. He then set a world's record at 25 yards, in ten seconds flat, in the thin air of Yosemite.

Cady saw that Duke got plenty of practice in the rough-and-rumble sport of water polo. He was an "invaluable man," for the LAAC, "as there are no polo players in the league who can dribble the ball away from him," one newspaper reported. "Kahanamoku also has endurance, due to his solid build and stature. He can afford to sprint and 'chase' other players throughout the game where another contestant of smaller proportions would tire much quicker."[1]

Kahanamoku made arrangements to go East in order to challenge Weissmuller, only to discover that turnabout was fair play. Just as Duke was rounding into form, Johnny fell sick. He was fatigued and developed a fever. Kahanamoku canceled his travel plans as Johnny lay bedridden and lost his prodigious appetite. One doctor diagnosed leakage of the heart.

"Weissmuller in Hospital; May Never Compete Again,"[2] the *New York Times* reported. Johnny's breakdown sidelined him for weeks, and Bachrach feared that he might never regain his form. But the spell passed. Whatever had ailed him—probably a bout with influenza—worked itself out of his system.

The two still had not raced, but now Kahanamoku held an advantage. The situation seemed to be following a familiar script. "Harry Hebner looked as if he would defeat the Duke, but Harry has long since hung up his racing suit for all time," one reporter commented. "Perry McGillivray defeated Duke in a warm pool in the East many seasons ago, and the world acclaimed him as the coming champion. But Perry has passed on like the rest. Wild Bill Harris and Norman Ross, Pua Kealoha and Warren Kealoha, all these have been rated above the Duke at one time or another, but the Duke can still smile his golden smile and take to the water with his old-time speed."[3]

Another contentious issue arose concerning Weissmuller's eligibility. Johnny was born in Europe and had come to the United States when he was seven months old. His parents had apparently not filed the legal paperwork for Johnny to become an American citizen—something that was required in order for him to qualify for the Olympics.

Right before the U.S. Olympic Trials of 1924, Illinois congressman Henry Riggs Rathbone questioned Weissmuller's citizenship status. The family assured the press that Johnny had been born in Chicago. Newspapers reported that the issue had been resolved, that is, until the city of Chicago was unable to produce the nonexistent birth record.

The family then purportedly doctored the records of Johnny and his younger brother Peter, who had been born in the coal-mining town of Windber, Pennsylvania, in 1905. The brothers "switched" names and birth order: Johnny's name became "Peter John," and he was now the younger brother; Peter became "John Peter" and was now the oldest child.[4]

Either the chicanery served its purpose or U.S. officials conveniently dropped the investigation because of Johnny's talent. Whatever the reason, Weissmuller was cleared to compete at the Olympic tryouts in early June.

Weissmuller remained haunted by this for his entire life. Perhaps fearful that he might be stripped of his medals if the facts were revealed, he concealed this deception to his grave. "No one—including his five wives, his three children, dozens of relatives, thousands of friends, or millions of fans—ever knew the full truth of the matter," his son concluded.[5]

After loosening up with a surfing exhibition in San Diego, Duke prepped for the matchup against Johnny at the West Coast Olympic trials at Brookside Park in the city of Pasadena. The whites-only pool was restricted except for one day per week, dubbed "International Day," when African Americans, Hispanics, Asians, and other ethnic groups were allowed to swim there. (The pool was promptly drained afterward.)

On May 18 Kahanamoku broke that barrier. He and water polo star Reginald Harrison matched strokes in the 100 meters, finishing in a dead heat in 1:02. Both men qualified for the national trials in Indianapolis.

Two of Duke's siblings, Sam and David, accompanied him there. David came along as trainer-masseuse-cheerleader; Sam, as a challenger to his throne. Sam was the most outgoing of the Kahanamokus, a musical savant who could sing or play any type of song. "You give him an instrument he's never seen before, he take it. He sit over there until he can play that damn thing," said their brother Louis. "Might take him half an hour, take him two hours. He's a professional. Any kind of instrument. Horn, saxophone, anything."[6]

Compact and muscular, Sam Kahanamoku was much smaller than Duke and twelve years his junior, closer in age to Johnny than to his older brother. While Duke was living in Los Angeles, Sam had emerged as Hawaii's top sprinter, with a personal best of 1:00.6 in the 100 meters. En route to the Olympic tryouts in Indianapolis, the Kahanamoku brothers stopped off in Chicago. Bill Bachrach graciously allowed them to work out at the Illinois Athletic Club, fully confident that Johnny had recovered from his illness. Weissmuller had broken his 100-meter mark earlier in the year in Miami with a blistering time of 57.4.

A last-minute shortage of funds within the U.S. Olympic committee raised the stakes. The budget allowed only twenty-four male swimmers to go to Paris, not thirty-six as originally planned. Competition for a coveted spot on the team was going to be fierce.

The U.S. Olympic Trials were held that year at the Broad Ripple, an amusement park located north of Indianapolis. The nation's largest concrete pool was Broad Ripple's popular centerpiece: the outdoor facility held 4.5 million gallons of water and measured 450 feet x 207 feet.

Sam Kahanamoku was considered an afterthought as the press hyped the Duke-versus-Johnny encounter as the "race of the century." The two posed for photographs in swimsuits and civilian clothes, almost as if they were about to fight for the heavyweight boxing crown. Beneath the headline, "'Hello, Duke'—'Hi, John,'" a caption read: "Johnny is in perfect trim. The

Duke still has a few pounds to spare. . . . Can the Duke comeback? Will youth prevail?"[7]

Another reporter parsed their styles. "Duke is never nervous at the start of a race and he has a way of shooting out ahead in the last 10 feet. Weissmuller, on the other hand, is often nervous before a race and, while he swims in record time and keeps a uniform pace, he has no burst of speed at the finish."[8]

Coach Bachrach was stiffly encased in a tight suit rather than his customary bathrobe. He scouted Johnny's every move, all the while dispensing last-minute instructions to the "human motor boats" from the Illinois Athletic Club. Duke was without the guidance of a personal coach. He was supported by the presence of his two brothers, but he was also preparing to vie against one of them.

Race day for the 100 meters, June 5, brought overcast skies and chilly temperatures, conditions that gave the hardened Midwesterners an edge over the shivering Hawaiians. Duke, Sam, and Johnny each won their first-round heats to qualify for the finals later in the day. Eliminated were the bold-type names of Norman Ross and "Stubby" Kruger.

That afternoon, just before the initial meeting between Kahanamoku and Weissmuller, the few hundred spectators who braved the damp weather deserted the shelter of the bleachers and massed at the edge of the Broad Ripple pool. They watched as Duke, Sam, and Johnny, along with Pua Kealoha and Jack Robertson of San Francisco's Olympic Club, climbed to the starting rail and walked to their marks.

Johnny was wedged between the two brothers: Duke on his left, Sam to his right. Bachrach fretted that the "Kahanamoku sandwich" might intimidate his young charge. Johnny swung his arms to shake out the nervousness.

The sky darkened. The drizzle turned to rain. The crowd hushed. The clickity-clack sound from the typewriters of the assembled reporters ceased.

"Ready!" the starter cried, and just before he pulled the trigger of his pistol, the swimmers jumped prematurely. False start.

The men climbed out of the pool and again readied themselves for the start. Their damp suits clung to their bodies.

Bang! This time the getaway was clean. Johnny surged to the lead, his head pivoting like a bobble head to see how close the others were lagging.

At the halfway mark, Johnny slipped underwater to make his turn, with Duke no more than four feet behind him.

Less than fifty meters to go. Johnny maintained his edge. Then he lost his concentration and, appearing to tire, drifted into the cord that separated the lanes. Bachrach nearly fell into the pool before Johnny corrected his course and aimed for the finish, still cleanly ahead.

Weissmuller touched first, his time of 59.4 beating Kahanamoku's mark from Antwerp by one second. Duke was second, ten feet behind, with Sam a close third. They converged around Johnny and congratulated him.

The first three finishers were selected for the U.S. Olympic team. As head coach of the American swimmers, Bachrach announced that he planned to enter Johnny in four events: the 100 and 400 meters, the 4x200-meter relay, and the water polo team.

Duke and Sam were disappointed to learn that they were entered in only one event, the 100 meters. Duke was snubbed for the relay, despite the fact that he had anchored the U.S. team that had won the gold in 1920 (and set a world record in the process), and for water polo, despite his standing with the LAAC team. He privately wondered whether Bachrach wanted his pupil to reap all of the Olympic glory.

Ten days later the American Olympic Committee held a farewell swimming carnival on Long Island. Johnny again swamped the Kahanamoku brothers by four and five yards, respectively, in the 100. Duke and Sam took some satisfaction in the 160-yard, mixed relay race, a rare chance for men and women to compete together in the same event. Their team defeated a foursome that featured Weissmuller and Gertrude Ederle.

Johnny had drawn first blood and held an edge entering the 1924 Paris Olympics. But not everybody was ready to count out Kahanamoku, beginning with Duke himself. He considered the Trials to be an opportunity to test Johnny's mettle and feel out his speed. What counted was the race for Olympic gold, when the pressure would be squarely on Weissmuller.

"The Duke has a faculty of being able to show startling speed at the psychological moment, and he probably won't regard that moment as having arrived until the big splash at Paris," the *Los Angeles Times* commented. "[Duke] said that he wouldn't be going strong until he got across to [France].

It won't be in the least surprising to see Duke capture the Olympic 100 meters for the third time in succession."[9]

Duke, Sam, Johnny, and the U.S. Olympic team sailed together to Europe on the SS *America*, its sides painted with "American Olympic Team," and with the country's cinematic sweethearts, Douglas Fairbanks and Mary Pickford, aboard. U.S. officials heeded the athletes' protests from 1920 and provided adequate accommodations.

On this, his third Atlantic crossing for the Olympics, Kahanamoku was familiar with the setup. The runners trained on a 220-yard cork track laid out on the promenade, the rowers pulled at stationary machines, and the boxers and wrestlers grappled on the mats. Duke, Sam, Johnny, and the other swimmers splashed in the canvas "pool" under coach Bachrach. Kahanamoku again entertained at night with choruses of Hawaiian melodies, this time joined by brothers Sam and Dave.

Nine days later the team arrived in Cherbourg, France. They were whisked onto two special trains to Paris and then transported by motorcar to the Rocquencourt estate just outside of Versailles. The male athletes were crowded together into concrete barracks, while U.S. Olympic officials occupied an adjoining chateau. An electrical fire broke out the first night. A villager who tried to douse the flames was killed, despite the rescue attempts of sculler Jack Kelly.[10] The next day, Bachrach had the swimmers moved to Colombes, near the site of the main Olympic Stadium, to ease the congestion.

On July 4, two days before the opening ceremony, the team celebrated Independence Day with a light workout. They were roused to battle by General John "Black Jack" Pershing, head of U.S. armed forces in Europe during World War I, who gave a short speech to rally the corps.

Neither Duke Kahanamoku nor Johnny Weissmuller required fiery rhetoric. They practiced stroke for stroke in the same pool and readied for the biggest moment of their athletic careers.

20

After the travails of Antwerp, the selection of Paris, "City of Light," as the host of the 1924 Olympics offered a glamorous sheen. "Paris was the place," as Gertrude Stein put it, although the absence of Stein's friend, Ernest Hemingway, who skipped the Olympics to watch the bullfights in Pamplona, temporarily lessened its literary firmament.

Pierre de Coubertin marked the return of the Olympics to his hometown by announcing his impending retirement as head of the International Olympic Committee. He exited on a high note after persuading the French ministry to support concomitant contests in music, architecture, painting, sculpture, and literature, and introducing the motto *Citius, Altius, Fortius* (*Faster, Higher, Stronger*) into the lexicon. A record forty-four nations participated in the 1924 Olympic Games, a sign that Coubertin's innovation had survived the war and become an institution (although Germany and the Soviet Union were still banned from competition).

Coubertin maintained a stubborn streak about what he considered to be the purity of his Olympic vision. Just as the entrée of women athletes had occurred over his protestations, so, too, he was unhappy over the launching of a sports carnival, in the mountainous terrain of Chamonix, France, in February of 1924. Winter sports had been included in the Summer Olympics program (ice hockey was introduced in 1920 in Antwerp), but the festival in Chamonix would be considered the first Winter Olympics.

American athletes had hoped to ogle the exotic showgirls who performed at the Moulin Rouge. Instead, they settled for panoramic views from the Eiffel Tower. "They kept us locked up, under constant guard, and all the guys called Olympic Village a high class Boy Scout camp,"[1] fumed Johnny Weissmuller, ever randy.

Duke Kahanamoku was passed over for the honor of carrying the American flag during the Parade of Nations in the opening ceremony, despite the fact that he was representing the United States for the third consecutive time and that he was the two-time defending champion in the 100 meters. Weight thrower Pat "Babe" McDonald did so for the second consecutive Olympics even though the "Prince of Whales" was not competing in Paris. American swimmers, however, voted Duke captain "by a big majority" over Weissmuller.[2]

As France celebrated Bastille Day, the swimmers converged at Le Stade Nautique des Tourelles, located high on a hill in the twentieth arrondissement. The outdoor pool featured an art deco interior and brick exterior, with filtered and heated water and a basin made from steel. The length of the pool was exactly fifty meters, which would become the standard distance for future Olympic swimming competitions. Spectator capacity was 10,000 and, with Parisians sweltering through July, Tourelles was a popular spot.

With his four events and with Bill Bachrach obsessing over his every twitch, Weissmuller was the busiest swimmer in Paris. On July 16 he won his 400-meter preliminary heat, took the semifinals the next day, and then won the gold medal the following day, downing Australia's latest sensation, Andrew "Boy" Charlton, and setting a new Olympic record.

Duke and Sam, meanwhile, attempted to qualify for the 200-meter breaststroke event, primarily to maintain their racing edge. This was not their preferred stroke or distance, and they finished nine seconds behind the leader. They did not make the final draw.

Preliminary heats for the 100 meters took place on July 19. Sam recorded the best time in the first round, in a leisurely 1:03.2, with Duke coming in at 1:04.2 and Johnny, at 1:03.8.

Later that day, in the semifinals, Duke stepped up the pace in 1:01.6, defeating his brother by .6 seconds. Weissmuller won his heat in a swift 1:00.8, with Arne Borg, the "Swedish Sturgeon," trailing him at 1:02.6.

The next morning, on Sunday, Johnny helped the United States set a new world's record and win the 4x200 relay over Australia and Sweden. That was mere prelude to the main event—the finals of the 100 meters—and the largest crowd of the Games to descend upon Tourelles.

Reporters mulled over whether Johnny had expended too much energy with the demanding schedule that Bachrach had outlined for Paris. They weighed the chances of Duke dashing Johnny's dreams. Duke's brother David privately wondered whether young Sam was prepared to spring a huge upset.

Bachrach paced nervously as the five finalists lined up along the starting mark: three Americans—Sam in lane 1, Johnny in lane 4, and Duke in lane 5—along with Borg in lane 2 and Japan's Katsuo Takaishi in lane 3. Ropes supported by cork floats separated each of the lanes.

At the gun, Johnny sprang ahead. His lean form was narrowly ahead of Duke, Sam, and Borg at twenty-five meters. He was slightly ahead at the midway point, but the race was too close to call.

Then, Weissmuller seized control. His youth and the endurance training that Bachrach had emphasized paid off as he dug into the water and extended his advantage after the turn. He never faltered and drove to the wall, touching ahead of Duke by a body length.

Johnny's time of 59 seconds flat set a new Olympic record. He decisively beat Duke, in 1:01.4, a second slower than his mark from 1920. Sam came in third at 1:01.8, with Borg in fourth place.

They climbed out of the pool and celebrated the second American sweep in four years. Duke wrapped himself in his robe, and he and Sam shook hands with Johnny and Bachrach. Less than an hour later, Johnny was back in action as the United States defeated Sweden, 3–2, for third place in water polo.

Duke had given his best effort and yet had fallen short. His consolation prize was the silver medal, as well as Sam's bronze medal, and he cheered on the two other Hawaiian swimmers on the U.S. team, Warren Kealoha (200-meter backstroke) and Mariechen Wehselau (relay), to gold medals. In total Bachrach guided American swimmers and divers to thirteen of the possible sixteen gold medals in Paris.

Afterward, Kahanamoku sought payback at a meet in England. In driving rain at Harrow-on-the-Hill, Johnny defeated him again, this time at 110 yards, with Duke settling into third place. He was never able to defeat Johnny in head-to-head competition.

The what-ifs surrounding the Paris Olympics surfaced later for Kahanamoku. What if he had started serious training earlier? What if he had incorporated more endurance workouts and more races into his routine? What if a personal coach, either Fred Cady or "Dad" Center, had accompanied him to France? And, perhaps most frustrating of all, what if he was in his prime when he met Weissmuller? Would they have pushed each other to train harder or to go faster?

Dejected but not discouraged, Kahanamoku held no residual resentment. He respected his rival's talent and drive and remained friendly with Johnny—and with Bachrach, who had exacted his own revenge after watching Kahanamoku defeat his Illinois Athletic Club swimmers in races over a span of twelve years—for the rest of their lives.

The bitterness of the setback lessened as the years passed. Duke offered several excuses for the defeat. He explained to one reporter that too much automobile driving and stepping repeatedly on the clutch and brakes had affected his muscles. "I realized that my legs might not stand up. I wasn't afraid of Weissmuller. I was afraid of my legs. Well, they didn't have the old kick, although Weissmuller was coming so fast then he might have beaten me anyway."[3]

Later, whenever he was asked about his defeat in 1924, Kahanamoku shrugged and leaned on a stock one-liner. "It took Tarzan to beat me," he said.[4]

Over time the hard-fought 100-meter Olympic finals gave rise to controversy and myth. Biographers of both Duke and Johnny have offered a well-worn tale concerning the start of the race, perhaps for dramatic effect. According to lore, when Weissmuller stepped to the starting mark, he found himself surrounded by the Kahanamoku brothers, with Duke on one side of him and Sam on the other.

"[Johnny] glanced at Duke on his right and Sam at his left. 'Which one of these two guys will run in front of me to let the other win?' he wondered," one biographer related. "He felt an uneasiness hard to shake, as he curled his toes over the edge of the pool."[5]

Then, Duke was said to have leaned over and exclaimed to Johnny: "Good luck! The most important thing in this race is to get the American flag up there three times. Let's do it!"[6]

Duke may well have wished Johnny good luck. They were rivals, not enemies. But the "Kahanamoku sandwich" configuration occurred at the U.S. Olympic Trials in Indianapolis, not in Paris. Black-and-white photographs published in the official report of the Games reveal that, while Johnny and Duke swam alongside one another, two other competitors—Sweden's

Borg in lane 2 and Japan's Takaishi in lane 3—were positioned between Sam and Johnny. Further, the lane dividers were now substantial enough to prevent blatant fouling.

Decades later another story surfaced. One of Sam's children, the late Jo-Anne Kahanamoku-Sterling, suggested that her father eased up and allowed Duke to take the silver medal. "[I]n Paris, Johnny Weissmuller was leading, my dad [Sam] was second, and Duke was third," she told an interviewer before her death in 2010. "My dad slowed down so Duke could.... They were going to disqualify my father for slowing down to allow his brother . . . but I look at it to where it's respect. That was his oldest brother, and in respect to his older brother he slowed down."[7]

The official report did not mention this incident. But with the brothers separated by three other swimmers and three lanes of roiling water, it is unlikely that Sam would have been able to see Duke, much less accurately judge his progress, from his side of the pool.

What is true is that Paris turned Weissmuller into a megastar. He was the undisputed king of the pool, with a personal haul of three gold medals and one bronze medal. With the exception of Finnish distance runner Paavo Nurmi, who won five gold medals, he was the most publicized athlete from the 1924 Paris Olympics.

Weissmuller's timing was impeccable. Sports and the Roaring Twenties were as well matched as Yankees and pinstripes. Stadiums and arenas were no longer cramped wooden firetraps; they were expansive concrete-and-steel cathedrals to play. College football was ascending beyond regionalism; golf and tennis were escaping the boundaries of the country club. The new medium of radio broadcast the action directly into America's living rooms. The Black Sox gambling scandal in baseball was becoming a distant memory.

Savvy promoters-cum-publicists like Tex Rickard, Christy Walsh, and C. C. Pyle dragged sports into the realm of entertainment. In what West-brook Pegler described as "The Era of Wonderful Nonsense," a generation of "Gee-whizzer" scribes saw their job as "godding up" the athletes for public consumption. Mere months after the 1924 Paris Olympics, Grantland Rice sat in the press box at a college football game and was moved to type the most memorable and hyperbolic opening line in the annals of sportswriting: "Outlined against a blue-grey October sky, the Four Horsemen rode again...."[8]

Journalist Paul Gallico called it the "golden age of sports," and finding larger-than-life heroes to "god up" wasn't difficult: baseball's Babe Ruth and Lou Gehrig, boxing champs Benny Leonard and Jack Dempsey, football's Red Grange, tennis stars Big Bill Tilden and Suzanne Lenglen, golf's Bobby Jones.

Swimmers fit neatly into the pantheon. When Gertrude Ederle, a gold medalist from Paris, became the first woman to swim the English Channel in 1926, she received a ticker tape parade in New York City. Gallico himself burnished Weissmuller's image, describing Johnny as "a dark-haired, dark-eyed Adonis"[9] while overlooking Weissmuller's controversial citizenship status (no small matter during a time of harsh anti-Germany sentiment).

"Swimming needed a Weissmuller," Gallico argued. "He was invented, carpentered and made for the sport which, up to then, had had only a Hawaiian beach boy, Duke Kahanamoku, to give a fillip of interest to a means of locomotion which at the turn of the century had been handicapped by Victorian notions of prudery."[10]

Weissmuller deserved all the praise that was lavished on him, but Gallico's comments reveal a deep-seated prejudice. He condescendingly described Kahanamoku as a "Hawaiian beach boy" and severely undervalued his contributions. It was Duke who popularized swimming as a glamour sport, starting in 1912 and extending through a decade of appearances at myriad meets and exhibitions across the mainland, not to mention in Europe and Australia. He jump-started competitive swimming in Hawaii, which became the dominant force at the 1920 Antwerp Olympics; when Kahanamoku moved to California, he helped establish the Golden State as the capital of aquatics this side of the Illinois Athletic Club.

Kahanamoku also competed with a handicap that Weissmuller could not fathom. Many years before nonwhite athletes like Joe Louis, Jesse Owens, and Jackie Robinson fought racism with courageous performances, Kahanamoku was a groundbreaking figure who was able to overcome—some would say transcend—racism. He swam at public pools where nonwhites were banned. When he swam at private clubs, he was often the only nonwhite person inside the building besides "the help."

This extended to the beach. It is little remembered today, but many of the spots where Kahanamoku swam and surfed in Southern California—specifically, in Los Angeles and Orange counties—were reserved for whites only. African Americans, for example, were confined to the Ink Well in Santa Monica and Bruce's Beach in Manhattan Beach. In the mid-1920s, when black business leaders started to build a summer resort south of Huntington Beach, the club was burned to the ground in a fire that many believe was started by the local chapter of the Ku Klux Klan.

Kahanamoku may have been Hawaii's most famous athlete, but he was often treated as a second-class citizen. That happened in Pittsburgh, in 1912, on his first trip to the mainland, when he was refused service because of his skin color. Diver Viola Hartman, the wife of LAAC swim coach Fred Cady, recalled that the same thing happened to Duke at a restaurant in Southern California in the 1920s. Only when Cady demanded that Duke be served did the waitress relent.[11]

In those years Kahanamoku was restricted from touring and competing in the deep South. (Weissmuller, by contrast, trained and swam in Florida.) His body and those of his brothers were prodded, measured, and studied by anthropologists who were associated with the eugenics movement from the era.[12] His "friends" at the LAAC called him "the submarine spook."[13]

Surely, it must have annoyed Kahanamoku to see members of the press fawn over Weissmuller and his accomplishments. But he never publicly complained. "*Mahape a ale wala'au*," he said. "Don't talk—keep it in your heart."

21

Duke Kahanamoku retreated to Hollywood, not Hawaii, after the disappointment of Paris. He signed a contract with Famous Players-Lasky Corporation, soon to be known as Paramount Studios. He was ready for his close-up.

Paramount was formed from the merger of two pioneering, show business minds. Adolph Zukor founded Famous Players Films to turn theatrical stars like Sarah Bernhardt into movie stars. Jesse Lasky was an ex-vaudeville performer whose partners were actor-turned-director Cecil B. DeMille and brother-in-law Samuel Goldwyn. DeMille's *The Squaw Man* was the first feature-length film to be shot in Hollywood, in 1914, in a small barn near Sunset Boulevard, leading other studios to abandon the East Coast for the mellow climes and diverse settings (mountains, deserts, beaches, urban life) of Southern California.

Studios like Famous Players-Lasky met the public's insatiable demand for "the flicks"—almost 100 million movie tickets were sold every week to a population then numbering 115 million—by creating a cavalcade of identifiable stars. Do you want yucks and chortles? Here's Roscoe "Fatty" Arbuckle and Buster Keaton. Adventure and romance? Look no further than Douglas Fairbanks, William Hart, and Rudolph Valentino. And, at a time when women were gaining the right to vote, screen sirens Clara Bow and Gloria Swanson were as invaluable to the studios' profit margins as their male counterparts.[1]

Movie stars had only one rival in stardom: athletes. Cinema embraced the physicality of sports—among the earliest offerings from Thomas Edison were displays of boxing and surfing—and some moguls figured it was worth bringing athletes, and their familiar names, to the screen. Sports stars were often cast as celluloid facsimiles of their stadium personae. Babe

Ruth played himself in *Headin' Home* (1920); Red Grange was Red Wade in *One Minute to Play* (1926).

Paramount counted on Kahanamoku's good looks and worldwide fame to drive box office winners. He appeared in approximately two dozen films during the 1920s, but it is impossible to tally the exact number because so many movies from the silent era are missing. Nearly three-quarters of the feature films produced between 1912 and 1929 cannot be found,[2] according to the Library of Congress, including Duke's earliest known film, *The Beachcomber* (1914).

Another lost silent film is *The House without a Key*, the first mystery story to feature a Chinese detective named Charlie Chan. The fictional character was based on Hawaiian-born Chang Apana, a real-life detective who served on the Honolulu Police Department at the same time as Duke's father.

The House without a Key was first published as a serial in the *Saturday Evening Post* and then as a book in 1925, after author Earl Derr Biggers conceived the plot while staying in Waikiki. The aha moment to unlocking the murderer's identity came with the realization that the killer must have swum ashore in order to commit the crime. Biggers invoked Duke Kahanamoku's name to highlight the suspenseful twist:

> "[Waioli] was one of our best swimmers, and for years they tried to get him to go to the mainland to take part in athletic meets, like Duke Kahanamoku," one character explained to another. "But he was a sentimentalist—he couldn't bring himself to leave Hawaii. Finally they persuaded him, and one sunny morning he sailed on the *Matsonia*, with a very sad face. When the ship was opposite Waikiki he slipped overboard and swam ashore. And that was that. He never got on a ship again. You see—"
>
> John Quincy was on his feet. "What time was it when we left the beach?" he asked in a low tense voice.[3]

Biggers' thriller was a best seller, and Pathé bought the film rights. The movie came out as a serial the following year with George Kuwa, a Japanese actor, playing Charlie Chan. Several publications have reported that Kahanamoku appeared in *The House without a Key*, but this cannot be confirmed since it is missing. (Several chapters of *Isle of Sunken Gold*, a serial released in 1927 that definitely featured Duke, are also lost.)

Another challenge in detailing Duke's filmography is that he some-times appeared as an uncredited extra. Kahanamoku reportedly played Native American Indians in two Westerns, *The Covered Wagon*, directed by James Cruze and released in 1923, and *The Iron Horse*, directed by John Ford and released in 1924. Both films do exist, but it is difficult to positively identify Duke on screen.

Kahanamoku often remarked that his first movie was *Adventure*, directed by Victor Fleming for Paramount, based on a novel by Jack London. He is featured rescuing the heroine, played by actress Pauline Starke, from danger. Fleming reportedly employed a special camera for an underwater scene involving Duke, who said he "nearly drowned" after swimming "four hundred yards with Starke to a ship and then, on the return swim, getting tangled in seaweed."[4]

Making *Adventure* was a serious workout for Kahanamoku. "In a single week during the filming of this production I took part in three fights, paddled a canoe until my arms ached, and swam a 440-yard course four times under conditions that called for every ounce of strength I possessed," he said. "All these things tend to keep my swimming muscles limber and to prevent me from becoming soft."[5]

Adventure was released in 1925, but the film is believed to be lost. A review in one Hawaiian newspaper noted that Duke looks "much more primitive than he used to when sitting at the desk outside of the governor's office [in Honolulu]."[6]

As might be expected, Kahanamoku was often cast as an "ethnic" char-acter. He donned a feathered headdress to play an Indian chief in *The Pony Express*, directed by James Cruze and starring Cruze's beautiful wife, Betty Compson, along with Wallace Beery, George Bancroft, and Ernest Torrence. Duke next appeared as Tamb Itam, a villager from the fictional South Seas country of Patusan, in the film adaptation of Joseph Conrad's *Lord Jim*.

In *Hula*, Kahanamoku played a Hawaiian ranch hand in a small role that showed off his horseback riding skills. *Hula* was based on a novel by Armine von Tempski, a young woman who grew up on a cattle ranch on Maui (although the film was shot on the estate of Elias "Lucky" Baldwin in Southern California). Fleming directed the picture, which starred his lover, Clara Bow, star of *The It Girl* and *Mantrap*. The highlight came in the opening reel, well before Duke's entrance, when Bow skinny-dips in a scene that established her devil-may-care character.

One reviewer wrote that "a prettier girl never wore a shredded wheat skirt," before adding, "Fleming has directed some very good pictures recently but this isn't one of them."[7] (Fleming later directed some very good pictures: *Gone with the Wind* and *The Wizard of Oz*.)

Living in Southern California and working in Hollywood agreed with Duke. He fine-tuned his golf game, teeing off with Babe Ruth and other celebrities, and socialized at soirees held at the Fleming manse, where nubile starlets made their attractions known. He was much in demand at a time when movie stars were adding backyard pools to their estates and making them de rigueur for the wealthy and the privileged.

Kahanamoku and John Ford, an up-and-coming director, started a lifelong friendship. The two were very different—Ford's benders were legendary, while Duke was a teetotaler—but Ford loved the sea and sailing and kept a residence in Hawaii. At one Southland beach, the pair hung out with mogul John Paul Getty, whom Ford described as "a skinny little guy who never picked up a check."[8] Later, after Ford became an established director, Kahanamoku crewed on the director's prized 106-foot ketch, the *Araner.*

When he was not called to the set, Kahanamoku was swimming for, or lifeguarding at, the Los Angeles Athletic Club. He surfed any chance he could, venturing to the South Bay cities where George Freeth had "walked on water." Venice and Long Beach were also popular spots, and Kahanamoku found sublime waves further south at Huntington Beach, then known as "oil city" for its plentiful derricks.

Everywhere Kahanamoku went he spread his knowledge of surfing and bodysurfing, even getting Clara Bow on a board. Duke's pal Tom Blake was among the first people to surf Malibu. When the Malibu Colony turned into a popular weekend escape for the Hollywood crowd, Kahanamoku visited frequently and reportedly taught Ronald Colman how to surf there.

In late April of 1925, Duke interrupted his surfing fun to face Johnny Weissmuller in a relay race held at the LAAC. Weissmuller was fresh from his victories at the national meet in San Francisco, and he and coach Bachrach were barnstorming the country to capitalize on Johnny's success. The much-hyped rematch wasn't close, as Kahanamoku and his squad were swamped by Weissmuller and his Illinois teammates.

Duke then had a beefy cameo in *No Father to Guide Him*, a Hal Roach two-reel film starring comedian Charley Chase (himself a member of the LAAC). Kahanamoku played a lifeguard who, when the camera first finds him, is strumming a ukulele with a flower behind his ear, surrounded by eight bathing beauties. Suddenly, he notices Charley Chase's character thrashing around in the water as if he were drowning.

Kahanamoku runs into the ocean and swims at top speed to save Chase, only to discover that Chase does not want to be rescued because, unbeknownst to Duke, he is not wearing a bathing suit. Slapstick hilarity ensues: Chase slugs Duke, knocks him out, and then drags him to safety. Pratfalls aside, the scene provides one of the few occasions when Kahanamoku was captured on film while swimming at top speed.[9]

After the shoot, Kahanamoku retreated to Corona del Mar, quite literally the crown jewel of surfing in Southern California. Located about fifty miles south of Los Angeles, in a secluded cove between Newport Beach and Laguna, Corona del Mar is separated from Newport Beach and the Balboa Peninsula by a narrow spit of water. A massive stone jetty, built at the mouth of the harbor, created a killer break along the south-facing beach.

Kahanamoku first surfed there in 1914, on one of his earliest trips to the Southland. The waves were consistently the best he had encountered outside of Waikiki. He returned as often as his schedule allowed after he, Tom Blake, and other LAAC members formed the Corona del Mar Surfboard Club in 1924. The nocturnal escapades to be had at the Rendezvous Ballroom, in nearby Balboa, were another draw.

On this lazy weekend in mid-June of 1925, Kahanamoku and fellow LAAC members Owen Hale, Gerard "Jerry" Vultee, and William Herwig camped in tents on the beach and readied their boards for some surfing action. Early on Sunday morning, Duke woke at around 6:40 to take a quick dip.

The surf was choppy. Near the entrance to Newport Harbor, local meteorologist Antar Deraga had placed a checkered flag, signaling danger to the pleasure fishing vessels plying the harbor. Deraga knew well how treacherous these conditions were. A year previous, almost to the day, the *Adieu* had capsized in the harbor because of heavy swells. Eight men lost their lives.

Captain Myron Bland apparently did not notice the warning flag as he steered the *Thelma* toward open water. Bland operated a cigar store in the city of Riverside, located sixty miles east of downtown Los Angeles, and led regular fishing excursions aboard the forty-foot, five-ton yacht that he owned with retired baseball star Clifford "Gavy" Cravath. On this summer day, Bland had sixteen passengers, all from Riverside, in search of schools of albacore.

As the *Thelma* rounded the end of the jetty, its twenty-five-horsepower motor chugging away, a monstrous groundswell slammed into the yacht. Bland tried to right the ship. The *Thelma* teetered on the crest of the wave, at nearly a forty-five-degree angle, before managing to slide down the other side.

They were safe for only a moment. From the beach Duke watched in horror as a green wall of water struck the boat. The heavy plate glass of the cabin shattered. Rigging flew overboard. The mast collapsed. Men were swept into the sea like bowling pins. Those who managed to grasp onto the railing screamed for help.[10]

Its motor swamped, the *Thelma* was defenseless against the ocean's fury. It was slammed yet again, this time by a wave estimated to be twenty feet high. The *Thelma* rolled completely over, from starboard to port, and swept toward the palisades.

"All went black," Bland recounted later. "I stood on my head, it seems, and all around me was water and blackness."[11]

Kahanamoku grabbed his surfboard and plunged into the sea. He furiously paddled toward the *Thelma*, bobbing about a quarter-mile from shore, and was half-blinded by the rush of water and debris. Panic-stricken passengers were struggling to stay afloat. Many were entangled in ropes and bent fishing equipment, their clothing and shoes a sodden burden. Others clung to the sides of the boat.

Duke grabbed one man and wrestled him onto the surfboard. There was room for another, and then a third, as he turned the plank into an emergency flotation device. Torrents of water broke over them as Kahanamoku propelled the board toward safety with urgent kicks. Hale and Vultee met him in the water and ferried the men to shore.

Duke turned around, inhaled mightily, and jumped on his board. He dug into the water toward the *Thelma*. He secured two flailing fishermen and maneuvered them onto his board, then kicked toward Hale, Vultee, and safety.

Deraga telephoned for assistance while his wife and a nurse, Mary Grigsby, wrapped the survivors in blankets and tried to resuscitate the unconscious men. Two bystanders, Charlie Plummer of Balboa and William McElhannon from Santa Ana, assisted in the rescue.

For a third time, Kahanamoku turned to the sea. He picked up stragglers and placed them on his board until, finally, he could do no more.

Bland and eleven passengers were rescued, with eight of them attributable to Duke. Five men perished that morning. Two of the bodies were never recovered. The *Thelma* was a battered wreck.

Kahanamoku, Hale, Vultee, and Herwig sat in stunned, exhausted silence as seemingly all of Riverside descended on the beach, followed by a swarm of reporters. They had one question: how had Duke managed to save so many lives?

He was far from forthcoming. "I do not know," he replied. "It was done. That is the main thing. By a few tricks, perhaps."[12]

Those were his only public remarks. Others spoke up for him. "But for the work of Kahanamoku and the others, we would have perished," survivor Fred Hock said. "The Hawaiian was a wizard, and he seemed to have everything in his hands, as we were fighting out there in the water. . . . At one time he had six of us on a large surfboard."[13]

"The Duke's performance was the most superhuman rescue act and the finest display of surfboard riding that has ever been seen in the world," said J. A. Porter, chief of police in Newport Beach.[14]

Later that afternoon, a heavy swell knocked out the warning light on the jetty. Kahanamoku, Deraga, and Hale again risked their lives to see that the light was saved and the mechanism salvaged.

That winter, the Hawaiian Society and the Los Angeles Athletic Club held a dinner to honor the rescuers. LAAC chief William May Garland presented Duke and the others with gold watches. Their reward notwithstanding, the rescue was seen as a milestone in the broader acceptance of the surfboard. Safety officials had previously viewed surfboards as a recreational oddity that only a few people, primarily Hawaiians, could master. Now the surfboard was seen as a device that could save lives.

As Duke put it, "[The rescue] helped sell the lifeguard service on the wisdom of keeping paddleboards at the guard towers. The boards soon became standard equipment on the emergency rescue trucks as well as at the towers. In short, some good sometimes comes from the worst of tragedies."[15]

Kahanamoku was too modest to mention that, on another occasion, he saved a surfer's life at Corona del Mar. "I lost my board in the huge waves and was caught in a series of oncoming combers under three feet of foam and unable to breath," Sam Reid remembered. "I thought I was gone until I saw Duke's strong brown arm come down and pick me up and put me on his board and catch a wave with me tandem toward shore to retrieve my board."[16]

The following year Duke was cast as a Pirate in *Old Ironsides*. With noted producer B. P. Schulberg in charge, Paramount had high hopes for the patriotic film, about the frigate USS *Constitution* that whipped the Barbary pirates of North Africa. Set to star were George Bancroft, Esther Ralston, Charles Farrell, and Wallace Beery.[17]

Paramount chief Adolph Zukor hired James Cruze to "out-epic" his hit, *The Covered Wagon*, wrangling "an extraordinary budget of $1.5 million" for *Old Ironsides*.[18] That sum increased with the implementation of Magna-scope, a crude magnifying projector lens that enlarged the images audiences saw on the screen.

Another $100,000 was paid to chewing-gum magnate William Wrigley for the use of Catalina Island, a mountainous resort that he owned about twenty miles off the coast of Southern California, as a stand-in for Tripoli. The crew lived on Catalina in "Camp Cruze," complete with a $75,000 electric generator to supply light and power to the mini-village of two hundred tents. The battle scenes were so noisy that Cruze had to give directorial instructions to the actors and crew using radio broadcasts.

On their breaks, Kahanamoku and Wallace Beery liked to take the actor's motor launch into deep water. They gave Esther Ralston her first experience in aquaplaning (an early version of waterskiing). "It was thrilling," Ralston said, "and although I fell off several times, I wasn't afraid because . . . Duke Kahanamoku was right there on Wally's boat to rescue me if I got into trouble."[19]

Kahanamoku found trouble early one morning as the wooden full-rigged ship that was the replica of the *Constitution* was towed into the Catalina

Isthmus. A heavy groundswell came up and "Old Ironsides" began to roll heavily. The fore shrouds gave way. The foremast snapped and went over the side, followed by the main and the mizzen masts.

Two men stationed in the main rigging—Max Koehler, an extra on the film, and rigger Christ Dorfs—fell one hundred feet into the water. Stunned, they floundered to free themselves from the jumbled mess of ropes, wires, and pulleys. Kahanamoku showed no hesitation. He jumped into the water, swam out to the two men, and brought them to safety. Shaken and bruised, Koehler and Dorfs received emergency treatment and survived.[20]

Unfortunately for Paramount, Duke could not rescue *Old Ironsides*. Despite an excellent cast, decent reviews, and Magnascope scenes that wowed audiences, Cruze's effort sank at the box office.

22

Even as he pursued his film career, Duke Kahanamoku continued to straddle the amateur-professional line as a swimmer. His participation with the LAAC, in the relay race against Johnny Weissmuller and the IAC squad in 1925, indicated that he was still considered to be an amateur. In January of 1927, he turned down an invitation to compete for the $25,000 first prize in William Wrigley's Ocean Marathon, a Catalina-Island-to-California-Coast exodus of about twenty miles, to preserve his eligibility.

And yet, with prodding from Hollywood friends and LAAC backers, Kahanamoku decided to turn pro in August of 1927. He organized a stage act that trumpeted him as the "Greatest Swimming Champion." A huge tank was built so that Duke and featured costars, including Marjorie Williamson, Lily Bowner May, and diver Viola Hartman (Fred Cady's wife), could perform and show off tricks.

The Hillstreet Theater in downtown Los Angeles was booked for the debut of the show. The LAAC newsletter noted that, as Kahanamoku "paddles into a new business," he hopes to sign with the Orpheum circuit and "tour the United States and Europe with a troupe of swimmers as vaudeville headliners."[1]

However, with scant funding or marketing muscle behind it, the act fizzled immediately and, again, Kahanamoku retained his eligibility. "This did not last long enough for Duke to make any money from the venture," Charley Paddock wrote.[2]

Kahanamoku sailed to Hawaii with Johnny Weissmuller, coach Bill Bachrach, and LAAC members in mid-August of 1927, right around the time that Clara Bow's nude scene in *Hula* was titillating audiences in theaters. What brought Duke home for the first time in years was the grand opening of the War Memorial Natatorium at the eastern end of Waikiki.

The long-gestating project had evolved from a statue to honor local men who had served and died during World War I into a memorial that also benefited the living. And what could be more beneficial for Hawaii than a state-of-the-art swimming stadium, built right into the ocean, complete with a hundred-meter saltwater pool, changing rooms, bleachers for 2,500 spectators, and a public park?

In effect, it was the Natatorium that Duke Kahanamoku built, and he delighted in reconnecting with friends and family, especially his aged mother, whose health had been slipping. Duke's brother David, the head of the Waikiki Beach Patrol, had married, and his brother Sam was engaged. Their youngest sibling, Sargent, was seventeen years old and making his own brand of mischief.

The dedication ceremony for the War Memorial Natatorium coincided with the national swimming championships and Kahanamoku's thirty-seventh birthday. Duke did not bother to compete in the meet. But he was accorded the honor of taking the ceremonial first plunge, and he swam a lap to great applause. "He hits the middle of the tank and starts down the middle," his brother Sargent remembered. "He goes about 20 yards and the waves come and hit the sides of the tank. . . . I mean, [those waves] were big—so big that I could take a 120-pound surfboard and ride them. . . . Nobody else, not even Johnny Weissmuller, could get in the middle of the pool and make waves like that."[3]

But Weissmuller stole the spotlight again, winning races from 100 meters to the half-mile. He defeated Hawaii's newest swimming sensation, Clarence "Buster" Crabbe, in the 440, broke his own world's record in the 100, and helped the IAC relay teams beat the Outrigger Canoe Club's squad.

Kahanamoku had nothing but praise for the new facility as "the first step on the way to a comeback of swimming in the Hawaiian Islands. Until now it has been almost impossible to develop young swimmers simply because of a lack of an adequate pool. . . . [Now] Hawaii will have a fit place in which to train its youngsters."[4]

A prime example was the youthful Crabbe, whose family had moved to Hawaii when he was two years old. He impressed Duke as "a coming world's champion." Duke also extolled Weissmuller as "a marvel. There's nobody can beat him right now. Just how long he will last, I cannot say. That's up to him and how he takes care of himself."[5]

As he admired the Natatorium and gazed out over the Pacific, Kahanamoku sounded wistful. "Someday I hope to return here to live permanently," he allowed, "although at the present time I cannot say just when that will be."[6]

The brief homecoming and the scent of competition reinvigorated Kahanamoku. Back in Los Angeles, he made plans for a comeback. His target: the 1928 Amsterdam Olympics, which were less than a year away. He began working out under Fred Cady's direction as friendly newspaper columnists hyped the return of "Duke of Neptune's Court" to the pool. "I haven't quite the speed I had at one time," he said, "but I do have the same stroke, and the proper stroke is everything."[7]

In truth he faced long odds to qualify for his fourth Olympic team in sixteen years. His fate was decided for him after he fell ill in May, beset by a long siege of influenza that bordered on pneumonia. He took to his bed at the Henry residence to recuperate. He missed crucial weeks of training on the eve of the U.S. Olympic Trials.

Kahanamoku finally admitted that he did not have the necessary fitness. "I trained for six months for the Olympic Games in 1924, and even then my legs went bad on me," he said. "In the last twenty-five yards of my race with Johnny Weissmuller my legs felt like a couple of dead weights. I'm resigning in favor of the younger fellows. I'm [nearly] 38, you know, and no spring chicken."[8]

For the first time since 1912, Kahanamoku did not qualify or compete at the Olympic Games. He followed the events in Amsterdam as Weissmuller won two more gold medals, defending his 100-meter crown in 58.6 and helping the United States triumph in the relay race. Duke's prediction about Buster Crabbe's potential was fulfilled as the Hawaiian (now swimming for Fred Cady at USC) took the bronze medal in the 1,500 meters.

Kahanamoku intimated that he was invited to play on the U.S. water polo team at the 1928 Olympics but turned down the offer because of work. He signed with Samuel Goldwyn to act in *The Rescue*, a silent film adapted from Joseph Conrad's novel. Costumed in a loincloth and wearing a necklace of human teeth, Kahanamoku appeared alongside stars Ronald Colman and

Lily Damita. A reel of this silent movie is lost, although Duke is reported to have filmed "an amazing water shot"[9] off Santa Cruz Island.

Later, long after he stopped trying to make it as an actor, Kahanamoku said that he "enjoyed working in the pictures." He appeared onscreen with Lon Chaney, Wallace Beery, Lupe Velez, Ronald Colman, Clara Bow, and a young Gary Cooper; the list of directors he worked with included Raoul Walsh, James Cruze, John Ford, and Victor Fleming. He socialized with them and golfed with them; he defended them from accusations of being "wicked Hollywood flappers."

"Why, the people in the films are regular folks, just the same as the ones that go to the 'movies' at night or matinee," he said. "As far as I can see human beings are pretty much the same the world over . . . good, bad, careless, and indifferent according to their ancestors and their own habits."[10]

That said, his was a marginal movie career. Kahanamoku was not permitted to "play" a swimming star without jeopardizing his amateur status. That severely curtailed potential roles, especially during the early years when he was establishing his screen reputation. Aside from brief scenes in *The Beachcomber*, *Adventure*, *No Father to Guide Him*, and *The Rescue*, Duke did not swim or perform stunts in the water. He was given few chances to display his sense of humor, his musicianship and dancing ability, or his physical presence.

A serial, or perhaps a series of short films, built around Duke as a surfer-lifeguard could have been produced without endangering his amateur status in swimming, but, alas, the cottage industry of surfing movies was many decades away. (Duke can be seen briefly surfing in Hawaii in *Around the World in Eighty Minutes*, a documentary produced by Douglas Fairbanks and Victor Fleming in 1931.)

Kahanamoku's name in Hollywood was just that—a name. Work was sporadic; he was not paid well. "He was courageous in his efforts," Charley Paddock said. "He worked long hours. And his labors were unrewarded. Now and then his name would be given screen credit. But in such a fashion that few associated Duke Kahanamoku, the greatest swimmer, with Duke Kahanamoku, the petty chieftain of a native group, or Kahanamoku the pirate, or Kahanamoku the soldier, or Kahanamoku the body guard of the hero."[11]

None of the films in which he appeared won major awards or were box office smashes. As Paddock pointed out, Duke was typecast as an "ethnic" character (including a Mexican caballero) in a slew of forgettable pictures, many of which are lost, including *The Lady of the Harem*,[12] *The Wanderer*, *Woman Wise*, *The Rescue*, *Eagle of the Sea*, *Her Summer Hero*, *Where East Is East*, *Wolf Song*, and *Easy Come, Easy Go*.[13]

"First I played a Hindu thief, then an Arab prince, and after that a Sioux chieftain," he said. "I was very surprised when at last I received an offer to play what I consider to be my most unusual part—that of a native-born Hawaiian."[14]

Los Angeles Times columnist Jim Murray summed up Duke's Hollywood stint with a pithy, but accurate, sentence: "His longest line was a death rattle."[15]

Curiously, one of the last films that Kahanamoku made showed off his acting potential. Director Bert Glennon, who often worked for John Ford as a cinematographer, offered Duke a small but key role in the all-talkie *Girl of the Port* (also known as *The Fire Walker*). In the film, Kahanamoku plays Kalita, a villager, and sports a Don King-like Afro while clad in a sarong. The action opens during a monsoon as Kalita escorts the heroine (Sally O'Neil) into a rough-and-tumble saloon. After the two exchange pleasantries and Kalita turns to leave the bar, the villainous McEwen (Mitchell Lewis) confronts him.

> McEwen: "Hey, you, Kalita."
> Kalita: "Yes, boss."
> McEwen: "When a black baboon like you carries bags for a white woman, he does it for money and nothing but, *sabe*?"
> Kalita: "Yes, boss."
> McEwen: "Well, there's your money." [Throws coin to the ground.] "Now pick that up before I skin the hide off you."
> Kalita: "Yes, boss."

Kalita bends to retrieve the coin, walks outside, and, as the rain lashes his face, throws down the coin in disgust.

Three statements of "Yes, boss." The first was delivered with a hopeful, can't-we-just-get-along note; the second with a resigned, almost lifeless tone; and the third, accompanied by a close-up of Duke's steely gaze, is an eloquent study in anguish.

As the dialogue indicates, the barrier that Kahanamoku could not overcome in Hollywood was racism. Duke arrived in Hollywood less than a decade after the release of *The Birth of a Nation*, a groundbreaking film for its technical innovations and one that also glorified the Ku Klux Klan. To that point, and long afterward, it was the highest-grossing movie in history. Duke left Hollywood not long after the introduction of "talkies," or sound films, in 1927, highlighted by actor Al Jolson, his face coated in black paint, in *The Jazz Singer*. Studio bosses would sooner sacrifice their casting couches than have Duke play a swashbuckling hero who vanquishes the bad guy and gets the girl.

Of course, when Hollywood stumbled upon a white "name" athlete whom they could mold into a movie star, they jumped at the opportunity. That person was none other than Johnny Weissmuller. Following his success at the 1928 Amsterdam Olympics, Johnny had not hesitated to turn pro after coach Bill Bachrach steered his protégé into signing a five-year contract to model and promote BVD swimwear at $500 per week.

The gig was an easy one, and Johnny excelled at being himself. He happened to be working in Los Angeles around the time that Metro-Goldwyn-Mayer was searching for a fresh face to play Tarzan, the vine-swinging character from the novels written by Edgar Rice Burroughs. The franchise was transitioning to talkies when Weissmuller took a screen test and landed the lead role opposite Maureen O'Sullivan. *Tarzan the Ape Man* was released in March of 1932, right before the start of the Los Angeles Olympics.

The loincloth-clad Weissmuller made six Tarzan movies for MGM and another six for RKO. He became a global icon outside the pool and earned a small fortune doing so. "Tarzan was right up my alley," he said. "It was like stealing money. There was swimming in it, and I didn't have much to say. How can a guy climb trees, say 'Me Tarzan, you Jane,' and make a million?"[16]

Kahanamoku never expressed public bitterness about this. But the fact that his archrival was able to land such a plum role, while his years-long apprenticeship in Hollywood amounted to little, was an insult. Years later Duke appeared in small parts in *Wake of the Red Witch* (1948), starring John Wayne, and *Mister Roberts* (1955), directed by John Ford. Otherwise, his movie career was *pau* (over).

23

Approaching the age of forty, with streaks of grey at his temples and the lines deepening on his face, Duke Kahanamoku had encountered another low point. He was too old to be a factor in the Olympics, and Hollywood had little use for him. Beyond memories and medals, he had only a small house to show for the sacrifices that he had made to pursue his swimming career and to promote Hawaii.

"Lady Luck has gone by," he wrote his brother David. "I've always heard she was fickle, but at least she was something wonderful I experienced—and now I go it alone without her."[1]

Hawaii and family called. His mother, nearing sixty years of age, was eager for her eldest son to be by her side. Local politicians lobbied for Duke to come home and dangled "honorable inducements commensurate with his fame and aquatic achievements." In May of 1929, both houses of the Territory's legislature adopted a resolution that welcomed "the prospect of Duke Kahanamoku's return and permanent residence in Hawaii, for, by his honorable conduct and prowess in many lands, he has added much to the 'honor lei' of the fair land that gave him birth."[2]

Kahanamoku finished shooting *Girl of the Port* and sailed to Hawaii on the *City of Honolulu* at the close of the year. His brothers greeted him at the harbor and sang Hui Nalu's fight song. They posed for photographs together, laughing, the tears in Duke's eyes almost hidden behind the *lei* that piled up around his ears.

"Home again, and this wonderful place to rest and play," he said. "No makeup, no excitement, no work for a time. Surfing, fishing, swimming and lots of play. I have been waiting for a long time to break away from the calcium lights."[3]

He moved back into the small house at 1847 Ala Moana Road and took stock. In many ways he was the same Duke who had left for Hollywood in 1922. He yearned for water like it was his lover. He paddled and surfed at familiar haunts. He swam long distances lazily and then flashed his speed. He slept for hours. He devoured poi and fresh fish.

Tom Blake, Duke's lifeguard pal from the Los Angeles Athletic Club, was now living in Waikiki. He used his time out of the water to study the antique surfboards at the Bishop Museum and then began experimenting with different woods—in particular, balsa—to make boards lighter and more maneuverable. Blake also tried hollowing out the boards to reduce their weight. He received a patent for his designs, and, by the early 1930s, two Los Angeles-based companies, Thomas Rogers and Pacific System Homes, started churning out the first commercial surfboards.[4]

Kahanamoku "had gone stale on surfriding," Blake observed, when Duke returned to Hawaii. "The ten-foot board held no thrill for him." He watched as Duke made a new model. Using an adze, a small ax, and a drawknife, Duke shaped a sixteen-foot board that weighed more than one hundred pounds. "He is an excellent craftsman and shapes the lines and balance of his board with the eye; he detects its irregularities by touch of the hand," Blake noted.[5]

Suddenly, Kahanamoku was "as enthusiastic a surfrider as ever" and, at the age of forty, did "some of the most beautiful riding I have ever seen on his new long board," Blake recalled. "The first big swell Duke caught went to his head like wine. He yelled and shouted at the top of his voice as he rode in. He was happy. It put new life into him and ever since his attitude towards surfriding has been as keen as when he was a boy."[6]

Kahanamoku's brothers delighted in schooling Duke in surfboard polo, a new game that Louis was credited with inventing. This was, essentially, water polo played while sitting on a surfboard, often in front of throngs of tourists on the beach.

"We'd let brother Duke have the ball and he'd try to paddle out to our goal and shoot and make a point," Sargent recalled, "but what Sam and I would do was put our hands around his surfboard underwater so he couldn't get away. He couldn't understand why he couldn't move and he'd get so mad."[7]

In other ways, Hollywood and his extensive travels had changed Kahanamoku. He was well aware of his status as a symbol of Hawaii and

Hawaiian culture, and with that came an appreciation of his public image. He took pride in his appearance at all times. He always looked elegantly turned out, even when he was wearing swimming trunks. He eschewed Hui Nalu, the hardscrabble club that he had helped launch, in favor of the teak furnishings of the Outrigger Canoe Club.

"It was somehow a shock to me," Sam Reid remembered. "He was used to dressing at the Los Angeles Athletic Club and his exclusive Beach Club in Santa Monica. There were not even towels at Hui Nalu, and while it is all right for a kid to dry off in the sun under the old hau tree, eventually, I guessed, we all have to change. As a man grows older, is there anything wrong in his wanting some of the material comforts in life? But somehow it disturbed me."[8]

As Kahanamoku adjusted to being home, he discovered that Waikiki was much changed. Hundreds of acres of wetlands had been drained, dredged, and paved for the creation of the Ala Wai Canal, a two-mile-long, 250-feet-wide, concrete-encased waterway that ran the length of Waikiki. The three freshwater streams that flowed into the area were now diverted into the canal and then funneled into the ocean. The duck ponds, taro fields, and rice paddies of Duke's youth disappeared, and the delicate aquaculture that had sustained families for generations vanished.

The Territory's future was inexorably tied to "development" and tourism. The vision of Hawaii as a safe playground—one that had "been carefully created, packaged and launched"[9] by the *haole*-controlled promotional agencies—was being realized, complete with a new airport to welcome the first trans-Pacific commercial flights. The Matson Navigation Company was building the Royal Hawaiian Hotel, right at the water's edge at Waikiki, for their well-heeled clientele. The gleaming "Pink Palace" could have doubled as a movie set, with coconut groves swaying in the breeze and the lilting sounds of Johnny Noble providing musical accompaniment to the gorgeous sunsets.

Hawaii's population, estimated to be about 192,000 in 1910, had almost doubled by 1930. Waikiki's beachboys stayed busy entertaining the tourists who came even in the throes of the Great Depression. Duke slipped into the role of beachboy emeritus, the man whom tourism industry leaders called on to entertain the movie stars, celebrities, and political figures who visited Hawaii: Charlie Chaplin, Clark Gable, Groucho Marx, the son of President Herbert Hoover, and the sons of President Franklin Roosevelt.

Duke made them feel at ease in no small part because he was as famous as they were. He discussed flying while dining with aviator Amelia Earhart. He and Babe Ruth placed a wreath on the tombstone of Alexander Cartwright, the father of baseball, at Oahu Cemetery, not far from where Duke's father was buried. He hoisted little Shirley Temple onto his broad shoulders when the child star came to Hawaii. "I call him 'Duke,' because the rest is too long," she said.[10]

Kahanamoku spent his own money buying bundles of genuine carnation *lei* and giving them to visitors. He entertained them with rides in an outrigger canoe, helped them balance on a surfboard, dined with them at the Outrigger Canoe Club, played golf with them on Oahu's first municipal course, escorted them to football games at the newly built Honolulu Stadium, and posed for endless photos.

Duke suffused them with *aloha* because he believed that promoting Hawaii was beneficial for fellow Hawaiians. That spirit became his calling card, literally, as he eventually printed his personal philosophy on business cards. "In Hawaii we greet friends, loved ones or strangers with ALOHA, which means with love," the text read. "ALOHA is the key word to the universal spirit of real hospitality, which made Hawaii renowned as the world's center of understanding and fellowship. Try meeting or leaving people with ALOHA. You'll be surprised by their reaction. I believe it, and it is my creed."[11]

Embracing *aloha*, however, did not improve Duke's job prospects. He was facing a situation that was familiar to elite athletes of a certain age. He needed something—a career, an outlet—that was commensurate with his celebrity status and provided him with the same type of inspiration and excitement that he found in the pool. This was no easy task, especially with Hawaii feeling the effects of the Great Depression.

In late 1930 mayor-elect George F. Wright, a Republican, appointed Kahanamoku to the post of superintendent of Honolulu *Hale*, the seat of the city and county government. "It no doubt would be pleasing for tourists to Hawaii who visit the city hall during their stay to be received by the one Hawaiian, above all others, who is known throughout the world," according to one report.[12]

The title was better than the actual job. Visitors were stunned to see Duke Kahanamoku, the heralded Olympian and symbol of Hawaiian manhood, sweeping the floors with a broom and mowing the grass under a blazing sun. His pay was $200 a month.

"Ha! Superintendent was nothing but 'official toilet cleaner,'" he said. "But at least I was my own boss."[13]

That Kahanamoku could find a silver lining in janitorial work ("I was my own boss") showed his essential and indomitable grit. But the menial job was a reminder that, for all he had done for Hawaii, he had ended up as just another brown-skinned servant.

Another dramatic change on Oahu was the buildup of U.S. armed forces. Some 20,000 troops were stationed in the Territory by the late 1920s, divided between the strategically vital naval base of Pearl Harbor, Fort DeRussy in Waikiki, Fort Shafter (located between Pearl Harbor and Honolulu), Hickam and Wheeler airfields, and the Schofield Barracks.

The relationship between longtime residents and young servicemen who were far from home was often tense, especially when alcohol became involved. Mary Paoa Clarke, Duke's cousin, described an early group of soldiers billeted at Fort DeRussy, adjacent to the Paoa-Kahanamoku homestead, as "very nasty." They insulted her father, saying, "'You dirty kanaka,' and all that. Oh, was terrible."

One solider tried to assault her father with an old-fashioned weight. Duke Kahanamoku Senior, her uncle, who was then serving on the Honolulu police force, "happened to come and grabbed him. Took him. . . . Oh, [they were] bad, those days. We were scared living there."[14]

From Here to Eternity, published in 1951, was James Jones' fictionalized account of his army days on Oahu prior to World War II. The regimental song in the novel captured the attitude of many young soldiers who were based at Schofield Barracks:

Oh, we wont come back to Wahoo [Oahu] any more.
No, we wont come back to Wahoo any more.
We will fuck your black kanaky,
We will drink your goddamned saki,
BUT we wont come back to Wahoo any more.[15]

The concentration of military might, and the tension this caused among local residents, came under national scrutiny after an incident on the night of September 12, 1931. Thalia Massie and her husband Tommy, a navy officer, were out drinking with friends. Thalia purportedly got into a squabble with another officer and ran off, leaving behind her husband and the party.[16]

What happened in the hour before a passing car picked up Thalia Massie, wandering along Ala Moana Road in Waikiki with a bruised face and a swollen lip, is unknown to this day. She claimed that several dark-skinned men forced her into a car and raped her.

Five young men of Hawaiian, Japanese, and mixed descent were picked up, questioned, and indicted on rape charges, even though Thalia Massie's story contained discrepancies that the police and the prosecution appeared determined to overlook. A tense trial followed. With the jury deadlocked, the Ala Moana trial was declared a mistrial. The five defendants were released on bail to await retrial.

Tommy Massie and Grace Fortescue, Thalia's mother, took matters into their own hands. With assistance from two enlisted men, they kidnapped one of the five accused men, Joseph Kahahawai, a native Hawaiian, and killed him while apparently attempting to coerce a confession. The National Association for the Advancement of Colored People (NAACP) called the murder a lynching.

The salacious details dominated national headlines, eclipsed only by the kidnapping and death of Charles Lindbergh's son in early 1932. Many commentators on the mainland scolded Hawaii for its allegedly casual attitude toward interracial couplings. There was "Lust in Paradise," raved *Time* magazine, which decried that the "yellow men's lust for white women had broken bonds."[17]

"The situation in Hawaii is deplorable," Hearst newspapers sensationalized, and "the whole island should promptly be put under martial law and the perpetrators of outrages upon women promptly tried by court martial and executed. Until such drastic measures are taken, Hawaii is not a safe place for decent white women and not a very good place for self-respecting civilized men."[18]

Kahanamoku had often been photographed surfing with white women; a full-page photo of Duke and Viola Hartman Cady, surfing tandem while she stood atop his shoulders, graced the cover of the *Los Angeles Times*

Magazine just before he left California.[19] In the aftermath of Joseph Kaha-hawai's murder, *Liberty* magazine published an article describing Hawaii as "A Paradise Gone Mad," with a photograph of Kahanamoku on a surfboard at Waikiki, with Jane Waite riding tandem on his shoulders. The pair are smiling and obviously enjoying the moment; the caption reads: "A white girl with a 'surf-board god'—that is, a Kanaka instructor."[20]

It was in this atmosphere that the Massie family, facing murder charges for the death of Joseph Kahahawai, hired famed attorney Clarence Darrow for their defense. Darrow was known for representing the underdog. He had defended Nathan Leopold and Richard Loeb in their murder trial, as well as the right to teach evolution in the Scopes Trial. He took the Massie case for no other reason than money, after having been nearly wiped out financially by the Great Depression.

Darrow arrived in Honolulu to great fanfare. Keen trial strategist that he was, he sought to shape the charged mood in his favor. And, what better way to do that than to sidle up to the most prominent Hawaiian of them all? Through local contacts, Darrow made arrangements to visit Waikiki. There, he donned a one-piece bathing suit, climbed into an outrigger canoe, and, his pale body covered by a white towel, rode to shore on the crest of a wave, with Duke Kahanamoku acting as steersman. A photograph of Darrow, beaming in the surf with Duke and several of his brothers, was published in newspapers from Honolulu to New York.

The publicity was a major coup for Darrow, who had managed to co-opt Duke's *aloha* spirit for his own beleaguered cause. Darrow was not as fortunate in court. He argued that the murder of Joseph Kahahawai was justifiable under the dubious argument that it was "an honor killing." His clients were found guilty, not of murder, but of manslaughter, a verdict that managed to outrage both sides. Their sentence was commuted to one hour in custody, which they spent in the office of the governor, before they and Darrow were whisked off to the mainland.[21]

An investigation later confirmed that Thalia Massie had probably con-cocted the original story. The original Ala Moana defendants were never retried. But the two trials and the senseless murder of an innocent young man profoundly scarred Hawaii, leading to a new sense of solidarity among the non-*haole* population.

24

During the proceedings of the Massie case, Duke's youngest sister, Maria Kahanamoku, died suddenly. The schoolteacher, who was only twenty-five years old, had recently gotten engaged. Her illness and death were wrenching for the family to endure. A life-sized statue of Maria was erected next to the grave site of Duke's father at Oahu Cemetery.

Feeling unmoored by his sister's death and underappreciated at home, Kahanamoku was thrown a lifeline by his friends at the Los Angeles Athletic Club. All of Southern California was gearing up for the 1932 Olympics in Los Angeles, an effort headed by the leaders of the LAAC. When Mercury clubmen Les Henry and Fred Cady invited Duke to help them, Duke decided to take a leave of absence and use the opportunity to make a final, improbable comeback.

"It is my innate desire to compete at one more Olympic aquatic carnival," he said. "Then and only then shall I retire from active competition in swimming."[1]

The notion was, frankly, absurd. Kahanamoku had skipped the 1928 Olympics in Amsterdam—at that time he was thirty-seven years old. Four years later, without having trained seriously during the interim, he was in no shape to challenge the nation's best swimmers.

Kahanamoku logged laps at the Natatorium and swam in the ocean at Waikiki in preparation for workouts under Fred Cady in Los Angeles. Then, in mid-July, he caught a plane to Cincinnati, hoping to catch lightning at the Olympic tryouts. "If I make the American team, I'm going to apply for the honor of carrying the flag [at the opening ceremony]," he said. "I think that would be the finest climax I could have to my career."[2]

Sunlite Pool in Cincinnati's Coney Island Park was a spectacular facility, easily the largest flat-surface pool in the nation. It was also open only to whites. Kahanamoku quietly broke the color barrier on the opening day of the trials when he toed the starting mark for the fourth qualifying heat of the 100-meter event.

His heart was willing, but his forty-one-year-old body was not. With Johnny Weissmuller watching poolside, the "grand old man" of swimming finished third in the Ohio heat, lagging behind Midwestern college boys who were half his age. Decades later, swim legends Mark Spitz and Janet Evans would learn the same lesson: making a comeback after the age of forty is nigh impossible.

"That's all right," Duke said with a grin. "I'm not as young as I used to be. I was really in there trying. It's the old story—the legs. They were okay for seventy-five meters. After that, it was just too bad."[3]

Kahanamoku returned to Los Angeles to help his adopted hometown celebrate the first Summer Olympics in the United States since St. Louis in 1904. President Herbert Hoover declined the honor of opening the Olympic Games, and the Great Depression limited the number of foreigners who were able to travel and compete in Los Angeles. The athlete who received the most pre-Games hype, distance runner Paavo Nurmi (and his nine Olympic gold medals), was suspended over charges of professionalism and was not eligible to participate.

Nurmi's absence from the track did not stop record crowds from filling the Los Angeles Memorial Coliseum and the other venues that were dotted around the region, including the spiffy new outdoor Swimming Stadium, adjacent to the Coliseum in Exposition Park, with capacity for 10,000 spectators. For sixteen days during the summer of 1932, Los Angeles organizers offered a unique blend of elite athleticism, stellar weather, civic enthusiasm, and Hollywood pizzazz. City leaders changed the name of Tenth Street to Olympic Boulevard in honor of the Los Angeles Games being the Tenth Olympiad. Douglas Fairbanks practically entertained the world, hosting countless parties and rallying his fellow movie stars to come out in force, including Will Rogers and Tom Mix, Buster Keaton and Joe E. Brown, Fay Wray and Tallulah Bankhead, and the entire cast of "Our Gang," featuring Pete the dog.

Before the opening ceremony, Kahanamoku reunited with Jim Thorpe at an "Old Champions" night at the Los Angeles Athletic Club. Thorpe had recently moved to Southern California. He was renting a small house in the suburb of Hawthorne and, following in Duke's footsteps, cobbling together a living by "playing" American Indians in B movies. He made headlines for the wrong reason after it was discovered that the American Olympic Committee had not reserved tickets for Thorpe, the man once hailed as the world's greatest athlete, to attend the Games.[4]

If Thorpe and Kahanamoku had defined the American Olympic effort in 1912, then the 1932 Games were defined by Mildred "Babe" Didrikson. In only the second Olympics that were open to women in track and field, the twenty-one-year-old wunderkind from Texas took two gold medals and one silver medal. She probably would have won another medal but for the rule that prohibited her from entering more than three events.

American women dominated in the pool as well, but the U.S. men faced a drought in the post-Kahanamoku and post-Weissmuller era. A young team from Japan, which huffed from oxygen tanks for energy, took five gold medals in six events, along with three silver and three bronze medals. "Little Brown Men Cinch to Win 100 Meters Final Today,"[5] read the headline in the *Los Angeles Times*, and the "Nipponese Paddlers" from "Cherry Blossom Land" did, ending the U.S. consecutive winning streak in the 100-meter event dating to 1908, with victories by Charles Daniels, Kahanamoku (twice), and Weissmuller (twice).

The one gold medal that eluded the Japanese team came in the 400, won by Buster Crabbe by a margin of one-tenth of a second. Kahanamoku and Weissmuller, who was then starring in theaters as Tarzan, were poolside to congratulate Crabbe. Their presence meant everything to Crabbe, who as a teenager had gone to Honolulu harbor to wave good-bye to Kahanamoku before the 1924 Paris Olympics. Duke was "my God," Crabbe said. "Every kid wanted to be like Duke Kahanamoku."[6]

The publicity that Crabbe received at the Olympics, together with his matinee idol's look, allowed him to follow in another path that Kahanamoku had forged and that Weissmuller had monetized. Instead of returning to Hawaii to become a lawyer, Crabbe signed with Paramount to play Kaspa the Lion Man in *King of the Jungle*, a rip-off of the Tarzan franchise. He also appeared in *Tarzan the Fearless*, a serial film released in 1933. Crabbe went on to have a long and lucrative screen career, starring as Flash Gordon and Buck Rogers.

Kahanamoku's primary duties leading up to the Olympics were to assist Les Henry and Fred Cady with the selection and preparation of the U.S.

water polo team. His loyalties were with the seven athletes representing the Los Angeles Athletic Club as they battled teams from the Hollywood, New York, and Illinois athletic clubs in a round-robin tourney held at Brookside Park pool in Pasadena.

When the Mercury club prevailed and was named the U.S. representative for the 1932 Games, the locals exulted. "A Los Angeles water polo team for the Los Angeles Olympiad!"[7]

During the Games, Duke roomed with goalkeeper Herbert Wildman in a bungalow in Baldwin Hills that constituted the first athletes' village erected for the Olympics. He attended the four matches played by the United States, which took third place behind Hungary (powered by one-legged star Oliver Halassy) and Germany. He also played with the American reserves in an exhibition match against a combined Hungarian-German squad.

Most researchers credit Kahanamoku with appearing in three Olympic Games (1912, 1920, and 1924). However, several historians maintain that Kahanamoku competed in four Olympics, claiming that he was "an alternate" on the water polo team in 1932. A search for definitive evidence to back up this assertion is inconclusive.

Kahanamoku's name does not appear on the rosters of the four matches involving the U.S. squad that were printed in the Official Report. The American Olympic Committee, which issued its own report, listed Duke as an alternate in one section, but it does not include Duke on the team in another section. Further, his name does not appear in the definitive article published in the *Los Angeles Times* that provided the names of the team's seven starters and four alternates.[8]

According to Charles "Doc" McCallister, an LAAC member who started every game on the back line, Kahanamoku tried out for the U.S. team, but he did not make the cut. "One [book] says he was a substitute on our team," McAllister said. "Well, he really wasn't. He was kind of an adviser or consultant, but he never really played on our team."[9]

Still, as the flame at the Los Angeles Memorial Coliseum faded, Kahanamoku could look back on one of the most eventful and inspiring Olympic careers in modern history. In his first appearance, in the 1912 Stockholm Olympics, he overcame daunting odds just to reach the tryouts on the mainland. He barely eluded disqualification in Stockholm before defeating a high-quality field of international swimmers, bringing glory and publicity to Hawaii and reenergizing American aquatics after the retirement of Charles Daniels.

He endured the cancellation of the 1916 Olympics, when he was at his physical peak, and maintained his amateur status despite numerous offers and temptations to cash in on his fame and turn pro. His perseverance was rewarded at the 1920 Olympics, when he led a Hawaiian juggernaut that swept the war-ravaged opposition in the chilly waters of Antwerp. In 1924, when he was thirty-three years old, he was still fast enough to finish second to compatriot Johnny Weissmuller, accurately acclaimed as the best swimmer of the first half of the twentieth century. His loss to Weissmuller, who was then in his prime, was perhaps more impressive than his showing at the 1920 Olympics.

His legacy extends beyond three gold medals, two silver medals, world records, and quadrennial controversies. He was the first Pacific Islander (and the first from the Pacific Rim) to achieve Olympic stardom, making him among the first non-white athletes to win international acclaim. He impressed fans, royalty, and the press not only with his times but with his grace and élan. Kahanamoku later said that his most cherished memento was the oak wreath that he personally received from King Gustaf V in Stockholm, tangible evidence that the beachboy from Waikiki had attained Olympic immortality.

Not long after his return from Los Angeles, Kahanamoku's post at Honolulu city hall was eliminated. He was offered another job with less pay, but he declined after discovering what his new title would be. "I would have stayed despite the salary cut," he said, "but when they decided to make me janitor it looked like an invitation to get out."[10]

One Democratic senator in the Hawaii Territory proposed giving Kahanamoku a pension of $350 a month for the rest of his life. This succeeded in turning Duke, a Republican appointee, into a political football. The Democrats "kicked Duke out of the city hall," the *Honolulu Star-Bulletin* argued, and then concocted the proposal to cover up "the shameful manner" in which they treated him."[11]

Kahanamoku declined to accept the pension. He then took over management of two Union Oil service stations, one in the Nuuanu area of Honolulu and one in Waikiki opposite the Royal Hawaiian hotel. "I did it because it was something to do," he shrugged. "The president of the company asked me if I wanted a job and I said, 'Heck yes, I'm not too proud to pump gas.'"[12]

He hung up a surfboard with his name emblazoned on it to catch the attention of passing motorists, and he took out newspaper advertisements in order to promote the business. He projected enthusiasm as he checked oil, wiped windows, and changed tires. Others saw his status as a massive comedown. A popular verse mocked him, noting that "the champion of Oahu" is now "pumping gasoline."[13]

Perhaps in response, songwriter Sol Bright and his "Holly-waiians" (featuring lap-steel guitar master Sol Hoopii) recorded "Duke Kahanamoku," an upbeat *hapa-haole* ditty that paid tribute to the swimmer with lyrics in English and Hawaiian. Kahanamoku is the "king of swimmers famous of the sea/mermaid beauties keep him company," and is "*kaulana* [celebrated] throughout the good *honua* [planet earth]," before the song concludes: "*Oi'a no'e ka'oi.*" ["He is the best."][14]

Kahanamoku's retirement from swimming did little to diminish his competitiveness. In May of 1934, he sailed from Honolulu to California on the *Manuiwa*, a sixty-foot staysail schooner owned by Harold G. Dillingham of the Pearl Harbor Yacht Club. Duke then helped ready the *Manuiwa* for a return voyage as an entry in the storied Transpacific Yacht Race (Transpac).

Duke and the rest of the crew were on deck on July 4 as they set sail in a light breeze from San Pedro, the port city south of Los Angeles, with the finish 2,225 miles away at the Diamond Head buoy off Oahu. A few days later, they encountered the "Pacific High," the airstream that blows strong and typically turns the Transpac into a downwind ride. The winds chased the *Manuiwa* west; Dillingham radioed about halfway across that they had moved so rapidly, they "worried about where our competitors may be."[15]

Thankfully, all of the yachts arrived safely. The *Manuiwa* did not cross the finish line first, but the trim schooner was placed first after corrective handicaps were tallied, in 13 days, 12 hours, 30 minutes, and 51 seconds, becoming only the second Hawaiian-owned yacht to win the biennial Transpac since its debut in 1906. While the victory wasn't as personally gratifying as his swimming triumphs, Kahanamoku wore a huge, weary grin after he and Dillingham were festooned with many *lei*.

25

Crewing for Harold G. Dillingham put Duke Kahanamoku in close quarters with one of Hawaii's most well-connected families. Harold's older brother, Walter, was considered the most powerful man in the Hawaii Territory. He owned the companies that had dredged the coral beds across the channel at Pearl Harbor and turned it into a modern base for the U.S. Navy, with room enough for the largest warships. He was also responsible for the dredging of the Ala Wai Canal that had transformed Waikiki into a tourist haven. Of course, Dillingham was savvy enough to buy chunks of real estate in Waikiki and turn a tidy profit once the property values there skyrocketed.

Not long after the victory of the *Manuiwa*, President Franklin Delano Roosevelt arrived in Honolulu on the USS *Houston*. Kahanamoku was chosen to head the welcoming party. Dressed in traditional garb that was symbolic of Kamehameha the Great, he led a flotilla of outrigger canoes that escorted the first sitting American president to visit Hawaii. Then, while President Roosevelt, a former assistant secretary of the navy, inspected the base at Pearl Harbor and congratulated his Harvard classmate Dillingham about the Transpac, Duke gave surfing lessons to two of President Roosevelt's sons, John and Franklin Jr.

Duke later brought his mother to attend a reception for the president. "When we came to the receiving line," Duke said, "and I introduced him to my mother, [FDR] said to me, 'I remember you very well. Saw you in New York [at a victory parade after the Olympics], saw you when you came out to meet me.' He had a very good memory, from what I hear. He remembers everybody."[1]

Kahanamoku's political connections soon extended beyond surfing with the president's sons and yachting with the *haole* elite. In the tense period on

Oahu following the two Massie-related trials, Kahanamoku was persuaded to run for elected office. He had dabbled in politics once before, losing a bid for the board of supervisors on the Republican ticket. This time, in the fall of 1934, Duke ran for sheriff of the city and county of Honolulu on the Democratic ticket.

He gave up the gas stations—a move he later regretted financially—and faced off against incumbent Charles Rose in the Democratic primary. Rose attacked Kahanamoku for his lack of experience, while Duke leaned on his upstanding reputation and Olympic glory. He enjoyed meeting with the people but not talking policy. He delivered his stump speech in both English and Hawaiian and kept his remarks brief, oftentimes under one minute. "Talk less," he said.[2]

Friends in the press supported his campaign. "[Duke] will never be a go-getter, I am afraid," Doc Adams wrote in the *Honolulu Advertiser*. "He probably hasn't even got a matched pen and pencil vest-pocket set. But somehow you can't help admiring his way of doing business. If I were his press agent I'd mention somewhere in my campaign material that a man who was a world famous athlete for years and in all that time never tried to figure out a way to pad an AAU expense account, ought to be a rather trustworthy person with whom to entrust the keys of the County jail."[3]

Kahanamoku narrowly defeated Charles Rose in a hard-fought primary and then rolled to victory over Republican Pat Gleason in the general election by about 3,000 votes. "He's Sheriff Duke Now," read the headline, and he immediately started a habit of buying postelection advertisements addressed to the people of Oahu. "Thank you for the great honor you have bestowed on me," one read. "I shall try to be worthy of your confidence. If at any time you are disturbed by things that seem to happen at the jail or office, please see me. I'm sure things can be straightened out to your satisfaction. Thank you and *Mahalo*."[4]

He took the oath of office in a conservative suit, his mother proud that her son was settling down and following in the law enforcement path of her late husband. The position carried prestige, not to mention a steady paycheck, but Kahanamoku had little policy-making authority as sheriff. He was responsible for the mundane tasks that keep the wheels of justice turning: serving summonses, overseeing the city and county jail and the bailiffs at the district courts, inspecting weights and measures, and supervising the morgue.

His first major decision was to extend an olive branch and appoint Charles Rose as his chief deputy. This backfired when Rose and his son were found to be complicit in numerous misdeeds and had to be sacked. Duke's foremost initiative was campaigning for the replacement of the ancient prison at Iwilei, which was so dilapidated that inmates routinely made their escape. He presented lawmakers with several potential locations for a modern facility. With public expenditures still restricted during the Great Depression, however, he was unsuccessful in persuading the legislature to allocate funds for the project.

As Kahanamoku scouted possible sites for a new jail and planned his reelection bid for sheriff, mother Julia's health worsened. He had taken her to lunch on Mother's Day, only to hear from sister Kapiolani and brother Sam soon afterward that she was feeling very low. By the time Duke reached home on the evening of June 4, 1936, she had passed away.

Julia was sixty-nine years old. She had had twelve children and had raised nine of them to adulthood, six of them men. In her quiet, devout, and unassuming way, she had been the bedrock of the family, especially following the death of her husband. She had fiercely supported Duke as he pursued his swimming career, made movies in Hollywood, and entered public service—just as she had supported her other children.

"Twelve of us kids, look at our mother," Louis said. "Small, little woman. . . . Oh, my mother was such a queen. She would never hurt us boys."[5]

The family assembled for a viewing at Williams Mortuary. Brothers, sisters, and cousins talked story, laughed, and cried together. They held a private service the next afternoon at Oahu Cemetery, next to their father's grave site, singing favorite songs. They decorated the plot with two truckload's worth of fresh flowers.

In 1936, for the first time since 1912, Kahanamoku did not train for the Olympics. Berlin finally hosted the Olympic Games, twenty years after its aborted attempt in 1916. In place of Grunewald Stadium, built before the start of World War I, German chancellor Adolf Hitler spared no expense in building a massive stadium to showcase the growing power of the Third Reich. He hid overt signs of his Nazi agenda in a successful attempt to persuade American Olympic officials—including, most prominently, Avery Brundage, the organization's chieftain—not to boycott the Games.

During the entirety of the Berlin Summer Olympics (as well as at the 1936 Winter Olympics in Garmisch-Partenkirchen), Hitler blanketed the surroundings with swastikas. Global politics extended to the pool, where Japanese and American men dueled for supremacy. Japan took three of six gold medals (and ten total medals), with the United States winning two gold medals and five medals in total. The "emergence of Japan as a great swimming nation," noted one observer, "is paralleled in a way by the rise of Japan as a great power."[6]

Without the star power of Kahanamoku, Weissmuller, or Crabbe, coverage of swimming slipped in the United States. The most famous American swimmer in Berlin was Eleanor Holm, who sailed to Europe as the defending 100-meter backstroker. Because of her excessive partying en route to Germany, Brundage banned her from swimming in Berlin.

Jesse Owens and his four gold medals, and the myriad medals won by other African American track stars, were the talk of the 1936 Olympics. But when the sprinter returned home, hailed as a national hero for humiliating Hitler and debunking Aryan propaganda, Owens would find that, like Kahanamoku and Thorpe before him, athletic glory did not guarantee him a decent job.

Decathlon gold medalist Glenn Morris, who was white, replaced Weissmuller as Tarzan, starring with Eleanor Holm in *Tarzan's Revenge* for 20th Century Fox. Owens was forced to race against horses to earn money. "Hollywood had no roles for a black Tarzan that Owens could fill," wrote one commentator.[7]

Notwithstanding his ongoing frustration with the conditions at the termite-infested jail, the job of sheriff suited Duke. The chores were not overly taxing, and the title impressed the tourists. He looked the part, with the gray at his temples adding a distinguished accent to his still-fit physique. Approaching fifty years old and still single, he was among the most eligible bachelors in Hawaii.

Journalist Ernie Pyle visited Hawaii in 1937 and noted that Kahanamoku "has kept his balance. He has never made a fool of himself. He has never stooped, nor lost his dignity. . . . [E]lecting Duke sheriff is about the only way Hawaii can reward one of its greatest sons for what he has been and what he is."[8]

Many residents viewed him as a unifying force. Physically imposing yet approachable, a figure to be trusted by everyone: *haole* and Asian, native and navy, *malihini* (newcomer) and *kamaaina* (long timer), wealthy and working class. He often ran for office unopposed and once found out about a primary victory when he was a passenger aboard a ship off Tahiti.

He took his duties as sheriff seriously. On trips to the mainland, Kahanamoku made a point of inspecting municipal jails. When he visited Alcatraz Island in San Francisco Bay, the warden informed him that, with the prison surrounded by water, criminals had little hope of escape. "He asked me if we had anything like it in Hawaii," Duke related, "and he seemed quite surprised when I said our main prison was built as far inland as we could get it. 'You see,' I explained, 'I am not the only Hawaiian who knows how to swim.'"[9]

Critics charged that the position was little more than a sinecure, a stratagem employed by the business elite to reward Duke's loyalty and co-opt his authentic Hawaiian roots to their law-and-order agenda. "Giving him the office of sheriff is merely to pay him a salary," one newspaper grumbled.[10]

Locals pointed out that Kahanamoku gave his brothers staff positions and that his underlings, including former baseball star F. Lang Akana and Leon Sterling (a cousin by marriage), handled the day-to-day operations. Duke shrugged, and he continued to be reelected every two years, like clockwork.

Soon there was talk about erecting a statue of him. Lew Henderson, who had accompanied Kahanamoku on his first trip to the mainland in 1912, organized an interisland effort "to commemorate the living ideals and clean sportsmanship exemplified by Hawaii's beloved swimmer."[11]

A renowned sculptor of athletes, R. Tait McKenzie, was commissioned to create a seven-foot bronze statue of Kahanamoku. Duke had posed for McKenzie at his Philadelphia studio back in 1912, before the Stockholm Olympics, when McKenzie snapped photos, took measurements of his body, and made a small sketch model. The artist proclaimed at the time that Kahanamoku was the finest physical specimen that he had ever encountered.

A twelve-inch version of the proposed $18,000 statue was displayed in Hawaii, and Henderson and "Dad" Center raised funds for its completion. They hoped to have it ready in time for the Hawaiian pavilion at the San Francisco World's Fair of 1939, a way to capitalize on Duke's popularity in bronze.

Kahanamoku scoffed at the idea. "Let that wait for a while," he told Ernie Pyle. "Wait till I'm dead."[12] But it was McKenzie who suffered a heart attack and died suddenly in 1938. The project was shelved, much to Duke's relief.

One advantage of being sheriff was that Kahanamoku had time to swim, surf, or paddle every afternoon. While others were sipping cocktails on the *lanai* (veranda), he was playing in the water. A group of visiting Australians had brought him a gift of a long, wooden "surf-ski"—a cross between a kayak and a surfboard. The carved-out space in the middle of the sixteen-foot-long craft had room for a couple of passengers. The rest of it was solid wood.[13]

The surf-ski was big enough for Kahanamoku to take out friends and tourists into the ocean. While they sat comfortably, he balanced on the front and paddled with a long canoe oar. This was an early, crude form of stand-up paddling (SUP), a recreational activity that the Ah Choy family was credited with originating at Waikiki Beach years later.

Kahanamoku also welcomed the fruit of his efforts to spread surfing in California. He had seeded the movement with his surfing displays and tutelage during the 1910s and 1920s; even the surfboards that he had shaped and left behind were put to use. A wave of young surfers, including Preston "Pete" Peterson, Lorrin "Whitey" Harrison, and Gene "Tarzan" Smith, integrated Duke's lessons and boosted surfing in Southern California in the 1920s and 1930s, abandoning places that were ruined because of construction or other issues (Long Beach, Corona del Mar) and establishing new epicenters in places like San Onofre, Palos Verdes, and Malibu.

Like Tom Blake and Sam Reid before them, they felt a calling to come to Hawaii, to experience the cradle of surfing, to soak up the local knowledge of Kahanamoku, his brothers, and the other beachboys. This generation was not content to stay within the cozy confines of Waikiki, however, and they joined with other exceptional and daring surfers in Hawaii—including Wally Froiseth, George Downing, Goodwin Murray "Buzzy" Trent, and John Kelly, among others—to challenge themselves at Makaha, tucked away on Oahu's West Shore, where wintertime swells created massive waves. A courageous few—some called them foolhardy—ventured further, to the unexplored wilds of Oahu's North Shore.[14]

These pioneers also experimented with shaping their boards differently and using lighter materials. John Kelly narrowed the tail and rounded the bottom of the boards; when the "V tail" models were unveiled in 1937, they changed the modality of surfing so that surfers could "attempt larger, faster, and more exhilarating rides."[15]

Kahanamoku served as the connective tissue between the traditions and methodology of ancient Hawaiian wave riders and the innovative designs and hot-dogging action that were beginning to roil surfing. He was more mentor, consultant, and cheerleader than innovator; he stuck with his long redwood board and stayed close to Waikiki.

He still played the stern guru. Dorian "Doc" Paskowitz, who first came to Hawaii to surf in the late 1930s, wanted to make a good impression in the water. One day, Paskowitz recalled, he pointed to the break known as Public Baths and said, "'Duke, I think I'll paddle out there and catch a few waves.' Duke sat on his board like a statue: never said a word.

"I paddled out and then, all of a sudden, the sea began to rise and the waves swelled," Paskowitz continued. "I'd seen nothing like that. I lost my cool. Lost my courage. I paddled in, my tail between my legs. I looked over and there was Duke, like the Sphinx, unsmiling, looking straight at me. In his eyes was [a message] as clear as the church bells of Rome: 'Did you learn something out there, *haole* boy?'"[16]

26

Surfers weren't the only visitors flocking to Hawaii in the late 1930s. Even as war threatened Europe again, tourists were coming in droves. Hotels on Oahu bloomed like bougainvillea. Long-distance air travel was in its infancy, but the adventurous (and well-heeled) were arriving on Pan Am's China Clipper flying boat.

Many were seduced by the *hapa-haole* music that was heard on "Waikiki Calls," a new radio show hosted by Webley Edwards (who often called on Duke to say a few words to the audience). Visitors danced to "Blue Hawaii" and "Sweet Leilani," Bing Crosby's Oscar-winning song from the film *Waikiki Wedding*. They snapped up the latest trend in casual wear: aloha shirts and muumuus, in brightly printed colors, featuring island motifs of pineapples, hula girls, volcanoes, and tropical foliage.

One prominent visitor was a willowy, striking young woman with honey-colored hair and almond-shaped blue eyes. Doris Duke was the only child of business mogul James Buchanan Duke, known as "Buck," and Nanaline Holt Inman. Buck took over his father's tobacco business and turned it into the American Tobacco Company, a conglomerate that monopolized the cigarette market at the turn of the twentieth century. (Duke Kahanamoku was featured on a cigarette card produced by one of his companies, Pan Handle Scrap, in 1913.) Buck started Duke Power, which supplied electricity throughout North and South Carolina, and helped found Duke University in Durham.

After Buck died in 1925, his fortune was principally divided between his daughter and the Duke Endowment. Doris Duke became, at twelve years old, "the richest little girl in the world," with her share of the estate estimated at more than $50 million (the equivalent of about $7 billion today).

She was twenty-two years old when she came to Hawaii in the summer of 1935, on her honeymoon tour of the world with husband James Cromwell, a man with political aspirations who was many years her senior. She was suspicious of strangers, but Duke and the Kahanamoku family, including sister Beatrice, made the couple feel so welcome that they extended their stay.

Doris fell in with the Kahanamoku *ohana*—and fell in love with Hawaii. They showed her how to perform hula and how to surf. They sang together, went fishing together, and ate together. They made her laugh. Hawaii was far removed from the society balls and stuffy dinner parties that were the staple, and bane, of Doris's life on the mainland. She could throw on a pair of slacks and sandals and go window-shopping on Kalakaua Avenue without being harassed by society columnists. In turn Duke and his family experienced the warm embrace of an American princess who lived without any budget and who answered to no one.

She returned the next year and purchased a nearly five-acre parcel of prime oceanfront land in the exclusive neighborhood of Kaalawai, on a stretch of the Oahu coast overlooking Diamond Head. She spared no expense in designing her dream house with architect Marion Sims Wyeth and then, once she got the necessary permits from the Hawaii Territory, hiring a small army of contractors, landscape architects, horticulturalists, and laborers to execute her every whim.

Shangri La was the first million-dollar private home built in Hawaii. The modern Persian palace was fit for a capitalist's heiress, a shimmering vision in white marble and glass that was tastefully stocked with an amalgamation of priceless tiles, artwork, and tapestries imported from Syria, Morocco, India, Spain, Turkey, Egypt, and Iran.[1] White crushed coral was used for the long, private driveway. A mature coconut grove was meticulously transplanted on the property.

Beyond the glass doors of the spacious living room was an outdoor pool that was "only a few nautical feet smaller than Lake Erie."[2] The diving board had a built-in elevator that cost a reported $35,000. Doris hired Fred Cady, Duke's coach from the Los Angeles Athletic Club, to teach her how to dive properly. David Kahanamoku and his wife moved into the caretaker's home to oversee the estate.

At the ocean's edge was a break wall and private harbor. A motor launch transported Doris and her surfboard around the point to Waikiki, a couple of miles away, where Sam Kahanamoku taught her how to surf. Doris was delighted when she and Sam won first prize in a tandem surfboard paddling race.

Sam and Doris were seen together often. He acted as her chauffeur, local liaison, and musical accompanist. When Doris decided to spend more time in Hawaii, and with Cromwell away on business, the pair reportedly became lovers. According to several sources, Doris Duke Cromwell and Duke Kahanamoku also became paramours.

"The Duke taught me the wonders of massage," she is quoted as saying in *Too Rich*, a book cowritten by her godson and nephew. "He had these massive strong hands, they were just a little rough from the water, and he would massage me in a strong but gentle way. I would lay on my stomach and he would rub my shoulders and back. Every place. Then he would turn me over and kiss me. Need I say more? . . . He was a man."[3]

An unauthorized biography by Stephanie Mansfield, titled *The Richest Girl in the World*, reported that it was an open secret that Doris and Duke were together while Cromwell pursued his political career on the mainland. "She was living with the great swimmer Duke Kahanamoku and the scandal was he was black," according to Eleanor Davies Tydings, wife of U.S. senator Millard Tydings from Maryland. "In those days, you didn't pal around with black men. When she was with him, she never saw anybody. And nobody wanted to have anything to do with her. . . . Nobody ever went in [Shangri La] and nobody ever came out. She was there with Duke and that was it."[4]

It was Kahanamoku who reportedly gave her the nickname "*lahi lahi*," translated as "soft as the wind." Doris later joked that it was "the Hawaiian way of saying, 'Lay me, Lay me!'"[5]

Doris Duke Cromwell's wealth allowed her to have a lifestyle that was unattainable for ordinary people, apparently including her choice of lovers. That the world's richest heiress allegedly took both Duke and Sam as lovers shocked and enraged Hawaii's *haole* elite. The sniping grew worse when Doris Duke Cromwell discovered that she was pregnant in late 1939 or early 1940. The implication of this development was as vast as the manicured grounds of Shangri La. Her child would be the presumptive heir to an immense fortune.

It is unclear whether Doris Duke Cromwell knew who the biological father of her child was or whether she revealed this information to anyone. At the time his wife was pregnant, James Cromwell was in New Mexico, about to travel to the Democratic convention in Chicago. He was named as the father in the birth index files in Honolulu, but he later denied paternity. "Everybody naturally assumed she was pregnant by me," he said. "I knew it wasn't me."[6]

Amid reports that the Cromwells were estranged, her biographers have speculated that the likeliest candidates were Duke Kahanamoku, Sam Kahanamoku, or another of Doris's lovers (perhaps actor Errol Flynn). These accounts suggest that her most immediate concern about having the child was that it would complicate future divorce proceedings with Cromwell. Presumably, if she delivered a biracial baby, the world would know that her husband was not the birth father.

And so, according to her biographers, she decided to terminate her pregnancy. The method she purportedly used: to go surfing with Duke Kahanamoku. "The surf was high and dangerous," one account reads. "Together they waded into the surf and paddled beyond the breakers. Doris stood on the board and surfed more recklessly than ever in her life. Spectators gathered on the shore watching the woman with the long blond hair in the treacherous waters. Again and again she paddled out through the heavy surf. Her tall body was lifted into the air and smashed into the curl of the giant waves. She was bruised and battered but she continued surfing. . . . By the time they reached the gleaming marble mansion, there was blood seeping though the fabric of her bathing suit."[7]

It is impossible to verify the details of this bizarre story. It is far-fetched that a woman so wealthy that she could afford to hire the best doctors to treat her safely and discreetly, whether in Hawaii, on the mainland, or in Europe, would terminate her pregnancy in such a public manner. It is also doubtful that surfing, no matter how strenuously it is done, would cause an immediate miscarriage.

Doris Duke Cromwell did deliver a baby girl on July 11, 1940, at Queen's Hospital in Honolulu. The child, born prematurely, weighed three-and-a-half pounds. She was named Arden Cromwell. She died the next day.[8] (Doris Duke never gave birth to a child thereafter.)

A brief article about the birth and death of Arden Cromwell noted that Doris Duke "entered [the hospital] on June 13 after returning from the

Mainland."[9] In other words, she would have been under doctors' care for nearly a month before the delivery of her child, casting doubt about the veracity of the absurd surfing tale.

Determining who fathered her child is equally problematic, and not just because of her many purported lovers. If she believed that her child was going to be biracial, as several of her biographers have attested, the identity of the father could perhaps be narrowed down to Duke and Sam Kahanamoku. Those with knowledge of the situation in Hawaii, including family members, believe that Sam was the more likely candidate. They note that he was the father of two children by his first wife; he also fathered a biracial daughter, born out of wedlock, in 1935 (a revelation that came many years after Sam's death).[10] Older brother Duke, on the other hand, apparently never fathered any children.

As the *Honolulu Advertiser* story indicated, Doris Duke Cromwell had recently returned to Oahu. She did not live at Shangri La for long stretches during 1939–40, including the crucial months preceding Arden's birth, when she was vacationing in Europe and staying at estates on the mainland. An examination of her travel itinerary during this time, preserved among her papers at Duke University, as well as an examination of Duke Kahanamoku's own diaries and date books kept at the Hawaii State Archives, indicate that it would have been nearly impossible for Doris Duke and Duke Kahanamoku to have conceived a child at that time.[11]

Another consideration casts doubt about the Duke-Duke configuration. Kahanamoku himself was involved in a serious relationship at this juncture. In fact, he and Nadine Alexander, a dance instructor at the Royal Hawaiian Hotel, were married on August 2, 1940—less than a month after the birth and death of Arden Cromwell. Doris Duke Cromwell herself attended the wedding; her date was Sam.

Would Duke Kahanamoku have married Nadine Alexander mere weeks after his child with another woman had died? Was their marriage a sham to protect Doris Duke Cromwell from scandal, as some have speculated?

From what is known about Duke Kahanamoku and from what is known about the dating history he enjoyed with his future wife, that scenario seems highly unlikely.

27

Nadine Alexander liked to say that she fell in love with Duke Kahanamoku before she met him. As a teenager in the 1920s, she was reading a popular movie magazine and happened upon a photograph of Douglas Fairbanks and Mary Pickford on the beach with Duke. "I thought, 'THAT's the man!'" she gushed.[1]

She was born in Cleveland in 1905, the daughter of entertainer parents. Her mother was with the Melbourne Opera Company, while her father was an American vaudeville performer. They met and married when he was touring Australia. Nadine spent much of her youth in Cincinnati. She eloped with her first husband when she was young. After the marriage ended in divorce, she traveled the world.

Nadine (pronounced "Nah-DEEN") was trained as a musician, but dance became her métier after she settled in New York City. She performed as a showgirl and then had her own ballroom act with a partner. She joined the Arthur Murray dance studio to learn how to be an instructor before Maya Boleyn recruited her to teach ballroom dancing at the Royal Hawaiian Hotel.

She arrived in Honolulu after Christmas in late 1938, planning to stay for one year. As she was getting ready to disembark, she caught sight of "a very good-looking dark man and this beautiful blonde girl next to him." Her companion said, "That's Sargent Kahanamoku, Duke Kahanamoku's brother," and Nadine immediately flashed back to the memory of her teenage crush. She thought, "That's the person I want to meet. Duke Kahanamoku."[2]

Nadine settled in at the Royal Hawaiian Hotel and tutored the Dillinghams and other *haole* families on footwork and rhythm. "I came over here to teach the missionaries how to dance," she quipped.[3] She couldn't help but run into the ubiquitous Kahanamoku brothers, all except Duke.

Finally, brother Sam introduced them in 1939. Their first date was dinner at Wo Fat's chop suey restaurant in Chinatown.

Duke was forty-nine years old; Nadine was thirty-four years old. She was vivacious, petite, pretty, and worldly. He calmed her fear of deep water, guided her into the ocean, and taught her how to surf. She led him out on the dance floor and showed him all the moves: rumba, tango, fox trot, the shag, the Lambeth Walk, and, later, the cha-cha-cha. He called her "Laka," after the goddess of hula.

"He was such a wonderful dancer," Nadine said. "He always said he had natural rhythm. We used to dance at the Royal Hawaiian for our pleasure and people would stop dancing just to watch us on the floor. He loved it when everyone would watch us."[4]

Local newspaper reporters noticed the budding romance and speculated that Norma Allen (her professional name) had snared Hawaii's most eligible bachelor. Kahanamoku issued a curt denial. "Why can't a fellow be seen with a girl without someone marrying him off right away?" he said. "Just forget about this marrying business."[5]

Duke was smitten. He had enjoyed numerous flings and romances, both in Hawaii and on the mainland, but for much of his adult life, he had focused on his swimming career. Now, approaching fifty years old and comfortably settled in the sheriff's office, the time seemed right to settle down.

Nadine, meanwhile, was said to be entertaining a marriage offer from a wealthy, younger man. She informed Duke about this. He responded, "Baby, come home," and she did. She let him know that an earlier miscarriage would make it impossible for them to have children. He said, "No, I don't want any."[6]

Their wedding was supposed to take place at the home of Chris Holmes, a wealthy friend of Duke's (and an heir to the Fleishman's Yeast fortune), but they realized that they would have to invite everyone on Oahu. So, instead, they snuck off to Kona, on the Big Island of Hawaii, and were married in a private affair at Mokuaikaua Church, the oldest in the Islands. Territorial Senator Francis I'i Brown, Duke's close friend, and Brown's girlfriend, hula dancer Winona Love, arranged the details.

The beaming bride wore a stylish dress, with matching hat, purse, and heels, and dozens of strands of white *pikake* (jasmine flower) that the groom draped around her neck. The guest list was small. Duke's oldest sister Bernice attended with her future husband, Gilbert Lee. Doris Duke Cromwell came with brother Sam (although Nadine later claimed the pair crashed the nuptials).[7]

Afterward, Francis Brown and Duke went off spearfishing, leaving Nadine behind in little more than a shack for fishing nets. "If you can imagine spending your honeymoon on two army cots that didn't even fit together," she laughed. "That was my honeymoon."[8]

Some in Nadine's family disapproved of her choice, "as if I had married an Australian aborigine,"[9] she said. She also endured evil looks and jibes from concerned *tutu* (grandmothers). "I remember they'd come up and point their fingers at me, 'Now you take care of our boy,'" she recalled. "Things like that. Warning me. I don't think they approved of him marrying a *haole*.[10]

Kahanamoku, too, was accused of betraying his heritage by marrying outside his race. Cynics snickered that, after the years spent acting in "*Haole*-wood" and competing for the Outrigger Canoe Club, Duke was permanently "*haole*-fied." Those jibes intensified when, right before the 1940 election, he switched his allegiance from Democrat to Republican, the de facto party of Hawaii's business interests.

"It's the most disgusting betrayal I've ever heard of," Democratic Party representative Arthur Trask said. "At the height of his fame as an athlete Duke tried to run for the board of supervisors as a Republican and was defeated. He came to us and we helped him and have elected him sheriff every time he has run.... You can say I am a very much disillusioned young man."[11]

Duke's bride attempted to take the fall. "His going over to the Republicans is all my fault," Nadine insisted. "I'm a strong Republican. You can blame me."[12] Her public loyalty notwithstanding, political insiders believed that it was Senator Francis Brown who counseled Duke to switch parties.

Kahanamoku easily won reelection in 1940 despite the flap. He maintained his GOP affiliation for the rest of his political career and made it his mission to push the Republicans to improve the public beaches and to build better parks and playgrounds.

The charge that Kahanamoku had, in effect, switched sides culturally is more nuanced. Duke learned to straddle different worlds during childhood, when pro-American forces took over the governance of Hawaii and changed the course of his life. This continued during the years he spent competing on the mainland (and in Australia and Europe) and performing in the movies, when he was often the only nonwhite person present. He became comfortable in this position, which gave him the opportunity to do what others could not: become a member of the Outrigger Canoe Club, hold the office of sheriff, and marry a white, divorced woman.

It's fair to say that, in gaining a level of fame that few swimmers or surfers have achieved, Kahanamoku grew apart from his roots. It's also true that, as a public and potent symbol of Hawaii, as someone who incorporated its past and its present, Duke was unwaveringly and ardently pro-Hawaii. His beliefs affected the culture such that the mainstream establishment moved to embrace him and his Hawaiian-ness.

Waterman Buffalo Keaulana remembers watching Kahanamoku going about his business in Waikiki as "a lot of *haole* just rush in and try to ask him questions. A lot of people like to be next to him. We stay away and let him be. The only time that you could really talk to him is when you were out in the ocean, when you're surfing or paddling, and then you say something."[13]

Duke and Nadine were deeply in love, but they were very different. He didn't know the whereabouts of all his trophies and medals. She saved every newspaper article published about him and every handwritten note that he left her, even ones as innocuous as, "I took $2 from your purse." She liked to gab about Hollywood; he was the silent type. She cooked him elaborate meals with fancy sauces. He shrugged and reached for the ketchup. Then he washed the dishes afterward.

They were a "very odd couple," said family friend Kenneth Brown, a nephew of Francis Brown. "Don't know how they got along together."[14]

"She was really kind of a party gal and Duke didn't care that much about all those parties and whatnot because he'd really rather be in the water," recalled Kimo McVay, Duke's manager in the 1960s. "It's that's simple."[15]

One day, Buster Crabbe remembered, he was on the beach with Duke and watching him sift handfuls of sand through his fingers. "A beachboy came and said, 'Your wife is on the phone. She wants to know when you're coming home to dinner,'" Crabbe said.

There was a pause. "'Tell her I haven't finished counting the sand yet,' Kahanamoku said."[16]

The couple moved into his rental place at the base of Diamond Head. Nadine soon realized that, when Duke had informed her that he was not wealthy, he was telling the truth. "Little did I know that not only was he poor, but he was also in debt. He had bills a mile high," she said.[17]

Indeed, while Kahanamoku's fame attracted promising endorsement opportunities, such arrangements did not translate into substantial revenue. In 1937 he signed a five-year contract with Branfleet, an apparel firm owned by Nat Norfleet and George Brangier. Branfleet was one of several upstart companies hoping to profit from the trend of "aloha shirts," the florid-patterned, garishly colored resort wear that tailor Ellery Chun had concocted at his clothier shop on King Street.

Chun's goods were custom-tailored. Branfleet produced factory-made shirts, muumuus, and swim trunks in a rough cotton weave that resembled hand-loomed linen. The company agreed to pay royalties on sales of its Duke Kahanamoku and Kahala lines. However, while Kahanamoku brought significant publicity to Branfleet whenever he was photographed wearing its products, his earnings over the length of the deal amounted to a pittance.

In September of 1940, just after the couple returned from their honeymoon, Kahanamoku was given a first-look opportunity at a new sporting-goods accessory for the water. He had met Owen Churchill in Southern California when they were members of the same yacht club. They crossed paths at the 1932 Los Angeles Olympics, where Churchill was captain of the U.S. yachting team and helmed the *Angelita* to the gold medal in the 8-meter class.

Afterward, during travels to the South Pacific, Churchill observed that swimmers and divers in Tahiti attached crudely constructed fins, woven from leaves, to their feet to increase their speed in the water. Churchill saw dollar signs. He returned home and developed "swim fins," which resembled the shape of the woven fins but were made from vulcanized rubber. He patented the invention, giving him the "exclusive right for manufacture and sale of anything that goes on the feet or hands for swimming aids."[18]

Churchill contacted Duke in the fall of 1940, as he was launching the business, with the idea that Kahanamoku's name and connections would help both of them. He sent Kahanamoku a pair of the swim fins and asked for assistance in introducing the "rubber feet" in Hawaii.

Kahanamoku tried them out in the water and replied enthusiastically in a letter to Churchill. "You have found something that the swimming public [will] take to like ducks," he wrote. "My wife was watching me, said that

I went like a streak."[19] In the same letter, Duke offered to be the exclusive sales agent of the swim fins in the Territory of Hawaii as well as in Australia and Japan. "You can draw up some kind of an agreement or contract," he wrote. "I would be very glad to handle this for you."[20]

Churchill declined the proposal, noting that "we cannot give any exclusive agencies." He offered Kahanamoku the opportunity to sell the swim fins on his own and make a $2 profit on every pair he sold. "With your reputation as a champion swimmer, and your social and business standing in the Islands," Churchill wrote, "you will sell most of the fins anyway and get the cream of the business."[21]

Kahanamoku delayed in responding to the offer, despite receiving at least one follow-up letter from Churchill. By December Churchill had gone ahead and appointed B. F. Schoen as exclusive sales agent for the swim fins in the Territory.

Feeling betrayed, Kahanamoku wrote back in early 1941 that he had "abandoned any idea of continuing plans for advancing the fins.... [Schoen] should do the 'pushing' and advertising of your fin."[22]

The two communicated no further. Churchill's swim fins became standard equipment for snorkelers and scuba divers, not to mention swim instructors and trainers, spear fishermen, and just about anyone working or having fun in the water. The venture netted Churchill a fortune.

With little income besides his sheriff's salary, Duke and Nadine turned to a friend for assistance. None other than Doris Duke Cromwell, who was underwriting her soon-to-be ex-husband's doomed bid for the U.S. Senate in New Jersey, advanced the couple the necessary $5,000 so that they could buy their own home. "She was kind enough to loan us the money, and she didn't want interest," said Nadine, who noted that she and Duke paid back every cent.[23]

Kahanamoku had one request as they searched for a new place. He wanted to live near the water. They chose a three-level, five-bedroom house at 114 Royal Circle, in an upscale enclave known as Kahala, not far from Shangri La, with space enough for an enormous bed made from *koa* wood. Black Point, as the neighborhood is called, was exclusively *haole* before Duke quietly integrated the area.

Sunlight filled the bank of large landscape windows that overlooked the ocean, and Duke was comforted by the sight and sound of water in motion.

He delighted in the views of Molokai, Lanai, and Maui, and he liked to watch the waves steaming toward Waikiki Beach, knowing he was just a few minutes' drive from his surfboard.

As the couple settled into Black Point, war was raging across Europe. Mainland reporters were speculating about when the United States was going to join the conflict against Germany, while Hawaiian-based newspapers focused on concerns over Japan's aggressive encroachment in the Pacific.

If you had asked Kahanamoku about the "Japanese threat" at that time, chances are he would have talked about the fast times the Japanese swimmers had recorded since the 1932 Olympics. He had witnessed their improvement when they came to Hawaii to test themselves against the local teams, and they were the early favorites to sweep the swim program at the 1940 Tokyo Olympics.

Japan bowed out as host, however, and soon the 1940 Olympic Games were called off due to the outbreak of war in Europe. Kahanamoku was chaperoning a group of Hawaiian swimmers on the mainland when he heard about Japan's withdrawal. He was particularly disappointed to hear about the cancellation of the 1940 Olympics, since he had missed out on competing in 1916 because of World War I. He knew all too well that athletes never can regain those lost, prime years.

Still, there was much for him to be excited about. Hawaiian swimmers were making their own splashy comeback, winning a third consecutive national title under coach Soichi Sakamoto (who was of Japanese ancestry). Sakamoto's scrappy young men of the Three Year Swim Club, who sometimes practiced in plantation irrigation ditches on Maui, viewed Duke as their model for success. Like Buster Crabbe before them, they memorized his times and yearned to match his Olympic accomplishments. Duke allowed his name to be used for the first annual outdoor Duke P. Kahanamoku Swimming Meet, held at the War Memorial Natatorium, in August of 1937, which gave local prospects, male and female, an opportunity to shine at home.

The Outrigger Canoe Club had completed construction of a new complex on Waikiki Beach, with a waterfront clubhouse, ample space for Duke's surfboards, and beach volleyball courts that were situated at the center of the action. It was exciting, too, that the multisport college kid from Pasadena,

Jackie Robinson of UCLA, was coming to Hawaii to play semipro football for the Honolulu Bears in the upcoming season.

Newly married to a smart and beautiful woman, with a secure job and a well-appointed home that offered sweeping views of his beloved Pacific, Kahanamoku was feeling content. It was the summer of 1941. Duke and Nadine were looking forward to a long period of peaceful bliss.

28

Morning sunlight was sneaking through the sheet of clouds hanging over Oahu as Duke and Nadine ate an early breakfast at the Snack Bar at the Outrigger Canoe Club. Duke was preparing for a yacht race later in the day, on a course that would take him from Waikiki Beach to Pearl City, site of the Pearl Harbor Yacht Club.

It was Sunday, December 7, 1941. A day like any other glorious day in Hawaii—until it wasn't.

"FDR WILL SEND MESSAGE TO EMPEROR ON WAR CRISIS," read the front page of that morning's *Honolulu Advertiser*.

The headline was soon yesterday's news. From carriers positioned about two hundred miles north of Hawaii, some three hundred and fifty Japanese fighters, torpedo planes, and dive-bombers were streaking toward Oahu, the distinctive red rising sun symbol visible on their wings as they hurtled down upon Battleship Row at Pearl Harbor, where the pride of the U.S. Navy was stationed, as well as the military installations at Hickam, Wheeler, Ewa, and Kaneohe.

So assured were Japan's pilots of their surprise attack that one of the pilots radioed the code word for success three times—"Tora, Tora, Tora"—even before the first bomb had landed at around 8 a.m.[1]

Billows of black smoke soon rose high above Pearl Harbor, accompanied by towering geysers of water caused by wayward bombs exploding in the sea. The sharp clap of antiaircraft guns mixed with the whinnying of dive-bombers strafing their targets. Sirens reverberated across Oahu. The stench of burning oil was overpowering.

Many residents initially mistook the clamor for the resumption of routine exercises conducted by the U.S. Navy. These maneuvers had been going on for months while high-level Japanese and American diplomats held meetings in Washington DC.

A simple message, repeated over and over, informed all of Hawaii that this was no drill. "This is the real McCoy! This is the real McCoy!" Webley Edwards said every few minutes on radio station KGMB, until the military ordered the popular disc jockey off the airwaves.

Kahanamoku made a phone call from the Outrigger Canoe Club to corroborate the news and then hurried back to tell Nadine: "Come on, baby, it's the real thing." They raced to City Hall. They could hear the blasts at Hickam and Wheeler, and they could see planes buzzing overhead. Kahanamoku went home to retrieve his gun.[2]

Rumors spread. The Japanese had landed at Diamond Head. The Japanese had stormed Waikiki. Questions went unanswered: Would the bombers return? Were enemy submarines lurking in the harbor? Could the United States protect Hawaii?[3]

Territorial governor Joseph Poindexter invoked the Hawaii Defense Act, which transferred powers to his office in the event of an emergency. A phone call from President Franklin D. Roosevelt, as well as pressure from the military, persuaded Poindexter to proclaim martial law that afternoon.

On Monday President Roosevelt went to Capitol Hill to address a joint session of Congress. "Yesterday, December 7, 1941—a date which will live in infamy—the United States of America was suddenly and deliberately attacked," he began, before asking Congress for a declaration of war. "Always will we remember the character of the onslaught against us," he said. "No matter how long it may take us to overcome this premeditated invasion, the American people in their righteous might will win through to absolute victory."[4]

Roosevelt's speech lasted six minutes. Less than an hour later, Congress voted to declare war on Japan. America had entered World War II.[5]

With charge of the coroner's office, Kahanamoku was witness to the devastation after the attack on Pearl Harbor. The county morgue was a small facility that was rented from Queen's Hospital. It had only four freezing compartments; Duke called it "inadequate" during normal times.

These were anything but normal times. Immediately afterward, when the death toll was unknown, Kahanamoku had the sobering task of inspecting Koko Head Park and nearby Kahauloa Crater with a bulldozer crew, in case a mass burial site was needed for upwards of 20,000 casualties. Thankfully, that wasn't necessary, but Kahanamoku and other officials spent sleepless days and nights scrambling to assess the destruction.[6]

Approximately 2,400 personnel were dead (including several dozen civilians), with another 1,150 or so wounded. Some twenty ships along Battleship Row were sunk or heavily damaged, with the USS *Arizona* sustaining the most serious casualties. Nearly two hundred aircraft were lost, many of them destroyed while they were still on the ground. Experts agreed that the casualties and damage would have been far worse if not for the fact that the U.S. fleet of aircraft carriers was absent from Pearl Harbor on December 7.

Hawaii became a war zone overnight. Lieutenant General Walter Short assumed command, and the military took over every aspect of governance, including the civilian courts. The right of habeas corpus was suspended. Hundreds of Japanese American citizens were taken prisoner and confined at the Honouliuli internment camp on Oahu, not far from Pearl Harbor.

A curfew was established and strictly enforced, with all homes blacked out after dark. Cars that were used in the evening had their headlights painted black except for a small spot. Gas masks were distributed. American currency was replaced with specially printed bills. Schools were closed for months. Gas rationing began. Censors read all incoming and outgoing mail.

"Oh, it was awful, just terrible," Nadine said. "It was miserable at the beginning."[7]

Tourism, the lifeblood of Waikiki, came to an abrupt halt. The Royal Hawaiian Hotel was leased to the U.S. Navy. The U.S. Army took over the Natatorium swimming facility for training purposes. Fort Ruger, on Diamond Head, was fortified with machine guns and sentries. Doris Duke Cromwell, who was stranded outside of Hawaii, permitted officers to use the grounds of Shangri La. Civilians pitched in to dig slit trenches along the shore and install rows of barbed wire along every beach, for protection against a possible invasion.

During World War I, Kahanamoku knitted scarves and raised money for the Red Cross by giving swimming exhibitions on the mainland. He was more directly involved this time, even though under martial law the Office of the Military Governor superseded his authority as sheriff. He worked closely with the Office of Civilian Defense, a wing of the Territorial government that supervised and coordinated transportation, communications, emergency, medical, and other services for residents.

One of his jobs was to help organize a citywide alert that simulated the conditions of an air attack on Honolulu during daylight hours. Girl Scout troops were recruited to act as the "casualties," under the chilling notion that "any air raid would probably include high altitude bombing—if not being confined entirely thereto—the innocent bystanders, the civilians in the city, would get what missed the target."[8]

Nadine went back to school to learn typing, bookkeeping, and shorthand. After gaining experience as a secretary at St. Andrew's Cathedral rectory, she worked in the censorship division at the post office. She was hired with Special Services, first at Maluhia and then at Fort Ruger. There was little opportunity for her and Duke to go dancing, but she volunteered at homecoming dances for marines and sailors, for officers and enlisted men, in order to help with morale.

Life during wartime eventually settled into normal routine. Kahanamoku could not leave the Islands, but he met with friends who were serving in Hawaii (swimmer Norman Ross, for one) or who were participating in the war effort. Director John Ford came over from Hollywood to produce a short movie for the U.S. Navy titled *December 7th* and then filmed a documentary, *The Battle of Midway*, in June of 1942, which won an Academy Award.

As the threat of another attack diminished, particularly after the Battle of Midway, rules governing curfews and other activities were relaxed. Duke and other swimmers and surfers gained access to the beach at Waikiki through openings "installed in the barbed wire," according to historian Barbara Del Piano, although "they were under strict orders from the military to be out of the water by sundown."[9]

"[The military] stopped us from everything," surfer Rabbit Kekai recalled. "They even stopped us going outside. We surfed, but they had a curfew. They shoot bullets at us. We had to catch the wave and come on in. Gotta get in. We used to throw firecrackers at them."[10]

The war "cramped surfing's style for long, too long," Kahanamoku noted. "Most all of the able-bodied young men who had been contributing to the fast development of the sport wound up in the military service or in defense plants. It was a time of vacuum for surfing."[11]

Kahanamoku turned to canoe racing. The president of the Outrigger Canoe Club, Walter Macfarlane, died unexpectedly during the war, and members decided to organize a regatta in his memory. Duke wanted to participate, but he needed to find five dedicated crew members.

He found them on the beach, sitting in front of the club. "Duke came up and said, 'Hey, you kids look like you are in good shape,'" Tom Arnott said. "'Do you want to learn how to paddle a canoe—really learn how to paddle a canoe?'"[12]

They soon discovered that Kahanamoku was a strict taskmaster. For training, they paddled all the way "from the old Outrigger along parallel to the beach up the Ala Wai Canal, back down the Ala Wai Canal, back up to the Outrigger," Arnott recalled. Then Duke had them circle a flag—positioned about a mile out in the ocean—and return to shore.

"We'd expect him to say, 'Right on, okay,'" Arnott said. "No way! We would go around again—and again—continuous to where we were in absolutely fantastic shape. No one could touch us."[13]

Kahanamoku took them out in a heavy canoe until about two weeks before the race, remembered paddler Thad Ekstrand. Then they switched to a lighter model made of *koa* wood. "It was like practicing with a medicine ball and then playing with a volleyball," Ekstrand said. "It made the canoe really move."[14]

The main event of the first annual Walter Macfarlane Memorial Regatta, held on July 4, 1943, was the "Senior Six" race. Kahanamoku and his team—Arnott, Ekstrand, Bob Bush, Jim Fernie, and Jack Beaumont—acknowledged the cheers of Outrigger Canoe Club members as they carried their racing canoe, a sleek thirty-nine footer named the *Leilani*, to the water's edge.[15]

The four-mile course consisted of three laps around the flags set out in the ocean. Thousands of servicemen and residents lined the beach in front of the Outrigger Canoe Club as the crews set out from shore.

It was, fairly quickly, no contest. With Kahanamoku as steersman, the *Leilani* swamped the competition. They were awarded a large silver bowl for their efforts, which Walter Mac's mother filled with champagne. Duke and the boys took turns drinking from it, savoring a rare, pleasurable moment during an otherwise somber time.

The race was more than a one-off event. Kahanamoku trained with his crew and pushed them to stay in shape before eventually turning over the steersman's duties to Alan "Turkey" Love. In the eight years that "Duke's Boys" paddled together, they took home the trophy seven times.

"[Duke had] the time, the energy, and the know-how to take a bunch of kids and teach them the important things in life," Ekstrand said. "It's hard to explain the respect we had for him. He was a great guy—a big, solid guy. There was nothing small about him, especially his heart."[16]

Martial law in Hawaii continued throughout the war. As the threat of a second attack on the Territory faded, many residents, journalists, and politicians came to believe that the military government was overstepping its authority. "While fighting for democracy on a dozen fronts," a U.S. Department of the Interior solicitor wrote in December of 1942, "we have dictatorship, quite needlessly—almost by accident, in one vital part of the United States of America."[17]

The debate became the basis of a legal case, *Duncan v. Kahanamoku*, which was eventually decided by the United States Supreme Court. The dispute began innocuously enough. Lloyd Duncan was a civilian shipfitter who worked at the U.S. Naval Base at Pearl Harbor. He was arrested in February of 1944, after he got into a dispute with two marine sentries. He was tried at a provost court, presided over by a naval officer, and convicted of assault and battery. He was sentenced to six months at the Honolulu County jail under the custody of Sheriff Kahanamoku.

Duncan appealed to the U.S. district court for a writ of habeas corpus. He challenged the legal authority of the military tribunal, claiming that the dangers that led to the declaration of martial law had passed. Duncan's lawyer, former Territorial Attorney General J. Garner Anthony, argued that the trial "was not in accordance with the constitution nor laws of the territory of Hawaii and is null and void."[18]

Kahanamoku, as sheriff, was served with an order to show cause in the case in March of 1944. He passed the order to city-county attorney Jean Gilbert. The military government asked for the immediate dismissal of the petition, with Admiral Chester Nimitz and others arguing that Hawaii remained in "imminent danger" of attack.

The district court ruled in favor of Duncan. "Congress may give the Territory of Hawaii any form of government it may see fit, conformable to Constitutional provisions, but no one in the War Department has such lawful power," Judge Delbert Metzger noted.[19]

Another convicted civilian, stockbroker Harry White, then filed his own writ of habeas corpus. White had been arrested, tried, and convicted for embezzlement before a provost court in 1942. He was sentenced to five years in prison. He, too, was freed because of the writ.

Government attorneys took the White and Duncan cases to the U.S. Court of Appeals for the Ninth Circuit. In November, the district court rulings were reversed. The two petitioners were joined into one case, *Duncan v. Kahanamoku*, which was argued in front of the U.S. Supreme Court on, appropriately enough, December 7, 1945.

By a 6–2 vote, the U.S. Supreme Court overturned the judgment of the court of appeals. "Courts and their procedural safeguards are indispensable to our system of government," Justice Hugo Black wrote for the majority in February of 1946. "They were set up by our founders to protect the liberties they valued. . . . The phrase 'martial law' as employed in the [Organic] Act, therefore, while intended to authorize the military to act vigorously for the maintenance of an orderly civil government and for the defense of the island against actual or threatened rebellion or invasion, was not intended to authorize the supplanting of courts by military tribunals."[20]

The decision represented a victory for individual freedom as well as a stinging repudiation of the military's position. "War does not authorize or excuse the military arm of government in operating counter to the Constitution of the United States," the *Honolulu Star-Bulletin* commented. "That principle written into the laws of a free people has again been upheld by the highest tribunal in the land."[21]

Kahanamoku, it should be noted, served only as the nominal defendant. He had no active involvement in the arrests, trials, or convictions of the plaintiffs, or with the appeals process. He expressed no opinion about the trial or its outcome in his personal papers. His participation began and ended with his name. But with his name attached to the military's side, the perception lingered that he supported authoritative rule, even in the waning days of the war.

Duncan v. Kahanamoku was a landmark case that exposed the roughshod treatment that Hawaii experienced during the war. The territorial status was a "special brand" that the people of Hawaii "were coming to regard as an overwhelming disability," according to historian Gavan Daws. "In relation to Americans living on the mainland they were second class citizens still."[22]

29

By the time the U.S. Supreme Court issued its ruling in *Duncan v. Kahanamoku*, World War II was over. The conflict in Europe concluded first, after Germany surrendered in May of 1945. Then, on August 6, 1945, a B-29 aircraft called the *Enola Gay* dropped a nuclear bomb on the city of Hiroshima. Three days later a B-29 aircraft known as *Bockscar* dropped a nuclear bomb on Nagasaki. With the Soviet Union poised to join the Pacific conflict on the American side, Japan surrendered unconditionally on August 14, 1945.

V-J Day was joyous for Americans everywhere, but it was perhaps sweetest in Hawaii and on Oahu, in the place where the war began so abruptly for the United States in December of 1941, where so many soldiers, sailors, marines, and air force personnel were based during the war, and, sadly, where the remains of so many fallen comrades were now buried.

Spontaneous celebrations started along Kalakaua Avenue in Waikiki and continued throughout the night and the next several days. GIs waved American flags and loudly honked their horns from passing cars. Beachboys and businessmen embraced in grateful elation. Copious liquor flowed in every tavern even as the bells of St. Augustine church tolled.

Kahanamoku had to contend with a multitude of drunks on V-J Day, but even that was a pleasurable chore for the sheriff's office. He soon was welcoming returning veterans as they mustered out of the service via Hawaii. One such soul was Louis Zamperini. He was a standout miler for the University of Southern California who finished eighth in the 5,000 meters at the 1936 Berlin Olympics. He had hoped to be the first man to run a mile in less than four minutes, but his dreams were dashed when he joined the U.S. Air Force just before the attack on Pearl Harbor.

Zamperini was adrift for weeks in the Pacific after the B-24 bomber in which he was flying crashed in waters north of Oahu in May of 1943. He staved off shark attacks and starvation before he was captured by the Japanese and taken to a hellacious prisoner of war camp.

Declared missing, Zamperini was assumed to be dead. When he was discovered alive after Japan's surrender, he was hailed as a hero. His final stop before reaching Los Angeles, and home, was Honolulu. "Hawaii was utopia," he recalled. "The place was awash in booze and girls and activity."[1]

Kahanamoku invited Zamperini for lunch and brought him to the comforts of the Outrigger Canoe Club. The former Olympians then went for a canoe ride at Waikiki Beach—just the two of them. "It was a privilege," Zamperini said. "He could paddle like six guys. Such a powerful man, easy-going."[2]

Duke's presence soothed Zamperini. "He knew what had happened [to me]," he said. "Everybody knew what had happened. But he never asked me about the war or anything. He was a big, gentle giant. It was good."[3]

After V-J Day, and after the protective barbed wire was removed from the beaches of Waikiki, Kahanamoku kept active. He was reelected sheriff in 1946 and 1948, running unopposed both times. He continued his quixotic campaign for a new county jail and morgue, and supported the cause of statehood, perhaps the defining political issue facing postwar Hawaii.

The sheriff's base salary of $436.66 per month was hardly munificent, so with Nadine's prodding, he looked for other income streams. He went to Los Angeles in mid-1948 in order to play a small role in *Wake of the Red Witch*, a Republic Pictures feature starring the "other" Duke, John Wayne. Kahanamoku received $500 per week for portraying—what else?—a sarong-clad tribal chief from the South Pacific.[4]

Kahanamoku's five-year contract with apparel maker Branfleet had expired during the war. Insurance salesman Elmer Leterman advised Kahanamoku to sign a new licensing deal with Cisco Casuals in 1949. In exchange for exclusive rights to the name of Duke Kahanamoku, the company agreed to manufacture a specialty line of aloha-wear, with Cisco Casuals paying royalties of 3.5 percent of net shipments.

"At long last, the Duke's going to help the Duke," Leterman said, boasting that the deal offered him "security for the rest of his days."[5]

Kahanamoku took advantage of every opportunity to promote the clothing line. He attended a lunch held for President Harry S. Truman at the Pearl Harbor Officers' Club in 1950, a stopover for Truman en route to a meeting on Wake Island with General Douglas MacArthur regarding the Korean War. When Duke found out that President Truman liked aloha shirts, he requested that Cisco Casuals send a shipment of them to the White House. The next year, President Truman appeared on the cover of *Life* magazine, wearing a loud shirt and a wide grin, with the headline, "The President of the United States: The Evolution of a Wardrobe."

In 1950, Cisco Casuals dispatched Duke and Nadine to the mainland, accompanied by beachboy Chick Daniels, to market the multihued aloha shirts. It was Kahanamoku's first visit to New York City since 1924, when he stopped there after the Paris Olympics, and he took in the changes of a quarter of a century. His golfing companion, Babe Ruth, had recently died, and the hardball talk in New York City now focused on Jackie Robinson, Roy Campanella, and Don Newcombe, the three African American players starring for the Brooklyn Dodgers, after Robinson broke Major League Baseball's color barrier in 1947. Madison Square Garden had moved uptown, to 50th Street, a block or so from the Broadway restaurant owned by Duke's pal, boxer Jack Dempsey.

Duke and Nadine took in *South Pacific* on Broadway, ate oysters at Toots Shor's, and schmoozed with the press corps. "I gave [burlesque star] Gypsy Rose Lee a lei," Kahanamoku told columnist Earl Wilson. "I explained to her husband, Julio de Diego, that it is a custom to kiss someone when you give them a lei. He agreed, and I kissed his wife."[6]

Cisco Casuals received extensive publicity after Kahanamoku appeared on Arthur Godfrey's TV and radio programs. Duke showed off a "howling" shirt, shed his shoes, and performed hula as Godfrey donned his own aloha shirt and strummed the ukulele. The two became close; when Kahanamoku journeyed to the mainland during the 1950s and 1960s, whether it was for business or pleasure, he often stayed at the entertainer's ranch in Leesburg, Virginia. Duke nicknamed him *"Minoaka"*—"Smiling One"—and "clubbed him over the head" until Godfrey, who picked up the ukulele while he was in Hawaii during the war, learned to pronounce it correctly [oo-ku-lei-lee].[7]

Later that summer, when the Outrigger Canoe Club threw an all-day bash for Duke's sixtieth birthday, Godfrey flew to Hawaii. The entertainer admitted to having a fear of deep water until Kahanamoku "taught me to play in the sea, to body surf, to spout like a whale, to frolic like a porpoise. He taught me to relax and enjoy, to utilize the power of the wave, to live in his joyful, wonderful world of water. And I'm sure it was this fearlessness, born of his long, intimate life in the sea, which gave him his relaxed, enviable peace of mind."[8]

The birthday celebration constituted a perfect-day scenario for Duke: volleyball, swimming, and surfing in the morning; canoe racing and talking story with friends and family in the afternoon; steak fry mixed with dancing in the evening. "Dad" Center helped organize the festivities, while Nadine, Duke's sister Bernice, and brothers David, Sargent, and Bill mingled with guests Lew Henderson, Judge Harry Steiner, "Tough" Bill, "Splash" Lyons, and John D. Kaupiko.

"Too bad the day wasn't long enough so I could have gotten in my yachting, horseback riding and golf," Duke said.[9]

At sixty years of age, Kahanamoku had found stability in and out of the water. He and Nadine were happily married and shared a beautiful home in a place he called "the navel of the world." His job was not overly taxing and provided a steady, if unspectacular, income. He had ample time for recreation and kept a busy social schedule with friends and family.

The equilibrium in his life stood in sharp contrast to the plight of Jim Thorpe. Like many of his contemporaries, Kahanamoku believed that his Olympic teammate had been treated callously by American sports power brokers after the 1912 Stockholm Olympics, beginning with Glenn "Pop" Warner and James E. Sullivan and continuing with Avery Brundage. Thorpe did enjoy an excellent professional football career after Stockholm, and in 1950 the Associated Press selected Thorpe as the greatest athlete of the first half of the century, but his besmirched reputation and wounded pride were never repaired.

Thorpe struggled with alcoholism and finding steady employment after his sports career ended. His later years constituted a "dismal stretch of odd jobs, unpaid bills, bar fights, broken homes," according to one biographer.[10] In 1953, not long after Thorpe was "rediscovered" with the release of a movie about his life (starring Burt Lancaster), he died virtually penniless in a trailer home in Lomita, California. He was sixty-five years old.

The humiliation continued after his death. Thorpe was not buried in his birthplace, on native land in Oklahoma, but in Pennsylvania, in an area he probably never visited while he was alive, after his third wife made arrangements with two communities to merge and name themselves "Jim Thorpe," for the sole purpose of boosting business. In death the world's greatest athlete was reduced to being a tourist sideshow.

Kahanamoku mourned his friend's passing. The following year, on the day he turned sixty-four, Duke went surfing at Waikiki. Perhaps he was feeling mortal after Thorpe's death, but when he spotted local photographer Clarence Maki on the beach, Duke asked him if he had any shots left in his camera. Maki said he had a couple of frames remaining on the roll, so Kahanamoku requested that he take his picture.

They paddled out together at Castle's break. Kahanamoku kept going, caught a wave, and came straight toward Maki and the Rolleiflex camera that he carried inside a handmade waterproof housing. The black-and-white picture is widely considered to be the last known photograph taken of Duke while surfing.[11]

Kahanamoku had a cameo role in *Mister Roberts*, directed by John Ford and starring Henry Fonda and Jack Lemmon, and was reelected sheriff in 1954. Then, three months after President Dwight D. Eisenhower suffered a heart attack in 1955, Duke suffered his own heart attack. He was rushed to Queen's Hospital in serious condition and was kept in an oxygen tent.

Letters of support poured into the hospital. An Atlanta serviceman, Ralph Chambers, wrote that he had been stationed at Schofield Barracks in the early 1920s. He went to Waikiki and was "having a rough time with a surfboard and someone came to me and said, 'Let me show you how to ride it.' And for about 30 minutes you gave me lessons in surfboard riding. I didn't know who you was until someone spoke to you and said, 'Hello, Duke.' And then I was told you was [the] champion swimmer. I was real thrilled."[12]

Kahanamoku rallied, and after ten days, he was allowed to go home to Black Point. Nadine found herself playing nursemaid, a role that she had to become accustomed to. "[Duke] had a lot of sickness beginning in the '50s," she said. "He suppressed everything; he kept everything inside, which is bad. It gave him a stomach ulcer and, unfortunately, it was a bleeding ulcer."[13]

Doctors told Kahanamoku to cut down on his consumption of poi. Later, when his diet was restricted to salt-free foods, he would "cheat all the time," according to Nadine. "I'd be cooking things without salt and watching him like a hawk. He didn't like me for it either. In fact, that's the only time we would have words, because I'd say, 'Look, you're not supposed to eat that, it's got salt in it.' He'd say, 'Well, everything has salt in it.' He was very bad about that."[14]

Kahanamoku was hospitalized again for asthma but was hale enough to travel to Australia on the invitation of a former swimming rival, Frank Beaurepaire, who was one of the chief organizers of the 1956 Melbourne Olympics. It was a homecoming of sorts for Nadine, whose mother was Australian, while Duke was making his first trip there since his historic tour of 1914–15.

The Olympic Movement again had survived war, as well as the cancellation of the 1940 and 1944 Olympics, with the torch reignited in war-ravaged London in 1948. A teenager from central California, Bob Mathias, stunned the world by winning the decathlon in London. Keen-eyed statisticians noted that Jim Thorpe's performance in 1912 would have been good enough to earn him the silver medal in London, thirty-six years later.

Japan and Germany were barred from competing at the so-called Austerity Games of 1948, and so the United States easily regained its edge in the pool. One of the brightest U.S. stars was Hawaiian-born Bill Smith, who won gold medals in the 400-meter freestyle and the 4x200-meter relay. Smith was a member of the Three Year Swim Club, training under innovative coach Soichi Sakamoto, but his childhood inspiration was watching Kahanamoku. "I used to hang around the Natatorium because it was a fun place to go," he said. "A lot of kids went there, and Duke was our role model. We all wanted to emulate what he had done."[15]

Ford Konno kept Hawaiian swimmers in the spotlight at the 1952 Helsinki Olympics by winning two gold medals and one silver medal, while his future bride, Evelyn Kawamoto, captured two bronze medals. Konno's teammate from McKinley High School in Honolulu, Bill Woolsey, also captured the gold medal in the relay, while Hilo's Yoshi Oyakawa set an Olympic record in winning the 100-meter backstroke.

In 1956, when Duke and Nadine traveled to Melbourne for the first Olympics to be held in the Southern Hemisphere, Kahanamoku took in as many swimming events as possible, including the silver-medal showing of Konno and Woolsey in the relay. They couldn't help but notice the first appearance of swim briefs for men, produced by local manufacturer Speedo. The skimpy suits helped produce much faster times than the prohibitive, bulky models worn during Kahanamoku's era. What impressed Duke the most was the win-at-all-costs commitment shown by the young swimmers and their embrace of advancements in training and nutrition. They shaved the hair on their bodies and their heads to reduce drag, lifted weights, swam laps several hours daily, and received full-time coaching. The best of the lot parlayed their talents into college scholarships. Smith, Konno, and Oyakawa all left Hawaii to swim for Ohio State University.

"I thought I trained hard," Kahanamoku said, "but I realized when I went down to the Olympics at Melbourne that I must have been fooling myself."[16]

The elevated status of surfing in Australia also impressed Kahanamoku. TV cameras and reporters accompanied Duke and Nadine as they journeyed to Freshwater, in northern Sydney, one of the beaches that he had surfed on his 1914–15 tour. There, Kahanamoku was reunited with Isabel Letham and Claude West, who had been teenagers when he had performed his tricks over forty years previously.

Claude ran to greet Duke and then pointed out Isabel. "She was streamlined when I saw her last," he joked. The trio posed for pictures in the clubhouse.[17]

West was now considered to be one of Australia's pioneering surfers and watermen. He had preserved the wooden board that Duke had shaped and bequeathed to him, a talisman that had survived fire and mishap to take its place among the country's most treasured sports mementos. "It's as good as the day I made it," Duke told West.[18]

Nadine and Duke journeyed to Singapore, Bangkok, Hong Kong, and Tokyo after the 1956 Summer Olympics as Kahanamoku received a hero's welcome during his first extended visit to Asia. He flew alone to Los Angeles to give advice about a planned travelogue about Hawaii.

The program was a ruse. When he walked through a Polynesian-themed set at NBC Studios in Burbank, California, Kahanamoku was greeted by TV personality Ralph Edwards. He found himself on stage and, without any preparation, the surprise subject of the TV show *This Is Your Life*, filmed in front of an audience that included familiar faces from his past: director John Ford and Los Angeles Athletic Club swim coach Fred Cady.

Edwards did the honors of recapping Kahanamoku's Horatio Alger-like life story, from humble origins to Olympic glory to Hollywood career to the sheriff's office. The usually stoic Kahanamoku blinked back tears as Nadine, sisters Bernice and Kapiolani, and all five of his brothers emerged from hiding backstage to embrace him. They chimed in with a rendition of "On the Beach of Waikiki," with brother Sam playing the guitar and Duke doing a graceful hula.[19]

A cavalcade of friends followed. "Dad" Center was introduced, as were "Ma" and "Pa" Henry. Johnny Weissmuller bounded onstage like an eager puppy to hug his old rival. No longer in the Hollywood spotlight (and working on his fourth marriage), Weissmuller was generously effusive. "This great guy gave me all the encouragement in the world," he burbled. "Yes, he made me take care of myself, stay in training and work out constantly. His main concern was not for personal glory, but that the United States team should win."[20]

A trio of middle-aged gentlemen whom Kahanamoku did not recognize came onstage. Edwards revealed that his staff had located three of the survivors whom Duke had saved from the wreck of the *Thelma* off Corona del Mar in 1925.

"I couldn't have lasted another five minutes if Duke hadn't rescued me," Edward Snead said. "I had a broken collar bone and a fractured shoulder."

Harry Ohlin chimed in. "Ever since 1925 we have followed Duke's career with great interest because if it weren't for him we wouldn't be here tonight," he said. "He risked his own life to save ours."

Kahanamoku shook their hands. "I've been waiting to see you," he said.

"I have waited 32 years to thank you tonight," Ohlin said.

Said Duke: "It's a long time, but it's wonderful."[21]

30

The return of surfers to the water after the war was slow, Kahanamoku recalled, because "the military returnees were occupied with finding jobs or returning to their interrupted education chores."[1] He was accurate about the war's effect on surfing, but even he could not foresee how dramatically the war changed surfing's future.

The death of Outrigger Canoe Club founder Alexander Hume Ford, just after V-J Day in 1945, proved to be the defining line between two distinct eras of surfing: from the restoration of a nearly extinct Hawaiian sport, primarily based in Waikiki, to the dissemination of something called "surf culture" around the globe, including components of fashion, music, film, travel, and business. Surfing's metamorphosis was sparked by innovations developed by and for the war effort. Wave forecasting was introduced when military strategists studied how to optimize amphibious landings, from North Africa to Normandy. By connecting facets of meteorology, oceanography, and geology—"weather, waves, and topography"—they were able to pinpoint "the three components of wave prediction: wind speed, fetch (the distance that wind travels), and duration," according to surf scholars Peter Westwick and Peter Neushul.[2]

Physicist Hugh Bradner created the rugged and flexible wet suit so that navy frogmen could withstand chilly underwater temperatures for long periods of time. Made of a synthetic rubber called neoprene, itself a by-product of wartime resourcefulness, the wet suit expanded surfing's reach beyond the balmy waters of Hawaii, especially after Santa Cruz-based Jack O'Neill and Redondo Beach-based twin brothers Bob and Bill Meistrell (whose dive shop business eventually became Body Glove) adapted it for recreational purposes.

Fiberglass, resin, and Styrofoam were materials that were used to reduce the weight of aircraft, enabling them to fly longer distances without refueling and thus penetrate deeper into enemy territory. Aerospace engineering student and surfer Bob Simmons applied that technology to surfboards, sandwiching foam between thin sheets of balsa wood. Simmons also utilized navy research about hydrodynamics to streamline the boards and to add a skeg (fin) underneath.

According to Duke, "much of the credit for surfboard improvements"[3] after the war belonged to Simmons, who died while surfing in 1954. Not long after his death, as Styrofoam and fiberglass became available for commercial applications, they supplanted wood in the manufacture of surfboards. Liquid plastic was poured into board-shaped molds. After it hardened, the "blank" was sanded into shape. Surfboard glassers then applied fiberglass and resin in order to reinforce and waterproof the boards.

The result was a revelation: light but super-durable boards, with curved bottoms, smoothed edges, and a skeg, which were relatively inexpensive to produce and allowed for greater maneuverability and speed in the water. The names of the top board manufacturers soon were as recognizable as the major surf breaks: Dale Velzy (initially with Harold "Hap" Jacobs) in Hermosa Beach, Dewey Weber in Venice Beach, and Hobie Alter in Dana Point.[4]

"When the short boards came around, they were calling me 'king of the hot-doggers," surfer Rabbit Kekai said. "Nobody used to do things like, come down and get inside the tube. Guys like Duke were just straight riders. Innovation you call that, from the old to the new."[5]

Beginning in the late 1930s and early 1940s, a select few expert surfers ventured from Waikiki and established Makaha, on the west side of Oahu, as a prime spot for big-wave surfing. That reputation was enhanced when Makaha hosted the first surfing contest of the modern era, with Honolulu-born and -raised George Downing winning the competition in 1954 and Rabbit Kekai prevailing the following year.

Few people outside of Hawaii had heard of Makaha, but that changed when a grainy photograph of Downing, Woodbridge "Woody" Brown, and "Buzzy" Trent barreling down a frothy fifteen-foot wave at Makaha appeared in newspapers on the mainland. Photographer Thomas "Scoop" Tsuzuki's black-and-white image was so dramatic—so epic!—that upon viewing the seething joyride, Fred Van Dyke, a twenty-two-year-old teacher in Santa Cruz, quit his job to chase giant waves at Makaha and the North Shore.[6] This young generation brought a daring élan to surfing, for whom waves "are not measured in feet and inches, they are measured in increments of fear," according to Trent.[7]

The cross-pollination between Hawaii and California continued after fledgling filmmaker Bud Browne shot surfing footage with a 16-mm camera during summer forays to Waikiki. Browne charged sixty-five cents for admission to watch surfing's first full-length documentary, titled *Hawaiian Surfing Movie*, and barnstormed up and down the California coast exhibiting the film. Browne supplied his own narration and a tape-recorded musical soundtrack to the action, as enthusiastic crowds cheered every wave and bemoaned every wipeout. Browne followed up his debut with *Trek to Makaha, Cat on a Hot Foam Board*, and *Gun Ho*.[8]

Several acolytes followed Browne, including Greg Noll, John Severson, Grant Rohloff, and Bruce Brown, as the surfing road movie format stoked excitement for waves. Severson took the next step forward by publishing the first magazine devoted to surfing, originally titled *The Surfer*, which highlighted surfing in far-flung places known only to mapmakers, like Mancora, Peru, and Jeffreys Bay, South Africa.

It was a novel that pushed surfing into the mainstream, and it came from an unlikely source. Screenplay writer Frederick Kohner was a Czech Jewish émigré who had fled the Nazis in the 1930s. He settled in Southern California where his brother, Paul, was a Hollywood talent agent.

Kohner had a teenage daughter, Kathy, who was learning to surf at Malibu. She regaled her father with colorful stories about hanging out with a gnarly bunch of surfers with nicknames like "Kahoona," "Don Pepe," and "Moondoggie." Kathy, who maybe stood five feet tall, was dubbed "Gidget," a mash-up of "girl" and "midget."

Bemused, Kohner stitched together the tales into a breathless romp that gave readers a peek into Southern California's surfing scene and a primer on teenage lingo. All is "bitchen" in Gidget's world, and the most "bitchen" of them is the great Kahoona, a character based on Terry "Tubesteak" Tracy, a surfer who lived in a makeshift shack on the beach.

In the novel, one of Gidget's friends describes Kahoona's surfing expertise: "He's been around from Peru to Nanakali [*sic*]. This here is bathtub stuff for him. Do you know that he's the only guy besides Duke Kahanamoku who came in on Zero break without spilling?"

"I had heard about the Duke because Scooterboy had his name on his board," Gidget recollects, "and Duke Kahanamoku is to surfing what the Babe is to baseball bugs."[9]

Gidget: The Little Girl with Big Ideas was published in 1957 and, like Earl Derr Biggers's *House without a Key*, the Charlie Chan whodunit from 1925 that also mentioned Duke in its pages, it became a best seller. Columbia Pictures released the movie version, *Gidget*, two years later, starring Sandra Dee and Cliff Robertson, with several insufferably cartoonish surfing scenes. Two sequels followed, including *Gidget Goes Hawaiian* and a TV sitcom, *Gidget*, with Sally Field in the mid-1960s.

The intermingling of surfing and popular culture proved to be a combustible mixture, with reverberations felt down the coast in Balboa, where Duke and his surfing pals from the Los Angeles Athletic Club had gone for nighttime entertainment in the 1920s, not far from his favorite surfing spot at Corona del Mar. There, inside the steamy Rendezvous Ballroom, the staccato sounds of guitarist Dick Dale and his band, the Del-tones, rocked and rolled like a chopping wave. In Dale's wake came the Surfaris ("Wipe Out"), the Bel-Airs ("Mr. Moto"), and the Chantays ("Pipeline"), as well as a group of five young men from the inland suburb of Hawthorne, California, with a name that evoked the golden yesteryear of Waikiki. These Beach Boys were *haole*, and their songs promised pleasure: "Good Vibrations," "Fun, Fun, Fun," "California Girls," "Catch a Wave," "Little Deuce Coupe."

Kahanamoku did surf Makaha on several occasions, according to Wally Froiseth, one of the pioneers there. He also experimented with foam boards, swapping with Peter Lawford when the actor came to Honolulu. "I took one wave and it was kinda tricky," he said. "I thought, 'Well, I better stick to my own solid board.' . . . I said to Peter, 'You better give me my board and you take your board back.' And that's the swap and that's the last I ever rode on one of these tricky boards they have."[10]

No longer the best or the most daring surfer in the water, Duke's role continued to evolve. He was surfing's Alexander Cartwright: the elder statesmen who dispensed advice to shapers and surfers alike, the essential and eternal link between redwood and foam, between Isabel Letham and Gidget, between *Waikiki Wedding* and "Wipe Out."

His influence was now felt primarily out of the water. Tubesteak and his ilk reveled in renouncing the nine-to-five grind and the grey flannel suit in favor of an alternative way. Call it youthful rebellion or ennui—with everyone from Holden Caufield to James Dean serving as role models—but they purposefully mimicked the lifestyle of Kahanamoku and the original beachboys by making the water and catching waves the center of their universe: comparing notes about which break was best that day, finding enough work to enjoy a simple but fruitful existence, strumming musical instruments at night before a raging bonfire, and chasing an endless summer.

Kahanamoku surfed less and less often, but the water remained his favorite haunt. He switched passions to sailing and boating, preferring to fish from a powerboat he named the *Nadu K*. He became infatuated with catamarans, another postwar innovation that was credited to big-wave surfer Woody Brown, who built the first modern "cats" in Hawaii along with Alfred Kumalae. Duke purchased a catamaran from Brown and learned to race it. He and his cousin, Leon Sterling, brought it to the mainland one summer to sail along the coast.

Duke sounded as enthusiastic as Alexander Hume Ford did about surfing when he gushed to Arthur Godfrey that sailing in the catamaran was "like riding the ice boats on the ocean—tremendous sport and lots of fun. . . . Boy, you have not experienced anything more thrilling. [I]magine sailing along on a twenty-footer better than 20 knots without motor-power of any kind but the wind."[11]

Later, on a boat trip to neighboring islands, Kahanamoku and the crew ran into rough weather in the Alenuihaha Channel, a hazardous crossing nicknamed the "I'll end you, ha-ha" channel. "There was four of us," said Henry Ayau, who worked with Duke. "We were hanging on just trying to stay in the boat as much as we can 'cause it was so rough and Duke was just standing there like nothing was phasing him. He turned to us: 'What's the mattah, boys? Too rough for you?' I tell you, that was a day I thought we were going to see the end of Hawaii."[12]

Kahanamoku continued to dispense wisdom in unpredictable ways. Long before he was selected to direct the 1984 Los Angeles Olympics, Peter Ueberroth was a top-notch water polo player who just missed making the 1956

U.S. Olympic team. He took up surfing when he visited Hawaii around this time, but he found that carrying the heavy boards was a chore. Duke advised him to "'get these little wheels, and then you walk down with your board like you have a suitcase,'" Ueberroth said. "It was like a miracle to me."[13]

Surfer George Downing recalled that Kahanamoku enjoyed sitting down against a tile wall at the Outrigger Canoe Club every afternoon around five o'clock. "I used to think, 'Why is Duke sitting by this wall all the time?'" Downing said to author Sandra Hall. "So one day I asked, 'Hey, Duke, you come down and sit by this wall all the time; it must be a special place.' And he said, 'Come. Come sit down with me.'

"So I went back and sat with him, and he said, 'Lean back.' So I leaned back and, oh, I got it. He never said anything to me, but I got what it was. During the day the sun used to heat this wall up and in the late afternoon the heat was radiating from this wall. So when you put your back against it, oh man, the relief of this heat coming through the wall. He looked at me and smiled, and never said anything because he knew I got it."[14]

31

Statehood was the seminal political issue in post–World War II Hawaii. When President Harry S. Truman visited in 1950, he campaigned for statehood for Hawaii and Alaska by emphasizing "their vital importance to the defense and welfare of the United States. They are both key positions in the national defense of the United States on its western borders. It is necessary that they have representation in the legislative bodies of the United States, in order to bring that lesson home to Congress."[1]

Truman's successor, Dwight D. Eisenhower, also endorsed statehood for Hawaii. Three times statehood bills passed the House, only to fail to reach the president's desk, due in large part to the displeasure expressed by Southern politicians with "the whole brown and white mosaic" of Hawaii,[2] where the population of about 500,000 people in 1952 was 40 percent Asian, 15 percent Caucasian, and 2.8 percent pure Hawaiian (along with 17 percent part Hawaiian).

Hawaii, too, was divided. Kahanamoku backed statehood, which was a key plank of the Republican Party platform, as did Democratic Party leaders. Many of the business moguls who controlled Hawaii's economy, including Walter Dillingham, opposed statehood, as did native Hawaiians who were still angered by the American takeover of the kingdom at the turn of the twentieth century.

After Alaska became the forty-ninth state, it was inevitable that Hawaii would follow. Approval from Congress came quickly in 1959, with President Eisenhower signing the Hawaii Admission Act on March 18. After the measure passed, Kahanamoku led a procession of the Royal Order of Kamehameha into Kawaiaha'o Church in Honolulu, across from the 'Iolani Palace, to give thanks.

The Reverend Abraham Akaka addressed the crowd, noting that "statehood brings great hopes" for many people. He also acknowledged that many felt alarmed by this step. "There are fears that Hawaii as a state will be motivated by economic greed," he said, "that statehood will turn Hawaii (as someone has said) into a great big spiritual junkyard filled with smashed dreams, worn-out illusions that will make the Hawaiian people lonely, confused, insecure, empty, anxious, restless, disillusioned—a wistful people."[3]

The decision was left to the citizens of Hawaii. The plebiscite ballot contained one question: "Shall Hawaii immediately be admitted into the Union as a state?" On August 21, 1959, three days before Duke's sixty-ninth birthday, Hawaii officially became the Aloha state.

Duke Kahanamoku had spent his entire life dealing with, and conforming to, what the writer Joan Didion described as "the pleasant but formidable colonial world in which a handful of families controlled everything Hawaii did."[4] The entrenched and interlocking business interests of the "Big Five" families and companies, and their accumulated wealth from their holdings in the sugar industry, shipping, tourism, and property development, continued to dominate much of Hawaii's economy. With statehood came dizzying change and new leaders.

Tourism boomed. In Kalia, the sleepy oasis where Duke was raised, the tiki-themed Waikikian Hotel opened on land that was leased from the Paoa estate. Industrialist Henry Kaiser bought up property there and built the Hawaiian Village, a Polynesian-styled playground of bungalows, swimming pools, nightclubs, and an aluminum-domed arena that sprawled across eighteen acres. Fronting the resort was a neat, man-made beach that Kaiser named for Kalia's favorite son, Duke Kahanamoku.

"Some day Waikiki beach is going to be the scene of one long hotel,"[5] said Jack London in 1915, and his prophecy was proving accurate. Arthur Godfrey decried the "tidal wave of tourism" and claimed that "if you really want to get sick, go out about five miles in a catamaran and just take a look. Why this place looks just like Pittsburgh."[6]

Locals, including many of Duke's siblings and relatives, left Kalia—and even Oahu—to live elsewhere. Duke himself questioned the direction in which Hawaii was headed even as he recognized that, as one of its key promoters, he had contributed to its current state. "I liked the old days better," he said. "Now the place is cluttered with people. People all over the place and it's not going to stop. There's no end to it. It's good economically, but it sure makes it crowded here."[7]

Kahanamoku was apprehensive about the viability of the Hawaiian people amid the transformations. "My concern is, 'Will we be in time to be able to hold our own?' because the present generation of Hawaiians must be fully prepared educationally and otherwise to meet the coming challenges," he noted in an undated, handwritten document.[8]

A new generation of politicians gained power, many of whom were of Asian descent, including Congressman Daniel Inouye and Senator Hiram Fong. When local voters approved a revised city-county charter that eliminated the sheriff's office, Kahanamoku was unceremoniously dumped from his job on December 31, 1960. Gone were his title and an annual salary of about $11,000. "I can't understand why they want to abolish this office," he said. "It will cost them a lot of money."[9]

Kahanamoku took small consolation in the fact that the issue he had campaigned for since he was first elected sheriff in 1934—the construction of a new, modern jail—finally happened, with the opening of a thirty-one-acre site in Halawa, built at a cost of $1.9 million. His quixotic dream took twenty-six years to be fulfilled, but it came only after he was out of office.

Kahanamoku stayed busy with myriad civic projects. He was a Rotarian and a Shriner who attended annual conventions wearing his favorite aloha shirts. He helped raise funds to erect a permanent shrine for the USS *Arizona*, which had not been disturbed since the attack on Pearl Harbor in 1941. Elvis Presley was recruited to give a benefit concert, and Duke contacted sports celebrities, including Willie Mays when the San Francisco Giants came to Hawaii for spring training, for assistance with the campaign. The dignified memorial opened in 1962 at a cost of about $500,000.

Kahanamoku's personal quest for financial stability continued. Just prior to statehood, Duke received a letter from Frank Walton, the deputy chief of police in Los Angeles and a former Olympic water polo player. Walton wrote that Los Angeles-based Belden Productions was eager to produce a "'Dragnet'-type TV show" in Hawaii that "would feature the Islands, their beauty and their music, with an undercurrent of the high adventure and drama that take place in connection with law enforcement."[10]

Dragnet, of course, was a police procedural drama set in Los Angeles that was a ratings winner in the early days of network television. Walton mentioned that Duke, as technical consultant, could count on $100 per TV script. "Such a show should go real well," Walton wrote. "I think it has good possibilities—would you like to try it?"

Kahanamoku replied positively. "The idea intrigues me," he wrote, "but would appreciate knowing more about the deal." He wondered if $100 "is all I can expect" if the show were to be produced.[11]

Walton responded that he was authorized to bump the offer to $250 "for each script on which they use the phrase 'Based on the official files of the Honolulu Sheriff' or some such phrase." If Duke also appeared as an actor, he would receive another $250 per episode.[12]

Kahanamoku equivocated about the offer, noting that his contract with Cisco Casuals gave the clothing company "the exclusive use of my name."[13] Belden Productions answered that objection by sending Duke a preliminary contract with language that allowed for previous licensing agreements under his name.

Negotiations then hit a snag. It is unclear whether Kahanamoku consulted with Cisco Casuals or legal representatives about the licensing question. Given the exposure that a TV show modeled after *Dragnet*, a huge national hit, would bring Cisco Casuals and its principal spokesperson, it is doubtful that the company would not support the project. Kahanamoku ended up declining to participate with Belden Productions, citing "other commitments which I feel might complicate matters."[14] Years later, a TV show with a similar concept, *Hawaii Five-O*, became a popular primetime show for CBS.[15]

Kahanamoku continued to promote the aloha clothing that was synonymous with the island lifestyle. When a visitor arrives in Hawaii, he boasted, "the very first thing he does is get the brightest colored aloha shirt he can buy. Nothing conservative satisfies him. The brighter, the better."[16] Their eye-popping designs disguised Kahanamoku's meager payouts. *Gentleman's Quarterly* magazine reportedly claimed that Cisco Casuals was paying Duke $30,000–35,000 annually in royalties. Duke scoffed at that figure. "If that were true, I wouldn't be here. I'd be traveling," he said.[17]

The *Los Angeles Times* reported that Kahanamoku made $20,000 a year "just lending his name to a sports shirt."[18] The *Honolulu Advertiser* reported that he earned approximately $100,000 over eight years from Cisco Casuals—or about $12,500 per year.

According to Kahanamoku, the published numbers were wildly inflated. He stated that he received $1,000 to $1,200 a month when the arrangement began in 1949, but then the amounts tailed off precipitously. "Sometimes I don't get anything," he said. "Last month I only got $11."[19]

Not long after Kahanamoku lost the sheriff's job, Honolulu mayor Neal Blaisdell put Duke on the city-county payroll as an "official greeter" at a salary of $8,256 a year. He logged thousands of miles as the public face of the fiftieth state, touring Vietnam, Burma, Japan, Thailand, India, Singapore, Indonesia, Cambodia, and the Philippines. When he landed in Stockholm while promoting air service between Sweden and the United States, he was hoisted onto the shoulders of two young, pretty girls. "Just like it was here in 1912," Duke joked.[20]

The greeter job enmeshed him in controversy after Arthur Godfrey complained about Kahanamoku's salary. "Hawaii should give Duke $25,000 a year and a car and require him to do nothing but appear at only the proper places," the entertainer said. "For all the dignity and honor that Duke has brought to Hawaii, giving him $25,000 would be just a gesture. And that wouldn't be charity, either."[21]

After Kahanamoku's death, Godfrey predicted, "Hawaii will probably go all out in erecting a $100,000 monument. Why not honor a living monument?"[22]

Godfrey's remarks were accurate (including his off-handed line about the statue). Kahanamoku had been content in the sheriff's office, despite its low salary, because the job came with an elevated level of public appreciation. Without that, he was forced to consider that Hawaii's power structure had failed to take care of him adequately, despite all he had done to boost their projects, a lifetime effort that began fifty years previously, in 1912.

"I am barely getting along," he admitted. "I agree that something should be done, but it is not my part to say anything. It takes a *malihini* [newcomer] like Arthur Godfrey to come here, look things over and speak the truth."[23] He pulled out his semimonthly check as greeter to show that he received only $262.41 after taxes. "I'm not getting the salary a lot of people think I'm getting," he said.[24]

Kahanamoku was unprepared for the outrage that ensued. Letters to the editor complained that his job was a cushy one, that he was being ungrateful when he grumbled about receiving a government paycheck just for "being Duke." Mayor Blaisdell was forced to defend the salary, noting that Duke also received a monthly pension of $286 for his tenure as sheriff.[25]

Speaking publicly about his financial plight was humiliating for Duke. He seldom revealed intimate details about his life. But as Hawaii entered the era of statehood, the controversy showed that even the legendary Kahanamoku was not immune to public rebuke.

32

At the age of seventy, unemployed for the first time since the Roosevelt administration, Kahanamoku was rescued from himself with help from his wife and Arthur Godfrey. They teamed him with businessman Robert Hoffman and musician-turned-promoter Kimo Wilder McVay to leverage and monetize Duke's good name.

McVay's genealogy reads like a minihistory of post-contact Hawaii. His great-grandfather was Samuel Wilder, who cornered the local supply of guano and then sold it as fertilizer on the mainland. Samuel Wilder married Elizabeth Kinau Judd, whose father was among the first missionary families to settle in Hawaii. In 1831, when Elizabeth was born, she was said to be the first white child born in Hawaii.

Kimo's mother, Kinau Wilder, grew up in Waikiki. She knew Duke from an early age, when he taught her "the rudiments of swimming form."[1] She married a navy ensign, Charles McVay, but the couple divorced in the 1930s. Captain Charles McVay commanded the USS *Indianapolis* during World War II. In the waning days of the war, the *Indianapolis* delivered parts of the atomic bomb that was dropped on Hiroshima. After the cruiser left the island of Tinian, a Japanese submarine fired two torpedoes that struck the *Indianapolis* and ignited the fuel tanks. The ship sank within twelve minutes, with approximately 900 survivors scattered in the water. Sharks attacked the wounded as their mates watched in horror. Captain McVay and about 315 men survived the ordeal. He was court-martialed and found guilty of not zigzagging in order to avoid being hit by the torpedo.

When Kimo wasn't attempting to clear his father's name,[2] he was a wheeler-dealer entrepreneur who played a mean piano and talked a big game. He had a reputation for spotting budding musical talent after he guided a local high schooler, Robin Luke, to create a hit with "Susie Darlin'."

Kimo McVay saw in Kahanamoku a worthy reclamation project and, no doubt, a chance to capitalize on Duke's global fame. With his mother's money behind the effort, McVay formed a corporation to exploit the opportunity, with the buy-in for Kahanamoku, one of the copartners, being his name. The group's first major venture was to pay a reported $250,000 to purchase Don the Beachcomber's tiki eatery at the International Marketplace, a sprawling, indoor-outdoor bazaar located in the heart of Waikiki.

The grand opening of Duke Kahanamoku's restaurant and nightclub came on September 1, 1961, after the Reverend Abraham Akaka delivered a blessing and Duke accepted the keys from his longtime friend Don Beach. Accompanied by a flurry of advertisements for brunch specials, McVay hired top-flight musical acts to entertain tourists and locals alike. Martin Denny brought his exotic sounds to the beach, along with Ed Kenney and The Surfers. The cover charge was $1.50.

Kahanamoku was ensconced in an office inside the restaurant beneath a banyan tree and dangling vines. The décor was Polynesian fantasy, featuring a thatched roof, bamboo walls, and an old battered desk covered with tapa cloth. Duke played the part of genial host. "When Jack Dempsey was out last time, he gave me a few tips on it," he said, referring to the champ's restaurant-bar in midtown Manhattan.[3]

The restaurant-club served as the hub for the myriad endeavors dreamed up by the peripatetic McVay. He started a company to produce a feature film based on Kahanamoku's life. (The film was never made.) He attached Duke to a "beachboy party" album of songs, recorded with Chick Daniels, Splash Lyons, Squeeze Kamana, Harry Robello, and Jimmy Hakuole. He negotiated with Cisco Casuals to buy back the rights to Duke Kahanamoku's name, reportedly for $15,000, and then signed a deal with local manufacturer Kahala to license a line of Duke Kahanamoku sportswear.

California-based Ventura International Plastics was recruited to make three models of Duke Kahanamoku surfboards. Nash Manufacturing agreed to fashion three types of Duke Kahanamoku skateboards, the "sidewalk offspring" of surfboards that were becoming popular among youth. An Asian company produced souvenir Duke Kahanamoku ukuleles; an eponymous foundation awarded scholarships to youngsters.[4]

In November of 1961 Kahanamoku hosted a Thanksgiving luau dinner for 230 foreign students attending the newly created East-West Center (EWC) at the University of Hawaii at Manoa. The EWC was a government-funded, "soft diplomacy" initiative to foster international exchange by bringing students from countries throughout Asia and the Pacific Rim to study in Hawaii. Kahanamoku sat in a huge peacock chair at the entrance to the restaurant, and he and Nadine personally greeted each student. The young men received an aloha shirt, and the young women received a muumuu. It is unclear whether Barack Obama, the lone African student at the university (and not officially connected with the EWC), attended the festivities. Obama and his young wife, Ann Dunham, had become parents to a son, also named Barack, in August.

The following year, Kahanamoku hosted another lavish spread for EWC students. A new grantee from Indonesia, Lolo Soetero, attended with his classmates.[5] Soetero later married Ann Dunham and became Barack Obama's stepfather. If Kimo McVay could have seen into the future, he surely would have arranged a photo op with Duke Kahanamoku and young Barack Obama. After all, when President John F. Kennedy visited Hawaii in 1963, McVay made sure that Duke was photographed with the president. McVay brayed that President Kennedy "didn't give a damn about anybody in the political thing of it. He wanted to talk to Duke. That was his hero."[6]

Duke's restaurant, as well as the luau with foreign students and the photo ops with presidents, generated much publicity. But the initial years of the enterprise were not financially successful. The branded surfboards could not compete against the quality boards crafted by expert shapers. The nightclub bled money as McVay searched for a popular act at a time when rock and roll was transforming the entertainment landscape. (Even Duke's efforts to unload the property in Waikiki that was given him in a trust after the 1912 Stockholm Olympics were stymied after the judge ruled that he must retain the property.)

In 1964, at around the time The Beach Boys were hitting number one on the charts with "I Get Around," McVay spotted a young entertainer performing in Waikiki. Born in Honolulu, with what he called a "chop suey" heritage, Don Ho got his musical start at his parents' lounge in Kaneohe, called Honey's Cafe after his mother, Emily "Honey" Ho. Don learned to play the organ at the bar, jamming with other local musicians and entertaining servicemen from the nearby marine base.

When Ho brought his keyboard and cocktail glass to a hole-in-the-wall in Waikiki, adoring and loyal crowds lapped up his "ain't no big t'ing" schtick. McVay took notice and tried to lure him to the International Market Place. Ho declined McVay's desperate entreaties—until Kimo returned with Kahanamoku.

"The Duke said maybe three words all year," Ho recounted, "but he gave me a big wet kiss and says to me, 'Son, come play for me at my place.' You can't turn the Duke down, so we agreed."[7]

Ho and his band, the Aliis, initially played the late-night slot. They were so successful that McVay made them the featured act. Ho and the Aliis jolted Oahu's staid nightlife and turned Duke's into Waikiki's hottest club. They were talented musicians, but they were also funky and funny, with a let's-get-buzzed-together, flip-flop-wearing vibe long before the likes of Jimmy Buffett took over that niche. When Ho cried "Suck 'Em Up," glasses emptied and cash registers trilled.

"Business is definitely up, thank the good Lord," McVay wrote Nadine shortly after Ho's arrival. "We'll need excellent months in July & August to keep afloat. . . . The picture isn't good, but at least not hopeless."[8]

33

Kimo McVay needed more than Don Ho to make the Duke-related businesses profitable, and he stumbled upon a potential gold mine when he accompanied Kahanamoku to the 1963 West Coast Surfboard Championships in Huntington Beach, California. The waves weren't much that weekend—none were over five feet—but traffic was bumper-to-bumper on Pacific Coast Highway by the pier.

The crowd gave Johnny Weissmuller a warm welcome, but it was obvious who they had come to see. When Duke Kahanamoku stepped onto the stage at the water's edge to congratulate the winners, McVay saw "30,000 or more teenagers, before any introduction was made, get off their *okole* ("butts"), stand and cheer wildly," he said. Duke is "the biggest thing in surfing, the newest and fastest growing sport in the world."[1]

Kahanamoku and Nadine flew to Sydney to attend the surfing championships in Australia. He received a rapturous reception for his role as the living pioneer of modern surfing, with large crowds lined up to get his autograph. He admitted to being "astounded at the amount of interest" in "the King of Sports"[2] and speculated that "maybe someday they'll add it to the Olympics. At least, I hope so. . . . I never dreamed it would grow this fast."[3]

The following year, when Huntington Beach hosted the U.S. surfing contest, Kahanamoku brought water from Waikiki to blend with the waters of Southern California, symbolically linking two of his surfing homes. He signed autographs from the moment his plane landed and brought down the house by kicking off his shoes and performing an impromptu hula to "Little Brown Gal." (ABC's "Wide World of Sports" taped the event.)

McVay astutely realized that, as the Baby Boomer generation came of age in the late 1950s and early 1960s, surfing was catching fire. Its image was about nonconformity, personal expression, freedom, and harmony with the natural world—ideas that were particularly attractive in the burgeoning counterculture. *Endless Summer* was not just the name of Bruce Brown's underground hit movie (complemented by graphic artist John Van Hamersveld's groovy poster). It was a lifestyle to aspire to: living to surf and surfing to live, with waves that are always free, brah.

The mainstream press and Madison Avenue advertising companies were taking notice. Tom Wolfe breathlessly wrote about Windansea's "Pump House Gang" from La Jolla, and *Sports Illustrated* splashed surfing images on its covers. Surfers and their surfboards were recruited to pose alongside cars and beers. Sensing an opportunity, McVay concentrated on surfing as a way to market products. He organized the Duke Kahanamoku surf club. For dues of five dollars, members would receive an official patch, a brass clubhouse key, a decal, a T-shirt, and an autographed photo. There was even Duke Kahanamoku after-shave cologne.

With surfing contests becoming more prominent, McVay recruited four young men to be the "officers" of Duke's surf club and compete on the circuit. Paul Strauch Jr., a local product, was half-Hawaiian and was studying for his college degree. He surfed in the classic Hawaiian style, with majestic poise, making long, sweeping, graceful turns. He was known for his "Cheater Five" trick: squatting low while sticking his left leg out toward the nose of the board.[4]

Joey Cabell, born and raised in Hawaii, was a precise, smooth surfer who thrived on adrenaline. Tall and lean, he started surfing at an early age and won the 1963 championships at Makaha. Cabell was a different sort of cat; he liked to leave the waves behind for the ski slopes of Aspen, Colorado, and he once entered a bullring in Peru, dressed in an aloha shirt and huaraches, to face off against a bull—and survived to tell the tale. Cabell was already planning for a career as an entrepreneur, having launched the Chart House restaurant chain while he was in his midtwenties.[5]

Brawny Fred Hemmings Jr., also born and raised in Hawaii, brought a football player's mentality to surfing. He was an aggressive and cerebral big-wave rider who had won at Makaha and numerous other contests. Hemmings was hired to be McVay's assistant, and he gained an insider's perspective on Kahanamoku that few were privy to. "Duke's essence was that of respect and love for the ocean and for the people that choose to make it a big part of their life," he said. "He was so grounded."[6]

Butch Van Artsdalen, a California transplant, was "a dark-haired Robert Redford," according to Hemmings.[7] Van Artsdalen was a goofy-footed and fearless surfer, among the first to master the fabled tube rides of Banzai Pipeline on the North Shore. "Butch was such an incredible athlete," said good friend and fellow surfer Mickey Muñoz, "but I don't think he cared that much about the game of competition. He just loved to surf. He was so good that he didn't use strategy."[8]

McVay outfitted Kahanamoku in an all-white suit and a bolo tie that accentuated his regal bearing. He color-coordinated the boys in matching aloha shirts; when they were grouped together, they looked like the surfing equivalent of The Beatles. They sat with Duke for Don Ho's gig at the Coconut Grove in Los Angeles and accompanied Duke to Disneyland. McVay rented a Rolls Royce—equipped with a surfboard rack—and had them chauffeured to Malibu. Kahanamoku tested the water, declared it was too cold, and went back to the car to take a nap.

On a visit to the factory that manufactured Duke-endorsed sneakers, they were informed that the machines adhered any type of material to the canvas in about twenty minutes. Kahanamoku instructed Hemmings to volunteer the shirt he was wearing and, voilà, a pair of floral-patterned "shirts on the toes" magically appeared for McVay to sell.[9]

Strauch helped Duke navigate through the countless meals and glad-handing. Kahanamoku took to wearing wraparound sunglasses, even at night, to disguise the fact that he sometimes fell asleep while in public. Strauch was always positioned to his right at the dinner table. When Duke was asked a question, Strauch's job was "to hit him with my left knee and repeat the question to him: 'Yeah, Duke, what was it like to win that first Olympic gold medal?'"[10]

Kahanamoku relished being part of the action, being relevant and revered. At one surfing contest in Huntington Beach, Strauch recalled, he and Kahanamoku watched as the disappointed third-place finisher received his prize. "The guy takes the trophy, doesn't shake the presenter's hand, walks past the [honorary beauty] queen, hurls the trophy into the garbage can, and stomps off the stage," said Strauch. "I said, 'Hey, Duke, did you see that?' He said, 'Yeah, Paul.' I said, 'What do you think of that?' expecting him to say, 'Not much sportsmanship.' He said, 'Gee, Paul, these guys really want to win. Isn't that fantastic? There really is nothing like winning.'"[11]

Cabell came away impressed that Kahanamoku "was never out front saying, 'I'm the Duke.' He was always in the back. His humbleness was a beautiful thing. We're lucky that he was who he was to show the rest of us the way to be."[12]

Closer to home, Kahanamoku assisted the environmental campaign of John Kelly, a surfboard pioneer and big-wave surfer. Kelly had founded Save Our Surf (SOS), a grassroots organization to prevent the sort of rampant development that despoiled coral reefs, surfing spots, and ocean resources of Hawaii. Duke joined the effort to oppose further development of Magic Island, between Waikiki and downtown Honolulu, writing to complain that the plans would "destroy twenty more surfing spots that are heavily used" and that the construction of a huge stone wall presents a "grave danger" to thousands of surfers. On this occasion, Kelly and SOS prevailed.[13]

Kelly's SOS group highlighted one major drawback to surfing's popularity. Environmentalists complained that formerly pristine surf spots were being overrun and ruined. Critics also decried the recreational drugs, including marijuana and LSD, that young surfers were bringing to the beach. "I think we have to teach a lot of these kids first to be gentlemen," Duke told *Surfer* magazine in 1965. "Gotta be clean cut youngsters, you know. And keep the rule and never get in trouble."

Duke Kahanamoku interrupted his cheerleading duties for surfing to fly to Japan for the 1964 Tokyo Olympics, the first time that the Games were held in Asia. The Tokyo Olympics served as Japan's coming-out party for its post-World War II reconstruction efforts. Television coverage of the Olympic Games had begun in earnest at the 1960 Rome Olympics, when CBS paid about $400,000 for the TV rights. In 1964, NBC paid more than $1 million to broadcast the Tokyo Olympics, using satellite technology to transmit the pictures and sounds. Pierre de Coubertin surely would have blanched at the money involved with his all-amateur Olympics.

In Japan, Kahanamoku was hailed as the original swim sensation of the Olympics. Old-timers recalled that he had encouraged Japanese swimmers during their burst of glory in the 1930s, not to mention his encouragement of Hawaiian swimmers of Japanese descent. Duke was delighted that Olympic organizers added volleyball, which was one of his favorite sports, to the official program (although beach volleyball would have to wait until 1996 to be part of the Olympics).

Duke also delighted in the swimming results, with Don Schollander leading the American men to seven gold medals. But it was increasingly apparent that swimming could not compete with surfing, at least in terms of media attention and youth interest. FINA, the governing body of swimming, had tried to grow the sport by adding countless relay events and disciplines. The butterfly became an Olympic event in 1956, and the individual medley was instituted in 1964. Female swimmers had many more opportunities than their counterparts in track and field; the women's 100-meter record of 58.9 seconds, set by Australia's Dawn Fraser in 1964, was faster than Duke's best time.

With the exception of the Olympics, however, when interest burbled for a few weeks, swimming did not attract large audiences or commercial opportunities. Antiquated amateur rules still prevented the biggest stars, like Americans Schollander and Donna De Varona and Australians Dawn Fraser and Murray Rose, from making a living in the pool. The prestigious private clubs from Kahanamoku's era, like the Illinois and Los Angeles athletic clubs, no longer sponsored elite swimmers or teams. The traveling aquatic shows made popular by Johnny Weissmuller, Eleanor Holm, and Esther Williams had disappeared; populist plunges, including the Sutro Baths in San Francisco, were being demolished. In the days before underwater camera technology, swimming did not lend itself to quality television coverage.

Competitive swimming ebbed in Hawaii as well. No Hawaiian qualified for the U.S. Olympic swim team in 1960 or 1964, breaking an appearance and medal streak that dated back to 1936. The Waikiki Natatorium that Kahanamoku and Weissmuller had inaugurated before a sold-out throng in 1927, the Beaux Arts symbol of Hawaiian aquatic prowess, was closed because of its crumbling condition.

The image of elite swimming was drudgery: the infinite laps, the victory margins measured by one one-hundredth of a second, the noxious chlorine. "The young people are too lazy," commented Kahanamoku, when asked about the state of swimming in Hawaii. "They would rather take a surfboard out than practice swimming."[14]

34

Kimo McVay's efforts to link Kahanamoku with surfing's youth-infused ethos coalesced around the first Duke Kahanamoku surfing contest, held at Sunset Beach on the North Shore of Oahu, in December of 1965. McVay hired Fred Van Dyke to organize the competition, and the big-wave surfer devised a unique format: an invitation-only meet that would be restricted to twenty-four top surfers from Hawaii, California, and Peru, including Kahanamoku's surf team quartet, as well as George Downing, Greg Noll, Mickey Muñoz, Mickey Dora, Dewey Weber, Kimo Hollinger, and Corky Carroll.

With such a top-quality field competing at such a storied locale, "The Duke" was trumpeted as "the Olympics of the Surfing World," with the winner receiving a golden statuette that was made by the same company that designed the Academy Awards. CBS agreed to televise the event (although the broadcast aired the following Easter).[1] When the competitors descended upon Honolulu, they were put up at the Moana Hotel and treated to a lavish steak dinner and party at Duke's restaurant.

Van Dyke patiently waited until the conditions were just right, and then declared that the contest would be held the next day. The twelve-foot waves were big and difficult during the morning preliminaries as Duke stationed himself on the beach and watched the dramatics unfold.

In the afternoon, when seventeen-year-old Jeff Hakman and the seven other finalists paddled out into brisk off-shore winds and rain squalls, the diminutive teenager looked like a child. Hakman proceeded to tear apart his favorite North Shore break—dropping, accelerating, climbing, and disappearing inside a curling wave—with what judge Buzzy Trent described as "the best ride I've ever seen at Sunset Beach. Jeff never made a mistake."[2]

Hakman won easily, Paul Strauch placed second, and Peru's Felipe Pomar was third. At the awards banquet the next evening, Duke and all of the surfers gathered to watch Bruce Brown's latest surfing flick, *Slippery When Wet*.

"The Duke" was an instant success. *Surfer* magazine rated the invitational above the Makaha contest, calling it "a marvel of organization, planning, and probably the greatest overall surfing ever put together in one competition."[3] As Fred Hemmings put it, "For the first time surfers were treated like the great athletes they were. The surfers weren't sleeping in the back of their cars."[4]

Kahanamoku was pleased, not only with the results, but also with how the contest legitimized the sport that he had popularized. "Surfing is good for [youth]," he said. "It keeps them off the streets. Surfing has helped Hawaii financially by attracting more people here and we have to take care of the boys and girls who take part in the sport."[5]

If there was any criticism of "The Duke," it was that only one full-blooded Hawaiian surfer, Kealoha Kaio, was selected to be part of the twenty-four-man field. The next year, local stars Eddie Aikau and Ben Aipa were invited to compete, reportedly at Kahanamoku's suggestion. The pair finished in sixth and seventh place, respectively, as Ricky Grigg took first, with Fred Hemmings third.[6]

"The Duke" turned into a professional event in 1967, with winner Mike Doyle receiving a check for $1,000. Joey Cabell became the only original member of Duke's surfing team to win the contest with his victory in 1969.

McVay's marketing strategy revolved completely around Kahanamoku, and it succeeded as long as Duke cooperated with the game plan. Kahanamoku had long resisted the entreaties of authors who wanted to interview him and ghostwrite his life story. McVay persuaded Duke to work with local journalist Joe Brennan and allow him to compile material for two books.

Kahanamoku visited Brennan at his seaside Waikiki apartment three times a week. Their conversations took place over the span of one year. That led to the publication of a biography titled *Duke of Hawaii* and a history-cum-guide called *Duke Kahanamoku's World of Surfing*. One local newspaper excerpted the entire biography in serial form.[7]

When Duke was healthy enough to make public appearances, he remained a publicity magnet. The Queen Mother of England stopped at the Honolulu airport, and Duke gave her a quick hula lesson. Photographs of the pair were published in newspapers around the world; they reminded Duke of his long connection to the British royal family, from the origin of his first name to the surfing lessons he gave the future King Edward VIII in 1920. Duke was feted in Santa Monica as part of the inaugural class that was inducted into the Surfing Hall of Fame, and he was celebrated in Ft. Lauderdale, Florida, when he joined Johnny Weissmuller and Buster Crabbe as charter members of the International Swimming Hall of Fame.[8]

McVay's all-or-nothing reliance on Duke, however, backfired whenever Kahanamoku's medical problems surfaced. He was hospitalized for ten days in March of 1962 because of stomach ulcers. In May of that year, he was hit in the head by the boom of his catamaran. After complaining of dizziness and headaches, he suddenly fell down and could not get up. He was rushed to Kaiser Hospital.

"They found there was something in his head," Nadine said. "It was terrible, the suspense. . . . We didn't know whether he was going to survive or not."[9]

Cerebral imaging showed that he had a massive blood clot that was displacing arteries and exerting tremendous pressure on the right side of his brain. Emergency brain surgery saved his life.

He spent weeks in the hospital, with Nadine at his side. His brothers and sisters visited frequently and were shocked at his condition. His eyes were rheumy. Skin sagged from his once powerful chest. His beautiful hair was shorn. He had no energy.

All around him were reminders of his mortality. Bill Bachrach, Johnny Weissmuller's coach and the leader of the Illinois Athletic Club, had recently died. John D. Kaupiko, a charter member of Hui Nalu, passed away in March of 1962. "Dad" Center, whom Duke out-swam in Honolulu harbor back in 1910 and who became his coach and trusted friend, succumbed in September of 1962.

Kahanamoku recovered slowly. Nadine took him to Kauai for uninterrupted rest. The headaches and dizziness disappeared. His leonine white mane grew back. Friends knew that he was feeling better when he joked about the *puka* ("hole") in his head from the surgery.

The ocean was once again his salve. He had to crawl into the water initially, supported by a cane, before he was able to float. He stayed busy tinkering with his equipment at the Waikiki Yacht Club and helped friends paint their boats. He never stopped sailing, fishing, or puttering around on the *Nadu K*, but Nadine no longer permitted him to go out to sea alone.

Kahanamoku maintained his surfboards, but he found that he could not manage his hefty wooden board. "Do me a favor," he told a friend. "Take my longboard out. Catch a few waves. It's been landlocked too long. Needs to get wet."[10]

In 1965, Kahanamoku underwent a prostate operation. Then in 1967 he entered Kaiser Hospital for bleeding ulcers. He needed five blood transfusions. An operation removed about 40 percent of his stomach. "A few prayers wouldn't hurt," Nadine told one reporter,[11] before Duke bounced back. "I thought I was *pau*," he admitted.[12]

Comments that Kahanamoku made in New York City, while attending the 1964 World's Fair to promote Hawaii, undermined McVay's efforts and made headlines for the wrong reasons. Almost seventy-four years old, with recurrent medical issues, he told reporter Eddie Sherman that he was planning to run for the United States Congress. "I want to do something for the people of Hawaii, and feel my election as Congressman would be a wonderful climax to my career."[13]

The announcement "had the effect of a bomb going off here," McVay wrote Nadine. "I have said nothing and done nothing about it at all, as I feel there is more than enough time to make a final decision after you return and we can discuss it in full, looking at the good and bad points involved."[14]

Kahanamoku changed his mind when he came home, no doubt after he received counsel from McVay and Nadine. "When I saw all that traffic there in New York I knew I couldn't go to Washington," he said. "What would I do? Here I can swim and sail and do my exercises. I think I can do more for the people here in Hawaii than I can in Washington."[15]

Two years later, in 1966, Kahanamoku threatened to run for lieutenant governor of Hawaii. In a disjointed interview, the seventy-five-year-old Kahanamoku announced that he would seek the governor's office instead. Once elected, he claimed, "I'll get my cabinet to run the government. Then I'll double-back, see, and become ambassador-at-large for the state of Hawaii. That's what I really want. But I got to go through it this way."[16]

He disclosed two motivations for seeking office. "I got to pay for food, taxes, gas for my car, everything," he lamented. And, he said, "We never had a Hawaiian governor before. When I'm *pau*, no Hawaiian left who can do it."

Asked to detail his views, Duke sounded like an out-of-touch senior citizen. The Republican Party platform? "I don't know anything about that.

I don't keep up with that." Taxes? "What about taxes?" he said. "Mine only go up, up, up. I wouldn't let it go higher unless some reason to put it up. Make the rich pay a little more. Not the poor." What about civic construction projects? "I want to build a sports hall of fame for trophies, pictures, history of athletes. I have a lot of things. But not only for my things."

Kimo McVay and his mother, Kinau Wilder, hastily arranged a press conference. Kinau Wilder announced that she was turning over her one-third share of Duke Kahanamoku enterprises, including the nightclub, to Duke and her son. "I cannot bear to see my beloved friend Duke subjected to any kind of political race at this time in his life—and my son Kimo be accused of pushing him into the political arena for personal gain," she said. "I do this simply because it will make Duke financially independent for the rest of his life."[17]

Kahanamoku buried his head in the crook of his elbow. When he straightened and faced the media, tears were rolling down his face. "This is what I want," he said. "It's sweet of you. It's a surprise to me, and I love you."[18]

An exuberant McVay took it from there. "I'm going to give him a new car and boat and $1,000 a month instead of the $400 he's been getting," he told reporters. "A minimum of $1,000 a month. Anything he wants."[19]

McVay arranged for an assistant to drive Duke around town and accompany him on boating and fishing excursions. "Kimo was the only one that really gave Duke the recognition and the support he needed," Fred Hemmings said. "Duke lived in royal style once he became part of Kimo's efforts. He had a Rolls Royce. He was oftentimes chauffeured around, and he was well taken care of."[20]

"People say I exploited him," McVay said. "Ha! He loved it."[21]

That McVay treated Kahanamoku with respect is beyond dispute. He also freed Duke from financial worry, allowing him to enjoy his final years. But this freedom came at a price. In exchange for the monthly stipend that McVay boasted that he "gave" Kahanamoku, Duke reportedly surrendered his interest in the restaurant and in the corporation to Kimo.

"A lot of people took my brother for a ride," Louis Kahanamoku said. "Duke was easy. Too goddamn easy."[22]

Others who knew Kahanamoku well held a more nuanced view. "You couldn't really take advantage of [Duke]," his friend Kenneth Brown said. "I know there were others around him who wanted him to be financially successful. But I never felt Duke had his heart in that. . . . He walked through a Western world, but he was always essentially Hawaiian."[23]

35

In August of 1967, when Duke Kahanamoku turned seventy-seven, McVay threw a birthday party that was over-the-top even for him. The cake was a sixteen-foot replica of a redwood board. Presents included a Silver Cloud Rolls Royce convertible, an exquisite handmade feather quilt, and a portrait painted by "big eyes" artist Margaret Keane. Duke's favorite gift was a portable generator for his boat, which was delivered on a tray with a red ribbon.

Don Ho appeared in an all-white outfit, and, as some 7,000 guests nibbled on teriyaki steak and sipped mai-tais, he and the Aliis led the room in a rousing version of "Happy Birthday."

Festooned with lei and standing before the throng on a stage with Nadine at his side, Kahanamoku stood smiling, tears brimming in his eyes. He reached out his arms as if to embrace the crowd. "This is a real luau," he said. "It was nice of you all to come."[1]

Duke Kahanamoku was content to putter on his latest boat, the *Nadu K. II*, a twenty-eight-foot cruiser with twin engines that he docked at the Waikiki Yacht Club. The yacht club was one of his regular haunts, along with the latest incarnation of the Outrigger Canoe Club, which had moved down the beach next to the Elks Club.

On Sunday nights, Duke and Nadine liked to frequent his restaurant for dinner and dancing. They dined there together on January 21, 1968, and Kahanamoku signed autographs for tourists at his usual table.

The next day, January 22, Duke joined brother Bill at the Waikiki Yacht Club. The two were fixing a little skiff that Duke had purchased, making measurements to put up a mast.

At about 2:30 in the afternoon, Bill was scraping paint from the boat while Duke rummaged for the keys to the Rolls Royce. A tourist from Europe approached Bill, but Bill could not understand what he was saying. The man pointed. Bill looked and saw Duke lying on his back, sprawled out behind the car.

Bill rushed to him. One eye was closed. Blood was coming from a wound at the back of his head. Bill searched for a pulse. He massaged his brother's chest and called to him. An ambulance was summoned, and Duke was taken to Kaiser Hospital.

He never regained consciousness and was pronounced dead that afternoon. He was seventy-seven years old. Doctors attributed the cause of his death to a heart attack, not to the head injuries suffered from the fall. Nadine collapsed when she heard the news. She woke up in the hospital.[2]

No one who was close to Duke was truly shocked at the news. His health had been shaky, and two of his brothers had recently succumbed to heart attacks. First it was Sam. The second-fastest swimmer of the Kahanamoku clan, and Duke's rival at the 1924 Paris Olympics, Sam had taken his charms and applied them to selling real estate before dying at the age of sixty-three in 1966. Then it was David, who died in 1967, not long after he became a hero for rescuing nine swimmers at Jones Beach in New York. David collapsed and died doing what he loved: paddling a canoe with friends in Waikiki.

Still, many found it difficult to believe that the indomitable symbol of Hawaii was gone. Tributes poured in from near and far. "He was my inspiration for many years and I'm proud to admit it," Don Ho said.[3]

"The Duke was just the Duke," con-man-turned-newspaper-columnist Sammy Amalu wrote. "Year in and year out, he never changed. Like Aloha Tower or Diamond Head or the beach at Waikiki, the Duke was always there. Just being himself. Just being Duke."[4]

"There is great sadness and mourning in Hawaii today," U.S. Senator Hiram Fong intoned from Washington DC. "Hawaii's most famous citizen . . . has passed away."[5]

"Whatever causes that ever-so-rare combination of native ability, skill and courage that makes a really good athlete, the Duke had it," the *Hartford Courant* noted. "He had that same rare genius that, in other fields, inspired a [Bill] Tilden from the Philadelphia main line and a Bobby Jones from the

Atlanta equivalent just as it did the peasant-born [Pavvo] Nurmi and the asylum-raised [Babe] Ruth."[6]

The *New York Times* invoked the reign of King Kamehameha. "To his own generation of Hawaiians," the newspaper concluded, "Duke Kahanamoku was sometimes looked upon as the personification of the prophecy of King Kamehameha, who in the late 19th century [sic] predicted the complete subjugation of the islands by the white man, but said that before the native Hawaiian race died out, one man would bring it fame."[7]

Five days after Duke's death, on Saturday, January 27, 1968, the skies above Oahu were steely gray. Rain fell in a heavy pitter-patter. The streets of downtown Honolulu were empty. Flags at government buildings hung at half-mast.

Kimo McVay declared that Kahanamoku's funeral would be open to all because he "belonged to everyone in Hawaii."[8] Actually, only the second half of the funeral was accessible to the public. Formal services were first held in Honolulu, where more than one thousand mourners and over one hundred honorary pallbearers packed into St. Andrew's Episcopal Cathedral. Nadine was joined by Duke's three surviving brothers, Bill, Louis, and Sargent, and his two surviving sisters, Bernice and Kapiolani, and their families; as well as numerous Paoa cousins and other relatives; Don Ho; friends from Hui Nalu and the Outrigger Canoe Club; and politicians.

A youngster played a single tone upon a nose flute. The sixty-five-member glee club from the Kamehameha Schools sang "Hawaii Aloha," a nineteenth-century ode that started as a dirge and ended in a chorus of celebration:

Happy youth of Hawaii
Rejoice! Rejoice!
Gentle breezes blow
Love always for Hawaii.[9]

Arthur Godfrey flew over from the mainland to deliver the eulogy, noting that "long ago Duke and I had made a pact: if he went first, I would be with him, and if I went first, he would be with me."[10]

Duke Kahanamoku was "the soul of dignity—*ali'i o ali'i*, the son of natural-born kings," Godfrey continued. "He gave these islands a new dimension, winning the respect of the world for himself and his people. What

Longfellow's *Hiawatha* and later Jim Thorpe had done for the American Indian, Paoa did for all Polynesians, especially Hawaiians."

According to Godfrey, Duke "loved people as only one who has really lived can love his fellows. His great physical strength alone would never have won his titles for him. It was that he had known defeat, that he had persevered with great courage to overcome the weaknesses of human frailty. And he knew so well how vicarious and empty are the lives of most. He had known and triumphed over one thousand heartbreaking disappointments, including—dear God help us—the stupid, blind, infuriating one of racism on the mainland."

After the service, a massive motorcade trailed a thirty-man police escort that moved slowly toward Waikiki. Thousands of people had gathered on the beach for the second part of the memorial. They stood quietly on the familiar crescent-shaped strip of white sand. Some were dressed in suit and tie. Others wore T-shirts and shorts. Long-haired teenagers in bare feet and aging beachboys with ruddy skin leaned against their surfboards. Shriners mingled with Masons. Tourists staying in the string of high-rise hotels lining Kalakaua Avenue peered down from the balconies.

Godfrey escorted Nadine to the water's edge in front of the Royal Hawaiian Hotel. She wore a white Hawaiian dress and veil underneath her raincoat, her reddened eyes shielded by dark sunglasses. She carried the urn that held her husband's ashes and placed it on a surfboard that rested upon a red-and-white outrigger canoe. Two white carnations lay on either side of the urn.

The Reverend Abraham Akaka, bare-legged and barefoot, wearing a wooden cross formed by two miniature surfboards, scooped sand from the beach and carefully poured some of it over the urn holding Kahanamoku's ashes. "It is written," he said, "God is aloha. And Paoa was a man of aloha. His life was gentle, and the elements so mixed in him that nature might stand up and say to all the world, 'This was a man.'"[11]

The gathered beachboys, under the direction of Splash Lyons, took their cue and joined in a version of "Aloha 'Oe," the traditional song of farewell composed by Queen Liliuokalani:

Farewell to you, farewell to you
The charming one who dwells in the shaded bowers
One fond embrace,

'Ere I depart

Until we meet again.[12]

Some two dozen outrigger canoes stood ready. The first boat held Duke's paddling team from the Outrigger Canoe Club, who had been young men when Duke first coached them in the 1940s but now were middle-aged. The steering seat, usually occupied by Duke, was left empty. His paddle was propped in the stern, twined with *maile* leaves.

Into the second boat stepped Nadine, holding the urn, followed by Reverend Akaka and Duke's brothers, who had changed into their swim-suits, with Sargent acting as steersman. Next came canoes loaded with cousins, nieces, nephews, business partners, politicians, and civic leaders.

The flotilla lifted into the restless waves, freeing them from the beach. Over one hundred surfers paddled out on their surfboards. An armada of small boats awaited them. The only sounds were the steady dipping of the oars into the water and the rain. Diamond Head loomed in the mist.

About a half a mile from shore, Sargent found that, no matter how hard he paddled, he could go no further. This was, it seemed, the place to stop. The other canoes drifted and bobbed like flotsam. The crew from a nearby Coast Guard cutter, dressed in formal whites, stood at attention by the rail. Paul Strauch Jr., from Duke's surf team, noticed other interested onlookers. "A bunch of sharks came in and circled right around where they had Duke's ashes," he said, noting that the shark was Kahanamoku's *aumakua* (traditional guiding spirit). "You could see them breaking the water. Not just one."[13]

Nadine held the small bronze box in her lap. She brought it to her lips and kissed it. She kissed it again and then slipped the box with her husband's remains into the turquoise waters that were his everlasting love.

A cloudburst appeared, as if the heavens above were offering their own lament. Family and friends lobbed flowers into the sea. A multicolored array of carnations, *pikake*, and orchids floated on the water's surface like an undulating carpet.

Moments passed. Tears and hugs were plentiful. Then the canoes turned around and took off toward shore. The oarsmen dug their paddles deep into the salty water, yelling and laughing in the rain, in one final sprint for Duke Kahanamoku as his earthly remains merged into the eternal waves, a waterman to the last and forever.

Epilogue

In the immediate aftermath of Duke Kahanamoku's death, a pall seemed to envelop Hawaii's oceanscape. A reporter who ventured to Waikiki to interview the beachboys on the anniversary of Duke's passing received a cool reception. "Duke Kahanamoku is a closed subject around here," Jimmy Hakuole said. "We old timers never talk about a beachboy once he passes away.... There's nothing left of what the old days used to be."[1]

The following year, Duke's widow Nadine sued promoter Kimo McVay. The lawsuit charged that when her husband signed away his interest in the restaurant and other businesses to McVay in exchange for a monthly stipend, he was "of unsound mind and incapable of understanding the documents he was induced to sign." The lawsuit further alleged that the agreement was executed "by the artifice and undue influence" of McVay and was "a fraud."[2]

As Nadine and McVay fought over Duke's estate in court, McVay and Don Ho ended up in litigation, too. Duke's nightclub was sold and then it folded. The Duke Kahanamoku Invitational, which reigned as the world's most prestigious surfing contest into the early 1980s and helped jump-start the formation of the professional surfing circuit, also faded away. "The thing just died," one organizer said, "a death of no sponsorship and lack of management."[3]

The concept of *aloha* that Kahanamoku embodied and preached fell out of favor. The increasingly militant (and even separatist) native population railed against the damage being done to Oahu's fragile ecosystem by rampant tourism and opposed the Vietnam War and the American military presence throughout Hawaii. They demanded reparations from the United States and supported the burgeoning sovereignty movement.

"The Aloha Spirit is facing extinction," one commentator wrote shortly after Kahanamoku's death. Hawaii had become "a sugar-coated fortress, an autistic Eden, a plastic paradise in which the militarism and racism of the American empire are cloaked by a deceptive veil of sunshine and flowers."[4]

The image of Kahanamoku as an accommodationist was now perceived as a liability, especially in an era when more overtly confrontational athletes were challenging the establishment: boxing champ Muhammad Ali, who refused to fight in Vietnam; track stars Tommie Smith and John Carlos, who raised their fists in solidarity with the Civil Rights Movement at the 1968 Mexico City Olympics just months after Kahanamoku's death; Curt Flood, who sued Major League Baseball over the reserve clause; and Merry Lepper, Roberta Gibb, and Kathrine Switzer, who were determined to enter and run marathons, even when women were banned from doing so.

Certainly, Kahanamoku was a man of his times. He relied on the assistance of others, in and out of the water, throughout his life: Bill Rawlins, "Dad" Center, and Fred Cady; his wife Nadine; Doris Duke; Arthur Godfrey; and Kimo McVay. He often felt beholden to them because he could not have survived without their financial largesse; without their support to send him to the Olympics and navigate the thicket of amateurism; without their help in setting up his political career; and without their marketing savvy in his business ventures.

But it is also true that his essence, his Hawaiian-ness, was never usurped. He was no minstrel puppet; he was his own man who quietly displayed a subversive side. As the first Hawaiian to compete in the Olympics and as the first Pacific Islander to win athletic glory in the modern era, he redefined what it meant to be an American. He took part in "The Mutiny of the *Matoika*," one of the first mass protests conducted by a group of athletes. When he was attacked in print, he sued one of Hawaii's most powerful businessmen and his newspaper. He integrated private clubs, pools, and public beaches, not to mention an exclusive Oahu neighborhood with his marriage to a white divorcée.

In overcoming the plantation-like oppression of the small-town racists who controlled Hawaii during much of the twentieth century, Kahanamoku provided hope after the loss of Queen Liliuokalani's monarchy and Hawaiian independence. He gave native Hawaiians a symbol of power, of *mana*, to believe in when they had scant few leaders or heroes. That he emerged so gracious, so regal-like, was his salvation and his strength. He possessed the ultimate trump card: a transcendent love for his home, what he called the "navel of the world," and a deep connection to its values, traditions, and teachings.

In the years following Duke Kahanamoku's death, Nadine became the point-person in preserving her husband's legacy, often assisted by surfer-turned-politician Fred Hemmings. Theirs was a multipronged effort that was designed to achieve lasting public recognition for Duke. Their initial approach was local; they backed campaigns to name city streets, pools, and swim meets in his name. Then they went national with their cause. A grassroots effort that was spearheaded by members of the Surfrider Foundation, an environmental group, lobbied for the creation of a U.S. postage stamp bearing Duke Kahanamoku's likeness. Art director Carl Herrman, a veteran surfer, shepherded the long-gestating project. He hired artist Michael Dees to paint a colorful portrait of a youthful-looking Kahanamoku, set against the backdrop of Diamond Head, from a black-and-white photo supplied by the Bishop Museum. The U.S. Postal Service issued the thirty-seven-cent stamp in 2002.[5]

The undertaking that was dearest to Nadine's heart was the creation of a statue in her husband's honor. This idea had been discussed since the late 1930s, but Duke himself quashed those plans. Several sculptors, from R. Tait McKenzie to his protégé Joseph Brown to artist Rosalie Young Persons, depicted Kahanamoku in miniature form. None were readied for public consumption.

"I still haven't got his statue," Nadine complained to one interviewer as the centennial of Kahanamoku's birth approached, "and I want it so badly. . . . There should be a statue of Duke somewhere on the Island. And a big one like King Kamehameha's across from the ['Iolani] palace."[6]

Finally, the Waikiki Improvement Association raised $200,000 and commissioned local art professor Jan Gordon Fisher to design a statue. On what would have been Duke's one-hundredth birthday, August 24, 1990, a large crowd gathered at Kuhio Beach Park for the unveiling of Fisher's work. Present were Nadine, an elegant widow of eighty-five years; Duke's two surviving brothers, Louis and Sargent; numerous cousins; assorted beachboys and politicians, including state representative Hemmings; and hundreds of supporters in aloha shirts and slippers.

The arrival of hula dancers and the chanter via outrigger canoes signaled the start of the ceremony. A covering was removed, and the bronzed Duke loomed above the sand: a muscular figure in swim trunks, with a decorative *lei* around his neck. An equally large bronze surfboard loomed behind him. The statue represented Kahanamoku in his three most prominent roles: champion swimmer, pioneer surfer, and ambassador of aloha.

"It's gorgeous," Nadine said to the crowd, her eyes hidden behind dark sunglasses. "I hope you will all come to the beach and visit him because he doesn't want to be lonely."[7]

Most residents applauded the tribute. But many felt its placement was inappropriate and disrespectful. Some wondered why the statue wasn't situated further down the beach, outside the Waikiki Natatorium that Kahanamoku had inaugurated in 1927, a position that might have prodded the state to repair the woebegone structure and restore it as a community gem.

The bronze Duke also was turned away from the ocean that he so loved. Instead, the statue faced inland, toward the hotels and shops fronting Kalakaua Avenue, with his arms outstretched. It was as if he were embracing traffic, fast-food outlets, and mobs of tourists.

This contradicted the most basic code of a waterman. "When I first came to the beach he taught me," Rabbit Kekai said. "The first thing he said to me was, 'Never turn your back on the ocean.'"[8]

"The beachboys are all *huhu* [angry]," champion surfer Rell Sunn, known as the Queen of Makaha, said. "They think it's wrong. It's not the Hawaiian way. They know Duke, and they think he should be facing the sea."[9]

The statue has become a tourist attraction in Waikiki, as has a statue of Duke surfing that Nadine helped to dedicate in Australia in 1994. The process of creating these monuments, of putting Duke Kahanamoku on a pedestal as it were, has had another, perhaps unintended effect: it has succeeded in shaping Kahanamoku's image exclusively in glowing terms. Subjects perceived as controversial, including Duke's alleged relationship with Doris Duke, have been deemed verboten by his acolytes. His display of sportsmanship at the 1924 Paris Olympics has been emphasized rather than his defeat in the race. Print the legend, indeed.

In 1997 Nadine Kahanamoku died at the age of ninety-two. The bulk of her estate, which reportedly was worth $3 million, went to the John A. Burns School of Medicine of the University of Hawaii at Manoa, to be used for scholarships. Duke's trophies and personal effects were distributed among several institutions, including the Kamehameha Schools, the Hawaii State Archives, and the Bishop Museum.

Before her death Nadine assigned the trademark to her late husband's name to a nonprofit organization that operates under the auspices of the Outrigger Canoe Club. The stated mission of the Outrigger Duke Kahanamoku Foundation (ODKF) is to assist local students with scholarships and to preserve and develop water sports with cultural significance to Hawaii. The trademark rights to Duke's name are now controlled by a California company called Malama Pono.

The resentment of many Kahanamoku relatives over this arrangement was palpable. They questioned why Nadine bequeathed control of Duke's name and likeness to people outside of the family and bemoaned the fact that they would not receive any benefit from projects derived from their name, including a successful chain of restaurant-bars (called Duke's) that stretches from Waikiki to Malibu.

"Our family name has been given out, and everybody has it but us," Harry "Didi" Robello, a grandnephew of Kahanamoku and the owner of a Waikiki-based beachboy business, told the *Los Angeles Times*. "We're all being used. We're being exploited."[10]

"People think that the Kahanamoku family got everything," one relative told me. "Nobody gave us nothing."[11]

Others saw the situation as another example of cultural imperialism, paralleling Hawaii's metamorphosis during Kahanamoku's lifetime. "It fits into a larger picture with corrosive, cumulative effects—a freeway here, a high rise there, a shopping center that partially blocks a mountain view, a gated community that closes off a beach access and ever-increasing real estate prices that prevent many indigenous islanders from buying homes," journalist Patti Paniccia noted. "To Hawaiians, the carving up of Duke's trademark represents not only the buying and selling of a name, but the buying and selling of Hawaii itself."[12]

One hundred and twenty-five years after his birth and nearly fifty years after his death, Duke Kahanamoku remains relevant. *Surfer Magazine* crowned him the "Surfer of the Century" in 1999. In 2000, *Sports Illustrated* selected Duke as the "greatest sports figure of the century" from Hawaii. In 2014, the National Portrait Gallery in Washington DC, declared Duke Kahanamoku to be among the one hundred "coolest" American icons.

"Cool" or not, Kahanamoku was unlike any other athlete, before or since, because he straddled disparate cultures, eras, and trends: the nineteenth and twentieth centuries; the Kingdom of Hawaii and the fiftieth state; wooden longboards and foam boards; woolen bathing suits and aloha shirts; silent movies and *Gidget*; Versailles, Pearl Harbor, and Vietnam. He knew Pierre de Coubertin and Peter Ueberroth; Alexander Hume Ford and Eddie Aikau; Jack London and James Michener; Cecil B. DeMille and Bruce Brown; Queen Liliuokalani and John F. Kennedy.

Few prominent athletes have been so intrinsically linked to one place and one culture. Fewer still have enjoyed such a meaningful relationship with water and, especially, with the Pacific Ocean—what one observer called "the islanders' great solace, escape and nourishment, the amniotic fluid that would keep them hedonistic and aloof, guarded, gentle and mysterious."[13]

It is only partly accurate that, as Duke put it, "out of the water I am nothing," but whether he was rescuing drowning victims or jumping into the ocean from the deck of an ocean liner for a dip or bodysurfing at Waikiki, or whether his remains were settling into that final resting place, Duke Kahanamoku was most comfortable in liquid, away from the exigencies found on land.

"How long were you on the beach?" a reporter asked Duke about five years before his death.

"All my life," he replied.[14]

ACKNOWLEDGMENTS

In Hawaii: I owe a debt of gratitude to Barbara Del Piano and her late husband, Tony, for providing me with a place to stay, correcting my mistakes, and treating me with aloha. Huge thanks to mentor and writer extraordinaire Don Wallace (and his wife Mindy) for advice, writing and otherwise, and for reading a first draft of the manuscript. Thanks to Earl "Pa'mai" Tenn for fielding questions and introducing me to the delightful Pi'ikea Miyamoto. Thanks to Sandra Hall for her graciousness and passion. Mahalo to those who spoke with me and/or facilitated research: "Buffalo" Keaulana (assist to his son Brian), "Rabbit" Kekai (assist to his wife Lynne), John R. K. Clark, Michael Ah Choy, Joey Cabell (assist to Yana Deaton), Mickey Muñoz, Jock Sutherland, Fred Hemmings, Keone Downing, the late Dorian "Doc" Paskowitz, John Zapotocky (assist to Alan Nemiroff), "Didi" Robello, Samuel "Bunny" Kahanamoku Jr., Ricky Lemke, Ron Haworth, Timothy Tovar DeLaVega, Lambert Wai (assist to Dan Ford), John Titchen, Troy Siruno. Stacey Naipo at the Kamehameha School Archives was very patient with my questions; John Lacy with the Outrigger Canoe Club; Melissa Shimonishi, Ricki Aikau, and Victoria Nihi at the Hawaii State Archives; DeSoto Brown, Alan Huapala Kapuaala, Tia Reber, and Leah Caldeira at the Bishop Museum archives (and for guidance above and beyond the call of duty); Barry Nakasone with the Department of Education; Dore Minatodani and Eleanor Kleiber with the Hawaiian and Pacific Collections, University of Hawaii at Manoa; Ron Okamura and Jennifer Asato at McKinley High School; Bruce Blankenfeld with Hui Nalu; Jim Fulton and Brent Imonen with OceanFest; Dr. Ricardo Trimillos, professor emeritus in Asian Studies and Ethnomusicology at University of Hawaii at Manoa; Ethel Alikapala Ward with East-West Center; and Hawaiian Islands Stamp and Coin.

On the mainland: Thanks to my agent, Rob Wilson, for believing in this project. Thanks to my editor at the University of Nebraska Press, Rob Taylor, and his assistant, Courtney Ochsner, for their efforts and patience, as well as support staff at Nebraska. In Los Angeles, LA84 Foundation's Anita DeFrantz, Patrick Escobar, Wayne Wilson, Michael Salmon, and Shirley Ito combine to operate the world's finest sports and Olympics research center. Mark Gunther of Kahanamoku Swimboat in El Segundo answered all of my questions and offered great advice. Paul Strauch Jr., member of Duke's surfing team and the executive director of the Surfing Heritage and Culture Center in San Clemente, encouraged my efforts at every stage, while SHCC's Dick Metz and Barry Haun were generous with their time and knowledge. Historian Jane Schmauss of the California Surf Museum in Oceanside facilitated my research and introduced me to the Henry family. Kim Stoner with the Santa Cruz Surfing Museum dug out long-buried articles about Kahanamoku and connected me with Northern California surfers. Steve Pezman, editor of the *Surfer's Journal*, was helpful throughout my research, and stamp designer Carl Hermann provided fascinating background about the U.S. stamp of Duke Kahanamoku. Thanks to the Henry family members (Mary, Mike, and Bill); Jill Thrasher with the Sherman Library in Corona Del Mar; Jenny Romero, Faye Thompson, Sandra Archer, Jeanie Braun, Sue Kane, and staff at the Margaret Herrick Library, Academy of Motion Pictures Arts and Sciences in Beverly Hills; the staff at the UCLA Film and Television Archives; Steve MacLeod with the Special Collections and Archives at UC Irvine; Elizabeth Dunn, Research Services Librarian, and staff at the David Rubinstein Rare Book and Manuscript Library at Duke University; Steven and Cory Hathaway of the Los Angeles Athletic Club; Heather Perez and Pat Rothenberg at the Atlantic City Free Public Library; Paul Burnett with Surfside Sports in Costa Mesa; director Cindy Cross with the International Surfing Museum in Huntington Beach, California; Carol Alhadeff with Perry Ellis (Jantzen); Bruce Wigo, president and CEO, and Dr. Ivonne Schmid, curator, with the International Swimming Hall of Fame in Ft. Lauderdale; Bert Lippincott with the Newport Historical Society; Steve Vaught with paradiseleasedblog.com; John Ansley, Gregory Wiedeman, and staff with Archives and Special Collections at Marist College, Poughkeepsie, New York; Barbara Flak with the Long Beach Historical Society and Eileen Pollis at the Long Beach Public Library (New York); Nancy Miller with the University of Pennsylvania archives; Adrienne Evans with the Superior Court of California; the staff at The Lilly Library, Indiana University, Bloomington (John Ford Papers); Katie Richardson, archivist with Special Collections, Pepperdine University Libraries; Douglas Westfall with The Paragon Agency; Deborah Sisum, Head of New Media, National Portrait Gallery, Smithsonian Institution; Dave Taube, assistant head, Special Collections, USC Libraries; Andrea Zomorodian, Cathedral administrator, St. John's Cathedral. Thanks to Jake Carton, Donald Love, Peter Neushul, Peter Westwick, Dr. Howard Berlin, Eric Stedman, Peter Ueberroth, Bill Mallon, David Wallechinsky, Bruce Jenkins, David Rensin, the late Louis Zamperini, James Gaddis, Christopher Rowland of the *Boston Globe*, Shaun Tomson, and Jack O'Neill.

From Australia: Thanks to John MacRitchie with the Manly Library in New South Wales; author Phil Jarratt; and Tina Graham, Local Studies Librarian at the Warringah Council Library.

Gathering photos and images for this book was no easy task. Thanks to Stacy Naipo, Davi Kunishige, and Sheree Espinueva at the Kamehameha Schools; DeSoto Brown and Tia Reber at the Bishop Museum; Tina Graham with the Warringah Council Library; George Lee, photo editor at the *Honolulu Star-Advertiser*; Elizabeth Dunn, with the David Rubinstein Rare Book and Manuscript Library at Duke University, and the Doris Duke Charitable Foundation; Ivonne Schmid with the International Swimming Hall of Fame; Faye Thompson and Sue Kane at the Margaret Herrick Library; Stephen Jensen and Sierra Campbell with the Chicago History Museum; Christina Rice and Kimberly Creighton at the Los Angeles Public Library Photo Collection; Douglas Westfall with The Paragon Agency; Kim Stoner with the Santa Cruz Surfing Museum; Linda Ruth Tosetti; and James Gaddis.

Thanks also to a patient crew of friends, writers, mentors, and editors: Lynell George, Kate and Ko Maruyama, Mack and Kristina Reed, Susan Reifer, Emily Green, Greg Burk and Deborah Drooz, Kateri Butler, Pamela Klein, Donnell Alexander, Randy Williams, Steve Kettmann, Jason Levin, Tim Toner, Eric and Rosa Harmon, Alex Lipkind, Steve Tager, Joan Spindel, Tom Sweeney, Bill Bunke, Glenn Stout, Karen Wada, Mary Melton, Paul and Patty Feinberg, Regino Chavez, Kevin Roderick, Bruce Bebb, Bobby Levins (photographer extraordinaire) and Jean Guccione, Terry and Mary Cannon, John Schulian, Ron Rapoport, Kit Rachlis, Kevin Nelson,

Kerry Yo Nakagawa, David Roth, Amy Inouye and Stuart Rapoport, Dewey Wigod, J. Peder Zane, Curtis Claymont, Michelle Linn Gust and Sam and Lois Bloom; and members of the Moore, Berman, Hazen, Davis, Shaw, Cooper, Cirino, Ito, and Hall families, including Lucy Ito and Rob Corn, Mark Cirino, Tonio Cirino, Constance Moore, Adam Hazen, Mort Davis, Daniel Shaw, and Tony Shaw. Thanks to the tireless indexer Shirley Ito.

Special thanks to my immediate family—Jessie and Andy Davis and Jennifer Davis Hall—and to Orly and Figgy. And, of course, to the boss of me, Flora Ito.

AUTHOR'S NOTE

This biography has its genesis in research that I conducted for my previous book, *Showdown at Shepherd's Bush*, which was about the 1908 London Olympics. One of the three main characters in that story, marathon runner Johnny Hayes, was a coach with the American team at the 1912 Stockholm Olympics, and so I read about those Games thoroughly.

Jim Thorpe, of course, was the unquestioned star of the 1912 Stockholm Olympics. Not far behind Thorpe was Duke Kahanamoku. He was written about nearly as much as Thorpe was in 1912, and the King of Sweden requested a private exhibition so that he could watch Kahanamoku swim. No doubt this was because of Kahanamoku's speed in the water, but it also was because of his exotic heritage.

Yet, while Thorpe has been the subject of numerous biographies, comparatively little has been published about Kahanamoku since his death in 1968. Much of that material was hagiography (replete with errors and omissions) and academic dissertations. These well-intentioned efforts gave short shrift to Duke's "other" careers: his stint in Hollywood making motion pictures in the 1920s and his job as the sheriff of Honolulu.

I cannot profess to have mined every aspect of Duke Kahanamoku's sprawling life. The family members, friends, and contemporaries who knew him best are dead. Several relatives and close friends whom I attempted to speak with, men and women who knew Duke personally and well, firmly but politely declined to speak with me, citing everything from their own infirmities to the anger they harbor about how the family was treated after his death.

Their decision was not surprising. Hawaii prefers to keep its stories to itself, especially where outsiders are concerned. I respect their choice. It is my loss. Because I do not speak or read Hawaiian, I was unable to read material from Hawaiian-language sources. That, too, is my loss.

A note on the text: I have taken the stylistic liberty of removing most ʻokina marks—the glottal stops found in Hawaiian spelling. Thus, *Hawaiʻi* is *Hawaii* and *Oʻahu* is *Oahu*.

NOTES

PROLOGUE
1. From *The Man Who Shot Liberty Valance*.
2. Author correspondence.
3. *Albany Times Union*, January 25, 1941.

CHAPTER ONE
1. Duke Kahanamoku, from his appearance on *This Is Your Life*, Show #234, taped on February 20, 1957, Ralph Edwards Collection, UCLA Film & Television Archives.
2. Quoted in James D. Nendel, "Duke Kahanamoku: Twentieth-Century Hawaiian Monarch: The Values and Contributions to Hawaiian Culture from Hawaii's Sporting Legend" (Master's thesis, Pennsylvania State University, 2006), 13.
3. Statement of Maria Kanehaikana Piikoi, Duke's first cousin, in Edwin North McClellan, "The Bronze Duke of Waikiki," *Forecast* (newsletter of the Outrigger Canoe Club), August 1950, 4.
4. McClellan, "Bronze Duke of Waikiki," 4.
5. Duke Kahanamoku, taped interview by Lowell Thomas Jr., 1950. James A. Cannavino Library, Archives & Special Collections, Marist College, Poughkeepsie NY.
6. 1900 Census Report; Duke Kahanamoku papers, Folder 28, Hawaii State Archives; and Louis Kahanamoku chapter in *Waikiki, 1900–1985: Oral Histories, Volume II* (Honolulu: University of Hawaii at Manoa, 1987), 855.
7. Robert Louis Stevenson, *Travels in Hawaii*, ed. A. Grove Day (Honolulu: University of Hawaii Press, 1973), 6.
8. *Honolulu Star-Bulletin*, August 23, 1963.
9. Mary Paoa Clarke chapter in *Waikiki: Oral Histories*, 661.
10. *Honolulu Star-Bulletin*, October 8, 1918.
11. *Waikiki: Oral Histories*, 858.

12. *Honolulu Advertiser,* October 8, 1961; and quoted in Peter von Buol, "Sargent Kahanamoku," *Tiki Magazine,* Winter 2006, 48.
13. David Malo, quoted in Gavan Daws, *Shoal of Time: A History of the Hawaiian Islands* (Honolulu: University of Hawaii Press, 1968), 106.
14. Population figures from Ralph S. Kuykendall, *The Hawaiian Kingdom* trilogy (Honolulu: University of Hawaii Press, 1967), 3:116.
15. Howard Wayne Morgan, *William McKinley and His America* (Kent OH: Kent State University Press, 2003), 225.
16. Kuykendall, *Hawaiian Kingdom,* 508.
17. Evan Thomas, *The War Lovers* (New York: Little, Brown, 2010), 51.
18. *New York Times,* November 20, 1893.
19. Julia Flynn Siler, *Lost Kingdom: Hawaii's Last Queen, the Sugar Kings, and America's First Imperial Adventure* (New York: Atlantic Monthly Press, 2012), xxx.
20. Letter written to President Cleveland's former secretary of state Richard Olney, quoted in Sarah Vowell, *Unfamiliar Fishes* (New York: Riverhead Books, 2011), 224.

CHAPTER TWO

1. *Honolulu Star-Bulletin,* January 23, 1968.
2. *Handicraft Journal,* January 1889. Kamehameha Schools archives (accessed online: http://kapalama.ksbe.edu/archives/historical/newspaper/handicraft .php).
3. Kamehameha Schools archives.
4. Kamehameha Schools archives. Duke's brother David graduated from Kamehameha Schools in 1914. Duke himself received an honorary diploma as a member of the class of 1910 at the graduation ceremony in May of 1959.
5. Duke Kahanamoku, with Joe Brennan, *Duke Kahanamoku's World of Surfing* (New York: Grosset & Dunlap, 1968), 69.
6. For Hawaiian surfing history and lore, see Tom Blake, *Hawaiian Surfriders 1935* (Redondo Beach CA: Mountain & Sea Publishing, 1983); John R. K. Clark, *Hawaiian Surfing: Traditions from the Past* (Honolulu: University of Hawaii Press, 2011); Ben Finney and James Houston, *Surfing: A History of the Ancient Hawaiian Sport* (San Francisco: Pomegranate Artbooks, 1996); Leonard Lueras, *Surfing: The Ultimate Pleasure* (New York: Workman Publishing, 1984); Patrick Moser, ed., *Pacific Passages: An Anthology of Surf Writing* (Honolulu: University of Hawaii Press, 2008); Matt Warshaw, *The History of Surfing* (San Francisco: Chronicle Books, 2010); various articles in *Thrum's Hawaiian Annual.*
7. Duke Paoa [Kahanamoku], "Riding the Surfboard," *Mid-Pacific Magazine,* January 1911, 5.
8. James King, "Surf Riding in 1778 at Kealakekua," excerpted in *Paradise of the Pacific* magazine, November 1936, 13.

9. Herman Melville, *Mardi and a Voyage Thither* (Boston: L. C. Page, 1923), 239 (originally published in 1849).

10. Mark Twain, *Roughing It*, in *The Complete Travel Books of Mark Twain*, ed. Charles Neider (Garden City NY: Doubleday, 1966), 762.

11. Reverend Henry T. Cheever, *Life in the Sandwich Islands* (London: Richard Bentley, 1851), 42.

12. Finney and Houston, *Surfing*, 53–57; Michael Scott Moore, *Sweetness and Blood: How Surfing Spread from Hawaii and California to the Rest of the World, with Some Unexpected Results* (Emmaus PA: Rodale, 2010), 9–10.

13. Hiram Bingham's "A Residence of Twenty-One Years in the Sandwich Islands," originally published in 1847, reprinted in Moser, *Pacific Passages*, 98.

14. Mark Twain, from a speech delivered in 1889. Paul Fatout ed., *Mark Twain Speaking* (Iowa City: University of Iowa Press, 1976), 244.

15. *The Friend*, August 1892, 50:57–60.

16. Duke Kahanamoku would have graduated from Kamehameha Schools with a grade 9 diploma if he had attended one more year.

17. Charley Paddock, "The Duke Again Is King," *New York Herald-Tribune*, June 9, 1929.

18. William McKinley High School student publication, *Black and Gold*, October 1909, 17.

CHAPTER THREE

1. Interview with Duke Kahanamoku, KGU, radio transcript in Duke Kahanamoku Collection (hereafter DKC), Folder 49, Hawaii State Archives.

2. Quoted in Grady Timmons, *Waikiki Beachboy* (Honolulu: Editions Limited, 1989), 69.

3. *New York Evening World*, July 17, 1918.

4. Kahanamoku, *World of Surfing*, 31–32.

5. "Rabbit" Kekai, quoted by Craig Stecyk and Steve Pezman in the *Surfer's Journal* (Winter 1994): 65–66.

6. *Long Beach Independent*, September 27, 1964.

7. Quoted in Joe Brennan, *Duke of Hawaii* (New York: Ballantine, 1968), 134.

8. Van Norden, "Hawaii for the White Man," *Mid-Pacific Magazine*, June 1911, 631.

9. Alexander Hume Ford, "Riding the Surfboard," *Mid-Pacific Magazine*, February 1911, 155.

10. Alexander Hume Ford, "Aquatic Sports," *Paradise of the Pacific*, December 1908, 19.

11. Alexander Hume Ford, "Riding the Surf in Hawaii," *Collier's*, August 1909, 17.

12. Jack London, "Riding the South Sea Surf," *Woman's Home Companion*, October 1907. Reprinted as "A Royal Sport," in *Stories of Hawaii*, ed. A. Grove Day (New York: Appleton-Century, 1965), 265.

13. In later versions of the story, the phrase "a black Mercury" was changed to "a brown Mercury."

14. London, "A Royal Sport," 274.

15. London, "A Royal Sport."

16. George Freeth's biographical information from Arthur Verge, "George Freeth: King of the Surfers and California's Forgotten Hero," *California History* (Summer–Fall, 2001); Matt Warshaw, *History of Surfing*; Peter Westwick and Peter Neushul, *The World in the Curl* (New York: Crown, 2013).

17. *Thrum's Hawaiian Annual*, 1911, 144.

18. *Thrum's Hawaiian Annual*, 1911, 146.

19. Ford, "Riding the Surf in Hawaii," 17.

20. Kahanamoku, *World of Surfing*, 31.

21. Duke Kahanamoku, quoted in numerous works, including Jim Heimann, *Surfing* (Cologne, Germany: Taschen, 2014).

CHAPTER FOUR

1. Duke Kahanamoku, interview by Lowell Thomas Jr., 1950, Marist College.

2. Quoted in *Surfer* magazine, March 1965, 17.

3. William Cottrell, oral history interview by William Kea, July 8, 1968, Historical Committee of the Outrigger Canoe Club, 6–7.

4. Kahanamoku, *World of Surfing*, 31–32.

5. Author interview with Richard "Buffalo" Keaulana, August, 2013.

6. *Surfer*, March 1965, 19.

7. *Mid-Pacific Magazine*, January 1911, 3.

8. *Mid-Pacific Magazine*, January 1911, 3.

9. *Forecast*, August 1950, 6.

10. *Evening World*, July 17, 1918.

11. *Los Angeles Times*, July 11, 1913.

12. *Oakland Tribune*, July 10, 1916.

13. Paul Gallico, *The Golden People* (Garden City NY: Doubleday, 1965), 55.

14. *Los Angeles Times*, October 23, 1913.

15. Sargent Kahanamoku, Outrigger Canoe Club Oral Histories, 18-7.

16. From Isaiah Walker, *North Shore Reign* (Honolulu: University of Hawaii Press, 2011), 112.

17. Sam Reid, "When the Hawaiians Ruled the Waves," *Surfer*, July 1968, 64. Hui Nalu fight song reproduced courtesy of Hui Nalu.

CHAPTER FIVE

1. Lueras, *Surfing: The Ultimate Pleasure*, 88.

2. Ted Kurras, "The Swimming Duke of Waikiki," *Sports Illustrated*, January 17, 1966, W3.

3. *Evening Bulletin (Honolulu)*, August 16, 1911.
4. *Pacific Commercial Advertiser*, August 20, 1911.
5. Sargent Kahanamoku oral history.
6. Timmons, *Waikiki Beachboy*, 70.
7. *Pacific Commercial Advertiser*, November 10, 1911.
8. *Pacific Commercial Advertiser*, November 10, 1911.
9. *Pacific Commercial Advertiser*, November 10, 1911.
10. *Pacific Commercial Advertiser*, November 10, 1911.
11. *Pacific Commercial Advertiser*, August 20, 1911.
12. *Pacific Commercial Advertiser*, January 8, 1912.
13. *Pacific Commercial Advertiser*, January 12, 1912.
14. *Hawaiian Star*, January 5, 1912.
15. *Hawaiian Gazette*, February 6, 1912.

CHAPTER SIX
1. Interview with Duke Kahanamoku, KGU; *Honolulu Star-Bulletin*, July 29, 1939.
2. Duke Kahanamoku, interview by Lowell Thomas Jr., 1950, Marist College.
3. *Pittsburgh Press*, February 26, 1912.
4. Duke Kahanamoku, interview by Lowell Thomas Jr., 1950, Marist College. Information about Duke and George Kistler from, among other sources, Ralph Wright, "A Historical Study of the Development of the Competitive Swimming of Hawaii up to 1916" (Master's thesis, University of Hawaii, 1947).
5. *Pacific Commercial Advertiser*, May 19, 1912.
6. *Honolulu Advertiser*, April 8, 1958.
7. *Boston Globe*, March 24, 1912.
8. Duke Kahanamoku, interview by Lowell Thomas Jr., 1950, Marist College.
9. *Honolulu Advertiser*, April 8, 1958.
10. *Los Angeles Times*, December 10, 1914.
11. *New York Sun*, February 21, 1916.
12. Various accounts, including the *New York Times*, February 20, 1916.
13. Unidentified newspaper, DKC, Folder 100, Hawaii State Archives.
14. *New York Tribune*, July 7, 1912. Ranjitsinhji was a legendary batsman who was born in British-controlled India and played international test cricket for England.
15. *Chicago Daily News Almanac and Year-Book for 1913* (Chicago: Chicago Daily News), 302.
16. *Chicago Examiner*, April 16, 1916, part 5, 2.
17. Brennan, *Duke of Hawaii*, 40–41.
18. *Honolulu Star-Bulletin*, June 19, 1937. McKenzie's relief, "Joy of Effort," showing three runners clearing a hurdle, was set into the wall at the Olympic Stadium in Stockholm in 1912.

19. *Pacific Commercial Advertiser*, May 25, 1912.
20. *Hawaiian Star*, March 8, 1912.
21. *Pacific Commercial Advertiser*, June 20, 1912.

CHAPTER SEVEN

1. *New York Times*, June 15, 1912.
2. Harold Wilson, "A Legend in His Own Mind: The Olympic Experience of General George S. Patton, Jr.," *Olympika: The International Journal of Olympic Studies* 6 (1997): 103.
3. *Hawaiian Gazette*, July 19, 1912.
4. *Honolulu Advertiser*, April 8, 1958.
5. Alan Katchen, *Abel Kiviat: National Champion* (Syracuse NY: Syracuse University Press, 2009), 126.
6. *Hawaiian Star*, June 21, 1912.
7. *Honolulu Star-Bulletin*, August 23, 1965.
8. James E. Sullivan, ed., *Spalding's Official Athletic Almanac for 1905* (New York: American Publishing, 1905), 257, 259 (accessed online: http://library.la84.org/6oic/OfficialReports/1904/1904Spal.pdf).
9. Bill Mallon and Ian Buchanan, *The 1908 Olympic Games: Results for All Competitors in All Events, with Commentary* (Jefferson NC: McFarland, 2000), 242.
10. Details about the 1912 Olympic Games in Stockholm from published interviews with Duke Kahanamoku; Swedish Olympic Committee, *The Official Report of the Olympic Games of Stockholm 1912* (Stockholm: Wahlstrom & Widstrand, 1912); James Sullivan, "What Happened at Stockholm," *Outing*, October 1912; Bill Mallon and Ture Widlund, *The 1912 Olympic Games: Results for All Competitors in All Events, with Commentary* (Jefferson NC: McFarland, 2000); newspaper clippings held at LA84 Foundation.
11. *New York Times*, September 29, 1910. Sheppard was a star runner, Sheridan was one of the "Irish Whales," and Sandow was a pioneering strongman.
12. *Harper's Weekly*, July 6, 1912.
13. *Detroit Free Press*, June 20, 1912.
14. *Mercury* magazine, January 1913, 58.

CHAPTER EIGHT

1. Details about the swimming competition in Stockholm from published interviews with Duke Kahanamoku, Swedish Olympic Committee, *Official Report of Olympic Games of Stockholm 1912*; Sullivan, "What Happened at Stockholm," *Outing*, October 1912; Otto Wahle, "Olympic Swimming," in *The Olympic Games Stockholm 1912*, ed. James E. Sullivan (New York: American Sports Publishing, 1912); Mallon and Widlund, *1912 Olympic Games*; newspaper clippings at LA84 Foundation.

2. Swedish Olympic Committee, *Official Report of Olympic Games of Stockholm 1912*, 716.

3. *New York Times*, July 8, 1912.

4. Wahle, "Olympic Swimming," *Olympic Games Stockholm 1912*, 161; Sullivan, "What Happened at Stockholm," *Outing*, October 1912, 22.

5. Duke Kahanamoku, interview by Lowell Thomas Jr., 1950, Marist College.

6. *Honolulu Advertiser*, April 8, 1958.

7. Kate Buford, *Native American Son: The Life and Sporting Legend of Jim Thorpe* (New York: Alfred Knopf, 2010), 131.

8. *New York Times*, March 18, 1917.

CHAPTER NINE

1. *Honolulu Advertiser*, April 8, 1958.

2. *Atlantic City Press*, August 11–19, 1912.

3. *Atlantic City Press*, August 11, 1912.

4. *Brooklyn Eagle*, August 26, 1912.

5. Freeth's claim appeared in an article in the *Hawaiian Gazette*, June 28, 1907.

6. *New York Times*, July 10, 1910.

7. Sam Reid, "When the Hawaiians Ruled the Waves," *Surfer* magazine, July 1968, 59.

8. Details about the victory parade from published interviews with Duke Kahanamoku; Sullivan, "What Happened at Stockholm," *Outing*, October 1912; newspaper clippings at LA84 Foundation; various newspaper and magazine reports.

9. *San Francisco Call*, September 23, 1912.

10. "School Notes," William McKinley High School student publication, *Black and Gold*, March 1912.

11. *Pacific Commercial Advertiser*, July 15, 1912.

12. *Pacific Commercial Advertiser*, July 11, 1912.

13. *Pacific Commercial Advertiser*, July 13, 1912.

14. *Honolulu Star-Bulletin*, July 12, 1912.

15. *Honolulu Star-Bulletin*, October 2, 1912.

16. *Maui News*, October 12, 1912.

CHAPTER TEN

1. *New York Tribune*, January 25, 1913.

2. *New York Tribune*, January 28, 1913.

3. *New York Tribune*, January 28, 1913.

4. Buford, *Native American Son*, 83.

5. *New York Tribune*, January 29, 1913.

6. *Honolulu Star-Bulletin*, August 23, 1965.

7. *New York Times*, September 8, 1907.

8. Melvin Sheppard, "Spiked Shoes and Cinder Paths: An Athlete's Story," *Sport Story Magazine*, May 1924, 107.

9. William O. Johnson, *All That Glitters Is Not Gold: An Irreverent Look at the Olympic Games* (New York: Putnam, 1972), 150.

10. *Maui News*, November 30, 1912.

11. *Maui News*, November 30, 1912; *Honolulu Star-Bulletin*, June 17, 1913.

12. "Meeting of the Duke Kahanamoku Fund Committee," minutes kept at the University of Hawaii, Manoa.

13. Information about the trust and the home are taken from contemporary newspaper articles and a lawsuit, Duke Kahanamoku vs. Bishop Trust Company, filed in Honolulu Circuit Court in 1964.

14. *Honolulu Star-Bulletin*, March 8, 1913.

15. *Los Angeles Times*, October 15, 1913.

16. Avery Brundage lost to Jim Thorpe in both the pentathlon and decathlon in 1912. Later, as the head of the International Olympic Committee (IOC), he denied appeals to return Thorpe's medals to his family. The IOC voted to restore the medals to Thorpe posthumously in 1982.

17. *Morning Oregonian*, November 3, 1913.

18. *Santa Cruz Evening News*, July 24, 1913; *Santa Cruz Sentinel*, July 29, 1913.

19. *Long Beach Independent*, July 12, 1913.

20. *Honolulu Star-Bulletin*, August 19, 1915.

21. *Los Angeles Times*, August 13, 1965.

22. *New York Herald Tribune*, June 9, 1929.

23. Handwritten note, reprinted in Claudine and Paul Burnett, *Surfing Newport Beach* (Charleston SC: History Press, 2013), 45.

CHAPTER ELEVEN

1. From Robert Allen, *Creating Hawaii Tourism* (Honolulu: Bess Press, 2004), 17. Also, see Timmons, *Waikiki Beachboy*.

2. Louis Kahanamoku oral history in *Waikiki, 1900–1985*, 871–72.

3. Sargent Kahanamoku told this anecdote to Dick Metz circa 1990; the board is displayed at the Surfing Heritage Foundation, San Clemente CA.

4. M. Leola Crawford, *Seven Weeks in Hawaii* (Chicago: Howard D. Berrett, 1913), 13.

5. Crawford, *Seven Weeks in Hawaii*, 31, 54.

6. *Hawaiian Gazette*, February 13, 1914.

7. *San Francisco Chronicle*, October 16, 1913.

8. *Hawaiian Gazette*, November 19, 1912.

9. *Hawaiian Gazette*, January 28, 1913.

10. *Honolulu Star-Bulletin*, April 8, 1914.

11. Sullivan, James E., ed. *The Olympic Games Stockholm 1912* (New York: American Sports, 1912), 246.
12. *New York Times*, March 13, 1915.
13. Honolulu-based photographer A. R. Gurrey, considered the forefather of surfing photography, snapped the photo of Duke Kahanamoku that was used in the poster sometime during 1910–14. Gurrey hand-assembled a pamphlet titled "The Surf-Riders of Hawaii," including several images of Duke surfing, which is believed to be the first publication devoted exclusively to surfing.
14. *Honolulu Star-Bulletin*, February 21, 1914.
15. *Honolulu Star-Bulletin*, March 10, 1914.
16. *Honolulu Star-Bulletin*, March 13, 1914.
17. Harry Hebner, "The Miracle Man of Swimming," *Tri-Color* magazine, September 1915, reprinted in Riess, *Sports in North America*, 367–68.
18. *Honolulu Star-Bulletin*, July 13, 1914, quoting account in the *San Francisco Examiner*.
19. *Oakland Tribune*, June 28, 1914.
20. *Los Angeles Times*, July 5, 1914.
21. *Motion Picture News*, November 22, 1914; Hobart Bosworth papers and photographs at the Margaret Herrick Library.
22. Duke Kahanamoku, interview by Lowell Thomas Jr., 1950, Marist College.
23. Duke Kahanamoku, interview by Lowell Thomas Jr., 1950, Marist College.
24. Duke Kahanamoku, interview by Lowell Thomas Jr., 1950, Marist College; *Los Angeles Times*, November 11, 1914.

CHAPTER TWELVE
1. *Los Angeles Times*, December 4, 1914.
2. From an article by Cecil Healy in *Sun*, December 15, 1914; Cecil Healy, *Referee*, December 16, 1914. Accounts of Duke's visit in Australia and New Zealand are available via http://trove.nla.gov.au/ and http://paperspast.natlib.govt.nz/ and posted at www.surfresearch.com.au. Other sources include interviews given by Duke Kahanamoku about this trip (his photo album is held at the Bishop Museum, as is Francis Evans's diary); Brennan, *Duke of Hawaii*, 85–102; Sandra Kimberley Hall, *Duke: A Great Hawaiian* (Honolulu: Bess Press, 2004); Sandra Kimberley Hall and Greg Ambrose, *Memories of Duke: The Legend Comes to Life* (Honolulu: Bess Press, 1995); Sandra Kimberley Hall "Duke Down Under," *Spirit of Aloha*, November 1994, 54–57; Sandra Kimberley Hall "The Million Dollar Surfboard," *Longboard*, April–May, 1996, 72–74; Phil Jarratt, *That Summer at Boomerang* (Melbourne: Hardie Grant Books, 2004).
3. Gary Osmond, "'Honolulu Maori': Racial Dimensions of Duke Kahanamoku's Tour of Australia and New Zealand, 1914–15," *New Zealand Journal of History* 44, no. 1 (2010): 22–34.

4. Cecil Healy, *Referee*, December 16, 1914.

5. See note 2 above, as well as http://www.surfresearch.com.au/00000100.html.

6. W. F. Corbett, *Sun*, December 24, 1914.

7. *Sunday Times* (Sydney), December 27, 1914.

8. Timmons, *Waikiki Beachboy*, 69.

9. Interview with Isabel Letham, by Roslyn Cahill, March 7, 1986, for Armidale College of Advanced Education, New South Wales, Australia, and with the Manly Library.

10. Quoted in Matt Warshaw, *The Encyclopedia of Surfing* (accessed online: encyclopediaofsurfing.com).

11. *Sun*, January 8, 1915.

12. *Richmond River Express and Kyogle Advertiser*, January 8, 1915.

13. *Sydney Morning Herald*, December 15, 1914.

14. *Sunday Times*, January 10, 1915.

15. *Dominion*, March 23, 1915.

16. The Bishop Museum papers; *Dominion*, March 13, 1915.

17. *Sun*, January 12, 1915.

18. "Foreword," by Duke Kahanamoku, in Jack Pollard, *The Surfrider* (New York: Taplinger Publishing, 1968).

CHAPTER THIRTEEN

1. *Honolulu Star-Bulletin*, March 31, 1915.

2. *New York Times*, August 17, 1914.

3. Frank Morton Todd, *The Story of the Exposition, Volume Three* (New York: G. P. Putnam's Sons, 1921), 111.

4. From *Honolulu*, the Chamber of Commerce monthly magazine, quoted in *Honolulu Star-Bulletin*, July 2, 1915.

5. Brennan, *Duke of Hawaii*, 103.

6. *Honolulu Star-Bulletin*, July 31, 1915.

7. *Honolulu Star-Bulletin*, August 3, 1915.

8. *Honolulu Star-Bulletin*, July 19, 1915.

9. Hawaiian-born educator Luther Gulick, the son of missionary parents, played a key role in the invention of both volleyball and basketball: he encouraged James Naismith to invent basketball and helped Morgan to develop volleyball.

10. Barbara Del Piano, *Outrigger Canoe Club: The First Hundred Years, 1908–2008* (Honolulu: Outrigger Canoe Club, 2007), 26.

11. From *The Sands of Time: The History of Beach Volleyball, Volume 1* (accessed online: http://www.bvbinfo.com/SandsSneak.asp?issue=1).

12. *Honolulu Star-Bulletin*, May 10, 1916.

13. *Hawaiian Gazette*, May 5, 1916.

14. *Honolulu Star-Bulletin*, April 27, 1916.
15. *Hawaiian Gazette*, May 12, 1916.
16. *Honolulu Star-Bulletin*, May 16, 1916.
17. *Honolulu Star-Bulletin*, June 2, 1916.
18. *Honolulu Star-Bulletin*, June 2, 1916.
19. *Honolulu Star-Bulletin*, June 2, 1916.
20. *Honolulu Star-Bulletin*, December 6, 1916; Hall and Ambrose, *Memories of Duke*, 98.
21. Brennan, *Duke*, 102.
22. Brennan, *Duke*, 102.
23. Brennan, *Duke*, 103.
24. *Honolulu Star-Bulletin*, March 22, 1916.
25. *Honolulu Star-Bulletin*, December 15, 1917.
26. DKC, Folder 80, Hawaii State Archives.

CHAPTER FOURTEEN
1. This was the title of a short book written by H. G. Wells, *The War That Will End War* (London: Frank & Cecil Palmer, 1914).
2. Kahanamoku, *World of Surfing*, 73.
3. *Honolulu Star-Bulletin*, September 4, 1924.
4. Blake, *Hawaiian Surfriders 1935*, 55. According to Blake, Duke surfed alongside "Dad" Center during the "Long Ride."
5. Clark, *Hawaiian Surfing*, 416.
6. Kahanamoku, *World of Surfing*, 74–75.
7. *Surfer*, March 1965.
8. Blake, *Hawaiian Surfriders 1935*, 55.
9. Brennan, *Duke*, 125.
10. Kahanamoku, *World of Surfing*, 77.
11. Clark, *Hawaiian Surfing*, 418.
12. Clark, *Hawaiian Surfing*, 418.
13. Kahanamoku, *World of Surfing*, 73.
14. Kahanamoku, *World of Surfing*, 80.
15. *Pacific Commercial Advertiser*, August 3, 1917.
16. Lili'uokalani, *Hawaii's Story by Hawaii's Queen* (Rutland VT: Charles Tuttle, 1964), 373–74.
17. Norman Ross, "Norman Ross Sr., Father and Friend," *Chicago Tribune*, May 3, 1968, 22.
18. *Honolulu Star-Bulletin*, September 4, 1917.
19. *New York Tribune*, August 7, 1918.
20. *Honolulu Star-Bulletin*, September 6, 1917.
21. *Honolulu Star-Bulletin*, September 6, 1917.

CHAPTER FIFTEEN

1. Brennan, *Duke*, 111.
2. *New York Tribune*, August 8, 1918.
3. *New York Times*, August 6, 1918.
4. *Hawaiian Gazette*, April 9, 1918.
5. Background about influenza is taken from Gina Kolata, *Flu: The Story of the Great Influenza Pandemic of 1918 and the Search for the Virus That Caused It* (New York: Farrar, Straus and Giroux, 1999).
6. Brennan, *Duke*, 113–15.
7. *Morning Oregonian*, October 28, 1918.
8. *New York Tribune*, Janaury 1, 1919.
9. *New York Tribune*, August 9, 1918.
10. Brennan, *Duke*, 117.
11. Brennan, *Duke*, 117.

CHAPTER SIXTEEN

1. *New York Times*, July 27, 1919.
2. *San Francisco Chronicle*, February 7, 1917.
3. *Pacific Commercial Advertiser*, October 29, 1919.
4. *Pacific Commercial Advertiser*, October 29, 1919.
5. Duke P. Kahanamoku v. Advertiser Publishing Company, No. 1277, Circuit Court First Circuit, 1920.
6. *Honolulu Star-Bulletin*, April 14, 1920; published interviews with Duke Kahanamoku, 1920–68; *Duke of Hawaii*, 141–54.
7. British crime writer Agatha Christie surfed in Hawaii in 1922. Kahanamoku was apparently not present.
8. John Lucas, "American Preparations for the First Post World War Olympic Games," *Journal of Sport History* 10, no. 2 (1983): 30–32. Other sources: *Report of the American Olympic Committee: Seventh Olympic Ganes, Antwerp, Belgium, 1920* (Greenwich CT: Conde Nast Press, 1921); *Olympic Games Handbook* (New York: American Sports Publishing: Spalding's Athletic Library, 1921); published interviews with Duke Kahanamoku and other members of the U.S. Olympic team; ephemera and oral histories from the LA84 Foundation; Bill Mallon and Anthony Bijkerk, *The 1920 Olympic Games: Results for All Competitors in All Events, with Commentary* (Jefferson NC: McFarland, 2003); Johnson, *All That Glitters*, 139–47; *The Olympic Century: The Official History of the Modern Olympic Movement* (Los Angeles: World Sport Research & Publications, 1995–2000); Lewis Carlson and John Fogarty, *Tales of Gold* (Chicago: Contemporary Books, 1987), 11–28; Roland Renson, *The Games Reborn* (Antwerp: Pandora, 1996); contemporary newspaper and magazine articles.
9. Copy of signed petition in DKC, Folder 69, Hawaii State Archives.

10. *Sports Illustrated*, December 17, 1979.
11. Program from the Swimming Hall of Fame induction ceremony, 1968, in DKC, Folder 80, Hawaii State Archives.
12. *Boston Globe*, August 25, 1920.
13. *New York Herald Tribune*, June 9, 1929.
14. Carlson and Fogarty, *Tales of Gold*, 18.

CHAPTER SEVENTEEN
1. Carlson and Fogarty, *Tales of Gold*, 20.
2. Antwerp held figure skating events and an ice hockey tourney. Among other factors, this led to the first Winter Olympics four years later.
3. *Report of the American Olympic Committee: Seventh Olympic Ganes, Antwerp, Belgium, 1920* (Greenwich CT: Conde Nast Press, 1921), 258.
4. Carlson and Fogarty, *Tales of Gold*, 19.
5. *Evening Public Ledger*, October 1, 1920.
6. Duke Kahanamoku, interview by Lowell Thomas Jr., 1950, Marist College.
7. Carlson and Fogarty, *Tales of Gold*, 75.
8. Mallon and Bijkerk, *1920 Olympic Games*, 302.
9. Vaudeville and Circus program, on board the *Princess Matoika*, from LA84 Foundation collection.
10. *Honolulu Advertiser*, January 19, 1994; *New York Times*, September 12, 2000. At the age of 103, legally blind and severely deaf, Prieste returned the flag, somewhat faded and tattered, to the International Olympic Committee after seventy-seven years.
11. *Oakland Tribune*, December 28, 1920.

CHAPTER EIGHTEEN
1. Brennan, *Duke*, 122.
2. Jantzen ads featuring Duke Kahanamoku appeared in the *Saturday Evening Post* (and other magazines) throughout 1922; *Printer's Ink* magazine, May 18, 1923.
3. *Washington Times*, May 6, 1922.
4. Kahanamoku also appeared on several trading cards: Felix Puton grocery set in 1920; Willard chocolates in 1924 (a set that also included Johnny Weissmuller); Greiling cigarettes in 1928; Gartmann cigarettes in 1931; Reemtsma cigarettes in 1932 (for the Los Angeles Olympics); and Goudey's "Sport Kings" series in 1933.
5. *Los Angeles Times*, July 4, 1922. Background research on Weissmuller: Johnny Weismuller Jr., *Tarzan My Father* (Toronto: ECW Press, 2008), 39–41; David Fury, *Johnny Weissmuller: Twice the Hero* (Waterville ME: Thorndike Press, 2001), 37–38; Narda Onyx, *Water, World & Weissmuller* (Los Angeles: VION,

1964), 30–55; Johnson, *All That Glitters Is Not Gold*, 148–51; Paul Gallico, *The Golden People* (Garden City NY: Doubleday, 1965), 219–33; "Johnny Weissmuller: From Olympic Champion to Tarzan," chap. in Michael Bohn, *Heroes and Ballyhoo: How the Golden Age of the 1920s Transformed American Sports* (Dulles VA: Potomac Books, 2010), 105–28.

6. *Evening World*, June 17, 1922.
7. Gallico, *Golden People*, 225.
8. Esther Williams, *The Million Dollar Mermaid* (New York: Simon & Schuster, 1999), 47–48.
9. *Washington Times*, July 19, 1922.
10. *Maui News*, May 16, 1922.
11. *Honolulu Advertiser*, July 11, 1929.
12. *Evening Public Ledger*, July 21, 1922.
13. *Los Angeles Times*, August 17, 1922.
14. *Honolulu Star-Bulletin*, March 18, 1922.
15. *Riverside Independent*, January 23, 1922.
16. *Los Angeles Times*, August 6, 1922.
17. *Los Angeles Times*, April 2, 1972.
18. Duke Kahanamoku, interview by Lowell Thomas Jr., 1950, Marist College.
19. Duke Kahanamoku, interview by Lowell Thomas Jr., 1950, Marist College.
20. *Screen & Radio Weekly*, December 8, 1935.
21. Author interview with Henry family members, 2013; author correspondence with the Superior Court of the County of Los Angeles, 2014; author visit to St. John's Cathedral, 2015.

CHAPTER NINETEEN

1. *Santa Monica Outlook*, March 28, 1923.
2. *New York Times*, July 30, 1923.
3. *Daily Telegram*, February 5, 1923.
4. Arlene Mueller, "Johnny Weissmuller Made Olympian Efforts to Conceal His Birthplace," *Sports Illustrated*, August 6, 1984; Weismuller, *Tarzan, My Father*, 38–40.
5. Weismuller, *Tarzan, My Father*, 40.
6. Louis Kahanamoku oral history.
7. *Indianapolis News*, June 5, 1924.
8. *Washington Post*, April 5, 1924.
9. *Los Angeles Times*, June 7, 1924.
10. Kelly won his third Olympic gold medal in Paris in 1924, after winning two gold medals in Antwerp in 1920. Another rower on the 1924 Olympic team was Dr. Benjamin Spock, who won the gold medal in Paris as part of the Yale University team in the eight-man shell with coxswain.

CHAPTER TWENTY

1. Onyx, *Water, World*, 66.
2. *New York Times*, June 26, 1924.
3. *San Francisco Examiner*, July 9, 1938.
4. Quoted in various sources, including Grady Timmons, "In Trim: Duke Kahanamoku," *Longboard Quarterly* (June–July 1994): 32.
5. Onyx, *Water, World*, 73.
6. Onyx, *Water, World*, 74.
7. Interview with Jo-Anne Kahanamoku-Sterling, from the documentary film *Duke Kahanamoku: Hawaii's Soul*.
8. *New York Herald Tribune*, October 18, 1924.
9. Gallico, *Golden People*, 225.
10. *Los Angeles Times*, March 15, 1964.
11. From Margery Voyer Cole, *Viola, Diving Wonder & Aquatic Champion* (Orange CA: Paragon, 2001); article about Viola Cady Krahn, *San Diego Union Tribune*, August 24, 2002; Viola Hartmann interview with Sandra Kimberley Hall, *Duke: A Great Hawaiian*, 53.
12. *Washington Herald*, August 9, 1921.
13. *The Mercury* newsletter, LAAC, June 6, 1923.

CHAPTER TWENTY-ONE

1. Film and Hollywood research conducted at the Margaret Herrick Library and the UCLA Film and Television Archive. Research material includes published interviews with Duke Kahanamoku and contemporaries; film magazines (including *Modern Screen, Motion Picture Magazine, Photoplay, Variety, Screenland*); Neal Gabler, *An Empire of Their Own: How the Jews Invented Hollywood* (New York: Anchor Books, 1988); Yunte Huang, *Charlie Chan: The Untold Story of the Honorable Detective and His Rendezvous with American History* (New York: W. W. Norton, 2010); Kevin Starr, *Material Dreams: Southern California Through the 1920s* (New York: Oxford University Press, 1990); Adolph Zukor, *The Public Is Never Wrong* (New York: G. P. Putnam's, 1953); Jesse Lasky, *I Blow My Own Horn* (New York: Doubleday, 1957); Joseph McBride, *Searching for John Ford: A Life* (New York: St. Martin's Press, 2001); Scott Eyman, *Print the Legend: The Life and Times of John Ford* (Baltimore MD: Johns Hopkins University Press, 2000).

Films viewed related to Duke Kahanamoku: *Around the World in Eighty Minutes, Big Jim McLain* (reportedly appears as actor), *Big Wednesday, Blue Surf-ari*, CBS *Sports Spectacular* (episode), *The Covered Wagon* (reportedly appears as actor), *A Deeper Shade of Blue, Doc Ball: Surfing's Legendary Lensman, Duke Kahanamoku* (KITV), *Duke Kahanamoku: Hawaii's Soul* (KGMB), *Duke Kahanamoku's World of Surfing, Duke the Legend* (KHET), *Eagle of the Sea* (appears as actor), *The Endless Summer, Gidget, Gidget Goes Hawaiian, Girl of the Port* (appears as actor), *Golden Breed, Hawaiian: The Legend of Eddie Aikau* (ESPN), *Hula* (appears as actor), *Iron Horse* (reportedly appears as actor), *The Man Who Shot Liberty Valance, The Medicine Man* (reportedly appears as actor), *Mister Roberts* (appears as actor), *No Father to Guide Him* (appears as actor), *Old Ironsides* (appears as actor), *Pau Hana Years: Hana Hou* (episode), *Point Break, The Pony Express* (appears as actor), *Portraits of Paradise, The Ride, Riding Giants, Step into Liquid, Tarzan the Ape Man, This Is Your Life* (episode), *Wake of the Red Witch* (appears as actor), *The Wanderer* (appears as actor), *Where East Is East* (appears as actor), *The Black Camel* (reportedly appears as actor).

2. David Pierce, *The Survival of American Silent Feature Films: 1912–1929* (Washington DC: Library of Congress and Council on Library and Information Resources, 2013).

3. Text of *House without a Key* (accessed online: http://gutenberg.net.au/ebooks 02/0200671.txt).

4. Michael Sragow, *Victor Fleming: An American Movie Master* (New York: Pantheon 2008), 105.

5. *Honolulu Star-Bulletin*, June 25, 1925.

6. *Honolulu Advertiser*, July 27, 1925.

7. From Audrey Chamberlin Collection, Scrapbook #38, Margaret Herrick Library.

8. *Honolulu Advertiser*, August 25, 1965.

9. The scene was reportedly shot at Venice Beach. You can glimpse actress Fay Wray (future star of *King Kong*) as the clubhouse attendant.

10. Rescue research conducted at The Sherman Library in Corona del Mar and the Riverside Public Library. Material includes published interviews with Duke Kahanamoku; *Mercury* newsletter, Los Angeles Athletic Club; contemporary newspapers, including *Balboa Times, Newport News, Riverside Daily Press, Santa Ana Register, San Diego Union, Los Angeles Times, New York Times, Honolulu Star-Bulletin*; *Time* magazine, June 15–25, 1925 and December 1925; Brennan, *Duke*, 150–56; Brennan, *Duke of Hawaii*, 166–78. These accounts contain discrepancies about the names of the survivors and of those who died. The *Riverside Daily Press*, for instance, reported that Philip Bengachea had been rescued; however, this particular name does not appear in other newspapers. I have relied most heavily on local newspapers (*Riverside Daily Press* and *Balboa Times*) for this narrative.

11. *Riverside Daily Press*, June 15, 1925.

12. *Balboa Times*, June 16, 1925.

13. *Riverside Daily Press*, June 15, 1925.

14. *Balboa Times*, June 16, 1925.

15. Kahanamoku, *World of Surfing*, 44. The deaths were deemed "accidental and unavoidable" at the inquest, and Bland was exonerated. The widow of Ralph

Farnsworth later sued Bland for $50,000 on grounds of negligence. The lawsuit was settled out of court.

16. *Honolulu Star-Bulletin*, October 22, 1955.

17. Also cast was George Godfrey, a standout African American boxer with the nickname of "The Black Shadow of Leiperville." Boris Karloff had a minor role, and Gary Cooper is said to have appeared as an uncredited extra.

18. Jesse Lasky, *I Blow My Own Horn* (New York: Doubleday, 1957), 178–79.

19. Esther Ralston, *Some Day We'll Laugh* (Metuchen NJ: Scarecrow Press, 1985), 96.

20. Duke was not able to prevent the death of Charles Davis, a seaman who was killed during the filming of a dynamiting scene.

CHAPTER TWENTY-TWO

1. *Mercury* newsletter, Los Angeles Athletic Club, August 3, 1927; *Honolulu Star-Bulletin*, August 17, 1927.

2. *New York Herald Tribune*, June 9, 1929.

3. Sargent Kahanamoku oral history.

4. *Honolulu Advertiser*, August 21–22, 1927.

5. *Honolulu Advertiser*, August 25–26, 1927.

6. *Honolulu Advertiser*, August 21, 1927.

7. *Honolulu Advertiser*, August 26, 1927.

8. *Los Angeles Times*, June 7, 1928.

9. *Photoplay*, March 1929.

10. Unidentified article, DKC, Hawaii State Archives.

11. Charley Paddock, "Why Athletes Fail in Pictures," *Photoplay*, September 1928, 124.

12. Years ago, one source mistakenly listed the film's title as *Lady of the Hare*. Other sources have repeated this error.

13. Others films that Duke reportedly appeared in include: *The Rough Riders, The Medicine Man*, and *The Cisco Kid*.

14. *New York Herald Tribune*, August 6, 1951.

15. *Los Angeles Times*, May 27, 1966.

16. Bohn, *Heroes and Ballyhoo*, 127.

CHAPTER TWENTY-THREE

1. Brennan, *Duke*, 159.

2. Proclamation in Duke Kahanamoku archive, Folder 448, the Bishop Museum.

3. *Honolulu Star-Bulletin*, December 20, 1929.

4. Paul Holmes, "Tom Blake Hollow Boards," in Guy Motil, *Surfboards* (Guilford CT: Falcon Guides, 2007), 141; Westwick and Neushul, *World in the Curl*, 72; Warshaw, *Encyclopedia of Surfing*.

5. Blake, *Hawaiian Surfriders*, 52, 62.

6. Blake, *Hawaiian Surfriders*, 58, 62.
7. Sargent Kahanamoku oral history.
8. *Surfer* magazine, July 1968, 65.
9. David Stannard, *Honor Killing: How the Infamous "Massie Affair" Transformed Hawaii* (New York: Viking, 2005), 23. Also, Daws, *Shoal of Time*.
10. *Modern Screen*, December 1937.
11. Aloha card in DKC, Hawaii State Archives.
12. *Honolulu Advertiser*, November 20, 1930.
13. *Honolulu Star-Bulletin*, August 23, 1965
14. Mary Paoa Clarke in *Waikiki, 1900–1985: Oral Histories Volume I* (Honolulu: Center for Oral History Social Science Research Institute University of Hawaii at Manoa, 1985), 654–55.
15. James Jones, *From Here to Eternity* (New York: Dial Press, 2012), 266.
16. Research about the Massie case: contemporary newspapers in Hawaii; Stannard, *Honor Killing*; Daws, *Shoal of Time*; Theon Wright, *Rape in Paradise* (Honolulu: Mutual Publishing, 2005); trial transcripts and more at the Clarence Darrow Collection at the University of Minnesota Law Library (accessed online: http://darrow.law.umn.edu/trials.php?tid=5).
17. *Time* magazine, December 28, 1931.
18. Quoted in Stannard, *Honor Killing*, 267.
19. *Los Angeles Times*, May 12, 1929.
20. *Liberty* magazine, March 26, 1932; see also DeSoto Brown, *Surfing: Historic Images from Bishop Museum Archives* (Honolulu: Bishop Museum Press. 2006), 131, where Brown notes that the surfer might be Sam Kahanamoku, not Duke. The photo is credited to Warren Tong.
21. Stannard, *Honor Killing*.

CHAPTER TWENTY-FOUR

1. *Honolulu Advertiser*, February 8, 1931. Original source was *Nippu Jiji*, a Japanese-language newspaper that was later known as *Hawaii Times*.
2. *Los Angeles Times*, June 28, 1932.
3. *New York Times*, July 14, 1932.
4. Buford, *Native American Son*, 174.
5. *Los Angeles Times*, August 7, 1932; *Pasadena Star News*, July 22, 1932.
6. Johnson, *All That Glitters*, 166, *Hartford Courant*, April 24, 1983.
7. *Los Angeles Times*, July 24, 1932.
8. *The Games of the Xth Olympiad, Los Angeles 1932, Official Report* (Los Angeles: Xth Olympiade Committee, 1933); *The American Olympic Committee Report: Games of the Xth Olympiad* (New York: American Olympic Committee, 1932), 71, 194; *Los Angeles Times*, August 4, 1932.
9. Charles McCallister oral history, LA84 Foundation.

10. *San Diego Union*, February 18, 1933.
11. *Honolulu Star-Bulletin*, February 18, 1933.
12. *Honolulu Star-Bulletin*, August 23, 1965.
13. Linton Freeman, "The Changing Functions of a Folksong," *Journal of American Folklore* 70, no. 277 (1957): 217 (accessed online: http://moreno.ss.uci.edu/~lin/6 .pdf).
14. "Duke Kahanamoku," words and music by Sol Bright, recorded by Sol Hoopii and His Novelty Quartet, Brunswick NY, 1935.
15. "Sport: Los Angeles to Diamond Head," *Time* magazine, July 30, 1934.

CHAPTER TWENTY-FIVE

1. Duke Kahanamoku, interview by Lowell Thomas Jr., 1950, Marist College.
2. Background on sheriff: Published interviews with Duke Kahanamoku; DKC, various folders, Hawaii State Archives and the Bishop Museum.
3. Undated article from DKC folder at the Bishop Museum.
4. DKC, Hawaii State Archives; *Van Nuys News*, October 10, 1936.
5. Louis Kahanamoku oral history.
6. *Japan Times* article from 1932, quoted in William O. Johnson "A Star Was Born," *Sports Illustrated*, July 18, 1984 (accessed online: http://www.si.com /vault/1984/07/18/643789/a-star-was-born).
7. Mark Dyreson, "Jesse Owens: Leading Man in Modern American Tales of Racial Progress and Limits," in *Out of the Shadows: A Biographical History of African American Athletes*, ed. David Wiggins (Fayetteville: University of Arkansas Press, 2006), 125.
8. Written by Pyle for Scripps-Howard newspapers, 1937, Hawaii State Archives.
9. *New York Herald Tribune*, August 6, 1951.
10. *Honolulu Times*, October 30, 1937.
11. *Honolulu Advertiser*, June 13, 1937.
12. Written by Pyle for Scripps-Howard newspapers, 1937, Hawaii State Archives.
13. Photographs of the original surf-ski found in Duke Kahanamoku archive at the Kamehameha Schools.
14. Research on the evolution of surfing from Blake, *Hawaiian Surfriders*; Warshaw, *History of Surfing*; Warshaw, *Encyclopedia of Surfing*; Lueras, *Surfing*; Clark, *Hawaiian Surfing*; Westwick and Neushul, *World in the Curl*; articles and interviews in *Surfer, Surfing, Surfer's Journal* magazines; legendary surfers website: http://files.legendarysurfers.com; author interviews.
15. Ben Finney and James Houston, *Surfing: A History of the Ancient Hawaiian Sport* (San Francisco: Pomegranate Artbooks, 1996), 76.
16. Author interview with Dorian "Doc" Paskowitz, August 2013. Paskowitz passed away in 2014.

CHAPTER TWENTY-SIX

1. Research about Shangri La and Doris Duke from Doris Duke Papers at Duke University; Pony Duke and Jason Thomas, *Too Rich: The Family Secrets of Doris Duke* (New York: HarperCollins, 1996), 92–101, 104–9, 114–21; Stephanie Mansfield, *The Richest Girl in the World: The Extravagant Life and Fast Times of Doris Duke* (New York: G. P. Putnam's Sons, 1992), 123–65; Ted Schwarz and Tom Rybak, *Trust No One: The Glamorous Life and Bizarre Death of Doris Duke* (New York: St. Martin's, 1997), 124–75; coverage of Arden Cromwell's birth and death in local newspapers; author visit to Shangri La.
2. *Oakland Tribune*, February 18, 1939.
3. Duke and Thomas, *Too Rich*, 105.
4. Mansfield, *Richest Girl*, 150.
5. Duke and Thomas, *Too Rich*, 100.
6. Honolulu Birth Index file (1940); Mansfield, *Richest Girl*, 161.
7. Duke and Thomas, *Too Rich*, 115.
8. Honolulu Birth Index file (1940); *Honolulu Advertiser*, July 14, 1940.
9. *Honolulu Advertiser*, July 14, 1940.
10. Author interviews and correspondence. Sonia Lien revealed that Sam Kahanamoku was her biological father in her memoir: Sonia Lien and K. D. Kragen, *From Alone to Aloha* (Seattle: Cedar Forge Press, 2011) (accessed online: http://www .alohasonia.com).
11. DKC, various folders, Hawaii State Archives; Doris Duke Papers at Duke University.

CHAPTER TWENTY-SEVEN

1. *Honolulu Advertiser*, August 13, 1990.
2. Nadine Kahanamoku oral history, 10.
3. *Honolulu Advertiser*, August 13, 1990.
4. Interview with Nadine Kahanamoku, by Janice Otaguro, *Honolulu* magazine, December 1988, 46.
5. *Honolulu Advertiser*, February 21, 1940.
6. Interview with Nadine Kahanamoku by Janice Otaguro, *Honolulu*, December 1988, 44; Nadine Kahanamoku oral history, 27.
7. *Honolulu Advertiser*, August 3, 1965.
8. Nadine Kahanamoku oral history, 13.
9. *Honolulu Advertiser*, August 3, 1965.
10. Nadine Kahanamoku oral history, 13.
11. *Honolulu Star-Bulletin*, August 30, 1940.
12. *Honolulu Star-Bulletin*, September 4, 1940.
13. Author interview with Buffalo Keaulana, August 2013.

14. From interview with Kenneth Brown in *Duke Kahanamoku: Hawaii's Soul*, documentary produced by Phil Arnone for KGMB, 2005.
15. From interview with Kimo McVay in *Duke Kahanamoku: Hawaii's Soul*.
16. *New York Times*, May 23, 1976.
17. Interview with Nadine Kahanamoku by Janice Otaguro, *Honolulu*, December 1988, 50.
18. Letter, September 19, 1940, DKC, Folder 9, Hawaii State Archives.
19. Letter, September 27, 1940, DKC, Folder 9, Hawaii State Archives.
20. Letter, September 27, 1940, DKC, Folder 9, Hawaii State Archives.
21. Letter, October 1, 1940, DKC, Folder 9, Hawaii State Archives.
22. Letter, January 14, 1941, DKC, Folder 9, Hawaii State Archives. Churchill swim fins are still being produced. The company is now owned by Wham-O.
23. Interview with Nadine Kahanamoku by Janice Otaguro, *Honolulu*, December 1988, 50; loan papers between Doris Duke and Duke and Nadine Kahanamoku.

CHAPTER TWENTY-EIGHT

1. Newspapers in Honolulu; eyewitness accounts and interviews published in newspapers and magazines (in Honolulu and by veterans groups), 1941–present; Walter Lord, *Day of Infamy* (New York: Henry Holt, 2001), 33.
2. Nadine Kahanamoku oral history, 6.
3. Lord, *Day of Infamy*, 160, 212.
4. FDR "Day of Infamy" Speech: SEN 77A-H1, Records of the United States Senate; Record Group 46; National Archives.
5. Lord, *Day of Infamy*, 209.
6. Robert Bobrow, "Remember Pearl Harbor?" *Los Angeles Times*, December 4, 1966.
7. Nadine Kahanamoku oral history, 7.
8. Communication from the Territorial Office of Civil Defense, November 4, 1943, DKC, Folder 56, Hawaii State Archives.
9. Barbara Del Piano, *Outrigger Canoe Club: The First Hundred Years, 1908–2008* (Honolulu: Outrigger Canoe Club, 2007), 58.
10. Author interview with Rabbit Kekai, December 2011.
11. Kahanamoku, *World of Surfing*, 45.
12. Thomas Arnott, oral history interview by J. Ward Russell, February 25, 1995, Historical Committee of the Outrigger Canoe Club, 6.
13. Thomas Arnott oral history, 6.
14. Grady Timmons, "Memories of Duke," *Midweek*, August 18, 2004, 38.
15. Metal heir Henry "Bob" Topping named the canoe in honor of his girlfriend. His brother, Dan, purchased the New York Yankees in 1945.
16. Grady Timmons, "Memories of Duke," *Midweek*, August 18, 2004, 55.

17. Quoted in Harry Schneiber and Jane Schneiber, "Taking Liberties," *Legal Affairs*, May–June 2003 (accessed online: http://www.legalaffairs.org/issues /May-June-2003/review_scheiber_mayjun03.msp).

18. *Landmark Briefs and Arguments of the Supreme Court of the United States, Constitutional Law*, vol. 42 (University Publications of America, 1977); J. Garner Anthony, *Hawaii under Army Rule* (Palo Alto CA: Stanford University Press, 1955); *Honolulu Star-Bulletin*, March 5, 1944; Brahan Houston, "Martial Law in Hawaii: A Defense of the War-Time Military Governor, *ABA Journal* 36 (October 1950): 825–28, 885–86.

19. Duncan v. Kahanamoku, 327 U.S. 304 (1946); Anthony, *Hawaii under Army Rule*, 78.

20. Duncan v. Kahanamoku, 327 U.S. 304 (1946).

21. *Honolulu Star-Bulletin*, February 26, 1946.

22. Daws, *Shoal of Time*, 381.

CHAPTER TWENTY-NINE

1. Louis Zamperini with David Rensin, *Devil at My Heels: A World War II Hero's Epic Saga of Torment, Survival, and Forgiveness* (New York: HarperCollins, 2003), 201.

2. Author interview with Louis Zamperini, February 2013; Louis Zamperini oral history, LA84 Foundation. Zamperini died in 2014.

3. Author interview with Louis Zamperini.

4. Several sources have stated that Duke appeared with John Wayne in another Republic Pictures film, titled *Big Jim McLain*, which was shot in Hawaii and released in 1952. I watched this movie on videotape and did not see Kahanamoku. His name is not listed in the credits.

5. Letter from Cisco Casuals, Duke Kahanamoku Collection, Folder 2, Hawaii State Archives; *Honolulu Advertiser*, January 11, 1950; Elmer Leterman, *Personal Power through Creative Selling* (New York: Collier Books, 1956), 10.

6. *New York Herald Tribune*, August 6, 1951.

7. *Washington Post*, November 10, 1953.

8. Arthur Godfrey's radio program, January 1968, Lowell Thomas Papers, Marist College.

9. *Honolulu Advertiser*, August 25, 1950.

10. Jack Newcombe, *The Best of the Athletic Boys* (New York: Doubleday, 1975), 246.

11. *Honolulu Advertiser*, November 20, 2010.

12. Letter from Ralph Chambers, DKC, Folder 15, Hawaii State Archives.

13. Nadine Kahanamoku oral history, 13.

14. Interview with Nadine Kahanamoku by Janice Otaguro, *Honolulu* magazine, December 1988, 49.

15. Hall and Ambrose, *Memories of Duke*, 38.

16. Undated article, DKC, Folder 123, Hawaii State Archives.

17. Isabel Letham oral history, 9; Hall and Ambrose, *Memories of Duke*, 42–43.

18. Sandra Hall, "The Million Dollar Surfboard," *Longboard* magazine, April–May 1996, 74.

19. *This Is Your Life*, Show #234, February 20, 1957, Ralph Edwards Collection, UCLA Film & Television Archive.

20. *This Is Your Life*.

21. *This Is Your Life*.

CHAPTER THIRTY

1. Kahanamoku, *World of Surfing*, 45.

2. Research on World War II and surfing from Westwick and Neushul, *World in the Curl*, 81–102.

3. Kahanamoku, *World of Surfing*, 48.

4. Warshaw, *Encyclopedia of Surfing*; Warshaw, *History of Surfing*; Lueras, *Surfing*; interviews posted on the legendarysurfers.com website; author interviews with Paul Strauch Jr., Mickey Muñoz, Rabbit Kekai, Joey Cabell, Jock Sutherland, and Buffalo Keaulana, 2011–14.

5. Author interview with Rabbit Kekai, 2011.

6. *Honolulu Star-Bulletin*, November 27, 1953; *Honolulu Star-Bulletin*, April 10, 2005; Warshaw, *History of Surfing*; Warshaw, *Encyclopedia of Surfing*.

7. Numerous sources, including Thomas Farber, *On Water* (New York: Ecco Press, 1996).

8. Bud Browne filmography available at: http://www.budbrownefilmarchives.com.

9. Frederick Kohner, *Gidget* (New York: Berkley Books, 2001), 41. Kohner probably meant Nanakuli, a surfing spot on Oahu.

10. *Surfer*, March 1965, 18; interview with Wally Froiseth available at: legendarysurfers.com.

11. Letters to Arthur Godfrey, 1954 and 1955, DKC, Folder 51, Hawaii State Archives.

12. Interview with Henry Ayau in *Duke the Legend* documentary, 1986, KHET.

13. Author interview with Peter Ueberroth, 2014.

14. Hall and Ambrose, *Memories of Duke*, 82.

CHAPTER THIRTY-ONE

1. From "Log of President Truman's Trip to Wake Island," October 13, 1950 (accessed online: http://www.trumanlibrary.org/calendar/travel_log/pdfs/wake50.pdf).

2. *Time* magazine, February 18, 1952.

3. Speech accessed online: http://www.akakafoundation.org/sermons.html.

4. Joan Didion, "Letter from Paradise," in *Slouching toward Bethlehem* (New York: Farrar, Straus and Giroux, 2008), 198.

5. Charmian London, *Jack London and Hawaii* (London: Mills & Boon, 1918), 257.

6. *Hawaiian Holiday*, August 23, 1959; *Honolulu Star-Bulletin*, August 6, 1961.
7. *Honolulu Star-Bulletin*, August 23, 1965.
8. Undated document, DKC, Folder 49, Hawaii State Archives.
9. Undated article, DKC, Folder 100, Hawaii State Archives.
10. Letter of April 15, 1958, DKC, Folder 50, Hawaii State Archives.
11. Letter of April 15, 1958, DKC, Folder 50, Hawaii State Archives.
12. Letter and contract dated August 20, 1958, DKC, Folder 50, Hawaii State Archives.
13. Letter of September 11, 1958, DKC, Folder 50, Hawaii State Archives.
14. Letter of November 3, 1958, DKC, Folder 50, Hawaii State Archives.
15. One of the characters from *Hawaii Five-O*, played by football-star-turned-actor Herman Wedemeyer, was named Duke in honor of Kahanamoku.
16. Letter of May 20, 1954, DKC, Folder 2, Hawaii State Archives.
17. *Honolulu Advertiser*, January 6, 1960.
18. *Los Angeles Times*, September 13, 1953.
19. *Honolulu Advertiser*, January 6, 1960; *Honolulu Star-Bulletin*, August 6, 1961.
20. *Honolulu Star-Bulletin*, April 23, 1961.
21. *Honolulu Star-Bulletin*, August 6, 1961.
22. *Honolulu Star-Bulletin*, August 6, 1961.
23. *Honolulu Star-Bulletin*, August 6, 1961.
24. *Honolulu Star-Bulletin*, August 6, 1961.
25. *Honolulu Star-Bulletin*, August 8, 1961.

CHAPTER THIRTY-TWO

1. Kinau Wilder, *Wilders of Waikiki* (Honolulu: Topgallant Publishing, 1978), 71. Also see "The Wilders of Waikiki" in Huang, *Charlie Chan*, 37–43.
2. McVay's reputation was restored, an absolution that came years after Charles McVay committed suicide in 1968.
3. *Honolulu Advertiser*, August 24, 1961.
4. *Honolulu Star-Bulletin* and *Honolulu Advertiser* articles; DKC, various folders, Hawaii State Archives.
5. Author interviews and email correspondence with former EWC students. My query to the press office of the White House about whether family members of President Barack Obama met or knew Duke Kahanamoku was not answered.
6. McVay interview from *Hawaii's Soul* documentary.
7. Lynn Cook, "The Don," *Hana Hou!* August–September 2003.
8. Letter dated June 17, 1964, DKC, Folder 5, Hawaii State Archives.

CHAPTER THIRTY-THREE

1. *Honolulu Advertiser*, October 11, 1963.
2. "Foreword," in Jack Pollard, *The Surfrider* (New York: Taplinger Publishing, 1968).

3. *Houston Chronicle*, April 17, 1966.

4. Author interviews with Paul Strauch Jr.; Alison Stewart, "The Duke Surf Team," *Makai Ocean Lifestyle*, August 2006, 7–10.

5. Author interviews with Joey Cabell; Matt Warshaw "At Speed," *Surfer's Journal* (Summer 1996): 64–79; Lisa Starr "The Speed Surfing of Joey Cabell," *Forecast*, February 1968.

6. Author interviews with Fred Hemmings Jr.; Paul Holmes, "Fred Hemmings: Full Power Dead Ahead," *Longboard Magazine*, June 2001, 59–66, 118–19.

7. Author interview with Fred Hemmings Jr.

8. Author interview with Mickey Muñoz; Steve Pezman, "Recollections of Butch," *Surfer's Journal* (Winter 1996): 93–102.

9. Fred Hemmings, *Soul of Surfing* (New York: Thunder's Mouth Press, 1997), 22.

10. Author interview with Paul Strauch Jr.

11. Author interview with Paul Strauch Jr.

12. Author interview with Joey Cabell.

13. *Honolulu Advertiser*, August 17, 1965; "Save Our Surf" digital collection (accessed online: http://digicoll.manoa.hawaii.edu/sos/index.php?c=1).

14. *Long Beach Independent*, September 27, 1964.

CHAPTER THIRTY-FOUR

1. Author interviews with contestants; contemporary articles in Honolulu newspapers; event program; articles that appeared immediately after the contest in *Surfer* and *International Surfing* magazines.

2. "'Duke' Contest Matches Hawaiian Surf-Great!!!" *Surfer*, March 1966, 24; *Honolulu Star-Bulletin*, December 16, 1965.

3. *Surfer*, March 1966, 23.

4. Author interview with Fred Hemmings Jr., 2013.

5. *Honolulu Star-Bulletin*, August 23, 1965.

6. "Eddie Aikau and Ben Aipa Make a Statement at the '66 Duke," by Sam George (accessed online: http://www.surfline.com/surf-news/eddie-aikau-and-ben-aipa-make-a-statement-at-the-'66-duke-1_118824). Stuart Holmes Coleman, *Eddie Would Go: The Story of Eddie Aikau, Hawaiian Hero and Pioneer of Big Wave Surfing* (New York: St. Martin's Press, 2001). Eddie Aikau won "The Duke" in 1977, four years after his brother Clyde took first place. Hakman won back-to-back titles in 1970 and 1971.

7. Until Brennan's work was published, only one full-length biography had been published: Earl Albert Selle, *The Story of Duke Paoa Kahanamoku* (The Golden Man Foundation, 1959). The book has been long out of print and was apparently disavowed by Duke.

8. Besides Duke, Weissmuller, and Crabbe, the inaugural class of the International Swimming Hall of Fame included Charles Daniels, Gertrude Ederle, and Adolph Kiefer.
9. Interview with Nadine Kahanamoku by Janice Otaguro, *Honolulu* magazine, December 1988, 47.
10. Hall and Ambrose, *Memories of Duke*, 54.
11. *Honolulu Advertiser*, February 16, 1967.
12. *Honolulu Advertiser*, February 1967.
13. *Honolulu Advertiser*, June 10, 1964.
14. Letter dated June 17, 1964, DKC, Folder 5, Hawaii State Archives.
15. *Honolulu Advertiser*, July 17, 1964.
16. *Honolulu Star-Bulletin*, June 3, 1966.
17. *Honolulu Star-Bulletin* and *Honolulu Advertiser*, June 3, 1966.
18. *Honolulu Advertiser*, June 3, 1966.
19. *Honolulu Advertiser*, June 3, 1966.
20. Author interview with Fred Hemmings Jr., 2013.
21. Timmons *Waikiki Beachboy*, 76.
22. Timmons, *Waikiki Beachboy*, 75.
23. Timmons, *Waikiki Beachboy*, 76.

CHAPTER THIRTY-FIVE

1. *Honolulu Star-Bulletin* and *Honolulu Advertiser*, August 25, 1967; *Sports Illustrated*, September 11, 1967; Brennan, *Duke*, 271–77; Brennan, *Duke of Hawaii*, 210–13; Ron Haworth, "Duke Kahanamoku: The Last Days," *Surfing*, June 1968, 46–49. Margaret Keane's portrait was used for "The Duke" contest poster in 1967.
2. Interview with Nadine Kahanamoku by Janice Otaguro, *Honolulu* magazine, December 1988, 54.
3. *Honolulu Star-Bulletin*, August 23, 1968.
4. *Honolulu Advertiser*, February 2, 1968.
5. "Eulogy to Duke Paoa Kahanamoku," Cong. Rec., January 23, 1968, S312–14.
6. *Hartford Courant*, January 26, 1968.
7. *New York Times*, January 23, 1968.
8. *Honolulu Star-Bulletin*, January 23, 1968.
9. "Hawaii Aloha," words by Reverend Lorenzo Lyons, with music by James McGranahan.
10. Eulogy by Arthur Godfrey, part of Lowell Thomas Collection, Marist College.
11. Address by Reverend Abraham Akaka, part of Lowell Thomas Collection, Marist College.
12. "Aloha 'Oe," words by Queen Liliuokalani.
13. Author interview with Paul Strauch Jr., 2014.

1. *Honolulu Advertiser*, January 19, 1969.

2. Nadine Alexander Kahanamoku v. Kimo Wilder McVay, Case #32392, filed on November 2, 1970, Circuit Court, Oahu.

3. Bruce Jenkins, *North Shore Chronicles: Big-Wave Surfing in Hawaii* (Berkeley CA: Frog, 1999), 133.

4. Francine du Plessix Gray, "The Sugar-Coated Fortress—II," *New Yorker*, March 11, 1972, 67. Also, from Francine du Plessix Gray, *Hawaii: The Sugar-Coated Fortress* (New York: Random House, 1972), 121.

5. Author interview with Carl Herrman, 2013; Carl Herrman as told to Steve Pezman "First Class: The Story behind the Duke Stamp," *The Surfer's Journal* (Spring 2002): 34–38.

6. Nadine Kahanamoku, oral history, 25–26.

7. *Honolulu Advertiser*, August 25, 1990.

8. *Honolulu Advertiser*, August 25, 1990.

9. *Honolulu Advertiser*, August 19, 1990.

10. Patti Paniccia, "In the Name of the Duke," *Los Angeles Times* magazine, November 16, 2003, 32.

11. Author interview.

12. Patti Paniccia, "In the Name of the Duke," *Los Angeles Times* magazine, November 16, 2003, 19.

13. Gray, *Sugar-Coated Fortress*, 145.

14. *Rotarian*, June 1962, DKC, Folder 129, Hawaii State Archives.

SELECTED BIBLIOGRAPHY

This bibliography includes sources that I found particularly helpful during my research. I also consulted many periodicals, and citations to those sources are provided in the endnotes.

LIBRARIES, ARCHIVES, MUSEUMS, CLUBS, AND INSTITUTIONS
Atlantic City Free Public Library
Bernice Pauahi Bishop Museum Library and Archives
Biola University Library
California Surf Museum
David Rubenstein Rare Book & Manuscript Library, Duke University
    Doris Duke Papers, Doris Duke Charitable Foundation Historical Archives
Edward Doheny Memorial Library (USC)
Frank Midkiff Learning Center, Kamehameha Schools
    Historical Archive
Glendale Public Library
Hamilton Library, University of Hawaii at Manoa
    Hawaiian & Pacific Collections
Hawaii Department of Education
Hawaii State Archives
Hawaii State Library
Hawaiian Historical Society
Honolulu Surf Museum
International Surfing Museum
James Cannavino Library, Archives and Special Collections, Marist College
    Lowell Thomas Papers
LA84 Foundation
Library of Congress
Long Beach Public Library (California)
Long Beach Public Library (New York)

Los Angeles Athletic Club
Los Angeles Public Library
Manly Library
Margaret Herrick Library, The Academy of Motion Picture Arts and Sciences
Mary Norton Clapp Library (Occidental College)
McHenry Library (UC Santa Cruz)
McKinley High School Library
New York Public Library
Oahu First Circuit Court
Oakland Public Library
Outrigger Canoe Club
Pasadena Public Library
Queens Public Library
Redondo Beach Public Library
Riverside Public Library
San Diego Public Library
San Francisco Public Library
San Jose Public Library
San Jose State University Library
Santa Cruz Public Library
Santa Cruz Surfing Museum
Santa Monica Public Library
Shangri La
Sherman Library and Gardens (Corona Del Mar)
Special Collections and Archives, Langson Library UC Irvine
Surfing Heritage & Culture Center
UCLA Film & Television Archive
    Ralph Edwards Collection
Venice-Abbot Kinney Branch Library

INTERNET RESOURCES
Australia and New Zealand surfing: www.surfresearch.com.au
Australia newspapers: http://trove.nla.gov.au/
Beachboys: http://www.surfcoastnews.com.au/2012/01/20/video-waikiki-beach-boys/
Clarence Darrow: http://darrow.law.umn.edu/trials.php?tid=5
Duke Kahanamoku: www.hawaiianswimboat.com
Family history: www.ancestry.com
HathiTrust Digital Library: http://www.hathitrust.org/home
Hawaiian swimming: www.hawaiiswim.org/legacy/ralphwright/toc1.html
Library of Congress (historic newspapers): http://chroniclingamerica.loc.gov
New Zealand newspapers: http://paperspast.natlib.govt.nz/

Olympics: www.olympic.org
Outrigger Duke Kahanamoku Foundation: www.dukefoundation.org
Save Our Surf digital collection: http://digicoll.manoa.hawaii.edu/sos/index.php?c=1
Song lyrics: www.territorialairwaves.com
Surfing history and interviews: http://files.legendarysurfers.com
Surfing videos: www.youtube.com
Surfing: www.surfline.com

BOOKS, ORAL HISTORIES, THESES

Allen, Gwenfread. *Hawaii's War Years, 1941–1945*. Honolulu: University of Hawaii Press, 1950.

Allen, Robert. *Creating Hawaii Tourism*. Honolulu: Bess Press, 2004.

The American Olympic Committee Report: Games of the Xth Olympiad. New York: American Olympic Committee, 1932.

Anthony, J. Garner. *Hawaii under Army Rule*. Palo Alto CA: Stanford University Press, 1955.

Benedict, Burton. *The Anthropology of World's Fairs: San Francisco's Panama Pacific International Exposition of 1915*. Berkeley: Lowie Museum of Anthropology and Scholar Press, 1983.

Biggers, Earl Derr. *House without a Key*. 1925. Accessed online at http://gutenberg.net.au/ebooks02/0200671.txt.

Black and Gold. McKinley High School publication, various years.

Blackburn, Mark. *Hula Girls & Surfer Boys, 1870–1940*. Atglen PA: Schiffer Publishing, 2000.

Blake, Tom. *Hawaiian Surfriders 1935*. Redondo Beach CA: Mountain & Sea Publishing, 1983.

Blossom, Laurel, ed. *Splash! Great Writing about Swimming*. Hopewell NJ: Ecco Press, 1996.

Bohn, Michael. *Heroes and Ballyhoo: How the Golden Age of the 1920s Transformed American Sports*. Dulles VA: Potomac Books, 2010.

Brennan, Joseph. *Duke of Hawaii*. New York: Ballantine Books, 1968.

———. *Duke: The Life Story of Duke Kahanamoku*. Honolulu: Ku Pa'a Publishing, 1994.

Brown, DeSoto. *Surfing: Historic Images from Bishop Museum Archives*. Honolulu: Bishop Museum Press, 2006.

Buford, Kate. *Native American Son: The Life and Sporting Legend of Jim Thorpe*. New York: Alfred Knopf. 2010.

Burnett, Claudine, and Paul Burnett. *Surfing Newport Beach: The Glory Days of Corona del Mar*. Charleston SC: History Press, 2013.

Carlson, Lewis, and John Fogarty. *Tales of Gold*. Chicago: Contemporary Books, 1987.

Cheever, Rev. Henry T. *Life in the Sandwich Islands*. London: Richard Bentley, 1851.

Cisco, Don. *Hawaii Sports: History, Facts, and Statistics.* Honolulu: University of Hawaii Press, 1999.

Clark, John R. K. *The Beaches of O'ahu.* Honolulu: University Press of Hawaii, 1977.

———. *Hawaiian Surfing: Traditions from the Past.* Honolulu: University of Hawaii Press, 2011.

Colburn, Bolton, Ben Finney, Tyler Stallings, C. R. Stecyk, Deanne Stillman, and Tom Wolfe. *Surf Culture: The Art History of Surfing.* Corte Madera CA: Gingko Press, 2002.

Cole, Margery Voyer. *Viola, Diving Wonder & Aquatic Champion.* Orange CA: Paragon Agency, 2001.

Coleman, Stuart Holmes. *Eddie Would Go: The Story of Eddie Aikau, Hawaiian Hero and Pioneer of Big Wave Surfing.* New York: St. Martin's Press, 2001.

Crawford, M. Leola. *Seven Weeks in Hawaii.* Chicago: Howard D. Berrett, 1913. Accessed online at http://books.google.com/books/about/Seven_weeks_in _Hawaii.html?id=exkNAAAAYAAJ.

Davis, David. *Showdown at Shepherd's Bush: The 1908 Olympic Marathon and the Three Runners Who Launched a Sporting Craze.* New York: St. Martin's Press, 2012.

Daws, Gavan. *Shoal of Time: A History of the Hawaiian Islands.* Honolulu: University of Hawaii Press, 1968.

Del Piano, Barbara. *Outrigger Canoe Club: The First Hundred Years, 1908–2008.* Honolulu: Outrigger Canoe Club, 2007.

DeLaVega, Timothy Tovar. *200 Years of Surfing Literature: An Annotated Bibliography.* Honolulu: Timothy DeLaVega, 2004.

———. *Surfing in Hawaii, 1778–1930.* Charleston SC: Arcadia Publishing, 2011.

Denney, Reuel, Francis Sydow, and Elmer Luke. "Olympic Hero Duke Kahanamoku: The Archetype of an Ethnic Achieving Popular Heroism." Research Paper, draft, 1974.

Didion, Joan. *Slouching toward Bethlehem.* New York: Farrar, Straus and Giroux, 2008.

Dinerstein, Joel, and Frank Goodyear III. *American Cool.* New York: DelMonico Books, 2014.

Duane, Daniel. *Caught Inside: A Surfer's Year on the California Coast.* New York: North Point Press, 1997.

Duke, Pony, and Jason Thomas. *Too Rich: The Family Secrets of Doris Duke.* New York: HarperCollins, 1996.

Dyreson, Mark. "Jesse Owens: Leading Man in Modern American Tales of Racial Progress and Limits." In *Out of the Shadows: A Biographical History of African American Athletes.* Edited by David Wiggins. Fayetteville: University of Arkansas Press, 2006.

———. *Making the American Team: Sport, Culture, and the Olympic Experience.* Urbana: University of Illinois Press, 1998.

Elwell, John, Jane Schmauss, and the California Surf Museum. *Surfing in San Diego.* Mount Pleasant NC: Arcadia Publishing, 2007.

Farber, Thomas. *On Water.* New York: Ecco Press, 1996.

Finney, Ben, and James Houston. *Surfing: A History of the Ancient Hawaiian Sport.* San Francisco: Pomegranate Artbooks, 1996.

Franks, Joel. *Hawaiian Sports in the Twentieth Century.* Lewiston NY: Edwin Mellen Press, 2002.

Fury, David. *Johnny Weissmuller: Twice the Hero.* Waterville ME: Thorndike Press, 2001.

Gabler, Neal. *An Empire of Their Own: How the Jews Invented Hollywood.* New York: Anchor Books, 1988.

Gallico, Paul. *The Golden People.* Garden City NY: Doubleday, 1965.

The Games of the Xth Olympiad, Los Angeles 1932, Official Report. Los Angeles: Xth Olympiade Committee, 1933.

Gault-Williams, Malcolm. *Legendary Surfers: A Definitive History of Surfing's Culture and Heroes,* vol. 1. Santa Barbara NC: CafePress, 2005. Chap. 10 accessed online at www.legendarysurfers.com.

Grannis, LeRoy. *Surf Photography of the 1960s and 1970s.* Los Angeles: Taschen, 2006.

Gray, Francine du Plessix. *Hawaii: The Sugar-Coated Fortress.* New York: Random House, 1972.

Gurrey, A. R., Jr. *The Surf Riders of Hawaii.* Restored edition, edited by Timothy DeLaVega, with text by Joel Smith and Sandra K. Hall. Honolulu: Timothy DeLaVega, 2014.

Hall, Sandra Kimberley. *Duke: A Great Hawaiian.* Honolulu: Bess Press, 2004.

Hall, Sandra Kimberley, and Greg Ambrose. *Memories of Duke: The Legend Comes to Life.* Honolulu: Bess Press, 1995.

Handicraft Journal, January 1889, Kamehameha Schools. Accessed online at http://kapalama.ksbe.edu/archives/historical/newspaper/handicraft.php.

Harris, Mark. *Five Came Back: A Story of Hollywood and the Second World War.* New York: Penguin, 2014.

Heimann, Jim. *Surfing.* Tachsen's 365 Day-by-Day. Cologne, Germany: Taschen, 2014.

Hemmings, Fred. *The Soul of Surfing.* New York: Thunder's Mouth Press, 1997.

———. *Surfing: Hawaii's Gift to the World of Sports.* Tokyo: Zokeisha Publications, 1977.

Hemmings, Kaui Hart. *The Descendants.* New York: Random House, 2007.

Honolulu City Directory (various years).

Huang, Yunte. *Charlie Chan: The Untold Story of the Honorable Detective and His Rendezvous with American History.* New York: W. W. Norton, 2010.

James, Don. *Surfing San Onofre to Point Dume.* San Francisco: Chronicle Books, 1996.

Jarratt, Phil. *That Summer at Boomerang*. Melbourne, Australia: Hardie Grant Books, 2004.

Jenkins, Bruce. *North Shore Chronicles: Big-Wave Surfing in Hawaii*. Berkeley CA: Frog Books, 1999.

Johnson, William O. *All That Glitters Is Not Gold: An Irreverent Look at the Olympic Games*. New York: G. P. Putnam's Sons, 1972.

Jones, James. *From Here to Eternity*. New York: Dial Press, 2012.

Kahanamoku, Duke, with Joe Brennan. *Duke Kahanamoku's World of Surfing*. New York: Grosset & Dunlap, 1968.

Kahanamoku, Nadine Alexander. Oral history interview by Alice Sinesky for The Watumull Foundation Oral History Project. Honolulu: The Watumull Foundation Oral History Project, ca. 1987.

Kampion, Drew. *Stoked: A History of Surf Culture*. Los Angeles: General Publishing Group, 1997.

Katchen, Alan. *Abel Kiviat: National Champion*. Syracuse NY: Syracuse University Press, 2009.

Klein, H. Arthur, and M. C. Klein. *Surf's Up!* New York: Bobbs-Merrill, 1966.

Kohner, Frederick. *Gidget: The Little Girl with Big Ideas*. New York: Berkley Books, 2001.

Kolata, Gina. *Flu: The Story of the Great Influenza Pandemic of 1918 and the Search for the Virus That Caused It*. New York: Farrar, Straus and Giroux, 1999.

Kozar, Andrew. *The Sport Sculpture of R. Tait McKenzie*. Champaign IL: Human Kinetics Books, 1992.

Kuykendall, Ralph. *The Hawaiian Kingdom* (trilogy). Honolulu: University of Hawaii Press, 1938, 1953, 1967.

———. *Hawaii in the World War*. Honolulu: Historical Commission, 1928.

Laderman, Scott. *Empire in Waves: A Political History of Surfing*. Berkeley: University of California Press, 2014.

Lasky, Jesse. *I Blow My Own Horn*. New York: Doubleday, 1957.

Lencek, Lena, and Gideon Bosker. *Making Waves: Swimsuits and the Undressing of America*. San Francisco: Chronicle Books, 1989.

Leterman, Elmer. *Personal Power through Creative Selling*. New York: Collier Books, 1956.

Letham, Isabel. Oral history interview by Roslyn Cahill for Armidale College of Advanced Education, New South Wales, Australia, March 7, 1986, and with the Manly Library.

Lien, Sonia, and K. D. Kragen. *From Alone to Aloha*. Seattle: Cedar Forge Press, 2011.

Lili'uokalani. *Hawaii's Story by Hawaii's Queen*. Rutland VT: Charles Tuttle, 1964.

Littlefield, Sharon. *Doris Duke's Shangri La*. Honolulu: Doris Duke Foundation for Islamic Art, 2008.

Lodge, David. *Paradise News*. New York: Viking, 1992.

London, Charmian. *Jack London and Hawaii*. London: Mills & Boon, 1918.

London, Jack. *Stories of Hawaii*. New York: Appleton-Century, 1965.

Lord, Walter. *Day of Infamy*. New York: Henry Holt, 2001.

Lueras, Leonard. *Surfing: The Ultimate Pleasure*. New York: Workman Publishing, 1984.

Lynch, Gary, and Malcolm Gault-Williams. *Tom Blake: The Uncommon Journey of a Pioneer Waterman*. Newport Beach CA: Croul Publications, 2013.

Mallon, Bill, and Anthony Bijkerk. *The 1920 Olympic Games: Results for All Competitors in All Events, with Commentary*. Jefferson NC: McFarland, 2003.

Mallon, Bill, and Ian Buchanan. *The 1908 Olympic Games: Results for All Competitors in All Events, with Commentary*. Jefferson NC: McFarland, 2000.

Mallon, Bill, and Ture Widlund. *The 1912 Olympic Games: Results for All Competitors in All Events, with Commentary*. Jefferson NC: McFarland, 2002.

Malo, David. *Hawaiian Antiquities*. Translated from the Hawaiian by Dr. Nathaniel Emerson. Honolulu: Bishop Museum Press, 1951.

Mansfield, Stephanie. *The Richest Girl in the World: The Extravagant Life and Fast Times of Doris Duke*. New York: G. P. Putnam's Sons, 1992.

Melville, Herman. *Mardi and a Voyage Thither*. Boston: L. C. Page, 1923.

Michener, James. *Hawaii*. New York: Random House, 1959.

Moore, Michael Scott. *Sweetness and Blood: How Surfing Spread from Hawaii and California to the Rest of the World, with Some Unexpected Results*. Emmaus PA: Rodale, 2010.

Morgan, Howard Wayne. *William McKinley and His America*. Kent OH: Kent State University Press, 2003.

Moser, Patrick, ed. *Pacific Passages: An Anthology of Surf Writing*. Honolulu: University of Hawaii Press, 2008.

Motil, Guy. *Surfboards*. Guilford CT: Falcon Guides, 2007.

Nendel, James D. "Duke Kahanamoku: Twentieth-Century Hawaiian Monarch: The Values and Contributions to Hawaiian Culture from Hawaii's Sporting Legend." Master's Thesis, Pennsylvania State University, 2006.

Newcombe, Jack. *The Best of the Athletic Boys*. New York: Doubleday, 1975.

Nicholson, Joy. *The Tribes of Palos Verdes*. New York: St. Martin's Press, 1997.

Noble, Valerie. *Hawaiian Prophet: Alexander Hume Ford*. Smithtown NY: Exposition Press, 1980.

Nunn, Kem. *Tapping the Source*. New York: Dell Publishing, 1985.

Obama, Barack. *Dreams of My Father: A Story of Race and Inheritance*. New York: Crown, 2004.

Okihiro, Gary. *Island World: A History of Hawaii and the United States*. Berkeley: University of California Press, 2008.

The Olympic Century: The Official History of the Modern Olympic Movement. Los Angeles: World Sport Research & Publications, 1995–2000.

Olympic Games Handbook. New York: American Sports Publishing: Spalding's Athletic Library, 1921.

Onyx, Narda. *Water, World & Weissmuller.* Los Angeles: VION Publishing, 1964.

Osmond, Gary, Murray Phillips, and Mark O'Neill. "'Putting up Your Dukes': Statues, Social Memory and Duke Paoa Kahanamoku," *International Journal of the History of Sport* (February 2006): 82–103.

Outrigger Canoe Club Oral Histories. Honolulu: Outrigger Canoe Club, various years.

Pierce, David. *The Survival of American Silent Feature Films: 1912–1929.* Washington DC: The Library of Congress and the Council on Library and Information Resources, 2013.

Pollard, Jack. *The Surfrider.* New York: Taplinger Publishing, 1968.

Pretor-Pinney, Gavin. *The Wave Watcher's Companion: From Ocean Waves to Light Waves via Shock Waves, Stadium Waves, and All the Rest of Life's Undulations.* New York: Perigee Book, 2010.

Pukui, Mary Kawena. *'Olelo No'eau: Hawaiian Proverbs & Poetical Sayings.* Honolulu: Bishop Museum Press, 1983.

Pyle, Ernie. *Home Country.* New York: William Sloane, 1947.

Ralston, Esther. *Some Day We'll Laugh.* Metuchen NJ: Scarecrow Press, 1985.

Reid, Sam. "Sam Reid Interview," by Michael Mandel, October 25, 1977, from the Santa Cruz Surfing Museum Collection. Santa Cruz: Santa Cruz Museum of Natural History, transcribed in 2000.

Rensin, David. *All for a Few Perfect Waves: The Audacious Life and Legend of Rebel Surfer Miki Dora.* New York: HarperCollins, 2009.

Renson, Roland. *The Games Reborn.* Antwerp, Belgium: Pandora, 1996.

Report of the American Olympic Committee: Seventh Olympic Games, Antwerp, Belgium, 1920. Greenwich CT: Conde Nast Press, 1921.

Riess, Steven. *Sports in North America, Volume 6: 1900–1920.* Gulf Breeze FL: Academic International Press, 1998.

Schwarz, Ted, and Tom Rybak. *Trust No One: The Glamorous Life and Bizarre Death of Doris Duke.* New York: St. Martin's Press, 1997.

Selle, Earl Albert. *The Story of Duke Paoa Kahanamoku.* Golden Man Foundation, 1959.

Shapton, Leanne. *Swimming Studies.* New York: Blue Rider Press, 2012.

Siler, Julia Flynn. *Lost Kingdom: Hawaii's Last Queen, the Sugar Kings, and America's First Imperial Adventure.* New York: Atlantic Monthly Press, 2012.

Smith, Chas. *Welcome to Paradise, Now Go to Hell: A True Story of Violence, Corruption, and the Soul of Surfing.* New York: itbooks, 2013.

Sprawson, Charles. *Haunts of the Black Masseur: The Swimmer as Hero.* New York: Pantheon, 1992.

Sragow, Michael. *Victor Fleming: An American Movie Master.* New York: Pantheon, 2008.

Stannard, David. *Honor Killing: How the Infamous "Massie Affair" Transformed Hawaii.* New York: Viking, 2005.

Starr, Kevin. *Material Dreams: Southern California through the 1920s.* New York: Oxford University Press, 1990.

Stevenson, Robert Louis. *Travels in Hawaii.* Edited by A. Grove Day. Honolulu: University of Hawaii Press, 1973.

Stout, Glenn. *Young Woman and the Sea: How Trudy Ederle Conquered the English Channel and Inspired the World.* New York: Houghton, Mifflin, Harcourt, 2009.

Sullivan, James E., ed. *The Olympic Games Stockholm 1912.* New York: American Sports Publishing, 1912.

Sullivan, James E., ed. *Spalding's Official Athletic Almanac for 1905.* New York: The American Publishing Company, 1905. Accessed online at http://library.la84 .org/6oic/OfficialReports/1904/1904Spal.pdf.

Swedish Olympic Committee. *The Official Report of the Olympic Games of Stockholm 1912.* Stockholm: Wahlstrom & Widstrand, 1912.

Thomas, Evan. *The War Lovers: Roosevelt, Lodge, Hearst, and the Rush to Empire, 1898.* New York: Little, Brown, 2010.

Thompson, Neal. *A Curious Man: The Strange & Brilliant Life of Robert "Believe It or Not!" Ripley.* New York: Crown Archetype, 2013.

Thrum's Hawaiian Annual. Honolulu: Star-Bulletin Printing, various years.

Timmons, Grady. *Waikiki Beachboy.* Honolulu: Editions Limited, 1989.

Todd, Frank Morton. *The Story of the Exposition.* New York: G. P. Putnam's Sons, 1921.

Tomson, Shaun. *Surfer's Code: 12 Simple Lessons for Riding through Life.* Layton UT: Gibbs Smith, 2011.

Twain, Mark. *Letters from Honolulu.* Honolulu: Thomas Nickerson, 1939.

———. "Roughing It." In *The Complete Travel Books of Mark Twain.* Edited by Charles Neider. Garden City NY: Doubleday, 1966.

Valentine, Tom, and Patrick Mahn. *Daddy's Duchess: The Unauthorized Biography of Doris Duke.* Fort Lee NJ: Lyle Stuart, 1987.

Verge, Arthur. "George Freeth: King of the Surfers and California's Forgotten Hero." *California History* 80, no. 2/3 (Summer/Fall 2001): 82–105.

Vowell, Sarah. *Unfamiliar Fishes.* New York: Riverhead Books, 2011.

Waikiki, 1900–1985: Oral Histories. Honolulu: Oral History Project, Social Science Research Institute, University of Hawaii at Manoa, 1987.

Walker, Isaiah. *Waves of Resistance: Surfing and History in Twentieth-Century Hawaii.* Honolulu: University of Hawaii Press, 2011.

Wallechinsky, David. *The Complete Book of the Summer Olympics.* New York: Overlook Press, 2000.

Warshaw, Matt. *The Encyclopedia of Surfing.* Available online at encyclopediaof surfing.com.

———. *The History of Surfing*. San Francisco: Chronicle Books, 2010.

Watson, Kathy. *The Crossing: The Glorious Tragedy of the First Man to Swim the English Channel*. New York: Jeremy P. Tarcher/Putnam, 2001.

Weissmuller, Johnny, Jr. *Tarzan, My Father*. Toronto: ECW Press, 2008.

Westwick, Peter, and Peter Neushul. *The World in the Curl: An Unconventional History of Surfing*. New York: Crown, 2013.

Wilder, Kinau. *Wilders of Waikiki*. Honolulu: Topgallant Publishing, 1978.

Willard, Michael Nevin. "Duke Kahanamoku's Body." In *Sports Matters: Race, Recreation, and Culture*. Edited by John Bloom and Michael Nevin Willard. New York: NYU Press, 2002.

Williams, Esther. *The Million Dollar Mermaid*. New York: Simon & Schuster, 1999.

Winton, Tim. *Breath*. New York: Farrar, Straus and Giroux, 2008.

Wolfe, Tom. *The Pump House Gang*. New York: Farrar, Straus & Giroux, 1968.

Wright, Katie. "Duke Kahanamoku: Cultural Icon." Masters Thesis, Center for Pacific Island Studies, 2005.

Wright, Ralph. "A Historical Study of the Development of the Competitive Swimming of Hawaii up to 1916." Masters Thesis, University of Hawaii, 1947.

Wright, Theon. *Rape in Paradise*. Honolulu: Mutual Publishing, 2005.

Yost, Harold. *The Outrigger: A History of the Outrigger Canoe Club 1908–1971*. Honolulu: Outrigger, 1971.

Young, Betty Lou. *Our First Century: The Los Angeles Athletic Club, 1880–1980*. Los Angeles: LAAC Press, 1979.

Yttergren, Leif, and Hans Bolling. *The 1912 Stockholm Olympics*. Jefferson NC: McFarland, 2012.

Zamperini, Louis, with David Rensin. *Devil at My Heels: A World War II Hero's Epic Saga of Torment, Survival, and Forgiveness*. New York: HarperCollins, 2003.

Zukor, Adolph. *The Public Is Never Wrong*. New York: G. P. Putnam's, 1953.

INDEX

AAU. *See* Amateur Athletic Union
aborigines, 91
Adams, Doc, 186
Admissions Act 1959, 226. *See also*
    Hawaii: statehood
Adrian, Tommy, 94, 130
Adventure (motion picture), 159, 169
Ah Choy Family, 190
Ahearn, Dan, 128
Aikau, Eddie, 242, 256
Aipa, Ben, 242
Akaka, Abraham, 227, 233, 249, 250
Akana, F. Lang, 189
Ala Moana Trial, 177
Ala Wai Canal, 174, 185, 209
Albert, King, 129, 134
Alenuihaha Channel, 134, 208
Alexander, Nadine. *See* Kahanamoku,
    Nadine
Alfred, Prince of Edinburgh, 5, 6
Ali, Muhammad, 252
Allen, Norma. *See* Kahanamoku, Nadine
"Aloha Oe" (song), 42, 52, 249
aloha shirt, 192, 201, 214, 228, 229, 234,
    237, 238, 254, 245
Alter, Hobie, 221
Amalu, Sammy, 247
Amateur Athletic Union (AAU), 40, 44–45,
    46, 87, 97, 98, 99–100, 113–14, 138–39,
    167; AAU swim meetings, 37, 39, 40, 46,
    99, 102, 113, 118, 122; Hawaii Chapter,
    35, 136; Hui Nalu membership, 35–36
amateurism, rules of, 74–75, 78
amateur status and eligibility, 42, 71, 73,
    75, 75–76, 77, 80, 102, 103, 104, 135–36,
    145, 166, 169, 180, 183

America, SS, 149
American crawl, 39
American Olympic Committee, 51, 69, 125,
    126, 128, 130, 146, 148, 149, 181, 182, 188
American Tobacco Company, 78, 192
Anthony, J. Garner, 210
Apana, Chang, 158
aquaplaning, 101, 164
Araner (yacht), 160
Arizona, USS, 207, 228
Arnott, Tom, 209
Around the World in Eighty Minutes
    (motion picture), 169
Atkinson, A. L. C., 77
Atlantic City, 3, 46–47, 66–68, 72, 78, 79,
    81, 96, 103
Australia, 2, 3, 33, 49, 55, 57, 60, 61, 63, 84,
    86, 90–91, 92, 94–96, 107, 124, 155, 190,
    199, 217, 218, 236, 254
Australian crawl, 33
Australian Swimming Union, 90
Ayau, Henry, 224

Bachrach, William "Big Bill," 76, 87, 88,
    99, 100, 102, 113, 125, 132, 136, 137–39,
    143, 144, 146, 147, 148, 149, 151, 152, 153,
    160, 166, 171, 243
Baden-Powell, Robert, 53
Baldwin, Elias "Lucky," 159
Bancroft, George, 159, 164
Banzai Pipeline, 238
Barry, Albert, 94, 130
Bartlett, William, 67
Bartley, R. M., 100–101
baseball, 20, 24, 64, 73, 74, 89, 155, 175,
    189, 223

bathing suit. *See* swim suits
The Battle of Midway (motion picture), 208
Beach, Don, 232
beachboy, 22, 35, 38, 82–83, 106, 136, 155, 174, 183, 190, 200, 212, 214, 224, 323, 249, 251, 254, 255
The Beach Boys (musical group), 223, 234
The Beachcomber (motion picture), 88, 158, 169
beach volleyball, 3, 12, 101, 107, 121, 141, 240
Beaumont, Jack, 209
Beaurepaire, Frank, 217
Beery, Wallace, 159, 164, 169
The Bel-Airs, 223
Belden Production, 228, 229
Benjamin, Robert, 103
Bennett, Mae Josephine, 84
Bernice Pauahi Bishop Museum. *See* The Bishop Museum
Berrett, Howard D., 83
Biggers, Earl Derr, 158, 223
Big Jim McLain (motion picture), 284n4
"The Big Kahoona," 222
big-wave surfing, 221, 224, 237, 239, 241
Billy Rose's Aquacade, 138
Bingham, Hiram, 19
Bishop, Princess Bernice Pauahi, 5, 15
The Bishop Museum, 133, 173, 253, 255, 271n2
Black, Hugo, 211
Black and Gold, 21
Black Point, 202, 203, 216
Blaisdell, Neal, 230, 231
Blake, Tom: Corona del Mar Surfboard Club, 161; friendship with Duke, 133, 141, 143, 160, 173; historian, 81, 133, 190; Los Angeles Athletic Club, 143; the "Long Ride," 108, 111; surfboards, 133, 141, 173
Bland, Myron, 162–63
Bleibtrey, Ethelda, 127, 131, 134
"Blue Hawaii" (song), 192
body surfing, 23, 67, 133, 160, 256
Bonhag, George, 59
Bonine, Robert, 24
Boomerang Camp, 92
Borg, Arne, 151, 152, 154
Boston Globe, 47, 127, 259

Bosworth, Hobart, 88
Bow, Clara, 157, 159, 160, 166, 169
Bradner, Hugh, 220
Branfleet, 201, 213
Brangier, George, 201
Brennan, Joe, 104, 119, 242
Brenner, Victor David, 45
Bretting, Kurt, 60, 61, 62, 66
Broad Ripple, 146, 147
"The Bronze Statue," 105
Brookside Park Pool, 145–46
Brown, Bruce, 222, 237, 242, 256
Brown, Francis I'i, 198
Brown, Joseph, 253
Brown, Kenneth, 22, 39, 200, 245
Brown, Woodbridge "Woody," 221, 224
Browne, Bud, 222
Bruce's Beach (Manhattan Beach), 156
Buckeye Lake, 137
Bush, Bob, 209

Cabell, Joey, 237, 239, 242
Cady, Fred, 144, 152, 156, 168, 177, 179, 181, 193, 218, 252
Cady, Viola Hartman, 156, 166, 177
Cann, Ted, 103, 138
canoes and canoe racing, 28, 42, 76, 83, 101, 124, 142, 159, 174, 178, 185, 209–10, 213, 247, 249–50, 254
Carlisle Indian Industrial School, 15, 16, 53
Carlos, John, 252
Carroll, Corky, 241
Cartwright, Alexander, 20, 175, 223
Castle, Alfred, 77
Castle, Harold, 30
Castle, James, 109
Castle, William R., 77
Castle & Cook, 30
Castle's (break), 108, 109, 216
Castles by the Sea (NY), 117
Castle's Pier, 125
Catalina Island, 164, 166
catamaran, 224
Cat on a Hot Foam Board (surfing film), 222
"Causes of the Decline of Ancient Hawaiian Sports" (Emerson), 20
Cavill, Arthur, 86
Cavill, Sid, 79
Cavill family, 33, 90

Center, George "Dad," 29, 37, 101, 107, 108, 133, 139, 152, 190, 215, 219, 252; coach and coaching, 113, 120, 125, 130, 139, 152; death of, 243
Chambers, Ralph, 216
Champion, Malcolm, 63
Chan, Charlie, 158, 223
Chaney, Lon, 169
Chantays, 223
Chaplin, Charlie, 132, 175
Charlton, Andrew "Boy," 151
Chase, Charlie, 161
Cheever, Henry, 19
Chicago, 43, 44, 46, 81, 102, 113
Chicago Almanac, 48
Chicago Examiner, 48
Chicago YMCA, 87
Chilton, Harvey, 99, 100
Christie, Agatha, 274n7
Chun, Ellery, 201
Churchill, Owen, 201–2; Churchill Swim Fins, 283n22
Cisco Casuals, 213–14, 229, 230, 233
citizenship status, 13, 138–39, 145, 155
City of Honolulu, 172
Clark, Henry, 102
Clarke, Mary Paoa (cousin), 8, 176
Clarkson, Magnus, 69
Cleveland, Grover, 13
Colman, Ronald, 160, 168, 169
Colony. *See* Malibu Colony
Compson, Betty, 159
Conrad, Joseph, 159, 168
Constitution, USS, 164
Coogan, Jackie, 141
Cook, James, 10, 18
Cooper, Gary, 169
Corbett, W. F., 93, 95
Corona del Mar, 3, 161, 164, 219, 223
Corona del Mar Surfboard Club, 161
Cottrell, William "Knute," 29, 30
Coubertin, Pierre de, 53, 54, 55, 56–57, 59, 65, 85, 86, 98, 120, 129, 133, 142, 150, 239, 256
The Covered Wagon (motion picture), 159, 164, 277
Cowells, Frances, 105
Crabbe, Clarence "Buster," 167, 168, 181, 188, 200, 203, 243
Cravath, Clifford "Gary," 162

Crawford, Minnie Leola, 83
Cromwell, Arden, 195–96
Cromwell, Doris Duke. *See* Duke, Doris
Cromwell, James, 193, 194, 195
Crosby, Bing, 192
Cruise of the Snark (Jack London), 24, 25–26
Cruze, James, 159, 164, 165, 169
cultural identity, Hawaiian, 3, 8, 10, 11, 14, 16–18, 21, 95, 174, 193, 200, 255
Cunha, George, 91, 92, 94, 99, 100
curfews, Hawaii, 208

Dale, Dick, 223
Damita, Lily, 169
The Dangerous Age (motion picture), 140
Daniels, Charles, 33, 38, 39, 40, 50, 56, 138, 181, 183, 288n8
Daniels, Chick, 214, 233
Darrow, Clarence, 178
Davison, Henry, 116
Daws, Gavan, 211
December 7th (motion picture), 208
Deerr, Noel, 83
Deerr, Rhonda (Wilson), 84
Dees, Michael, 253
Dee Why Beach, 93
Del Piano, Barbara, 208
The Del-tones, 223
Dempsey, Jack, 3, 126, 134, 155, 214, 233
Denny, Martin, 233
Deraga, Antar, 161, 163
Desborough, Lord, 55, 62
Detroit Free Press, 58
Diamond Head, 109, 125, 184, 193, 200, 206, 207, 247, 250, 253
Didion, Joan, 227
Didrikson, Mildred "Babe," 181
Diego, Julio de, 214
Dillingham, Harold G., 184, 185, 197
Dillingham, Walter, 226
Dole, Sanford, 13
Domain Baths, 9, 130
Don the Beachcomber (restaurant), 233
Dora, Mickey, 241
Dorfner, Olga, 144
Dorfs, Christ, 165
Downing, George, 104, 111, 151, 190, 221, 225, 241, 257
Dowsett, Beatrice, 105–6

Dowsett, Marion "Babe," 105–6
Dowsett Family, 112
Doyle, Mike, 242
Drew, Howard, 57
"Duke" (name and namesake), 5
The Duke (surfing competition), 241–42
Duke, Doris, 192–96, 199, 202, 252, 254
Duke, James B., 78, 192
"Duke de Crawlstroke," 63
"Duke Kahanamoku" (song), 184
Duke Kahanamoku Aquatics Complex, 1
Duke Kahanamoku Beach, 1
Duke Kahanamoku Fund Committee, 77
Duke Kahanamoku Invitational, 251
Duke Kahanamoku Lagoon, 1
Duke Kahanamoku's (restaurant), 1, 232,
    233, 234, 241, 245, 246, 251
Duke Kahanamoku surf club, 237
Duke Kahanamoku's World of Surfing
    (Brennan), 242
Duke Kahanamoku v. Advertiser
    Publication Corporation, 123, 136, 274n5
Duke Kahanamoku v. Bishop Trust
    Company, 270n13
Duke of Edinburgh. See Alfred, Prince of
    Edinburgh
Duke of Hawaii (Brennan), 242
Duke P. Kahanomoku Swimming Meet,
    203
Duke's (restaurant). See Duke
    Kahanamoku's (restaurant)
Dunbar, Addie, 84–85
Duncan, Lloyd, 210
Duncan v. Kahanamoku, 210–12
Dunham, Ann, 234

Eagle of the Sea (motion picture), 170
Earhart, Amelia, 175
Eastman, Ruth, 135
East-West Center, University of Hawaii, 234
Easy Come, Easy Go (motion picture), 170
Ederle, Gertrude, 148, 155, 288n8
Ed Kenny and the Surfers, 232
Edward, Prince of Wales, 124, 243
Edwards, Ralph, 218–19
Edwards, Webley, 192, 206
Eisenhower, Dwight D., 216, 226
Ekstrand, Thad, 209, 210
Elizabeth, Queen Mother, 242
Emerson, Nathaniel, 20

Encino Country Club, 143
Endless Summer (motion picture), 237
environment, 239, 253
Evans, Francis, 91, 92, 94
Evening World, 138

Fairbanks, Douglas, 140, 149, 157, 169,
    180, 197
Famous Players-Lasky Corporation, 157.
    See also Paramount Studios
Farrell, Charles, 164
Federation Internationale de Natation, 56
Fern, Joseph J., 77
Fernie, Jim, 209
Ferris, Daniel, 126
Field, Sally, 223
films. See Kahanamoku, Duke Paoa: motion
    picture film career; motion pictures
Finland, 55, 51, 52, 58, 61, 62, 63, 64, 65
Finney, Ben, 81
The Fire Walker (motion picture), 170
Fisher, Jan Gordon, 253
Fleming, Victor, 159, 160, 169
Flood, Curt, 252
flutter kick, 34
Fonda, Henry, 216
Fong, Hiram, 228, 247
Ford, Alexander Hume, 24, 25, 27, 28, 31,
    32, 34, 41, 42, 43, 83, 107, 123, 220, 224,
    256
Ford, Edsel, 105
Ford, John, 159, 160, 169, 170, 171, 208,
    216, 218
Fortescue, Grace, 177
Frank, Alvin, 142
Freeth, George: coaches Duke, 87; death
    of, 120; first to surf Atlantic City, 68;
    first to surf California, 27, 120; in
    California, 27, 79, 80, 160; friendship
    with Duke, 29, 32, 42, 68, 79, 79–80, 87,
    120; Jack London's descriptions of, 26–
    27; Los Angeles Athletic Club, 87; on
    mainland with Duke Kahanamoku,
    42, 68, 87–88; surfing in Hawaii,
    25, 29, 32; teaches Jack London and
    Alexander Hume Ford, 25–27
Freshwater Beach, 3, 92, 93, 218
Frizell, R. E., 46
Froiseth, Wally, 190, 223
From Here to Eternity (Jones), 176–77

Gable, Clark, 175
Gallico, Paul, 34, 138, 155
Garland, William May, 142, 163
Gaynor, William, 69
Genoves, Vincent "Zen," 42, 43, 44, 45, 46
Getty, John Paul, 160
Gibb, Roberta, 252
Gidget (motion picture), 223, 256
Gidget (TV show), 223
Gidget Goes Hawaiian (motion picture), 223
Gidget: The Little Girl with Big Ideas (Kohner), 223
Gilbert, Jean, 210
Girl of the Port (motion picture), 170, 172
Glennon, Bert, 170
Godrey, Arthur, 214, 224, 227, 230, 232, 248–49, 252
Golden Age of Sport, 154–55
Goldwyn, Samuel, 157, 168
golf. *See* Kahanamoku, Duke Paoa: golf
Grand Olympic Auditorium, 142
Grigg, Ricky, 242
Grigsby, Mary, 163
Gun Ho (surfing film), 222
Gurrey, A. R., Jr., 31, 72, 271n13
Gurrey's (photo studio), 72
Gustaf V, King of Sweden, 59, 62, 63, 64, 70, 183

Hakman, Jeff, 241
Hakuole, Jimmy, 233, 251
Halassy, Oliver, 182
Hale, Owen, 161, 162, 163, 173
Hall, Sandra, 225
Hall of Fame, 233, 288n8
Handley, Louis de Breda, 102
Hands around the Pacific, 25
Handy, Jamison, 87
Harmon, Millard, 118
Harper's Weekly, 58
Harris, Bill, 125, 130, 131, 145
Harrison, Lorrin "Whitey," 190
Harrison, Reginald, 146
Harrow-on-the-Hill, 152
Hartford Courant, 247
Hartman, Viola, 156, 166, 177
Hawaii: Admissions Act 1959, 226; annexation of, 13, 21, 174, 210; cultural identity, 3, 8, 10–11, 14, 16–18, 21, 48, 82, 95, 97, 100, 123, 127, 174, 193, 200, 227, 252, 255–56; martial law, 206, 210, 211; military in, 107, 116, 176–77, 205, 206, 207, 208, 210–11; origins, development and history, 2, 10–14, 112, 174, 226–27; promoting of, 3, 24–25, 27, 31–32, 41, 71–72, 76, 86, 92, 98, 99, 100, 104, 123, 133, 172, 174, 175, 244; statehood, 72, 213, 226–27, 228, 231; tourism, 1, 3, 72, 76, 82, 86, 97, 107, 122, 135, 174, 175, 185, 192, 207, 227, 251, 254; World Wars, during, 107, 117, 203, 205–7, 212; World's Fair, exhibited at, 6, 12, 87–98, 100, 190, 244
"Hawaii Aloha" (song), 248
Hawaiian Centennial Swim Meet, 125
Hawaiian culture and identity, 8, 11–12, 14, 17, 18, 20, 28, 48, 52, 100, 107, 142, 174, 189, 191, 200, 207, 227–28, 237, 245
Hawaiian Defense Act, 206
Hawaiian "Dragnet," 228–29
Hawaiian Gazette, 84
Hawaiian kick, 34
The Hawaiian Society, 163
Hawaiian Sugar Planters' Association, 83
Hawaiian Surfing Movie (motion picture), 222
Hawaiian Trail and Mountain Club, 25
Hawaiian Village, 227
Hawaii Five-O (TV show), 229
Hawaii Promotion Committee, 78, 86
Healani Boat Club, 29, 37, 38, 113
Healy, Cecil, 60, 61, 62, 63, 90, 91, 92, 95, 130, 131
Hebner, Harry, 52, 63, 87, 100, 125, 138, 145
Hemmings, Fred, Jr., 237–38, 242, 245, 253, 254
Henderson, Lew, 42, 43, 45, 45, 46, 47, 49, 189, 190, 215
Henderson family, 66
Henning, Dr. Oscar, 140, 141
Henning, Thor, 140
Henry, Bill, 142
Henry, Les, 79, 87, 141, 142, 179, 181, 219
Henry, Madge, 142, 219
Henry Waterhouse Trust Company, 77
Herald, William, 131
Herrman, Carl, 253
Her Summer Hero (motion picture), 170
Herwig, William, 161
Hill, William W., 66, 90

Hillstreet Theater, 166
Ho, Don, 234–35, 236, 246, 247, 248, 251
Hock, Fred, 163
Hollinger, Kimo, 241
Holm, Eleanor, 188, 240
Holmes, Charles, 198
Honolulan, SS, 42
Honolulu Advertiser, 186, 196, 205, 229
Honolulu Bears, 204
Honolulu High School, 21
Honolulu Police Department, 8, 97, 158, 176
Honolulu Stadium, 175
Honolulu Star-Bulletin, 71, 77, 84, 103,
    106, 114, 117, 124, 183, 211, 259
Honouliuli Internment Camp, 207
Hoopii, Sol, 184
Hoover, Herbert, 175, 180
Hoppe, Willie, 103
Hotel Australia, 91
The House without a Key (book and
    motion picture), 158, 223
Houston, USS, 185
Hui Nalu: AAU membership, 35; club
    history, 30, 32, 35–37, 38, 41, 42, 80, 82,
    87, 88, 108, 174, 243, 248; club name,
    29, 80; club song, 36, 172; supporting
    Duke, 70, 71, 72, 77, 79
Hula (motion picture), 159
hula dancing, 72, 100, 193, 198, 198, 214,
    219, 236, 242, 254
Huntington, Henry, 27
Huntington Beach, 27, 80, 156, 160, 236,
    238, 236
Hustace, Curtis, 30
Hustace, Harold, 30
Huszagh, Kenneth, 45, 52, 60, 61, 62–63
Hygeia Pool, 46, 67

IAC. *See* Illinois Athletic Club
Illinois Athletic Club (IAC), 76, 87, 88, 99,
    102, 113, 125, 136, 137, 138, 146, 147, 153,
    155, 166, 167, 182, 243
Impossible Mrs. Bellew (motion picture),
    140
Indianapolis, USS, 232
influenza, 118–19, 120, 144, 168
Ink Well (Santa Monica), 156
Inman, Bill, 89
Inman, Nanline Holt, 192
Inouye, Daniel, 228

Inter-Allied Games 1919, 121
International Olympic Committee, 33, 54,
    56, 78, 85, 142, 150
Iolani Palace, 226, 253
Irish American Athletic Club, 74
The Iron Horse (motion picture), 159
Isle of Sunken Gold (motion picture), 158

Jacobs, Harold "Hap," 221
Jantzen swimsuit, 135
Johnson, Jack, 49, 74, 91
Judd, Elizabeth Kinau, 232

Kaahumanu Society, 8
Kahahawai, Joseph, 177, 178
Kahala (Black Point), 202–3
Kahala (sportswear), 201, 233
Kahanamoku, Beatrice (sister), 7, 105, 112,
    198, 215, 219, 248
Kahanamoku, David Piikoi (brother), 7,
    66, 101, 107, 112, 124, 146, 149, 152, 167,
    172, 193, 146, 215
Kahanamoku, Duke Halapu (father), 4,
    5, 6–7, 8, 9, 12, 15, 33, 46, 49, 65, 70, 71,
    77, 97, 103, 187; death of, 111–12; Duke
    name, 5; Kamehameha relationship,
    5–6; policeman, 8, 97, 111
Kahanamoku, Duke Paoa: amateur
    status and eligibility, 42, 71, 73, 74,
    75–78, 88, 95, 102, 103, 104, 136, 139,
    166, 169, 183, 252; athleticism, 29, 34,
    38, 45–46, 47–48, 87, 117, 247; birth
    and youth, 4–5, 7–9, 13, 15, 16, 20–21;
    and Blake, Tom, 108, 111, 133, 141, 143,
    160, 161, 173; as captain of the 1924
    U.S. Olympic Team, 151; and Center,
    George ("Dad"), 29, 37, 101, 107, 113–14,
    1120, 125, 130, 152, 190, 215, 219, 243;
    citizenship, 13; cultural and ethnic
    identity, 8–9, 17–18, 22, 48, 123, 127,
    170, 173–75, 200, 208, 245, 252; death
    of, 247; earnings, erroneous accounts
    of, 229–30; economic and financial
    challenges, 106, 139, 202, 228, 230,
    244–45; education and schools, 16, 20–
    21; employment, 72, 82, 104, 120, 136,
    139, 170, 175, 176, 183–84, 186, 188, 230;
    endorsement opportunities, 78, 135–36,
    201, 213, 229 238; eulogy by Arthur
    Godfrey, 248–49; fictionalized

stories of, 48, 84–85, 96, 153–54; and Freeth, George, 29, 32, 42, 68, 79, 79–80, 87, 120; funeral of, 248–49; golf, 160, 169, 174, 214, 141, 143; Hall of Fame inductions, 243, 288n8; Hawaiian royalty, 5–6, 8, 21, 140, 185, 248; health and medical issues, 118, 216–17, 243, 244; hula dancing, 72, 100, 193, 198, 198, 214, 219, 236, 242, 254; influenza, 118–19; King Kamehameha significance, 5–6, 8, 20–21, 140, 185, 226, 248; learning to surf, 23–24; learning to swim, 4, 9, 33–34; legend, 2, 3, 5, 21, 80, 96, 108; letter writing, 16, 42, 50, 52, 45, 49, 89, 112, 201; lifesaving, 42, 46, 83, 117, 162–63, 164, 219; Los Angeles Athletic Club, 81, 87, 143, 144, 156, 160, 161, 163, 166, 179; the "Long Ride," 2, 108–11; media accounts of, 3, 38–39, 47, 48, 58, 67, 70, 80–81, 85, 88, 92, 94, 111, 114, 138, 144, 155, 237; military enlistment, 116–18, 119; motion picture film career, 1, 3, 21, 88, 140, 157–59, 161, 164–65, 168–70, 171–72, 173, 180, 219, 261, 277n1, 284n4; Olympic Games 1912, 50–53, 58–65; Olympic Games 1920, 125–34; Olympic Games 1924, 149–54; Olympic Games 1932, 179, 180–82, 201, 203, 275n4; Olympic Games 1956, 96, 217, 224–25; Olympic Games 1964, 239–40; 100-meter swimming final (1924), 152, 153–54; physical descriptions, 34, 35, 37, 47, 48, 49, 83, 91, 110, 117, 137, 138, 189; politics and political involvement, 183, 185, 186, 188, 199, 213, 226, 228, 245, 252; popularizing surfing and swimming, 4, 9, 80, 120, 155, 242; professional leanings, 76, 77, 78, 95, 103–4, 134, 135, 136, 166, 183; racism, experience of, 12, 40, 49, 88, 156, 171, 169; Duke Kahanamoku's (restaurant), 1, 3, 234, 241, 233; retirement, 179, 184; returns to Hawaii, 71–72 (1912), 88–89 (1914), 95, 97, 101 (1915), 112 (1917), 120 (1918), 133–34 (1920), 166–67 (1927), 172 (1929), 183 (1933); rights to his name, 213, 233, 245; rumors of marriage proposals, 84–85, 105–6; schools and education, 15–16, 19, 20, 21, 22, 23, 70, 108, 264n4, 265n16;

song and poetry about, 100, 184; sportsmanship and humility, 30, 52, 61, 86, 114, 139, 153, 189, 239, 255; statue of, 1, 3, 167, 179, 189–90, 230, 253, 254; surfboard design and construction of, 23, 34, 92, 111, 163, 221, 223, 256; surfing Atlantic City and East Coast, 46–47, 67–69, 78, 79; surfing Australia, 92–93; surfing exhibition, 67–69, 78, 79–80, 92, 93, 95, 145; surfing New Zealand, 94–95, 96; surfing technique, skill and knowledge, 23–24, 30–31, 34, 47, 67, 80, 91, 92–93, 108–11, 117, 162–63, 164, 173, 191, 223, 224, 225; swimming exhibitions, 42, 45, 66, 67, 80, 84, 137, 207, 261; ukulele playing, 45, 48, 52, 72, 82, 94, 100, 105, 117, 161, 214, 233; water and wave knowledge, vii, 4, 9, 17, 22, 30, 34, 38, 39, 109 156; water polo, 132, 182–83; wedding of, 196, 198–99; Weissmuller rivalry, 76, 138–39, 143–45, 146, 147–49, 160–61; world records, 86, 94, 114, 117, 131

Kahanamoku, Julia Paakonia Lonokahikini (Paoa) (mother), 5, 6, 7, 8, 13, 42, 71, 72, 111, 112, 116, 120, 134, 167, 172, 185, 186, 187

Kahanamoku, Kapiolani (sister), 5, 7, 107, 219, 248

Kahanamoku, Louis (brother), 7, 9, 83, 112, 146, 173, 187, 245, 254

Kahanamoku, Maria (sister), 7, 179

Kahanamoku, Nadine (Alexander) (wife), 196, 197–200, 202, 204, 205, 206, 207, 208, 213, 214, 215, 216, 217, 218, 219, 234, 235, 236, 243, 244, 246, 247, 248, 249, 250, 251, 252, 253, 254, 255; wedding of, 196, 198–99

Kahanamoku, Samuel "Sam" Alapai (brother), 111, 139, 140, 146, 147, 148, 149, 151, 152, 153, 154, 167, 173, 187, 194, 195, 196, 198, 199, 219, 247

Kahanamoku, Sargent (brother), 8, 9, 35, 39, 83, 112, 167, 173, 197, 215, 248, 250, 254

Kahanamoku, William "Bill" (brother), 7, 8, 93, 112, 123, 135, 215, 246–47, 248

Kahanamoku Fund, 41

Kahanamoku kick, 34

Kahanamoku-Sterling, JoAnne (niece), 154

Kaio, Kealoha, 242
Kaiser, Henry, 227
Kalanianaole, Jonah Kouio, 30
Kalehuawehe (break), 109
Kamana, "Squeeze," 233
Kamehameha, King, 2, 5, 6, 8, 10, 17, 20,
    50, 72, 140, 26, 253
Kamehameha School for Boys, 15, 16, 20,
    21, 23, 248, 255, 264n4, 265n16
"kanaka" (derogatory expression), 12, 26,
    27, 49, 58, 61, 176, 178
Kaupiko, John D., 214, 243
Kawaiaho'o Church, 226
Kawamoto, Evelyn, 217
Kealoha, Pua, 121, 125, 130, 131, 145, 147
Kealoha, Warren, 125, 131, 139, 145, 152
Keaulana, Richard "Buffalo," 30, 200
Keaweamahi, George "Tough Bill," 30
Keaweamahi, "Steamboat Bill," 30
Kekai, Albert "Rabbit," 23, 208, 221, 254
Kelii, John, 113, 114, 116, 121
Kellerman, Annette, vii, 33, 90
Kelly, Jack, 127, 134, 149
Kelly, John, 190, 191, 239
Kennedy, John F., viii, 234, 256
Kenney, Ed, 232
Kiefer, Adolph, 288n8
King, Bill, 29
King, James, 18
King of the Jungle (motion picture), 181
Kistler, George, 45–46, 49, 65, 66, 81, 102
Kiviat, Abel, 52, 57
Koehler, Max, 165
Kohner, Frederick, 222
Kohner, Kathy, 222
Kohner, Paul, 222
Kolehmainen, Hannes, 63–64
Konno, Fred, 217, 218
Kruger, Harold "Stubby," 99, 100, 113, 116,
    125, 147
Kuhio Beach Park, 253
Kumalae, Alfred, 224
Kuwa, George, 158

LAAC. See Los Angeles Athletic Club
The Lady of the Harem (motion picture),
    170
Lane, Clarence, 99, 100, 113, 116, 121, 125
Lane, Fred, 90
Langer, Ludy, 80, 88, 103, 125

The Latest in Life Saving (motion picture),
    80
Lawford, Peter, 223
lawsuits, 136, 251
Lazaro, Francisco, 65
Lee, Gilbert, 198
Lee, Gypsy Rose, 214
Lemmon, Jack, 216
Lepper, Merry, 252
Leterman, Elmer, 213
Letham, Isabel, 93, 96, 218, 224
libel suit against Pacific Commercial
    Advertiser, 134
Liberty (magazine), 178
Life (magazine), 135
lifeguard and lifeguarding, 35, 80, 141,
    160, 161, 164, 169, 173
life saving and rescue, 29, 30, 42, 46, 47,
    61, 80, 83, 85, 88, 116–17, 162–64, 165,
    219, 247
Liliuokalani, Queen, 13, 42, 112, 113, 249,
    256
London, Jack, 24, 25–28; and Freeth,
    George, 26; surfing, 25–27, 31–32
Long Beach (CA), 27, 80, 160, 190, 258
longboard, 23, 244
Longfellow, Wilbert, 116
"Long Ride," 2, 108–11
Longworth, William Bill, 60, 61, 62, 90, 94
Lord Jim (motion picture), 159
Los Angeles Athletic Club (LAAC), 79, 81,
    87, 156, 163, 173, 174, 179, 180, 182, 193,
    218, 223; Mercury Swim Club, 80, 142,
    143, 160–61, 166, 179, 182, 240; Mercury
    water polo team, 144, 148, 182
Los Angeles Memorial Coliseum, 142,
    180, 182
Los Angeles Riviera Country Club, 143
Los Angeles Times, 77, 81, 88, 90, 148, 170,
    181, 182, 229, 255
Los Angeles Times Magazine, 177
Love, Alan "Turkey," 210
Love, Winona, 198
"Lust in Paradise" (Time), 177
Lyall Bay, 95
Lyons, "Splash," 215, 233, 249

Makaha, 221, 222, 223, 237, 242
Maki, Clarence, 216
Malibu, 27, 160, 190, 222, 238, 255

Malibu Colony, 160
Mallon, Bill, 132
Malo, David, 11
Mansfield, Stephanie, 194
Manuiwa (schooner), 184, 185
Mardi and a Voyage Thither (Melville), 18
Marshall Field's, 43
Marx, Groucho, 175
Massa, Mario, 61
Massie, Thalia, 177, 178
Massie, Tommy, 177
Massie trial, 177, 178
Matsonia, 88, 89, 103, 158
Matson Navigation Company, 71, 89, 174
May, Lily Browner, 166
Mayer, Louis B, 140
Mays, Willie, 228
McAlister, Charles "Snow," 93, 96
McCallister, Charles "Doc," 182
McCurdy, Wallace, 69
McDermott, Mike "Turk," 47, 48, 52, 62, 66
McDonald, Pat "Babe," 52, 129, 151
McElhannon, William, 163
Mcfarlane, Walter, 209
McGillivray, Perry, 52, 60, 61, 62, 63, 88, 99, 100, 102, 131, 145
McGrath, Matt, 52
McInerny, 70
McKenzie, R. Tait, 49, 189–90, 267n18
McKinley, William, 12, 13
McKinley High School, 21, 70, 217
McVay, Charles, 232
McVay, Kimo Wilder, 200, 232–33, 234–38, 241, 242, 243, 244, 245–46, 248, 251, 252
Meany, Helen, 132
Melville, Herman, 18, 26
Mercury, 81
Mercury Swim Club. *See* Los Angeles Athletic Club: Mercury Swim Club
Merrick, Owen, 117, 118, 119
Mersereau, Verna, 84
Metzger, Delbert, 210
Michener, James, 82, 256
Mid-Pacific Carnival 1914, 86
Mid-Pacific Magazine, 31–32
military in Hawaii. *See* Hawaii: military in
Miller, Edward "Dude," 35–36, 38, 41, 42, 43, 46, 82

Million Dollar Pier, 66, 78
missionaries, 11, 12, 19, 197
Mister Roberts (motion picture), 171, 216
Moana Hotel, 22, 24, 28, 29, 30, 82, 110, 124, 241
Mobile, 133
Mokuaikaua Church, 198
Morgan, William, 101
Morris, Glenn, 188
Moses, Helen, 125
Moss, Edward Bayard, 58
Motion Picture News, 88
motion pictures, 157–59, 161, 164–65, 168–70, 171–72; surf-themed, 222–23, 237, 256. *See also* Kahanamoku, Duke Paoa: motion picture film career
Mountbatten, Louis, 124
"Mr. Moto" (song), 223
Muñoz, Mickey, 238, 241
Muriwai Beach, 95
Murphy Mike "Silent," 45, 53
Murray, Jim, 170
Myrtles Boat Club, 29, 37, 101

NAACP (National Association for the Advancement of Colored People), 177
Nadu K., 224, 243
Nadu K. II, 246
Naismith, James, 49
Nash Manufacturing, 233
National Championship 1914, 87–88
National Championship 1915, 97–98, 99–100
National Championship 1917, 113–14
National Championship 1922, 138–39
Native American Indians: athletes, 15–16, 33, 53, 54, 57, 73, 249; cast in films as, 49, 83, 159, 181
Neushul, Peter, 220, 259
New Brighton Beach, 95
Newport Beach, 27, 80, 161, 163
New South Wales Amateur Swimming Association, 92, 94–96
New York, ss, 66
New York Athletic Club (NYAC), 33, 39, 51, 56, 67, 87
New York Times, 13, 61, 68, 75, 86, 118, 121, 144, 248
New Zealand, 92, 94–96

nicknames: "The Big Kahoona," 222; "The Bronze Statue," 105; "Duke de Crawlstroke," 63
Nimitz, Chester, 210
Noble, Johnny, 174
No Father to Guide Him (motion picture), 161, 169
Noll, Greg, 22, 241
Norconian Resort Supreme, 143
Norfleet, Nat, 201
Northern Pacific, 126
North Shore (Oahu), 222, 238, 241, 241
Nurmi, Paavo, 154, 180, 248

Oahu, 1, 6, 7, 10, 17, 20, 21, 22, 105, 109, 112, 138, 139, 175, 176, 184, 186, 191, 192, 193, 196, 198, 205, 207, 212, 213, 221, 227, 235, 241, 248, 251, 252, 262
Oahu Cemetery, 112, 175, 179, 187
Oahu College, 16. *See also* Punahou School
Oakland Tribune, 88
Obama, Barack, 234, 286n5
Obama, Barack, Sr., 234
OceanFest carnival, 1
ODKF. *See* Outrigger Duke Kahanamoku Foundation
Office of Civilian Defense, 208
Ohlin, Harry, 219
Old Ironsides (motion picture), 164, 165
Olympians from Hawaii, 121, 133, 217
Olympic Club, 70, 79, 87, 147
Olympic Games 1896, 53–54, 55
Olympic Games 1900, 39, 54, 56
Olympic Games 1904, 33, 35, 39, 54, 56, 98, 180
Olympic Games 1908, 25, 33, 35, 55, 56, 57, 62, 65, 181, 261
Olympic Games 1912, 2, 40, 46, 50–53, 58–66; closing ceremony, 63; competition, 59–63, 58–65; Hawaiian newspaper account, 70; opening ceremony, 59; swimming venue, 60; travel to, 51–53, 58
Olympic Games 1916, 71, 85; cancellation of, 86, 102, 103, 107, 120, 183, 203
Olympic Games 1920, 125–35, 276n10; competition, 130–31; opening ceremony, 129; swimming venue, 130;

training for, 120, 121; travel conditions, 126–28; water polo, 132
Olympic Games 1924, 139, 143, 146, 148–55, 168, 181, 182, 183, 247, 255, 276n10; captain U.S. Team, 151; competition, 152, 153–54; opening ceremony, 149, 151; swimming venue, 151
Olympic Games 1928, 168, 171, 179
Olympic Games 1932, 142, 179, 180, 182, 183, 201, 203, 275n4
Olympic Games 1936, 188, 212
Olympic Games 1940, cancellation of, 203, 217
Olympic Games 1948, 217
Olympic Games 1956, 156, 217, 218, 224–25, 240
Olympic Games 1964, 239–40
Olympic Games 1968, 252
Olympic Trials, U.S., 125, 145–46, 179–80
Olympic Winter Games 1924, Chamonix, 150
O'Neil, Sally, 170
O'Neill, Jack, 220
"On the Beach of Waikiki" (song), 219
Organic Act 1900, 13, 213
O'Sullivan, Maureen, 171
outrigger canoe. *See* canoes and canoe racing
Outrigger Canoe Club, 28–29, 30, 31, 32, 37, 71, 101, 107–8, 116, 120, 124, 122, 125, 136, 167, 174, 175, 199, 200, 203, 205, 206, 209, 213, 214, 220, 225, 246, 248, 250, 255; excluded membership, 28, 29, 31, 38, 71, 108; membership in, 107–8, 200
Outrigger Duke Kahanamoku Foundation (ODKF), 255
Owens, Jesse, 2, 155, 188
Oyakawa, Yoshi, 217, 218

Pacific Commercial Advertiser, 41, 70, 121–23, 125, 134, 136, 274n5
Pacific Olympiad, 123
Pacific System Homes (surfboards), 173
Paddock, Charley, 80, 127, 134, 139, 166, 169
Paka, Toots, 45
Palama Club, 113
Panama-Pacific International Exposition, 97–98. *See also* World's Fair 1915
Pan Handle Scrap, 78, 192, 275n3
Paniccia, Patti, 255–56

Pan-Pacific Union, 25
Paoa, Julia. *See* Kahanamoku, Julia
    Paakonia Lonokahikini (Paoa)
Paoa family, 6, 7, 8, 14, 70, 77, 111, 227, 249
parade(s), 55, 69, 71, 79, 133, 155, 185
"A Paradise Gone Mad" (*Liberty*), 178
Paramount Studios (formerly Famous
    Players-Lasky), 157, 158, 159, 164, 165
Parkhurst, Anita, 135
Paskowitz, Dorian "Doc," 191
Pathé, 158
Patton, George S., Jr., 52, 58
Pearl Harbor, 9, 12, 24, 42, 101, 117, 176,
    185, 205–7, 210, 214, 256; attack on,
    205–7, 228
Pearl Harbor Yacht Club, 184, 205
Pegler, Westbrook, 154
Perkins, Irmgard Harbottle, 14
Pershing, John "Black Jack," 149
Persons, Rosalie Young, 253
Peterson, Charles, 89
Peterson, Preston "Pete," 190
Philadelphia, 45, 66, 81, 98
Philadelphia Canoe Club, 47
Phillips, Coles, 135
photographs of Duke Kahanamoku, 1, 2,
    20, 31, 32, 38, 39, 49, 58, 67, 78, 83, 88, 96,
    100, 107, 108, 117, 124, 135, 136, 139, 140,
    146, 153, 172, 175, 177–78, 189, 197, 201,
    216, 234, 242–43, 253, 271n13, 281n13
Pietri, Dorando, 74
Piikoi, Maria, 104
"Pipeline" (song), 223
Pittsburgh, 44, 45, 49, 50, 78, 102, 156
Pleasant, Frank Mount, 57
Plummer, Charlie, 163
Poindexter, Joseph, 206
political parties and candidate, 183, 189,
    199, 200, 213, 216, 226, 228, 244
Pomar, Felipe, 242
The Pony Express (motion picture), 159
pools. *See* swimming pools
popularity of surfing, 27, 31–32, 68, 80,
    236–37
popularity of swimming, 33, 39, 56, 120,
    155, 240
Porter, J. A., 163
Portolá Festival, 79
postage stamp, 253
Presley, Elvis, 228

Prieste, Haig "Hal," 132–33, 275n10
Princess Matoika, 126, 133, 252
prison in Iwilei, 186, 187, 188, 189, 213, 228
professionalism in sport, 2, 42, 73, 74, 75,
    76, 171, 180
Public Baths, 191
Public Works, 82, 97, 104, 120
"Pump House Gang," 237
Punahou School, 16, 108, 139. *See also*
    Oahu College
Pyle, C. C., 154
Pyle, Ernie, 189, 190

Queen Emma Estate, 28
Queen Kaahumanu Elementary School, 15
Queen's (beach), 110
Queen's Hospital, 195, 206, 216

racial tension between military and
    locals, 176, 177
racism, 2, 12, 28, 29, 40, 48–49, 58, 61, 83,
    91, 155–56, 171, 176, 178, 249, 252
Raithel, Arthur, 88, 100
Ralston, Esther, 164
Ramme, Walter, 61, 62
Ranjitsinhji, 48
Rathbone, Rigg, 145
Rawlins, William "Bill," 34, 35, 36, 38, 39,
    41, 42, 65, 71, 77, 79, 91, 102, 103, 104,
    113, 122, 123, 252
Reciprocity Treaty 1887, 12
Red Cross, 116–17, 118, 119, 207
Redlands Municipal Pool, 143
Redondo Beach, 27, 80, 220
Redondo Hotel, 27
Redondo Plunge, 80
Redondo Reflux, 81
Reid, Sam, 68–69, 164, 174, 190
Rendezvous Ballroom, 161, 223
Renown, HMS, 124
Republic of Hawaii. *See* Hawaii:
    annexation of
The Rescue (motion picture), 168, 169, 170
Retzer, George, 58
Rice, Grantland, 154
The Richest Girl in the World (Mansfield),
    194
Rickards, Tex, 154
"Riding the South Sea Surf" (London),
    25, 265n12

"Riding the Surfboard" (Ford), 31, 32
Riggin, Aileen, 127, 129, 162
rights to name, 213, 233, 245, 255
Ripely's "Believe It or Not," 108, 127
Ripley, Robert, 108, 127
Robello, Harry "Didi," 255
Robello, Harry S., 233
Robertson, Cliff, 223
Robertson, Jack, 147
Robinson, Jackie, 2, 155, 204, 214
Rockaway Beach, 67–68
Roger, Will, 180
Rogers, Thomas, 173
Rohloff, Grant, 222
Roosevelt, Franklin, Jr., 185
Roosevelt, Franklin Delano, 175, 185, 206, 232
Roosevelt, John, 185
Roosevelt, Theodore, 12, 43, 53, 55, 69, 98
Rose, Charles, 97, 186, 187
Rose, Ralph, 52
Ross, Norman "The Big Moose," 113–14, 116, 119, 121, 125, 128, 130, 131, 132, 133, 135, 137, 145, 147, 208
rowing, 3, 21, 32, 34, 107, 121, 122
Royal Hawaiian Hotel, 174, 183, 196, 197, 198, 207, 249
Royal Order of Kamehameha, 226
royalty, legendary Hawaiian connection, 5, 6, 48
Rubien, Fred, 118
Ruddy, Joe, 67
Ruth, George Herman "Babe," 3, 108, 126, 134, 155, 157–58, 160, 175, 214, 223, 248

sailing (boating, crewing, yachting), 3, 184, 185, 205, 224, 243, 245, 246
Sakamoto, Soichi, 203, 217
Sandow, Eugen, 57, 268n11
San Francisco, 43, 44, 70, 79, 81, 87, 97, 98, 98, 99, 100, 117, 119, 160, 189, 190, 240
San Francisco Call, 86
San Francisco Examiner, 88
San Francisco Giants, 228
Santa Cruz, 19, 27, 30, 79, 80, 220
Santa Cruz Island, 169
Santa Monica, 141, 156, 243
Santa Monica Beach Club, 141, 174
Sanville, F. H., 46
Saturday Evening Post, 136, 158

Save Our Surf (SOS), 239
Schulberg, B. P., 164
sculling, 32, 101
Seaside Hotel, 24, 28
Selective Service Act 1917, 116
Sennett, Mack, 80, 132
Seven Weeks in Hawaii (Crawford), 83
Severson, John, 222
Shangri La, 194–96, 202, 207
Sheppard, Mel "Peerless Mel," 57, 75, 78, 268n11
Sheridan, Martin, 57, 74, 268n11
sheriff, Honolulu, 186, 187, 189, 190, 198, 199, 200, 202, 207, 210, 212, 213, 216, 219, 228, 229, 230, 231
Sherman, Eddie, 244
Shinyo Maru, 120
Short, Walter, 207
Shryock, John, 46
Simmons, Bob, 221
Singlehurst, Tom, 101
skateboard, 3, 233
Slippery When Wet (motion picture), 242
Small, Robert "Bud," 86, 88
Smith, Bernyece, 104–5, 119
Smith, Bill, 217
Smith, Gene "Tarzan," 190
Smith, Ronald Quay, 101
Smith, Tommie, 252
The Snark, 24, 26
Snead, Edward, 219
Sockalexis, Andrew, 57
Soetero, Lolo, 234
Southern California, 3, 27, 68, 79, 79, 81, 87, 88, 96, 141–42, 155, 156, 157, 159, 160, 161, 164, 179, 180, 190, 201, 222, 236
Spanish-American War, 13
Speedo, 218
Sports Illustrated, 237, 256
sportsmanship and humility, 30, 52, 61, 86, 114, 139, 153, 189, 239, 255
Stade Nautique d'Antwerp, 130
Le Stade Nautique des Tourelles, 151
St. Andrews Episcopal Church, 208, 248
Starke, Pauline, 159
statue of Duke, 1, 3, 167, 179, 189–90, 230, 253, 254
Steel Pier, 67
Steiner, Harry, 30, 215
Sterling, Leon, 189, 190

St. John's Episcopal Church, 142
Strauch, Paul, Jr., 237, 238, 242, 250
Sullivan, Frank, 87
Sullivan, James E., 35, 39, 46, 51, 52, 54, 55, 56–57, 61, 64, 69, 73–74, 75, 85, 98–99, 126, 127, 131, 215
Sunday Times (Sydney), 94
Sunlite Pool, 179
Sunn, Rell "Queen of Makaha," 254
Superintendent Honolulu Hale, 175–76
Surfaris, 223
surfboard polo, 173
surfboards: Blake, Tom, 133, 141, 173, 190–91; Duke's construction of, 23, 34, 47, 92, 95, 104, 109–10, 111, 121, 218, 223, 244, 246; fiberglass, 221; history and design, 16, 18–19, 23, 28, 34, 68, 79, 91, 92, 93, 133, 136, 141, 163, 173, 191, 221, 223, 234, 256; lifesaving, used for, 162–63; longboard, 23, 108, 116; production, 233; shortboard, 19, 221; Valspar, 136; wood construction, 18, 23, 68, 93, 136
surf culture, 18, 19, 30, 82–83, 220, 224, 237
Surfer (magazine), 222, 239, 242, 256, 259
surfing: big-wave, 221, 224, 237, 239, 241; Blake, Tom, 111, 141, 160; competition, 28, 236–38, 239, 241–42; Corona del Mar, 161; decline of, 19, 20, 32, 208, 220; described by authors, 18–19, 20, 26–27; early surfers in Atlantic City, 68; early surfers in California, 19, 27, 68, 120; early surfers in Newport, 27, 80; early surfers in Malibu, 160; etiquette, rules, safety, 30; exhibition by Duke, 67–69, 78, 79–80, 92, 93, 95, 145; Freeth, George, 27, 68, 120; Hall of Fame, 243; health and fitness, 25, 34, 42, 121; in popular culture, 26, 31, 222–23, 233, 237, 242, 254; the "Long Ride," 2, 108; origins and development of, 3, 10, 16–20, 23–24, 25, 27, 28, 30–31, 32, 120, 190–91, 220–22; permission and permits, 67, 91, 92; popularity of, 31, 32, 140, 141, 160, 163, 169, 190, 236, 240, 242; promoting Hawaii, 3, 32, 38, 68, 96, 98, 135, 136, 242; tandem, 3, 23, 93, 164, 177–78, 194; teaching and lessons, 82, 83, 104, 105–6, 124, 133, 135, 141, 160, 178, 185, 190, 193, 198, 216 243; wet suit, 220
Surfing Hall of Fame, 243

surfing in popular culture, 26, 31, 222–23, 233, 237, 242, 254
Surfrider Foundation, 253
surf-ski, 190, 281n13
surf-themed motion pictures and films, 222–23, 237, 25
Sutro, Adolph, 99
Sutro Baths, San Francisco, 79, 88, 99, 240
Swanson, Gloria, 140, 157
"Sweet Leiani" (song), 192
swim fins, 201–2
swimming: ability, skill and training, 33–34, 46, 47, 87, 94, 102, 106, 144, 168; competitive open water, 45, 50, 125, 137; exhibition, 42, 45, 66, 67, 80, 84, 137, 207, 261; Hall of Fame, 243, 288n8; history of competitive, 3, 33, 36, 44, 55, 78, 81, 88, 138, 143, 155, 24; promote Hawaii, 50, 76, 98, 123; open water swimming, 34, 58; women athletes, 56, 127, 181, 240; popularizing the sport, 118, 120, 155; strokes, 33, 39, 56 61, 102
swimming in Olympic Games. *See* Kahanamoku, Duke Paoa: Olympic Games 1912–1932; Olympic Games 1896–1964
swimming pools, 2, 27, 35, 40, 44, 45, 46, 55, 67, 70, 79, 99, 102, 130, 137, 137–38, 139, 143, 145–46, 146, 147, 151, 155, 167, 168, 179, 179; Olympic venues, 56, 60, 130, 151
swimsuits, 1, 34, 49, 134, 135, 201, 218, 246
Switzer, Kathrine, 252

Taft, William, 43, 69
Tait, Clair, 117
Takaishi, Katsuo, 152, 154
tandem surfing. *See* surfing
Tarzan (character), 153, 171, 181, 188
Tarzan the Ape Man (motion picture), 171, 181
Tarzan the Fearless (motion picture), 181
Taylor, Henry, 56
Taylor, John Baxter, 57
Temple, Shirley, 175
Terrace Garden Restaurant, 69
The Territory. *See* Hawaii: annexation of
Tewanima, Louis, 57, 64, 78
Thelma (yacht), 162–63, 219

This Is Your Life (TV show), 218–19
Thompson, Robert, 51, 52
Thorpe, Jim, 16, 53, 188, 217, 249, 261, 270n16; death of, 216; disqualification, 73–74, 75, 76; economic and personal struggles, 215–16; Olympic Games 1912, 53, 57, 64, 65, 69; Olympic Games 1932, 180–81
Three Year Swim Club, 203, 217
Thurston, Lorrin A., 6, 12, 41, 70, 123
Toots Shor's, 214
Torrence, Ernest, 159
tourism. *See* Hawaii: tourism
Tracy, Terry "Tubesteak," 222, 224
trading cards. *See* Pan Handle Scrap
Transpacific Yacht Race (Transpac), 184
Trask, Arthur, 199
Trek to Makaha (surfing film), 222
Trent, Goodwin Murray "Buzzy," 190, 221, 222, 241
Trudgen, John, 33
Truman, Harry S., 214, 226
Tsuzuki, Thomas "Scoop," 221
Tukino V, Tureiti Te Heuheu, 95
Twain, Mark, 18–19, 29, 26
Tydings, Eleanor Davies, 194
Tydings, Millard, 194

Ueberroth, Peter, 224–25
Uhl, Eleanor, 130
ukulele, 8, 30, 45, 214
Union Oil service stations, 183–84
United Carriage Company, 6
University of California Los Angeles, 143, 204
University of Hawaii, 234, 255
University of Pennsylvania, 45, 53, 259
University of Southern California, 144, 168, 212
Unmack, William, 86
U.S. Army Quartermaster Corps, 135
Usborne, Gordon, 98
U.S. Olympic Trials 1920, 125
U.S. Olympic Trials 1924, 145, 146–48
U.S. Olympic Trials 1932, 179
U.S. Postal Service, 253
U.S. Supreme Court, 210

Valentine & Company, 136
Valspar, 136

Van Artsdalen, Butch, 239
Van Dyke, Fred, 241, 222
Van Hamersveld, John, 237
Velez, Lupe, 169
Velock, Jack, 134
Velzy, Dale, 221
Venice Beach, 27, 80, 221
Ventura, SS, 90
Ventura International Plastics, 233
Vogue, 135
volleyball, 3, 20, 101, 107, 121, 141 203, 209, 215, 240, 272n9; beach volleyball, 3, 12, 101, 107, 121, 141, 240
Von Tempski, Armine, 159
Vosburgh, William, 100
Vultee, Art, 80
Vultee, Gerard "Jerry," 161, 163

Wagner, Honus, 74
Wahle, Otto, 39–40, 46, 50, 51, 57, 61, 64–65, 67, 125
Waikiki, 1, 7, 8, 13, 15, 24, 38, 71, 76, 104, 106, 108, 120, 158, 174, 178, 179, 185, 232; home in, 76–78, 82, 102, 112, 234; meaning of, 7; Waikiki Beach, 4, 17, 28, 32, 190, 203, 208, 213, 227
Waikikian Hotel, 227
Waikiki Beach Patrol, 135, 167
"Waikiki Calls" (radio show), 192
Waikiki Improvement Association, 253
Waikiki School, 14
Waikiki Wedding (motion picture), 192, 224
Waikiki Yacht Club, 243, 246
Waite, Jane, 178
wakeboarding, 101
Wake of the Red Witch (motion picture), 171, 213
Walker, Tommy, 96
Walker, William, 96
Walsh, Christy, 154
Walsh, Raoul, 169
Walter Macfarlane Memorial Regatta, 209
Walton, Fred, 228
The Wanderer (motion picture), 170
War Memorial Natatorium, 167, 168, 179, 203, 207, 217, 240, 257
Warner, Glenn "Pop," 73, 74
water and waves, understanding of, vii, 4, 9, 17, 22, 30, 34, 38, 39, 109, 156, 220

waterman, 4, 6, 22, 30, 34, 72, 120, 200, 218, 250, 254; waterwomen, 30
water polo, 29, 39, 45, 55, 56, 57, 67, 87, 121, 130, 132, 143, 144, 146, 148, 152, 168, 173, 182–83, 224, 228; Olympic Games participation, 132, 148, 168, 182–83
water skiing, 101
wave-riding. *See* surfing
Wayne, John, 171, 213
Webb, Matthew, 33
Weber, Dewey, 241
Wehselau, Mariechen, 152
Weightman Hall, 46
Weissmuller, Johnny: citizenship status, 137, 145, 155; childhood and early years, 137; childhood illness, 137; competitive swimming, 136, 137–39, 166–67; Hall of Fame induction, 243, 288n8; Illinois Athletic Club, 76, 137, 138, 146, 166; influenza, 144, 137; learn to swim, 137; motion picture opportunities (Tarzan), 171, 181; 100-meter swimming final (1924), 152, 153–54; Olympic Games 1924, 149–54; Olympic Games 1928, 168; popularity of, 154–55; professional career, 171, 240; success in Hollywood, 171; rivalry with Duke, 76, 138–39, 143–45, 146, 147–49, 160–61; swimming technique, training, skill, 17, 138, 156, 181; *This Is Your Life*, 219; trading cards, 275n4; water polo, 52
West, Claude, 95, 96, 218
West Coast Surfboard Championship 1963, 236
Westwick, Peter, 220
wet suit, 220
Where East is East (motion picture), 170
White, Harry, 211
Wickham, Aleck, 33
Wilder, Kinau, 232, 245
Wilder, Samuel, 232
Wildman, Herbert, 182
Wilhelmina, 71
Williams, Esther, 138, 240
Williams, George, 53

Williamson, Marjorie, 166
William Wrigley's Ocean Marathon, 166
Wilson, Earl, 214
Wilson, Woodrow, 43, 69
Windansea, 237
Winter, Kenneth, 29
"Wipe Out" (song), 223
Withington, Leonard, 122–23
Wolfe, Tom, 237
Wolf Song (motion picture), 170
Women's Home Companion, 25
women's participation in Olympic Games, 56–57, 127, 131, 148, 150, 181, 240
Woodrow, Wilson, 118
Woolloomooloo Bay, 94
Woolsey, Bill, 217, 218
Worcester Telegram, 73
"World Champion Athletes" (trading cards), 78
World's Fair 1893, 6–7, 12
World's Fair 1904, 98
World's Fair 1915, 97, 98, 99, 100 *See also* Panama-Pacific International Exposition
World's Fair 1939, 190
World's Fair 1964, 244
World War I, 85, 90, 98–99, 113, 116–17, 118; cancellation of Olympic Games, 86, 103, 107, 120, 183
World War II, 205–8, 210; cancellation of Olympic Games, 203, 205–7, 212
Wright, George F., 175
Wrigley, William, 113, 164, 166
writ of habeas corpus, 207, 210–11
W. W. Dimond Company, 6
Wyeth, Marion Sims, 193
Wylie, Durack, 90
Wylie, Mina, 90

Yamada, Koji, 103
Yosemite, 144
Young, John, 66

Zamperini, Louis, 212–13
Zukor, Adolph, 164